OXFORD STUDIES IN EUROPEAN LAW

Series Editors

PAUL CRAIG

Professor of English Law at St John's College, Oxford

GRÁINNE DE BÚRCA

Professor of Law at New York University School of Law

The Concept of State Aid Under EU Law

OXFORD STUDIES IN EUROPEAN LAW

Series Editors: Paul Craig, Professor of English Law at St John's College, Oxford and Gráinne de Búrca, Professor of Law at New York University School of Law

The aim of this series is to publish important and original research on EU law. The focus is on scholarly monographs, with a particular emphasis on those which are interdisciplinary in nature. Edited collections of essays will also be included where they are appropriate. The series is wide in scope and aims to cover studies of particular areas of substantive and of institutional law, historical works, theoretical studies, and analyses of current debates, as well as questions of perennial interest such as the relationship between national and EU law and the novel forms of governance emerging in and beyond Europe. The fact that many of the works are interdisciplinary will make the series of interest to all those concerned with the governance and operation of the EU.

OTHER TITLES IN THIS SERIES JUSTICE IN THE EU

The Emergence of Transnational Solidarity
Floris de Witte

The Euro Area Crisis in Constitutional Perspective
Alicia Hinarejos

The European Fundamental Freedoms
A Contextual Approach
Pedro Caro de Sousa

National Identity in EU Law
Elke Cloots

The Constitutional Foundations of European Contract Law
A Comparative Analysis
Kathleen Gutman

The Criminalization of European Cartel Enforcement
Theoretical, Legal, and Practical Challenges
Peter Whelan

Fundamental Rights in Europe
Challenges and Transformations in Comparative Perspective
Federico Fabbrini

The Principle of Loyalty in EU Law
Marcus Klamert

Constitutional Pluralism in the EU
Klemen Jaklic

EU Consumer Law and Human Rights
Iris Benöhr

The Principle of Mutual Recognition in EU Law
Christine Janssens

The Coherence of EU Free Movement Law
Constitutional Responsibility and the Court of Justice
Niamh Nic Shuibhne

European Law and New Health Technologies
Edited by Mark Flear, Anne-Maree Farrell, Tamara Hervey, and Thérèse Murphy

European Agencies
Law and Practices of Accountability
Madalina Busuioc

The Legal Effect of EU Agreements
Mario Mendez

The Foundations of European Union Competition Law
The Objective and Principles of Article 102
Renato Nazzini

The Emergence of EU Contract Law
Exploring Europeanization
Lucinda Miller

Participation in EU Rule-making
A Rights-Based Approach
Joana Mendes

Regulating Cartels in Europe
Second Edition
Christopher Harding, Julian Joshua

Religion and the Public Order of the European Union
Ronan McCrea

The Concept of State Aid Under EU Law

From internal market to competition and beyond

JUAN JORGE PIERNAS LÓPEZ

OXFORD
UNIVERSITY PRESS

OXFORD
UNIVERSITY PRESS

Great Clarendon Street, Oxford, OX2 6DP,
United Kingdom

Oxford University Press is a department of the University of Oxford.
It furthers the University's objective of excellence in research, scholarship,
and education by publishing worldwide. Oxford is a registered trade mark of
Oxford University Press in the UK and in certain other countries

First Edition published in 2015

Published in the United States of America by Oxford University Press
198 Madison Avenue, New York, NY 10016, United States of America

British Library Cataloguing in Publication Data
Data available

Library of Congress Control Number: 2015942289

ISBN 978–0–19–874869–4

Foreword

This book is a unique attempt to trace the evolution of State aid policy through the analysis of its central and crucial element, the concept of State aid itself. It combines a fine and thoughtful legal discussion of carefully selected judgments with a wide historical perspective.

Other scholars have described the development of European policies over time or discussed changing features of the case-law of the Court of Justice in its different periods. Here, these accounts are verified and refined through the magnifying glass of a sharp legal analysis. The concept of State aid represents an ideal topic for such an enquiry, because of its importance for the economic constitution of the European Union and because of the abundance of interesting judgments covering more than fifty years. A clear perception of the policy context, an accurate statement of the arguments and a meticulous dissection of the formulas used by the Court cast a new light both on the technical choices of the judges and on their broader policy implications.

The analysis shows that, case after case, the contours of a notion consistently described as objective have been progressively defined, rectified or altered by the Court of Justice. While such a pattern is relatively frequent, indeed inevitable, whenever judges are called upon to apply unspecified legal concepts, the concept of State aid is specially suited for judicial creativity. First, the European treaties provide for strong, centralised control on certain forms of State intervention in the economy while leaving considerable latitude for determining the precise scope of such a mechanism, precisely through the definition of State aid. Second, the peculiar nature and role of State aid control, at the crossroads between internal market rules and competition policy, provides ample space for different conceptions of its aims and of its purview. Third, the various constituent elements of the notion – advantage, selectivity, State origin, distortion of competition, effect on trade – lend themselves to a variety of readings and to an even greater number of combinations and permutations. The Court of Justice has largely taken advantage of these opportunities, in a long series of judgments extending or reducing the concept of State aid from time to time by different techniques. Successive judgments have also expressed different views of the relationship of State aid control with other treaty provisions and policies, or of its encroachment upon the powers of Member States, particularly in the area of taxation. This book provides a critical assessment of these interventions, without hesitating to condemn some of them or to anticipate that certain interpretations are bound to be reversed in the future.

According to the author, the Luxembourg judges have often reacted to the Commission's attempts to use the instrument of State aid control at the service of more general policy aims and priorities. One may wonder whether these impulsions, through the adoption of State aid decisions or through the submission of observations in references from national courts for a preliminary ruling, have always been conscious and consistent, in other words whether the Commission has indeed pursued a coherent adjudicatory and judicial strategy. But undeniably, the two institutions have entertained over the years a rich and fruitful dialogue, with phases of substantial agreement and occasional episodes of divergence. The positions expressed by the Member States and by private litigants, the activity of national courts and the academic debate have provided further input and have also influenced the outcome of individual cases, thus contributing to the progressive refinement of the concept of aid by the Luxembourg judges.

This fascinating account of the various avatars of the concept of State aid constitutes an apt reminder that, here more than in other areas, the case-law is not frozen. Further developments will inevitably retouch or even reverse certain principles that are considered as established. Such a humbling lesson is particularly important at a time when the Commission has for the first time endeavoured to put forward an interpretative notice on the notion of State aid, still to be finalised. The Commission's intention is to increase clarity by distilling the teachings of the Court or, in their absence, the orientations resulting from its own practice. Whether the notice, once adopted, will also contribute to the stability of the case-law, remains to be seen. In any event, such a piece of work must be periodically revisited and adapted, if it is to remain useful and to perform its function of guidance for stakeholders and practitioners.

Drawing on his significant and multiple experiences, Juan Jorge Piernas López has thus provided not only a remarkable scholarly achievement, with an insightful assessment of law and practice over many decades, but also a salutary reminder of the evolutionary nature of economic law and of its constant links with public policy objectives.

Vittorio Di Bucci*

* Member of the Legal Service of the European Commission since 1991. Director, head of the State Aid and Antidumping Team from 2010 to 2015. Any opinions expressed are personal and do not necessarily reflect the views of the European Commission.

Series Editors' Preface

The law relating to State aid has been central to the European Economic Community (EEC) from its very inception. This centrality reflects the underlying policy of preventing attainment of a single market from being hindered through aid, in its multiple forms, being given by states to their own undertakings. A very considerable body of case law has developed over the years, matched by an attendant body of scholarship grappling with the core precepts used by the courts. The sophisticated legal literature has more recently been complemented by works that seek to take a broader perspective on the law relating to State aid. This monograph by Piernas López comes in the latter category.

The book takes a dynamic approach to State aid, tracing its historical routes to mercantilism, followed by an analysis of the travaux préparatoires insofar as they relate to this topic. The author advances three interesting theses, which provide the cornerstone for the subsequent analysis.

The first is that the legal concept of aid has evolved not primarily because of different interpretations of the economic foundations of this concept, but rather as a result of the policy priorities of the European Commission over time, combined with difficulties encountered by the Commission in enforcing the State aid rules. Drawing on the work of political scientists, the author identifies four periods in the evolution of State aid policy: the first period, from 1958 to the early 1970s; the second period, from the early 1970s to the mid-1980s; the third from the mid-1980s to the mid-1990s; and the final period being the mid-1990s to the present.

The first thesis is complemented by the second, whereby the author contends that the evolution of the concept of aid has also been influenced by the evolution of the European Court of Justice's (ECJ) case law and that it tracks the way in which the ECJ has dealt with other areas of economic law, such as the free movement of goods and competition.

The third thesis flows from the first two, in that the author contends that the concept of aid analysed in the preceding manner is helpful in understanding decisions in seminal cases. The cases are integrated into an analysis of how the judgments fit with the main policy initiatives of the Commission and the general jurisprudence of the Court during the period in which the case was laid down.

The law relating to State aid will doubtless continue to occupy the time of the Commission and generate legal challenges before the EU courts. This work will enrich our understanding of this concept and the way in which it has evolved over time.

Paul Craig and Gráinne de Búrca

Acknowledgements

This book is by no means the sole outcome of my doctoral work during four years at the European University Institute (EUI). I have profited from the support, guidance, advice, and friendship of many people, and they deserve, at the very least, to be mentioned at this point.

I am particularly indebted to my thesis supervisor, Giorgio Monti, without whom this book, based on my Ph.D thesis, would have been a very different and far poorer document. He has helped me in many ways in the past few years, from suggesting relevant readings to discussing thoughts and reviewing multiple drafts. More importantly for me, Giorgio has supported this project since the beginning. In particular, he has believed in using policy and history to understand the law, an approach this book defends. I owe a great deal to him. I am also grateful to Heike Schweitzer, my first supervisor, for her support in the early days of my doctorate. In addition, I would like to thank the members of my examining board, Professors Piet Jan Slot, Andrea Biondi, and Hans-W. Micklitz, for having kindly agreed to review the thesis on which this book is based.

Other people have also contributed to this book by generously offering to discuss some ideas or parts of my work with me. They have helped me at different stages of this process. I thank EUI Professors Marise Cremona, Bruno de Witte, Petros C. Mavroidis, Hans-W. Micklitz, Loic Azoulai, Ruth Rubio, and Miguel Poiares Maduro in this regard. Also within the EUI, I would like to pay a singular tribute to Luca Rubini, truly a master of the subject of my doctoral thesis. He possesses great reserves of modesty (and patience), listening to me instead of teaching me over the last years. Similarly, I would like to highlight the generosity of Judge Allan Rosas and Judge Koen Lenaerts for agreeing to discuss my preliminary conclusions during my traineeship at the Court of Justice of the European Union in the summer of 2012 at the Cabinet of Advocate General Pedro Cruz Villalón. I am greatly indebted to the Advocate General for giving me this opportunity and to Daniel Sarmiento for accompanying me on this enriching experience. I also benefited immensely from the opportunity to discuss my thesis with members of the legal service of the European Commission—Francisco Santaolalla Gadea, Vittorio di Bucci, and Christophe Giolito, the latter who is guilty of helping me finish the 2009 Florence Marathon!

Gratitude is also owed to other people who commented on a previous presentation of my research at the 10th session of the Dubrovnik Seminar 'Advanced issues of European Law', especially Siniša Rodin, Monica Claes, Christophe Hillion, and Steven Blockmans. Also thanks to the staff of the EUI Library and of the Historical Archives of the European Union. I would like to mention in particular Evangelia, Machteld, and Ruth, all of whom made the historical part of my thesis possible. Francoise Thauvin, from the EUI Academic Service, supported me throughout my doctorate, and Rossana Lewis at the Law Department provided valuable assistance in the last stages of the thesis on which this book is based. Special thanks go to my closest friends at the EUI, to Gonzalo, Emilie, Fernando, Mateja, Mislav, Jerneja, Chiara, Lisa, Alex, Marina, Tamara, Juana, Germán, and Teimuraz, who made my years in Florence some of the best of my life.

I also owe a lot to Cesáreo Gutiérrez Espada, my first professor in International and European Law at Murcia University, for awakening my interest in these subjects, for supporting every step of my career, and for offering me his precious advice and invaluable friendship. I am also indebted to María José Cervell, from whom I have learned a great deal as an academic and as well as a person. Friends, many of them, in Murcia, in Brussels, and from Harvard Law School, have made this book possible with their constant encouragement. Elías is certainly one of them, also Pierantonio, Andrés, Carlos, Ángel, Miguel, Víctor, Valentina, and Agus.

Of course I want to thank my family, starting with my parents, who have given everything to me and never asked for anything in return, for their love, their effort, the example they set, and their generosity. I want to thank also my sister, Paqui, her husband Antonio, and their daughther Ana, who have always backed my projects and helped me and our parents to feel close while being far away. Thanks too to the rest of my family, to my uncles, aunts, cousins, and especially my grandparents, those physically with us and those in our hearts; all are key touchstones for me. I would like to thank Dorothy and Fernando for welcoming me as a son, for the many great conversations on a thousand topics, and particularly for the very generous and loving way in which they have accepted and supported the fact that their daughter lives in Europe with me. Thanks also in this regard to Monica, Mary Fer, Isa, Memo, Alan, Juan Fer, Matilda, and Jimena for the wonderful moments that we spend together every time we meet.

Finally, I want to thank very specially Dorothy, my wife, my love, my life. Since we met at the EUI she has been my friend, my confidante, my strength, and my happiness. She has also made me recognize worlds other than our own, about the millions of anonymous heroes, from women to migrants and people with disabilities who live among us, often unappreciated. This book is dedicated to you, and to the first pages of that dream we are writing together, to our son Alonso and to our daughter Elena.

Contents

Table of Cases

Page numbers in **bold** indidcate extended analysis. *n* = footnote.

Table of Statutes

n = footnote.

INTERNATIONAL AGREEMENTS

EUROPEAN LEGISLATION

Conventions/Treaties/Agreements

Directives (in chronological order)

Regulations (in chronological order)

Decisions, Communications, Resolutions etc.

NATIONAL LEGISLATION

Germany

Italy

United Kingdom

United States

BILATERAL /MULTILATERAL AGREEMENTS

List of Abbreviations

AG	Advocate General
BAA	British Aggregates Association
BEPS	Base Erosion and Profit Shifting
BIAC	Business and Advisory Committee (to the OECD)
BPOT	Business Property Occupation Tax
CFI	Court of First Instance
ECJ	European Court of Justice
ECOFIN	Economic and Financial Affairs Council
ECSC	European Coal and Steel Community
EDF	Electricité de France
EEA	European Economic Area
EEC	European Economic Community
EFTA	European Free Trade Association
EMU	Economic and Monetary Union
EU	European Union
FDI	Foreign Direct Investment
FNE	Fonds National de L'Emploi
FT	France Télécom
GATT	General Agreement on Tariffs and Trade
GDP	Gross Domestic Product
ITO	International Trade Organization
MEIP	Market Economy Investor Principle
OECD	Organisation for Economic Co-operation and Development
R&D	Research and Development
SAAP	State Aid Action Plan
SAM	State Aid Modernisation
SGEI	Services of General Economic Interest
SMEs	Small and Medium-size Enterprises
TFEU	Treaty on the Functioning of the European Union
WTO	World Trade Organization

PART I

1
Introduction

Article 107(1) of the Treaty on the Functioning of the European Union (TFEU) provides that 'Save as otherwise provided in the Treaties, any aid granted by a Member State or through State resources in any form whatsoever which distorts or threatens to distort competition by favouring certain undertakings or the production of certain goods shall, in so far as it affects trade between Member States, be incompatible with the internal market.' This article declares 'any aid' (or State aid, as it is usually called) *a priori* incompatible with the internal market. Article 107(1) TFEU does not define 'aid'. The Court of Justice has clarified that this notion requires the following criteria to be met:

> First, there must be an intervention by the State or through State resources. Second, the intervention must be liable to affect trade between Member States. Third, it must confer an advantage on the recipient. Fourth, it must distort or threaten to distort competition.[1] The Court of Justice has also clarified that the advantage conferred must be selective as it has to favour 'certain undertakings or the production of certain goods.[2]

This article has not been modified since its introduction in the European Economic Community Treaty of 1957, save for the draftsman substituting the phrase 'internal market' in place of 'common market'.

This book is concerned with the legal concept of State aid encapsulated in this provision. It was borne out of the concern that European institutions and practitioners alike refer to it as if this concept had been immune to the evolution experienced by the context in which it has been applied: the internal market. Indeed, while the evolution and even transformation of the Common Market from the early 1960s to the present is unanimously recognized, Commission decisions, court judgments, and textbooks explain the notion of aid today through a number of formulas mostly laid down by the Court of Justice in the 1960s and 1970s.[3] Similarly, other formulas concerning the notion of aid have appeared

[1] See in this regard, eg, C-280/00 *Altmark* [2003] ECR I-7747, para. 75.

[2] See, eg, C-409/00 *Spain v Commission* [2003] ECR I-1487.

[3] This is the case for the notion of aid (and advantage) laid down by the Court in 1961 in case C-30/59, *De Gezamenlijke Steenkolenmijnen in Limburg v High Authority of the European Coal and Steel Community*, [1961] ECR 1, for the notion of selectivity for which reference is usually made

more recently in the case law of the Court, such as the Market Economy Investor Principle or the concept of selectivity coined by the Court in the *Adria-Wien* judgment, yet no explanation is usually given as to the factors that led to the emergence of these more recent formulas, or what changes they brought with respect to the previous ones.

Against this seemingly static legal background, the literature of political science on State aid policy makes evident how dynamic the evolution of this policy has been. Political scientists show that the State aid policy has served different goals over time and that the development of this policy has been heavily influenced by the difficulties that the European Commission has encountered in enforcing the State aid rules due to the Member States' reluctance to make these rules effective.

Likewise, against this apparently unchanging legal background, some judges of the Court of Justice have identified a number of phases or periods in the case law of the Court based on its general approach during those periods. In other words, they have observed an evolution in the case law of the Court of Justice. Similarly, some authors have observed an evolution of the case law of the Court in relation to some important economic law provisions of the Treaty, such as the provisions on free movement of goods and competition provisions.

This book tries to reconcile the legal and policy narratives described above in relation to the concept of aid. It argues that the study of the policy of State aid provides a more holistic understanding of the current legal concept of aid because this concept, despite its static appearance, has evolved and has done so mainly in line with the policy priorities of the European Commission in this field, but also as a result of the enforcement difficulties that the Commission has experienced in the application of these rules. Secondly, the book argues that the evolution of this concept has also been influenced by the evolution of the case law of the Court of Justice in different periods of the integration process. Indeed, the book argues that the concept of aid, as with other economic law provisions of the Treaty, is not *fixed or stable, but instead fluid*, and has been influenced by the political and economic context in which it has been applied.[4]

In order to show the validity of these claims, Part I (Chapters 1–3) of the book provides an analytical framework that includes an historical account of the origin of subsidy control in Europe, a review of the legislative history of today's Article 107 TFEU, and a study of the evolution of State aid policy. This framework is then

to the judgment in Joined Cases C-6/69 and C-11/69, *France v Commission*, [1969] ECR 523, and shortly after in 1974 in case 173/73, *Commission v Italy*, [1974] 703, for that of State resources in 1977 in case C-78/76, *Steinike & Weinlig v Federal Republic of Germany*, [1977] ECR 00595, or effect on trade in 1980 in case C-730/79, *Philip Morris v European Commission*, [1980] ECR 02671.

[4] We have borrowed the terminology of Gráinne de Búrca in De Burca, G., 'Unpacking the concept of discrimination in EC and international trade law', in Barnard, C., and Scott, J. (eds), *The Law of the Single European Market: Unpacking the Premises* (Hart Publishing, 2002) 181 at 182, where she held that 'A common misapprehension is to assume that these concepts-protectionism, discrimination market access etc.—have relatively fixed or stable meaning... On the contrary, consideration of the development of the EC internal market... over time suggests that the concepts themselves are eminently fluid and that their construction is capable of changing as the economic and political context in which they are being interpreted alters.'

discussed in Part II (Chapters 4–7) in relation to the main formulas established by the Court concerning the concept of aid, which allows the reader a better understanding of why these formulas emerged and why they did so at a particular time in light of the policy and legal context in which they appeared. In so doing, the book places the legal concept of aid in the broader economic and political context in which it has been applied. Finally, Part III of the book reviews the main conclusions drawn from the two previous parts and includes a case study related to the State aids granted to the financial sector during the most recent crisis.

This book is thus concerned with providing the reader with a richer understanding of the current formulas that depict the concept of aid through the prism of policy and enforcement considerations. It is not aimed at devising an abstract test for the concept of aid or for any of its criteria. Nevertheless, by providing a closer look at the interests and reasons that underpinned the emergence of the formulas that are used to define the concept of aid, this book may offer some useful tools to help decide some cases in the future as it provides a number of elements by which to judge whether the application of a particular formula to the facts of a given case is justified in the light of the objectives that led to the adoption of the formula at issue. Finally, this chapter includes a brief review of the relevant literature, followed by a summary of the book's argument and chapter synopses.

1. Literature Review

Legal literature on the concept of State aid is by now abundant. Contributions tend to study the criteria included in this concept as it has been shaped by the case law of the Court of Justice. In this regard, most contributions discuss one or more of the criteria mentioned, namely: State resources, advantage, selectivity, distortion of competition, or effect on trade, often in response to a particular development in the case law of the Court of Justice.[5] Authors tend to emphasize the broad meaning that the Court of Justice has given to this concept, applicable to most forms of State intervention (ie fiscal, social, and monetary measures), and to underline the tension existing between the breadth of the concept, based on the effects of State intervention and not on the form it takes, and the decision of the Court to exclude regulatory measures from its scope.

[5] See, eg, Slotboom, M., 'State Aid in Community Law: A Broad or Narrow Definition?' (1995) *European Law Review* 289; Biondi, A., 'Some Reflections on the Notion of "State Resources" in European Community State Aid Law' (2007) *Fordham International Law Journal* 1426; Bacon, K., 'State Aids and General Measures' (1997) *Yearbook of European Law* 269; Bartosch, A., 'Is there a Need for a Rule of Reason in European State aid law?: Or How to Arrive at a Coherent Concept of Material Selectivity?' (2010) *Common Market Law Review* 729; Vesterndorf, B., 'A Further Comment on the New State Aid Concept as this Concept Continues to be Reshaped—Pearle—A Further Piece of the State Aid Puzzle?' (2005) *European State Aid Law Quarterly* 393; Baquero Cruz, J., and Castillo de la Torre, F., 'A Note on PreussenElektra' (2001) *European Law Review* 489; Miro, P., 'The Requirement of Selectivity in the Recent Case-law of the Court of Justice' (2012) *European State Aid Law Quarterly* 335.

There is also a significant body of literature that has analysed the concept of State aid in relation to a particular form of State intervention in the economy. In this regard, the application of the concept of State aid to tax measures is one of the most studied topics.[6] Similarly, the relationship between the concept of State aid and social measures[7] or between this concept and State participation in the economy has also been examined in detail.[8] In the same vein, many contributions have covered the relationship between the concept of State aid and the financing of public services, particularly since the adoption by the Court of Justice and the General Court of a number of contradictory rulings relating to these services in the early 2000s.[9]

More recently, and this time due to a policy initiative by the European Commission (the so-called State Aid Action Plan (SAAP)), the concept of State aid has been the subject of several studies from an economic perspective. Papers, articles, and books studying the economic rationale of the granting and control of subsidies, as well as the economic foundations (or lack thereof) of some of the legal interpretations of the criteria included in the concept of State aid, have appeared in considerable volume.[10] They have enriched a discussion that has been for a long time predominantly occupied by legal narratives.

[6] See, eg, Quigley, C., 'General Taxation and State Aid', in Biondi, A., Eeckhout, P., and Flynn, J. (eds), *The Law of State Aid in the European Union* (OUP, 2004) 207; Schön, W., 'Taxation and State Aid Law in the European Union' (1999) *Common Market Law Review* 910; Bacon, K., 'Differential Taxes, State Aids and the Lunn Poly Case' (1999) *European Competition Law Review* 384; Bourgeois, J.H.J., 'State Aids, Taxation Measures and Specificity. Some Thoughts', in Dony, M., and De Walsche, A. (eds), *Mélanges en hommage à Michel Waelbroeck*, Vol 2 (Bruylant, 1999) 765; Di Bucci, V., 'Direct Taxation'—State Aid in Form of Fiscal Measures', in Rydelski, M.S. (ed.), *The EC State Aid Regime: Distortive Effects of State Aid on Competition and Trade* (Cameron May, 2006) 73; Nicolaides, P., 'Fiscal State Aid in the EU: The Limits of Tax Autonomy' (2004) *World Competition* 365; Nicolaides, P., 'Fiscal Aid in the EC: A Critical Review of Current Practice' (2001) *World Competition* 319.

[7] Biondi, A., and Rubini, L., 'Aims, Effects and Justifications: EC State Aid Law and Its Impact on National Social Policies', in Dougan, M., and Spaventa, E. (eds), *Social Welfare and EU Law* (Hart Publishing, 2005) 79; Davies, P., 'Market Integration and Social Policy in the Court of Justice' (1995) *Industrial Law Journal* 49; Atanasiu, I., 'EC State Aid Policy with Respect to Soft Budgetary Constraints: Tax and Social Security Contribution Payment Arrears' (2005) *European State Aid Law Quarterly* 597.

[8] See, eg, Abate, A., 'Privatisations et déréglementations en droit communautaire' in *EC State Aid law—Le Droit des Aides d'État dans la CE, Liber Amicorum Francisco Santaolalla Gadea* (Kluwer Law International, 2008) 239; Atanasiu, I., 'Chronopost II: The Application of the Market Economy Investor Principle in Reserved Sectors' (2008) *European State Aid Law Quarterly* 571; Khan, N., and Borchardt, K.D., 'The Private Market Investor Principle: Reality Check or Distorting Mirror?' in *EC State Aid law/Le droit des aides d'État dans le CE: liber amicorum Francisco Santaolalla Gadea* (Wolters Kluwer Netherland 2008) 109; Anestis, P., and Mavroghenis, S., 'The Market Investor Test', in Rydelski, M.S. (ed.), *The EC State Aid Regime: Distortive Effects of State Aid on Competition and Trade* (Cameron May, 2006) 109.

[9] See, eg, Szyszczak, E., 'Financing Services of General Economic Interest' (2004) *Modern Law Review* 982; Biondi, A., 'Justifying State Aid: The Financing of Services of General Economic Interest', in Tridimas, T., and Nebbia P. (eds), *European Union Law for the Twenty-First Century*, Vol. II (Hart Publishing, 2004); Bovis, C.H., 'Financing Services of General Interest in the EU: How do Public Procurement and State Aids Interact to Demarcate between Market Forces and Protection' (2005) *European Law Journal* 79.

[10] See, eg, Crocioni, P., 'Can State Aid Policy Become more Economic-Friendly?' (2006) *World Competition*, 89; Neven, D., and Verouden, V., 'Towards a More Refined Economic Approach in State

The SAAP has led to an interesting discussion in the literature on the objectives and the nature of the State aid rules, which includes a significant discussion on the interpretation of the concept of aid that would best suit those objectives and the rules' nature. Among the scholars two groups can be distinguished. One group defends the view that State aid rules have more in common with the internal market than with competition rules, which leads to a limited role for economics in the State aid field, as in the case of the internal market field.[11] By contrast, another group of commentators proposes to introduce more economics in the analysis of distortions of competition produced by State aid measures and in this way to complete the trend towards an effects-based approach to the competition rules enshrined in the Treaty, of which the State aid rules would also form part.[12]

Fewer contributions have discussed the concept of aid in a broader context; that is, in relation to other legal rules or policy objectives of the European Union. Ross and Winter have discussed recent developments of the concept of State aid in the light of the decentralization of the European competition rules that has taken place since the early 2000s.[13] Similarly, Biondi and others have discussed some of the criteria included in this concept in relation to the prohibitions and justifications provided for the internal market rules.[14]

Aid Control', in Mederer, W., Pesaresi, N., and Van Hoof, M. (eds), *EU Competition Law*, Volume IV, State Aid, Book One (Claeys & Casteels, 2008) 99; Garcia, J., and Neven, D., 'Identification of Sensitive Sectors in which State Aid may have Significant Distorting Effects', Report for the HM Treasury, UK, 2004; Nitsche, R., and Heidhues, P., Study on Methods to Analyse the Impact of State Aid on Competition, Report prepared for the European Commission, Directorate General for Economics and Financial Affairs (Final Report ECFIN/R/2004/004): Bruxelles (2005).

[11] Buendia Sierra, J.L., 'Not Like This: Some Skeptical Remarks on the "Refined Economic Approach" in State aid', in Proceedings of Fourth Experts' Forum on New Developments in European State Aid Law, 18 and 19 May 2006, European State Aid Law Institute (Lexxion, 2006) 59; Buendia Sierra, J.L., and Smulders, B., 'The Limited Role of the "Refined Economic Approach" in Achieving the Objectives of State Aid Control: Time for Some Realism', in *EC State Aid Law—Le Droit des Aides d'État dans la CE, Liber Amicorum Francisco Santaolalla Gadea* (Kluwer Law International, 2008) 18.

[12] Derenne, J., and Merola, M. (eds), *Economic Analysis of State Aid Rules—Contributions and Limits* (Lexxion, 2007); Friederiszick, H.W., Röller, L.H., and Verouden, V., European State Aid Control: An Economic Framework, in Bucirossi, P. (ed.), *Handbook of Antitrust Economics* (MIT Press, 2008) 625; Hancher, L., 'Towards an Economic Analysis of State Aid' (2005) *European State Aid Law Quarterly* 425; Ahlborn, C., and Berg, C., 'Can State Aid Control Learn from Antitrust? The Need for Greater Role for Competition Analysis under the State Aid rules', in Biondi, A., Eeckhout, P., and Flynn, J. (eds), *The Law of State Aid in the European Union* (OUP, 2004) 41.

[13] Ross, M., 'State Aids: Maturing into a Constitutional Problem' (1995) *Yearbook of European Law* 79; Ross, M., 'State Aids and National Courts: Definitions and Other Problems—a Case of Premature Emancipation?' (2000) *Common Market Law Review* 401; Ross, M., 'Decentralization, Effectiveness, and Modernization: Contradiction in Terms?' (2004) in Biondi, A., Eeckhout, P., and Flynn, J. (eds), *The Law of State Aid in the European Union* (OUP, 2004) 85; Winter, M., 'Redefining the Notion of State Aid in Article 87(1) of the EC Treaty' (2004) *Common Market Law Review* 475.

[14] Biondi, A., and Eeckhout, P., 'State Aid and Obstacles to Trade' in Biondi, A, Eeckhout, P., and Flynn, J. (eds) *The Law of State Aid in the European Union* (OUP, 2004) 103; Biondi, A., and Farley, M., 'The Relationship between State Aid and the Single Market' in *Research Handbook on European State Aid Law* (Edward Elgar Publishing, 2011) 277.

Finally, a smaller amount of contributions have dealt with the legal concept of State aid as a whole, thus dealing with an analysis of all the criteria included in today's article 107(1) TFEU. Beyond contributions in textbooks[15] and journal articles,[16] a seminal book that forecasted a significant amount of future developments of the case law, was written by Scheuing in 1974.[17] More recently, Rubini has published an in-depth analysis of the concept of State aid, probably the most complete critical contribution to the study of this concept published thus far.[18] He conducted a comparative analysis of the concept of aid with that of subsidy in the context of the World Trade Organization (WTO). His study analyses the many forms of government action covered by both sets of rules and highlights how often in both the WTO and European Union frameworks the legal definition of aid or subsidy is conflated with the justifications given for granting them. Recently, De Cecco has published a monograph entitled *State Aid and the European Economic Constitution*.[19] This book analyses the concept of aid in the broader context of the role and purpose of the State aid regime within the economic constitution, and the differences and similarities that this regime has with the anti-trust and the internal market rules.

The contributions hitherto discussed have analysed the legal concept of aid from a predominantly static perspective; that is, from the study of the law as it stands at the moment of the analysis.[20] They also analyse this concept by focusing on legal sources, particularly the case law of the Court of Justice, coupled with economic insights. This book seeks to contribute to the existing literature

[15] Recently a number of excellent textbooks on State aid have been published. They cover all the relevant Commission decisions, Court judgments, and compatibility instruments (guidelines, block exemption regulations, etc) concerning State aid rules. Their task is, naturally, to provide a complete account of the case law, not to examine it in detail from a critical perspective. Nevertheless they also tend to include some critical remarks. Among already classic works are: Keppenne, J.P., *Guide des aides d'état en droit communautaire: réglementation, jurisprudence et pratique de la Commission* (Bruylant, 1999); Hancher, L., Ottervanger, T., and Slot, P.J., *EU state aids*, 4th edn (Sweet & Maxwell/Thomson Reuters, 2012); Quigley, C., *European State Aid Law and Policy*, 2nd edn (Hart, 2009); Dony, M., Renard, F., and Smits, C., *Contrôle des aides d'État*, 3ème édn (Editions de l'université de Bruxelles, 2007). See for other recent contributions Mederer, Pesaresi, and Van Hoof (eds), *EU Competition Law—Volume IV: State Aid*, op. cit.; or Bacon, K. (general ed.), *European Community Law of State Aid* (OUP, 2009).

[16] See, eg, Quigley, C., 'The Notion of a State Aid in the EEC' (1988) *European Law Review* 242; Plender, R., 'Definition of Aid', in Biondi, A., Eeckhout, P., and Flynn, J. (eds), *The Law of State Aid in the European Union* (OUP, 2004) 3.

[17] Scheuing, D.H., *Les aides financiers publiques aux enterprises en droit francaise et européen* (Editions Berger-Levrault, 1974).

[18] Rubini, L., *The Definition of Subsidy and State Aid: WTO and EC Law in Comparative Perspective* (OUP, 2009).

[19] De Cecco, F., *State Aid and the European Economic Constitution* (Hart, 2013). See also the recent article based on a chapter of this book written by De Cecco, F., 'State Aid and Self-Government: Regional Taxation and the Shifting Spaces of Constitutional Autonomy', in Shuibhne, N.N., and Gormley, L. (eds), *From Single Market to Economic Union: Essays in Memory of John A. Usher* (OUP, 2012) 221.

[20] For an exception to the static analysis, see the thesis of Arpio Santacruz, J.L., *State Aids in the European Community: Framework Exceptions and Implications for National Economic Policies*, doctoral thesis defended at the European University Institute in 1996.

by studying the concept of aid from a dynamic perspective; that is, by examining the criteria included in the concept of aid as it has been interpreted by the case law of the Court of Justice in different periods of the process of European integration, and by bringing to the analysis not only legal sources but also historical and political-science literature. In this regard, the periods chosen for analysis have been those identified by political scientists who have studied the evolution of State aid policy. Similarly, the book provides a brief historical account of the reasons for granting and for controlling subsidies as well as a study of the legislative history of the current Article 107(1) TFEU. These sources enrich the analysis and facilitate a better understanding of the current concept of aid and its evolving character. Indeed, this book seeks to contribute to the existing literature by analysing the legal concept of aid through the prism of the policy and enforcement considerations that have determined the evolution of the State aid policy. The book also attempts to add to the existing literature by analysing the evolution of this concept in light of the evolution of the case law of the Court of Justice as described by some of its judges. In sum, the book aims to complement the existing literature by discussing the historical, policy, and enforcement considerations that may explain the current legal concept of aid.

2. The Argument

This book presents three principal and related strands of argument. First, it is proposed that the legal concept of aid, despite its alleged objective character based on economic considerations, has evolved and has done so not because of a different interpretation of the economic foundations of this notion but as a result of the policy priorities of the European Commission, which change over time, coupled with the difficulties that the Commission has encountered in enforcing the State aid rules. Second, the book argues that the evolution of the concept of aid has also been influenced by the evolution of the case law of the Court of Justice and that the evolution of this concept tracks the way the Court has handled mainstream fields of European economic law such as the free movement of goods or the competition law provisions. Third, this book argues that the study of the evolution of the concept of aid in light of the two previous frameworks (evolution of policy and of case law) provides not only a holistic knowledge of this concept but it is also useful in deciding difficult cases. This is the case because an approximation of the policy objectives and interests present before the Court when it laid down a particular formula concerning the concept of aid does more than help understand the reasons that may have underpinned that particular formula. It also gives guidance as to how that formula should be applied in the future in accordance with those reasons, in more than a ritualistic fashion. It emphasizes that the formulas are a means to an end, not the ends themselves.

In order to assess the validity of these arguments, for each of the criteria included in Article 107(1) TFEU this book identifies a number of cases in which the Court of Justice laid down for the first time a formula that has since become a standard way of depicting a particular criterion.[21] For each of the cases identified a policy and enforcement context is given. In particular, the book will look at the period in which the different formulas that today integrate the concept of aid emerged, the objectives pursued by the State aid rules during that period, as identified in the chapter devoted to the evolution of the State aid policy (Chapter 3), and at the policy considerations at stake in the case under review. Finally, in the assessment of each of these cases reference will often also be made to the general approach of the case law of the Court during the relevant period and to the original interpretation of the criterion under review, as can be ascertained from the study of the legislative history of the current Article 107(1) TFEU and early academic sources.

The book thus looks at a selection of cases which have been carefully chosen among all relevant State aid cases regarding definition, all of which have been reviewed by the author. The main criterion for this selection has been, as mentioned, that in each given case the Court coined for the first time in the selected judgment a formula that has since become the standard formula to refer to a particular element of the notion of aid. Moreover, each case analysis is not just a case note but is an integrated analysis of how the judgment at hand fits with the main policy initiatives of the Commission and the general jurisprudence of the Court during the period in which the case was laid down. Finally, only cases from the Court of Justice, and not from the General Court, have been included in the selection for three main reasons: (i) because only the case law of the Court of Justice can be traced back to the early years of the European Economic Community, (ii) because the Court of Justice is the ultimate interpreter of EU Law—and this has become particularly evident in recent years in the State aid field in which the General Court and the Court of Justice have disagreed in some important cases, and (iii) because the Court of Justice remains the only Court with jurisdiction to give preliminary rulings,[22] and some of the most important cases in the State aid field have appeared in this form.

The analysis of the criteria of the concept of aid will follow the order in which, it is submitted, the Commission and the Court of Justice usually conduct it: whether there has been an advantage, if this advantage is selective, granted by a State or through State resources, and ultimately whether it may distort competition and affects trade. In this regard, as a former Advocate General, President of the Court of First Instance, and current Judge of the Court of Justice held, European courts usually start the analysis of the concept of aid by asking the

[21] The book does not deal with the concept of economic activity in the State aid field but this concept is of paramount importance for the application of the concept of aid as it only applies to undertakings pursuing an economic activity. See, for the important role of economic activity in the State aid field, eg the recent case C-288/11 P, *Mitteldeutsche Flughafen AG and Flughafen Leipzig-Halle GmbH v Commission* [2012] nyr.

[22] See Information Note on references from national courts for a preliminary ruling (2011/C 160/01) at I.3.

question of whether a given advantage is selective, leaving to the end the issue of the distortion of competition.[23]

A. The concept of aid and the policy priorities of the European Commission

The first argument defended by this book submits that the legal concept of aid has evolved in accordance with the policy priorities of the European Commission. These priorities have been identified in the work of a number of political scientists that have divided the evolution of State aid policy into a number of periods: (i) first period (from 1958 to early 1970s), (ii) second period (from early 1970s to mid-1980s), (iii) third period (mid-1980s to mid-1990s), and the (iv) fourth period (from mid- to late 1990s to the present).[24]

In this regard, the concept of aid during the first period was initially restricted to financial measures affecting the costs of production of undertakings operating in the sectors most exposed to intra-community trade, such as the textile sector, and to financial measures that directly damaged the interests of out of State traders such as export aid or para-fiscal measures,[25] which were also the first cases that reached the Court in this field.[26] This concept of aid thus mirrored the policy priorities of the European Commission during the early years of application of the Rome Treaties, namely the establishment of the Common Market through the elimination of all discriminatory barriers to trade. In the same vein, the weight given by the Commission to the effect on trade criteria during the early years is indicative of the early focus on measures that could have an appreciable impact on trade.

Similarly, the policy priorities of the Commission during the second period of State aid policy (early 1970s to mid-1980s) were concerned with the recovery of

[23] Cruz Vilaca, J., 'Material and Geographic Selectivity in State Aid—Recent Developments' (2009) *European State Aid Law Quarterly*, 444.

[24] See Lavdas, K.A., and Mendrinou, M.M., *Politics, Subsidies, and Competition: The New Politics of State Intervention in the European Union* (Edward Elgar, 1999); Doleys, T., 'Fifty Years of Moulding Article 87: The European Commission and the Development of EU State Aid Law & Policy (1958–2008)', Paper prepared for presentation at the 11th Biennial International Conference of the European Union Studies Association in Marina Del Ray, CA, 2009; See Mederer, 'Evolution of State Aid Control' in Mederer, Pesaresi, and Van Hoof (eds), *EU Competition Law, Volume IV, State aid, Book One*, op. cit., 19; or Blauberger, M., 'Of "Good" and "Bad" Subsidies: European State Aid Control through Soft and Hard Law' (2009) *West European Politics*, 719 See also the recent periodization of the evolution of State aids by a legal scholar Tosato, G.L., 'L'evoluzione della disciplina sugli aiuti di Stato', in Schepisi, C. (ed.), *La modernizzazione della disciplina sugli aiuti di Stato: il nuovo approccio della Commissione europea e i recenti sviluppi in materia di public e private enforcement* (G. Giappichelli, 2011) 3.

[25] Para-fiscal levies are charges levied for a specific purpose; for example, the promotion of national industry. They may be disadvantageous for foreign undertakings because they usually do not benefit from the purported purpose.

[26] See, for export aid, Joined Cases C-6/69 and C-11/69 *Commission v France* [1969] ECR 523; and for para-fiscal levies Case 47/69 *Government of the French Republic v Commission* [1970] ECR 487.

the competitiveness of the European industry after the oil crisis and the reduction of the heavy burden represented by part of the public sector. These priorities led to the application of the advantage criterion of the notion of aid to the activities of the public undertakings through the Market Economy Investor Principle (MEIP) test which complemented the Transparency Directive, adopted in 1980. The fact that this test was not the result of a new understanding of the economic concept of advantage is evident because the test had already been outlined by the Commission in 1963,[27] yet seldom used until the 1980s.[28] The beginning of the systematic application of the MEIP test represents the start of a trend that has since materialized, a trend towards the application of State aid rules to prevent distortions of competition between competitors through individual aid rather than distortions of trade between national economies through sectorial aid, aid to exports, or para-fiscal levies, as was the case in the first period.

During the third period (mid-1980s to mid-1990s), the Commission profited from the momentum created by States supporting the 1992 programme of further integration, and sought to tighten the State aid control. The Commission confirmed the trend initiated in the previous period and applied the State aid rules with an increasing focus on aid being given to companies in competition with other companies in a given Member State (intra-jurisdictional competition), and less focus on aid granted to help them to compete against undertakings placed in other Member States (inter-jurisdictional competition). The formulas adopted by the Court during this period also reflect this more competition-oriented approach. In this regard, in the FNE (Kimberley Clark)[29] case the Court upheld a concept of selectivity based on the discretion enjoyed by the public authorities, thereby initiating a trend towards a discrimination-like test for selectivity that was also easier to understand for competitors of the beneficiary undertaking. Similarly, in the *SFEI* judgment the Court adopted a notion of aid that made all State measures, and not only capital injections, subject to review under market conditions.[30] In the same vein, the Court diminished the evidence that the Commission had to put forward in relation to the distortion of competition and effect on trade criteria, concluding also that a *de minimis* rule in the State aid field could not be

[27] See the Reply to Parliamentary Question No. 48 of Mr Burgbecher, 30 July 1963, OJ 2235/63: '*Au cas où la puissance publique renonce, en tout ou en partie, a la rémunération du capital propre d'une entreprise d'État ou de toute autre entreprise publique, un telle renociation pourrait, le cas échéant, être considérée comme une aide d'État. De l'avis de la Commission, ceci pourrait se concevoir dans la mesure ou un propriétaire ou actionnaire privé se trouvant dans une situation comparable et agissant en vertu de considérations d'ordre économique, ne renoncerait pas—ou ne renoncerait que dans un mesure limitée—á la rémunération de son capital propre; autrement dit, la renonciation a laquelle consentirait la puissance publique résulterait en l'occurrence non pas considérations d'ordre économique, mais de motifs d'ordre politique.*'

[28] Second Report on Competition Policy (Office for Official Publications of the European Communities, 1973) at point 124.

[29] C-241/94 *France v Commission* [1996] ECR I-4551 at 24.

[30] Case C-39/94, *Syndicat français de l'Express international (SFEI) and others v La Poste and others* [1996] ECR p. I-03547 at 60: 'in order to determine whether a State measure constitutes aid, it is necessary to establish whether the recipient undertaking receives an economic advantage which it would not have obtained under normal market conditions'.

accepted, and this in cases of aid to a single undertaking,[31] thus furthering the trend towards the applications of the State aid rules as competition rules.

Finally, during the fourth period, initiated in the mid- to late 1990s, the most significant policy initiative pursued by the European Commission has been the use of the State aid rules to combat harmful business taxation.[32] The Court has supported this initiative by upholding the selectivity test proposed by the European Commission, including as regards the justification by the nature or general scheme in several judgments.[33] However, in this last period the Court has been sensitive to other goals now included in the Treaties, such as the respect for the special role of Services of General Economic Interest (SGEI) in the Union, included since the Amsterdam Treaty, or the respect for the national (constitutional) identity of Member States, now included in Article 4(2) TEU. These other treaty provisions may help explain judgments decided during this period, such as *Altmark* or *Chronopost*[34] concerning SGEIs, or *Azores* and *UGT-Rioja*,[35] related to the respect for regional government and the national constitutional identity of Member States, in which the Court has balanced the orthodox application of the State aid rules with the more recent goals. To conclude, it is perhaps too early to assess whether the fourth period has led to a new phase after the 2004 State Aid Action Plan and the Commission's response to the banking crisis in 2008. The changes triggered by these initiatives seem to be, at least thus far, more concerned with the criteria for aid compatibility than with definitional issues, although the banking crisis has also led to important clarifications on the notion of aid which are discussed in the case study included in Part III of the book.

B. The concept of aid and the evolution of the case law of the Court of Justice of the European Union

The second argument defended by this book submits that the evolution of the concept of aid has also been influenced by the evolution of the case law of the Court of Justice as described by some of its judges.

In this regard, Judge Koopmans has noted that during the 1950s and 1960s the case law of the Court of Justice was characterized by institutional issues such as the direct effect of Treaty provisions or the independence of the High Authority

[31] Case C-142/87 *Belgium v Commission (Tubemeuse)* [1990] ECR I-00959 at para. 43; C-301/87 *France v Commission ('Boussac')* [1990] ECR I-307.

[32] See Conclusions of the ECOFIN Council Meeting on 1 December 1997 concerning taxation policy—Official Journal C 002, 06/01/1998 P. 0001–0006; 'The Council held a wide-ranging debate in the light of the Commission communication entitled "A package to tackle harmful tax competition in the European Union", which takes stock of a discussion initiated by the Commission at the informal meeting of Ministers for Economic Affairs and Finance in Verona in April 1996 and given more substantial shape at the informal meeting in Mondorf-les-Bains in September 1997'.

[33] See for all, C-88/03 *Portugal v Commission* (Azores) [2006] ECR I-7115 at 81.

[34] Case C-280/00 *Altmark* [2003] ECR I-7747; Joined Cases C-83/01 P, C-93/01P, C-94/01/P *Chronopost* [2003] ECR p.I-6993.

[35] C-88/03 *Portugal v Commission* (Azores) [2006] ECR I-7115 and UGT Rioja C-428/06 to C-434/06 *UGT-Rioja and Others* [2008] ECR I-06747.

(and the Commission) from Member States, more than on substantive ones. He referred to this period as *institutional*.[36] Similarly, the few cases on State aid decided during this period were concerned with institutional issues such as the direct effect of today's Article 108 TFEU.[37] The Court's preference for institutional issues was also made clear by the way in which the Court dealt with the few substantive issues brought before it during this period, namely, by issuing broad principles purporting to assert the Commission competence in this field rather than to clarify the substance of the notion of aid.[38]

Secondly, Judge Koopmans claimed that the case law of the Court during the 1970s could be referred as *instrumental* 'to realising the European treaties' general aims'.[39] Examples of instrumental judgments handed down during this period include the *ERTA*,[40] *Dassonville*,[41] and *Continental Can* decisions.[42] Similarly, in the State aid field the Court decided during this period some of the most important judgments for the concept of aid such as the *Italian textiles*[43] and the *Steinike* and *Weinlig*[44] cases, both instrumental as they clarify important notions concerning all the criteria of the concept of aid and, more generally, because they clarify the role of the State aid rules within the Treaty architecture. Also from this period is the *Van Tiggele* decision.[45] This decision was also instrumental to the Commission enforcement priorities, both in the internal market and in the State aid fields, and, as a matter of fact, the decision of the Court matched the outcome sought in the Commission's pleadings.

Thirdly, during the 1980s, the Court became less activist, requiring more evidence from the Commission in order to uphold its decisions. Koopmans referred to this period as one of a *return to minimalism*.[46] Similarly, in the State aid field this period coincided with the first annulments of State aid decisions precisely due to defective motivation or poor legal basis.[47]

Fourthly, towards the end of this decade, the success of the internal market programme led to a time of *euphoria*, as underlined by Judge Everling,[48] in which

[36] See Koopmans,T., 'The Role of Law in the Next Stage of European Integration' (1986) *International and Comparative Law Quarterly*, 925 at 926–7.

[37] See Case 6/64 *Flaminio Costa v E.N.E.L.*, ECR, P. I-0114.

[38] For an example of this approach, see Joined Cases C-6/69 and C-11/69 *Commission v France* [1969] ECR 523.

[39] See Koopmans, 'The Role of Law in the Next Stage of European Integration', op. cit. at 927.

[40] Case 22/70 *Commission v Council* (ERTA) [1971] ECR 263.

[41] Case 8/74 *Procureur du Roi v Benoît and Gustave Dassonville* [1974] ECR 00837

[42] Case C-6/72 *Continental Can v Commission* [1973] ECR 215.

[43] See Case 173/73 *Italy v Commission* [1974] ECR 709.

[44] Case C-78/76 *Steinike & Weinlig v Federal Republic of Germany* [1977] ECR 00595.

[45] Case 82/77 *Van Tiggele* [1978] ECR 25 at paras 24–25.

[46] See Koopmans, 'The Role of Law in the Next Stage of European Integration', op. cit. at 930.

[47] See Case 323/82 *Intermills v Commission* [1984] ECR 3809, Joined Cases 296 and 318/82 *Netherlands and Leeuwarder Papierwarenfabriek v Commission*, [1985] ECR 809, and C-290/83 *Commission v France* [1985] ECR 439.

[48] See Everling, U., 'On the Judge-made Law of the European Community's Courts', in O'Keeffe (ed.), *Judicial Review in European Union Law: Liber Amicorum in Honor of Lord Slynn of Hadley* (Kluwer, 2000) 36 at 39.

the Court adopted bold decisions such as *Francovich*. In the State aid field, the Court supported the Commission's bold submissions concerning the absence of a *de minimis* rule and the presumption that operating aid always distorts competition and affects trade in the *Tubemeuse* and *Boussac* judgments.[49]

Fifthly, during the 1990s, Judge Everling observed a more cautious approach in the Court's case law.[50] In this context, marked by the difficult ratification of the Maastricht Treaty, cases such as *Keck* or *Meng* were decided in the internal market and competition fields, and *Sloman Neptun* was decided in the State aid field, representing the first serious conceptual disagreement between the Commission and the Court in the field.[51] In any event, this case has been confirmed several times in different contexts and it will be argued in this book that the Court's finding was justified under the general architecture of the Treaty.

Finally, towards the end of the 1990s, after the ratification of the Amsterdam Treaty, Judge Everling has claimed that a more balanced approach can be observed in the Court's case law.[52] The book argues that a similar approach can be observed in the case law on State aids and cases such as *Altmark, Chronopost*, or *Azores* can be cited as examples of this new trend. Nevertheless, the Court has remained generally supportive of the European Commission during this period, which for this reason we consider as a period of *balanced instrumentalism*.

C. Application of the study of policy and enforcement considerations to future cases

The third argument defended throughout the book submits that the study of the policy and enforcement considerations that have affected the evolution of the concept of aid is not only enriching from an intellectual point of view but also useful to decide difficult cases. The study of those considerations is thus a *criteria provider* because it bestows elements useful to understand why a particular formula applicable to the case at hand seems to have been established in the first place and therefore whether its application to the given case would be coherent with those original reasons. Two examples will help make this point at the end of the book. Both are cases recently decided by the Grand Chamber of the Court of Justice: the *Gibraltar* and the *EDF* judgments.[53]

[49] Although even in this propitious context the Court refused in the latter the Commission's submission in the sense that illegal aids should be deemed incompatible just because of their illegality (because they were granted without prior notification to the Commission).

[50] See Everling, 'On the Judge-made Law of the European Community's Courts', op. cit. at 39.

[51] Joined Cases C-72/91 and C-73/91 *Sloman Neptun* [1993] ECR I-887.

[52] See Everling, 'On the Judge-made Law of the European Community's Courts', op. cit. at 39.

[53] Joined Cases C-106/09 P and C-107/09 P *Government of Gibraltar v Commission* [2011] ECR not yet published (nyr); and Case C-124/10 P *European Commission v Électricité de France (EDF) and Others* [2012] ECR nyr.

3. Chapter Synopses

This chapter presents an introduction to the book, a summary of the argument, and synopses of the chapters that follow.

Chapter 2 is divided into two parts. The first provides a brief historical account of the first forms of systematic intervention in the economy through subsidies, and of the initial attempts to control and limit the granting of subsidies. The aim is to give an overview of the main reasons that underpinned the first granting of subsidies and also the initial attempts to control and limit public subsidies. The second analyses the development of the control of subsidies since the Second World War and the main objectives behind the introduction of subsidy rules in the General Agreement on Tariffs and Trade (GATT), the European Coal and Steel Community (ECSC), and finally the EEC (European Economic Community). Finally, this includes a section concerned with the legislative history of Article 92 EEC as can be inferred from the Spaak Report and the Val Duchesse conference in which the final wording was given to the prohibition of State aid in the EEC. The chapter also includes the earliest definition of subsidy, found in an international Treaty of 1902, presented with a view to offering the reader an understanding of how the objectives of subsidy control were translated into a legal provision at that time. The main aim of this chapter is to give the reader an approximation of the knowledge concerning subsidies that was available to the drafters of the Rome Treaties in 1957 when they included Article 92 EEC in the Treaty, to the goals that they attached to the introduction of this article, and to the original interpretation of the criteria included in the current Article 107(1) TFEU. From this original understanding of the concept of aid, we will start our analysis of the formulas that have appeared in the case law to characterize each of the criteria of the concept of State aid.

Chapter 3 gives an overview of the evolution of the Commission's policy on State aids. The chapter is mainly based on the work of several political scientists who have divided the evolution of this policy into a number of periods. Their work is complemented by a review of Commission's documents, such as guidelines, surveys, and annual reports, and of scholarly commentaries and articles published during the different phases. This chapter shows how hazardous the development of State aid policy has been. The evolution of State aid policy is divided into four periods. The first period runs from 1958 to the early 1970s. This period was characterized by the Commission's focus on the elimination of barriers to trade and discrimination between undertakings in different Member States in a context of general States' hostility towards State aid compliance, which contributed to a selective and largely weak enforcement of these rules by the European Commission. The second period runs from the early 1970s to the mid-1980s. The Commission, in the absence of a State aids procedural regulation (rejected by the Council first in 1966, and for the second time in 1972), in the presence of the oil crisis, and with Member States unwilling to cooperate, accepted playing a pragmatic and low-profile role towards State aids until 1975–76. The Commission considered that the national protectionist measures adopted during the early years after the oil crisis would be temporary and therefore decided against active intervention. However, by 1978 the Commission recognized that the economic problems of Member States were 'of a basic structural nature', and that they had to be addressed at Community, not national, level. The arrival of more liberal Commissioners for Competition, such as Frans Andriessen (1981–85), also marshalled in the direction of a harder line towards State intervention in the economy, particularly in relation to the activities of public undertakings and in their financial relations with the State. The third period, which runs from the mid-1980s to the mid-1990s, is recognized as a crucial period in the development of State aid policy, which benefited from the Member States' support for the 1992 project of completing the single market. The stricter approach to State aids was also part of a 'public turn' that included the application of Article 90 EC and of the competition rules to State action supporting anti-competitive conduct, as public barriers were considered at this point more numerous and capable of distortion than the remaining private ones. The fourth period, running from the mid-1990s to the present day, is characterized by a number of initiatives purporting to make State aid control more efficient and transparent, through the adoption of legal procedural rules—almost forty years later than in the anti-trust field (with the early Regulation 17/62)—and through the focus on a number of so-called horizontal goals (Lisbon Agenda goals)—such as those concerning research and development and environmental protection towards which State aid should be channelled. The period is also characterized by the Commission's and the Council's determination to address harmful taxation measures through the State aid rules, a goal that was supported by the issuing of a communication on State aids and direct business taxation in 1998.

Chapter 4 applies the historical, policy, and enforcement considerations described in the previous chapters to the study of the formulas that are most commonly cited in the case law in relation to the notion of advantage. The chapter gives an account of the broad concept of aid given by the Court in 1961, based on the context of the ECSC Treaty which withdrew from Member States and gave to the Community the exclusive jurisdiction to grant aids in the coal and steel sectors. Member States were thus prevented from intervening by any means in the coal and steel sectors. As Advocate Lagrange put it: 'They [had] lost jurisdiction.'[54] The chapter also offers an explanation of the emergence of the MEIP test in the case law of the Court in the mid-1980s as an outcome of the change of focus and priorities of the European Commission supported this time by the Council. The chapter provides a background to the emergence of the concept of aid, including a notion of advantage in the mid-1990s that is based on the extension of the MEIP test to all transactions of the State, not just capital injections. Finally, the chapter concludes with the issue of the notion of advantage in the context of SGEI. In

[54] Opinion of Advocate General Lagrange, C-30/59 *Steenkolenmijnen v High Authority* [1961] ECR 3 at 42.

this regard, the chapter shows that the Commission refused to take a systematic position on this issue, not only by refusing to act on complaints lodged before it, but also by refusing to submit pleadings before the Court in difficult cases such as *Chronopost* or *Altmark*. This in turn led to a judge-made notion of advantage in this context that takes into consideration several goals now included in the Treaties and not only the most efficient application of the State aid rules.

Chapter 5 applies the historical, policy, and enforcement considerations described in Part I of the book (Chapters 1–3) to the study of the formulas that are most commonly cited in the case law in relation to the notion of selectivity. The chapter reviews the different formulas concerning selectivity that have appeared in the case law of the Court in different periods, from the broad notion of selectivity defended by the Court in the 1960s, according to which only measures applicable to all undertakings in a Member State could escape the notion of selectivity, to the current discrimination-like test for selectivity coined by the Court in the *Adria–Wien* judgment. The first formula, very broad, was context-specific and was never applied in a systematic way by the Commission beyond export aid. The second, still broad yet less so than the previous one, was developed in a context of systematic enforcement of the State aid rules and was therefore more manageable and attractive for the new actors in this field, private applicants, who started to appear more often before the Commission and the Court during the 1990s when formerly reserved sectors were being liberalized. Finally, policy considerations are also discussed in relation to the decisions of the Court in recent judgments such as *British Aggregates*, *Gibraltar*, or *Azores*, this latter judgment being also discussed in relation to the respect for the national constitutional identity of Member States including self government that Article 4(2) TEU now protects.

Chapter 6 applies the historical, policy, and enforcement considerations described in Part I of the book to the study of the formulas that are most commonly cited in the case law in relation to the notion of aid granted by a State or through State resources. In this regard, the chapter reviews the functional interpretation of this criterion that has led the Court to accept as State resources not only public but also private bodies instituted by the State to administer the aid in the early *Steinike and Weinlig* case. The same interpretation has also led the Court to accept that the financial burden included in this provision may fall on the public or private distributors of aid mentioned earlier and therefore not directly on the State. However, this criterion is most widely known for being the main point of disagreement between the Commission and the Court, concerning in particular whether regulatory measures should be considered as State resources. The analysis carried out shows that this disagreement only arrived in the early 1990s with the *Sloman Neptun* judgment as the Commission had, prior to that date, also required a financial burden for the State under today's Article 107(1) TFEU. The chapter advances some reasons as to why the Commission defended that position during the 1960s until the 1980s and why it may have decided to change it in the 1990s. It also provides an explanation to the case law of the Court on this particular aspect and concludes that the Court's limitation of the effects-based formula in this case is justified by reference to the general architecture of the Treaty. Finally, the chapter discusses the *Preussen Elektra* judgment in the light of the recent case law of the Court such as *France Télécom*, and concludes that it might be overruled in the near future, as the latter case law concerning this criterion seems to indicate, in line with the new tendency of the Court in Gibraltar and other judgments towards less formalism and the sanctioning of certain *regulatory techniques*.

Chapter 7 applies the historical, policy, and enforcement considerations described in Part I of the book to the study of the formulas that are most commonly cited in the case law in relation to the notions of distortion of competition and effect on trade. The analysis of these criteria, usually considered jointly by the Commission and the European Courts since *Philip Morris*, in context shows that originally the standard of proof required from the Commission for each of these two criteria was thought to be quite different. The distortion of competition element was almost automatically met because this criterion was originally interpreted as meaning any impact on costs or prices. However, the effect on trade criterion was the most difficult to fulfil of all the criteria enshrined in today's Article 107 TFEU in the early days as the wording of that article requires an actual effect to be demonstrated, and this ought to be shown with statistical data on exports and imports.[55] The chapter argues that the continuous reduction of the evidentiary requirements related to these criteria may have been motivated by the fact that Member States were boycotting the implementation and enforcement of these rules, as the Court had sanctioned in several judgments and some judges had openly criticized in public. The chapter also gives an explanation to the two largely isolated judgments in which the Court has annulled a Commission decision for the faulty motivation of the effect on trade criterion: the *Leeuwarder* and *Intermills* cases. The chapter argues that these cases were motivated not only by the certainly defective reasoning of the Commission decisions at stake but also by the general approach of the Court towards the Commission during this period and the fact that the judgments concerned a new and important test, the MEIP. Finally, the chapter discusses the changing path followed by the *de minimis* rule in the evolution of the concept of aid, first seemingly admitted by the Court, then rejected explicitly and finally admitted again, and traces theses changes to the different policy, enforcement, and even political considerations that have surrounded the introduction of this rule in the State aid field.

Using a case study, Chapter 8 analyses the impact of the 2008 financial crisis on the notion of aid from a policy and legal perspective. The chapter shows

[55] See Catalano, N., *Manuel de droit des Communautés Européennes*, 2nd edn (Dalloz, 1965) at 495. See also Quadri, R., Monaco, R., Trabucchi, A. (eds), *Trattato istitutivo della C.E.E. Comentario* (Giuffrè, Milano, 1965, vol. II) at 720. See also eg the statement by the Court in 1961 concerning the position of the High Authority as to the difference between the EEC and the ECSC Treaties: 'The applicant's arguments are somewhat similar to those of the defendant [High Authority]. It emphasizes that the Treaty establishing the European Coal and Steel Community, in contrast to that establishing the European Economic Community, prohibits subsidies regardless of whether they have a tangible effect on the common market. This deprives the statistical arguments of the intervener of most of their weight.' See case C-30/59, *De Gezamenlijke Steenkolenmijnen in Limburg v High Authority of the European Coal and Steel Community* [1961] ECR 1 at 13.

that during the crisis the European Commission has applied a broad notion of aid based on the virtual inapplicability of the MEIP, the so-called pollution theory and the fulfilment of the State resources criterion when public authorities made declarations announcing the support to be granted to banks. This approach towards the notion of aid allowed the Commission to consider as State aid most of the national measures adopted during the crisis, and therefore to advance some regulatory objectives, beyond the protection of competition and of the integrity of the internal market, during the compatibility analysis of those measures under Article 107(3)(b). The chapter also discusses the fact that the Court of Justice rejected the pollution theory defended by the Commission as a matter of principle in *ING*. The Court has also in this context shown to have '*une certain idée des aides*', which can only be fully understood by looking at formulas identified in the previous chapters in the context in which they first appeared.

Chapter 9 weaves together the historical, economic, legal, and policy considerations discussed in Parts I and II of the book in relation to the legal concept of aid. The chapter summarizes the conclusions of the inductive approach followed in order to study the formulas that depict this concept today. In doing so, the chapter attempts to bring to the legal debate over this concept the context that has determined its evolution and current meaning. The chapter thus familiarizes today's reader with the interests and objectives present at the time when a number of significant formulas concerning the concept of State were adopted. This approximation allows us to understand the current definition of State aid in a way that the exclusive analysis of the case law fails to provide.

2

Origins of Subsidy Control

This chapter provides a brief historical account of the granting and control of subsidies in Europe. This introductory section offers an overview of the reasons that have underpinned the granting of aids or subsidies and their control since the institutionalization of this form of intervention in the economy until the signing of the Rome Treaties in 1957. The aim is thus to provide the reader with an approximation of the reasons that may have motivated the introduction of Article 92 EEC and its particular wording.

1. Subsidy Control before the Second World War

A. The granting of subsidies: some historical notes

(1) The rise of mercantilism and the systematic granting of subsidies

State aids, or subsidies, have been granted for centuries. References to subsidies granted for political and military purposes can be dated back to the Roman Empire.[1] Yet, the beginning of the systematic granting of subsidies as a form of intervention in the economy is commonly associated with mercantilism and, more particularly, with the French mercantilist Jean-Baptist Colbert (1619–83), controller general of finance under King Louis XIV of France.

The '*mercantile system*' was the name given by Adam Smith to the economic measures undertaken by modern states to reinforce their power through State intervention in the economy from the sixteenth to the seventeenth centuries. The common policies advanced by mercantilism included the protection of national industry, the promotion of exports, and the achievement of a positive balance of trade that would allow the accumulation of precious metals such as gold and silver. Many of these policies had been adopted earlier by some medieval cities, yet

[1] See, eg, Gordon, C.D., 'Subsidies in Roman Imperial Defence' (1929) *Phoenix*, 60; Brogan, O., 'Trade between the Roman Empire and the Free Germans' (1936) *The Journal of Roman Studies*, 195; or Blockley, R.C., 'Subsidies and Diplomacy: Rome and Persia in Late Antiquity' (1985) *Phoenix*, 62. See also the famous work by Machiavelli, N., *The Prince*, Chapter XVI, translated by Bull, G. (Penguin Books, 1999) at 51, in which reference is also made to the *generosity* of many rulers and to the benefits and risks associated with this policy.

it was not until after the second half of the seventeenth century that mercantilism became widespread among the nation-states.

In the context of the emergence of the nation-state after the Peace of Westphalia (1648), mercantilists argued that the enrichment of a State could only be achieved at the expense of others.[2] This zero-sum game prompted the rise of barriers to trade and the public fostering of exports in several nation-states. These ideas also favoured, according to some authors, military conflicts between nation-states in an unprecedented manner.[3] France pioneered this system of barriers with the introduction of tariffs on English and Dutch manufactured goods. Colbert's plan was to create incentives for internal production at the expense of imports, and to foster exports. To attain these goals, national industry, best represented by the publicly supported '*manufactures*', received fiscal exceptions, favourable credits, honorary titles, low-interest loans, production subsidies, and '*primes a l'exportation*' (export bonuses).

Mercantilism was in fact not only an economic doctrine but also a political one. According to Colbert, only by reintroducing trade and by developing internal production would a country become richer and hence more powerful at the expense of others.[4] The social advantages of a positive balance of trade in terms of employment were also emphasized.[5] Indeed, as it is still the case, traders welcomed public funding. Financial support to industry also yielded a positive political impact to the grant authority who at the time was the king. To this end, all financial aid, even the smallest amount, was presented as a manifestation of the king's recognition and generosity.[6]

[2] See Comín, F., Hernández, M., and Llopis, E. (eds), *Historia económica mundial: siglos X–XX*, 2nd edn. (Barcelona, 2009) at 98 and 148.

[3] See, eg, Lahaye, L., 'Mercantilism', in the *Concise Encyclopedia of Economics*, available at: <http://www.econlib.org/library/Enc/Mercantilism.html>: 'During the mercantilist period, military conflict between nation-states was both more frequent and more extensive than at any other time in history.'

[4] Colbert, J.B. (1664), *Memorandum on Trade*, 'I believe everyone will easily agree to this principle, that only the abundance of money in a State makes the difference in its greatness and power.' An English version of the Memorandum is available at: <http://www.fordham.edu/halsall/mod/1664colbert.html>.

[5] Ibid. 'Aside from the advantages that the entry of a greater quantity of cash into the kingdom will produce, it is certain that, thanks to the manufactures, a million people who now languish in idleness will be able to earn a living. An equally considerable number will earn their living by navigation and in the seaports'.

[6] Necker, for example, noted that '*ce procédé plait beaucoup aux négociants: vu leur nombre… il est politique de se conformer a leur gout* (Trans. 'This process is highly appealing to traders : considering their number… it is good policy to adjust to their taste) [In the same vein subsidies were] '*une des plus sages dépenses de l'État* [and their reduction] *ne saurait jamais être compète parmi les économies bien entendus* (one of the wisest expenditure of the State [and their reduction] can never be considered among the reasonable savings)'. See Scheuing, D.H., *Les aides financiers publiques aux entreprises en droit francaise et europeen* (Editions Berger-Levrault, 1974) at 36. See also Necker, J., 'Sur la legislation et le commerce des grains', in Galiani, F. De Condillac, E.B., De Condorcet, J.A.N. (eds), *Melanges d'economie politique II* (Guillaumin, ed., 1848) at 315. See also Wathelet, M., and Partsch, P.E., 'Delimitation des contours de la notion d'aide d'état en droit communautaire' in *Les aides d'état en droit communautaire et en droit national* (Brussels, 1999) 1 at 3–12.

Mercantilism was also introduced in other European States. In Spain, for example, the protectionist principles of mercantilism, and in particular the State intervention in the economy through subsidies, were introduced with the arrival of the French Bourbon dynasty in 1700. The new economic ideas resulted in the establishment in Spain of several *Reales Manufacturas* that needed as much injection of capital as the French ones to remain active. In this vein, subsidies of several million *Reales* were granted to the *Manufacturas* due to their reported inefficiency.[7] Similarly, in England, mercantilism was based on the Navigation Acts that restricted foreign shipping, particularly from the Netherlands, in trade between England and its colonies. For example, the Staple Act of 1663 established the obligation on the colonies to acquire their goods from England. Subsidies, or bounties, were also granted to protect '*infant industries*' such as the linen and iron manufactures.[8]

(2) *The decline of mercantilism and the mutation of subsidies*

The degree of application of the mercantilist policies was largely dependent on the economic and military capacity of each nation-state to prevent foreign products from penetrating national borders. In this fashion, mercantilism was quite heterogeneous in modern Europe.[9] Moreover, by the mid-eighteenth century, there was a gradual shift in economic thinking towards free trade as a better way to achieve price stability, and towards a change from direct subsidies to consumers to incentives to agrarian producers. This led to a reduction in the overall level of subsidies. At the same time, a significant price increase of essential supplies made it almost impossible for municipalities to continue granting subsidies to products such as bread and other essential items. These factors, together with others such as the reduction in transport costs, favoured the partial liberalization of internal and external commerce.[10]

After that period, in the less interventionist nineteenth century, the State was seen as an agent for industrialization. Most States tried to imitate the British model and resources were increasingly granted to foster industrialization while liberalizing factors of production.[11] Accordingly, the focus of subsidies shifted

[7] See in this regard, eg, Llopis, E., in Comín, F., Hernández, M., and Llopis, E. (eds), *Historia económica mundial: siglos X–XX*, 2nd edn (Crítica, 2009) at 145 where the author refers to an expenditure of 180 million Reales only to sustain the *Real Fábrica de Paños de Guadalajara*. See also, Vicens Vives, J., *Manual de historia económica de España* (Editorial Vicens Vives, 1985) at 478–79.

[8] See, for the infancy argument (1740), 'On the Neglect of Trade and Manufacture' *Scots Magazine*, II; 476. See, for the reference, Viner, *Studies in the Theory of International Trade* (A. M. Kelley, 1975) at 72. The infant industry argument was also to be found in Steuart, J., *An Inquiry into the Principles of Political Economy* (James Williams and Richard Moncrieffe, 1767) I, 302 ff., 381, and in Tucker, J., *Instructions for Travellers* (London, 1757) at 33. Viner adds that Adam Smith was overcritical with the infant industry argument in his *Wealth of Nations*, Cannan, E. (ed.), (Methuen & Co., Ltd, 1904) at I, 422 ff.

[9] See Comín, Hernández, and Llopis (eds), *Historia económica mundial: siglos X–XX*, op. cit. at 148.

[10] Ibid. at 149.

[11] Ibid. at 229.

towards large amounts of aid for the deployment of infrastructure, particularly railways, for which it was agreed that not only public companies and public subsidies but also private operators and resources should be involved in order to share risks and costs.[12] Indeed, although some forms of protectionism remained during the nineteenth century, notably tariffs and subsidies, export bounties, at least in the form known during the seventeenth and early eighteenth centuries, largely disappeared during the early years of nineteenth century.[13] Export subsidies were replaced by more nuanced forms of public support that could be referred to as indirect export bounties. Indirect bounties took the form of refunds and grants of drawbacks upon the export of commodities or goods.[14]

These more sophisticated forms of subsidies were also in line with the trend towards the reduction of barriers to trade through free trade agreements signed in Europe during the nineteenth century. The main promoter of free trade was Great Britain. After having obtained economic and military supremacy in the mid-nineteenth century, Great Britain was poised to reap the benefits of free trade, more so than any other State. In this vein, in 1860 Great Britain and France entered into the Cobden–Chevalier Treaty, a free trade agreement that would be soon followed by others in which the Most Favoured Nation Clause was inserted.[15] However, British economic superiority did not last for very long and, by 1880, the rise of new economic powers such as Germany and the United States threatened British industry, which started to demand the reintroduction of tariffs by its government.[16] Protectionist measures were also introduced in Germany during the Second Reich (1871–1914), ranging from tariffs to the legalization of industrial cartels, and in France, with the rise of the wheat tariffs in 1887 and the introduction of the Méline tariff in 1892.

Protectionism and subsidies increased substantially with the beginning of the First World War, and even more so in the aftermath of the Great War. Massive subsidies were granted for multiple purposes, including commercial credit, shipbuilding, rail and air transport, exports, and housing.[17] The increase of subsidies during the aftermath of the First World War was not an isolated phenomenon but rather it was embedded in the general trend towards protectionism that dominated

[12] Wathelet and Partsch, 'Delimitation des contours de la notion d'aide d'état en droit communautaire', op. cit. at 7. See also Scheuing, D.H., *Les aides financiers publiques*, op. cit. at 37–39.

[13] Viner, J., *Dumping: A Problem in International Trade* (A.M. Kelley, 1990) at 163.

[14] Ibid. at 163–64. Viner divides them into three types: '(a) refunds, upon the export of commodities which had been subjected to internal excise taxation, of amounts in excess of the taxes which had actually been collected upon them; (b) refunds, upon the export of goods manufactured from imported materials upon which import duties had been imposed, of drawbacks of duty in excess of the amounts of import duties which had actually been collected upon the materials from which they were made; and (c) grants of drawbacks upon the export of goods made from materials of a kind subject to duty upon importation, even though the materials actually used in their manufacture or production were of domestic origin and not imported.'

[15] See Comín, Hernández, and Llopis (eds), *Historia económica mundial: siglos X–XX*, op. cit. at 230.

[16] Ibid. at 262.

[17] See, for a summary of the different laws adopted in France, Scheuing, *Les aides financiers publiques*, op. cit. at 40–41.

the mid-1920s. Protectionists measures adopted during this period included the enactment of tariffs and quotas, and a 'second wave' of international cartelization.[18] In fact, the interwar period was characterized by 'beggar-thy-neighbour' policies such as competitive devaluations and protectionists policies interestingly championed by the US (for example, the Smoot–Hawley Tariff Act of 1930). These policies, together with other crucial factors such as the Treaty of Versailles conditions and the 1929 crisis, resulted in the most recessive economic period in terms of world Gross Domestic Product (GDP) and GDP per capita since industrialization.[19]

Notwithstanding, it is after the Second World War that subsidies in Europe achieved the dimension that they still have today. Several reasons justify this development; the need to rebuild national industries and infrastructure after the War, the influence of the Marshall Plan, which required the establishment of a national distribution network of funds, different national planning experiences, and the ideological movement towards a more interventionist State model.[20]

In sum, this brief account shows that subsidies have traditionally been granted to enhance political power, both internal (pleasing merchants and allies) and external (increasing national revenues through exports),[21] to promote particular industries (such as military and textile) or enterprises (retribution or premiums for particular military or industrial success),[22] to develop State infrastructure (rail, roads, ports), and to increase employment. The account also shows that subsidies have been largely embedded in more general economic policies that were often dependent on the strength, not only economic but also military, of each country to put them forward. Similarly, not only external pressures but also internal ones, such as lobbying by merchants and consumers of essential items, have often

[18] See for an account of the political and economical situation of this period, eg, Gerber, D.J., *Global Competition: Law, Markets, and Globalization* (OUP, 2010) at 19–24. Viner refers to the enactment of several national antidumping laws in the early 1920s that were applicable not only to dumping proper but also to bounties and subsidies (eg New Zealand and Australian antidumping legislation of 1921, or the United States Tariff Act of 1922). See Viner, *Dumping: A Problem in International Trade,* op. cit. at 187. As to the first wave of international cartelization that followed the Great Depression of the 1870s and 1880s, see Gerber, *Global Competition,* op. cit. at 24. See also Conish, W.R. 'Legal Control over Cartels and Monopolization 1880–1914: A Comparison', in Hohn, N., and Kocka, J. (eds), *Law and the Formation of Big Enterprises in the 19th and 20th Centuries* (Gottingen, 1979) at 280–305.

[19] See Comín, Hernández, and Llopis (eds), *Historia económica mundial: siglos X–XX,* op. cit. at 287.

[20] Wathelet and Partsch, 'Delimitation des contours de la notion d'aide d'état en droit communautaire', op. cit. at 5.

[21] In this regard, Henry Home suggested in 1774 that the export bounty on corn would not only stimulate production and export in England, but it would also hurt French agriculture and therefore France in case of war. See Home, H. (Lord Karnes), *Sketches of the History of Man* (Edinburgh, 1774) Vol. I, 491 ff. See also on this account Viner, *Studies in the Theory of International Trade*, op. cit. at 70.

[22] Subsidies were also granted as a form of retribution/incentive or premium to the most active undertakings under Napoleon. See Scheuing, *Les aides financiers,* op. cit. at 35–46. See also Catherine, R., and Gousset, P., *L'état et l'essor industriel; du dirigisme colbertien a l'économie concertée* (Berger-Levrault, 1965) at 100.

justified the granting of subsidies. Finally, this brief overview also offers some evidence as to the many forms that subsidies may adopt (direct, indirect, fiscal, more and less sophisticated, to consumers, to production, etc) that may have ultimately led to their prohibition, as we will see in the next section.

B. The control of subsidies: some historical notes

(1) From Turgot to the Second World War

Some of the problems arising from the granting of subsidies were noticed very quickly. Anne Robert Jacques Turgot, Louis XVI's controller-general of finances, warned his king about the dangers of a generous policy regarding subsidies as early as 1774. In a famous letter, Turgot concluded that the shortcomings of the royal policy on subsidies were not limited to the reduction of the State's treasury. In fact, Turbot underlined that the 'gracious' policy also entailed unfair discrimination between the beneficiaries of the subsidies (the minority with access to the Crown), and the payers of those subsidies (the majority without that access).[23]

Similar concerns were raised in England after the second half of the eighteenth century in relation to the export bounty on corn.[24] The granting of subsidies was also criticized by Adam Smith in his famous *Nature and Causes of the Wealth of Nations* of 1776. He noted, in an entire chapter devoted to bounties, that their effect 'like that of all the other expedients of the mercantile system, can only be to force the trade of a country into a channel much less advantageous than that in which it would naturally run of its own accord.'[25] Smith therefore claimed that subsidies should cease or, as at second-best, be given on production rather than export because in this way people would only be 'taxed' once because the price of the product would be lower for domestic consumption.

In a similar vein, by the end of the nineteenth century importing countries of subsidized products started to consider export bounties, whether direct or indirect,

[23] 'Your Majesty knows that one of the largest obstacles to the economy is the multiple requests He is continuously assailed with, unfortunately authorized thanks to the too great facility of his predecessors to welcome them. It is necessary, Sire, to arm yourself against your kindness with your kindness itself; to consider those from whom this money comes you can distribute to your courtiers, and compare the misery of those from whom it is sometimes required to tear off it by the most rigorous executions, with the situation of those who have more titles to obtain your liberalities.' Letter of Turgot to the King, 24 October 1774. The original text in French of this letter, together with an English translation, is available at: <http://users.skynet.be/cedesguin/turgot.htm>. See also Scheuing, *Les aides financiers publiques*, op. cit. at 37.

[24] This bounty was firstly granted in 1673 and subsequently systematized by the corn law of 1689 and remained in place until 1814. See Viner, *Studies in the Theory of International Trade*, op. cit. at 69–71

[25] The chapter is available at: <http://www.bartleby.com/10/405.html>. Luca Rubini notes that, in the United States, Alexander Hamilton's view in his 1791 Report on Manufacturers was also similar to that of Adam Smith. See Rubini, L., *The Definition of Subsidy and State Aid: WTO and EC Law in Comparative Perspective* (OUP, 2009) at 3. For a passage of this report, see Jackson, J.H., *The World Trading System—Law and Policy of International Economic Relations* 2nd edn (MIT Press, 1997) at 417.

as injurious and unfair to their domestic industries. Consequently, these countries first tried to have these bounties abolished through the introduction of anti-bounty clauses in bilateral treaties with export subsidizers countries.[26] These clauses have been considered as the antecedents of bounty-countervailing and antidumping legislation.[27] They could also be considered as the most remote predecessors of the European State aid rules as they were originally entered into mainly by European States alone.[28] In any event, the introduction of anti-bounty clauses proved wholly inefficient in practice because those States formally obliged by them continued to grant subsidies in the same fashion. This failure may have been due, at least partly, to the lack of enforcement mechanisms or penalties in case of incompliance with these good-faith obligations.[29]

Interestingly, the same States would overcome the enforcement shortfall in a very short time, at least in relation to one commodity, namely sugar. In this regard, by the end of the nineteenth century, some European States and the US were engaged in a subsidy race for the production and export of sugar. The relevance of this industry for massive employment explains why this costly competitive measure became a matter of national priority. The strong protectionism that developed led to the formation of cartels 'which allowed the sugar manufacturers and refiners to charge prices at home that insured handsome profits and led to still further expansions of the sugar industry'.[30] Indeed, this 'first wave'[31] of cartels had the explicit goal of 'artificially elevating the price of sugar in the internal market, and restraining its depreciation'.[32]

In this context, as the main importer of sugar at the time, Britain sought to secure the abolition of cartels or, as it finally happened, to make them economically unfeasible through a Convention.[33] Britain's bargaining position against the

[26] Ibid. at 166–68. According to this author, by 1923, twenty-nine treaties contained rules on subsidies, seven of them being signed after 1900.

[27] Ibid. at 166–68.

[28] Indeed Viner refers to treaties entered into by France, Austria, Italy, Switzerland, and Germany. The first treaty mentioned by Viner dates from 1862 and was concluded by France and the German Zollverein (the German Customs Union), although in this case the commitment was only given by one party, namely France. The first mutual anti-bounty commitment was signed three years later between Austria and the German Zollverein. An early example of anti-bounty clause written in French may be found in the 1904 Treaty entered into by Italy and Switzerland. This clause made the granting of export subsidies dependent on the consent by the other party: '*Chacune des Parties Contractantes s'engage par contre, a ne pas accorder des primes d'exportation, pour aucun article et sous quelque titre ou quelque forme que ce soit, sauf consentement de l'autre Partie*'. See Viner, *Dumping: A Problem in International Trade*, op. cit. at 168.

[29] Ibid. The failure of abolishing bounties through these clauses led to the enactment of countervailing duties on import commodities which had received direct or indirect export subsidies (eg the United States Tariff Act in 1890, the Belgium bounty-countervailing provision in 1892).

[30] See Taylor, B., 'The Brussels Sugar Convention' *North American Review* (1909) 347 at 347.

[31] This phenomenon of international cartelization that followed the Great Depression of the 1870s and 1880s was repeated in a more extensive and significant fashion after the Great War. See Gerber, *Global Competition*, op. cit. at 24. See also Conish, 'Legal Control over Cartels and Monopolization 1880–1914', op. cit. at 280–305.

[32] Art. 2 of the By-Laws of the German cartel, quoted by Priaux, F., *La Question des Sucres et les Conventions Sucrières de Bruxelles*, Thèse de Doctorat (Faculté de Droit), Université de Rennes, Rennes, 1910, at 63.

[33] See Moura Filho, H.P., 'Pioneering Multilateralism: The Sugar Agreements 1864–1914', paper presented at the XVI International Economic History Congress, Helsinki, Session 109, 2006

adamant Austro-Hungarian and German counterparts, which were reluctant to surrender their cartels, was strong because it could give preference to its colonies against the bounty-fed 'Germanic' sugar, and this decision would have harmed the business of those nations' cartels.[34] Nevertheless, the awareness of a clear collective action dilemma concerning the abolition of subsidies was notorious as no single country dared to abolish them unilaterally.[35]

The dilemma was resolved, after some unsuccessful attempts,[36] in March 1902 when Germany, Austria–Hungary, Belgium, France, Italy, Holland, Sweden–Norway, Britain, and Spain (which did not finally ratify it) signed the Brussels Sugar Convention. Luxembourg and Peru ratified it in 1903, Switzerland in 1906, and Russia finally joined under a specific arrangement in 1907. The Convention prohibited all direct and indirect bounties for the production and export of sugar. The definition of bounty laid down by the conference was quite broad. Article I stated:

> The High Contracting Parties engage to suppress, from the date of the coming into force of the present Convention, the direct and indirect bounties by which the production or exportation of sugar may profit, and not to establish bounties of such a kind during the whole continuance of the said Convention. For the application of this provision, sugar-sweetened products, such as preserves, chocolates, biscuits, condensed milk, and all other analogous products containing in a notable proportion, artificially incorporated sugar, are assimilated to sugar. The preceding paragraph applies to all advantages derived directly or indirectly, by the several categories of producers, from State fiscal legislation, and in particular to (a) Direct bonuses granted on exportation. (b) Direct bonuses granted to production. (c) Total or partial exemptions from taxation which profit a part of the products of manufacture. (d) Profits derived from excess of yield. (e) Profits derived from too high a drawback. (f) Advantages derived from any surtax in excess of the rate fixed by Article III.[37]

at 11. It is available at: <http://mpra.ub.uni-muenchen.de/5208/>. For an explanation of the close relationship between the abolition of cartels and the adoption of the Brussels Sugar Convention see, eg, Notz, W., 'International Private Agreements in the form of Cartels, Syndicates and other Combinations' (1920) *The Journal of Political Economy*, 658 at 676.

[34] As Pigman explains: 'It became clear to the other conferees that Britain was negotiating at what Westminster regarded as a genuinely critical moment for the economies of the West Indian colonies and was prepared to impose colonial preferences on their behalf, even at the expense of low-priced sugar for British consumers and sugar-using industries…As the conference encountered delays, Lansdowne warned in late February 1902 that if an agreement was not reached, the upcoming annual budget would contain subsidies for colonial sugar…German negotiator Baron von Thielmann argued to Reichstag deputies, who feared that British colonial preferences on sugar would edge German sugar out of the Bristish market, that only by signing the proposed sugar convention could Germany avoid British colonial sugar preferences.' See Pigman, G.A., 'Hegemony and Trade Liberalization Policy: Britain and the Brussels Sugar Convention of 1902' (1997) *Review of International Studies*, 185 at 198–99.

[35] See Viner, *Dumping: A Problem in International Trade*, op. cit. at 178.

[36] See, eg, the Sugar Convention entered into between Great Britain, France, Holland, and Belgium of 1864.

[37] See Convention between Great Britain, Germany, Austria, Hungary, Belgium, Spain, France, Italy, Netherlands, and Sweden, relative to Bounties on Sugar, signed at Brussels, 5 March 1902 (International Convention Relative to Bounties on Sugar, 5 March 1902, 191 Consolidated TS 56, 1902 Foreign Relations of the United States 80).

The broad sweep of this Article and its reference to direct and indirect support was underlined by an author in 1909.[38] In this context, the US Supreme Court also observed in 1903 that bounties could be direct,

> as where a certain amount is paid upon the production or exportation of particular articles…or indirect, by the remission of taxes upon the exportation of articles which are subjected to a tax when sold or consumed in the country of their production, of which our laws, permitting distillers of spirits to export the same *without payment of an internal revenue tax or other burden* (emphasis added).[39]

Importantly, together with this broad definition, the Brussels Sugar Convention created for the first time a permanent commission where all signatories were represented, to monitor the execution of its provisions and to issue binding decisions by majority voting.[40] Perhaps surprisingly at the time, this pioneering system was very successful and worked as expected for at least ten years.[41] The importance of this Convention thus goes beyond the substance of the agreements. Indeed, it proved, just before the Great War, that multilateralism was both beneficial and possible, and could yield benefits for all participants and was able to trump domestic industrial pressure to maintain subsidies[42] and the collective action dilemma of different nations abolishing subsidies unilaterally.

After the Great War, and until the Second World War, the world's economic situation was disastrous and the political situation was certainly not propitious for any multilateral agreement on economic matters. Against this context, a significant effort was made to identify and remove obstacles to international trade, including subsidies, in order to improve the economic situation. This took the form of a World Economic Conference promoted by the League of Nations in 1925. The conference sought to gather the largest possible number of experts on international economic issues from the different States members of the League. Importantly, these experts could not be officials or politicians of the different States involved because they would have supported the official line of their respective governments. Rather, they had to be the most influential experts from private practice or academia. The strategy behind this idea was to influence public opinion through the authority of the experts involved.[43] The Conference finally took place in Geneva in May 1927 and gathered 194 experts

38 See Taylor, 'The Brussels Sugar Convention', op cit. 351. See also Martineau, G., 'The Brussels Sugar Convention' (1904) *The Economic Journal*, 34 at 41.

39 Supreme Court of the United States in 1903, case *Robert E. Downs, Petitioner, v United States*, 187 U.S. 496 (1903). The notion of mitigating a burden, of indirect bounty, would be upheld by the Court of Justice of the European Communities in 1961.

40 See Art. VII of the Convention which starts as follows: 'The High Contracting Parties agree to establish a Permanent Commission charged with supervising the execution of the provisions of the present Convention…'.

41 As to the success see, eg, Taylor, 'The Brussels Sugar Convention', op. cit. at 347, in reply to some critics of the Convention: 'The only effect the Convention has had on prices has been to bring them to the level of economic conditions which they had not under the bounties.' In relation to the duration of the effects of the Convention, in 1912 Great Britain withdrew from its obligations under the agreement. Subsequently Italy withdrew in 1915, France in 1918, and Holland in 1920.

42 See in this regard, Pigman, 'Hegemony and Trade Liberalization Policy', op. cit. at 199.

43 The strategy was explained by the director of the economic section of the League, Sir Arthur Salter, in the following terms: 'it may be hoped [that] the public opinion of the world will realize

from fifty states.[44] As has been claimed, 'it was here that the idea of using law to protect global competition emerged as a prominent international issue',[45] thus almost two decades before the adoption (and demise) of the Havana Charter and the entering into force of the General Agreement on Tariffs and Trade (GATT).

The experts gathered in Geneva agreed on the distortive and inefficient character of subsidies and recommended the desirability of their reduction. In the terms of the Final Report, 'The Conference draws the attention of the various Governments to the true nature of direct or indirect subsidies, which are merely a palliative, and expresses the hope that Governments will, so far as possible, refrain from having recourse to them.'[46] The experts knew that their advice would not be followed immediately. However, their efforts were not limited to the content of the final report of the Conference. They also intended to show that it was possible to work collaboratively for the cause of peace, of which economic stability was and remains a close relative.[47]

Unfortunately, as we know, neither economic nor political peace was secured. Indeed, soon after the Conference the need for financial aid and the incentives for more national protectionist measures were dramatically augmented by the 1929 crisis. In this regard, France adopted '*des interventions spectaculaires*',[48] and the US adopted the ultra-protectionist Smoot–Hawley Tariff Act of 1930. In sum, the time was simply not ripe for the adoption of the sound recommendations of the Conference. However, the identification of the *true nature* of subsidies, as the case of other impediments to trade and competition, including cartels, was never forgotten, not least because some of the experts and participants of the Conference would, after the Second World War, also be involved

that it is essential, in the public interest, that the unanimous advice of the most authoritative body of persons who could be found should be adopted; and will insist that economic policies should be modified as they recommend'. See Salter, A., 'The League's Contribution' in Salter, A., and Boyden, R.W. (eds), *The Economic Consequences of the League: The World Economic Conference* (London, 1927) at 8, quoted by Gerber in *Global Competition*, op. cit. at 25.

[44] See Hill, M., *The Economic and Financial Organization of the League of Nations* (Carnegie Endowment for International Peace, 1946) at 47.

[45] For an account of this conference from a global competition viewpoint, see Gerber, *Global Competition*, op. cit. at 24–31.

[46] The World Economic Conference, Geneva, May 1927, Final Report (C.E.I.44 (1)) League of Nations at 27.

[47] As the president of the Conference said: 'We have worked loyally together to secure economic peace, on which, indeed, political peace depends. This Conference is an assembly of persons who have been brought into touch with realities—always harsh and often disappointing—but with realities in which truth, sooner or later, always prevails. Our advice and recommendations will in all probability not be followed immediately on the scale we would desire. Great movements frequently experience many difficulties at the outset. But we are convinced that our work is based on true principles, and on the determination to ensure to the best of our power both the peace and the prosperity of the world.' See Runciman, W.L., 'The World Economic Conference at Geneva' (1927) *The Economic Journal* 465 at 472. See also Gerber, *Global Competition*, op. cit. at 24–31.

[48] Scheuing, *Les aides financiers publiques*, op. cit. at 41. See also James, E., 'L'État au secours des entreprisses défaillantes' (1932) *Revue d'economie politique*, 1511.

in influential policy and legal discussions, including those held at the Court of Justice of the European Union.[49]

The sources reviewed show that some risks relating to the granting of subsidies were soon identified, namely; (i) the inefficient waste of scarce resources in non-productive industries; (ii) the unfair redistribution of subsidies between the beneficiaries (few industries or merchants) and the costs to most industries and citizens of subsidies, and, related to the latter; (iii) the problems derived from the fact that few had access to the grantor authority, often the king (what we could call today the influence of lobbies and the result of regulatory capture); and (iv) the distorting effect that subsidies, and particularly export subsidies, had on both international trade and international relations. The account also shows that although the problem of collective action was identified and was even tackled for a single commodity (sugar) through the establishment of a supranational control of subsidies, the political scenario prevented the necessary economic cooperation to enrich all countries. Again, the brief overview reveals how dependent subsidies are on wider economic and political conditions. In this vein, forty years before the GATT's adoption the message was already clear: 'political peace' would only come after 'economic peace' was secured.

2. Subsidy Control after the Second World War

A. The GATT

Apart from the Treaties entered into at the end of the nineteenth century and during the first years of the twentieth century, subsidies were only controlled, if at all, at national level.[50] The supranational control of subsidies for more than one commodity started with the GATT.

[49] For example, Jacques Rueff, a French economist who worked as a judge for ten years at the Court of Justice since its formation, served from 1927 to 1930 as a member of the Economic Section of the Secretariat of the League of Nations and was therefore necessarily aware of the discussions and conclusions of the Conference. He was the Judge-Rapporteur of the important 1961 *miners' bonus* case (C-30/59) for the concept of aid. Similarly, the first president of the Court of Justice, Massimo Pilotti, was deputy secretary general of the League of Nations 1932–37 and thus he was probably aware of the final report of the World Economic Conference.

[50] Indeed, it could be said that the national control of subsidies is as old as the granting of subsidies itself. In this regard, Colbert noted in the seventeenth century that there had to be some control of subsidies in order to avoid the misuse of public funds. In Colbert's own words [control rules] '*sont toutes nécessaires, non seulement parce qu'elles assurent la vérité et empeschent la surprise, qui d'ailleurs seroit trop facile, mais mesme qu'elles rendent la grace du rou publique et convenient tous les autres marchands a bastir pour en jouir*'. (Trans. 'control rules are all necessary, not only because they provide the truth and avoid surprise, which also would be too easy, but they also make the King's grace public and it is convenient for all other merchants to be able to profit from it'). See letters of 5 and 26 December 1670, and privilege of 17 February 1671, cited by Scheuing, *Les aides financiers publiques*, op. cit. at 36 and note 8.

The GATT is the unexpected result of US efforts to prohibit all non-tariff barriers to trade while limiting tariffs through international negotiations.[51] Non-tariff barriers to trade were to be abolished through a comprehensive binding code governing world trade, the International Trade Organization (ITO) Charter, also known as the Havana Charter. The US policy underpinning such a code was to a large extent a belief in free, non-discriminatory, trade between nations as a safeguard against war.[52] The project was ambitious, covering not only traditional trade issues but also rules on employment, commodity agreements, competition, services, and investment. Economic peace and development appeared again as important conditions for political peace.[53]

As is now known, the Havana Charter never entered into force. The US Congress failed to ratify the ITO after a number of attempts and President Truman announced in 1950 that the Charter would not proceed. Many States refused to adopt the Charter because they were still keen on protectionist measures, but many also wished to influence international politics by favouring some trading partners and discriminating others.[54] Moreover, by this time market-economy and planned-economy, developed and underdeveloped countries, held very different trade views from each other and this too contributed to the Charter's demise. Finally, the failure to set up a proper institutional framework that would ensure enforcement of the Charter was also considered decisive in its collapse.

Therefore, what was originally an exclusive agreement on tariffs, concluded in 1947—even before the start of the negotiations of the Havana Charter—and entered into force in 1948, appeared as the only instrument that could fill the gap for the non-tariff barriers, including subsidies, the elimination or reduction of which was provided for in the Havana Charter.[55] In this context, the GATT rules on subsidies were envisaged as a complement to the rules concerning customs duties.[56] The idea behind these rules was that liberalization of trade through the reduction of tariff customs could be offset by domestic support.[57] States could resort to subsidies while other trade barriers, easier to identify and monitor, were

[51] Dam, K., *The GATT: Law and International Economic Organization* (University of Chicago Press, 1970) at 12–13.

[52] See the speech of US Under Secretary of State Summer Welles delivered before the Foreign Affairs Council, Cleveland, Ohio, 28 September 1940, 'many attempts...have been undertaken by this country to induce the nations of the world to return to a sane economic order—to halt the armaments race—and to reestablish in international life the standard of morality and law...one of the surest safeguards against war is the opportunity of all peoples to buy and to sell on equal terms and without let or hindrance of a political character, we have never ceased to offer our full participation and cooperation in such a general economic program', available at: <http://www.ibiblio.org/pha/policy/1940/1940-09-28a.html>.

[53] See, in this regard, the words of the Department of State of the United States. The summary analysis of the ITO charter carried out by the Department of State is available at: <http://www.fraser.stlouisfed.org/docs/historical/martin/17_07_nd1.pdf>.

[54] Dam, *The GATT*, op. cit. at 13.

[55] See United Nations document E/Conf. 2/78, Arts 25–28.

[56] See Les parties contractantes a l'Accord général sur les tarifs douanières et le commerce IBDD, suppl., No. 10 at 219. See also, Scheuing, *Les aides financiers publiques*, op. cit. at 249 and footnote 1.

[57] Ibid. at 249.

abolished.[58] However, the original rules on subsidies introduced by the GATT were quite limited and considerably less strict than those provided for in the Havana Charter.[59] The original 1947 GATT rules on subsidies merely established some reporting obligations and a possibility of countervailing duties.[60] Nevertheless, the main provision on subsidies, Article XVI GATT, was amended during a 1954–55 review in order to introduce some commitments to reduce export subsidies.[61]

Finally, it should be noted that a definition of subsidy did not seem to be necessary or feasible at this point, neither for the ITO nor for the GATT. Rather to the contrary, an encompassing concept of subsidy, capable of covering several forms of public intervention, seemed preferable, as was stated by the Report of a Panel on Subsidies in 1961.[62]

B. The ECSC rules on subsidies

In 1951 the Treaty of Paris establishing the European Coal and Steel Community (ECSC) introduced the first prohibition of subsidies related to the European integration project,[63] in particular Article 4(c) of this Treaty, the application of which was naturally limited to the coal and steel industries. According to this provision (all) subsidies were deemed incompatible with the common coal and steel market, thus subsidies were strictly and unconditionally banned.[64]

[58] Luengo Hernández de Madrid, G.E., *Regulation of Subsidies and State Aids in WTO and EC Law—Conflicts in International Trade Law* (Kluwer Law International, 2007) at 42. A similar meaning has been given in the EU to State aids, their importance increasing as other impediments to trade are eliminated in the Common Market.

[59] The rules provided for in the Havana Charter included an obligation to notify general subsidies, a prohibition of export subsidies for non-primary products, while domestic subsidies remained lawful, and the limitation of export subsidies for primary products. However, even at the ITO Charter negotiations, derogations from the subsidy rules were proposed by the US delegation, the driving force of the ITO in order to protect domestic farm programs. This attempt was considered a proof of hypocrisy by the other negotiating parties. See Dam, *The GATT*, op. cit. at 131.

[60] Sykes, A.O., 'The Economics of WTO Rules on Subsidies and Countervailing Measures', Chicago, John M. Olin Law and Economics Working Paper No. 186 (2nd Series) May 2003 at 12–13.

[61] With respect to subsidies on 'primary products', the obligation was to avoid the application of subsidies that resulted in a nation obtaining a 'more than equitable share of world export trade.' For products other than primary products, the obligation was to avoid subsidies that resulted in a price for exportation of a product that was below the price charged for the like product in the domestic market. See Sykes, 'The Economics of WTO Rules on Subsidies and Countervailing Measures', op. cit. at 13.

[62] L/1442 and Add.1-2, adopted on 21 November 1961, 10S/201, 209, para. 23; see also MTN. GNG/NG10/W/4 at 49: 'it was neither necessary nor feasible to seek an agreed interpretation of what constituted a subsidy. It would probably be impossible to arrive at a definition which would at the same time include all measures that fall within the intended meaning of the term in Article XVI without including others not so intended... In any event the Panel felt that the lack of a precise definition had not, in practice, interfered with the operation of Article XVI'.

[63] Treaty Establishing the European Coal and Steel Community, Art. 4(c), 18 April 1951, 261 UNTS 140.

[64] The wording of this provision reads as follows: 'The following are recognized as incompatible with the common market for coal and steel and shall accordingly be abolished and prohibited

The ECSC Treaty was quite interventionist given that its intention was to replace national aid to the coal and steel industries by aid granted at Community level,[65] as the Court of Justice noted.[66] The ECSC was indeed supranational, as it was based 'on full delegation of sovereignty to a common organ of the six countries'.[67] In fact, the notion of aid laid down in Article 4(c) did not contain any criteria or qualification for its compatibility, which promoted the recognition of its immediate application by the Court, the forerunner of the notion of direct effect.[68] Indeed, the fact that the ECSC Treaty did not require any sort of distortion of competition, selectivity criteria, or *de minimis* rule has also been observed by the European courts.[69]

within the Community, as provided in this Treaty: subsidies or aids granted by States, or special charges imposed by States, in any form whatsoever.'

[65] See Davignon, E., 'Subsidies and Competition in the European Union', in Stuyck, J., Abraham, F., and Goemans, Ch. (eds), *Subsidies and Competition in the European Union: Generale Bank Lectures 1994–1995* (Leuven University Press, 1996) 1 at 11–13. See also Luengo Hernandez de Madrid, *Regulation of Subsidies and State Aids in WTO and EC Law*, op. cit. 292.

[66] '[The ECSC Treaty] intends to reserve to the Community institutions and withhold from the states the right to grant, within the community, subsidies or aids and to impose special charges in any form whatsoever. The strict wording of article 4 itself emphasizes the exclusive character of the community's jurisdiction within the Community.' See C-30/59 *Steenkolenmijnen v High Authority* [1961] ECR 1, para. 22. See also in this regard, Ehlermann, C.D., 'State Aids under European Community Competition Law' (1994) *Fordham International Law Journal*, 408 at 412.

[67] See Address given by Gaetano Martino, Italian Foreign Minister in Rome, 18 January 1957: Martino, G., 'From the ECSC to the Common Market.' Ministerio degli affari esteri (ed.). *Gaetano Martino e l'Europa, Dalla Conferenza di Messina al Parlamento europeo* (Istituto poligrafico e zecca dello stato, 1995. Translated by the CVCE) 66–78 at 66: 'when the Treaty Establishing the European Coal and Steel Community was negotiated and concluded six years ago, the governments of the day... intended that Treaty to be based on full delegation of sovereignty to a common organ of the six countries. They spoke... of a supranational authority.' See also the opinion of Judge Jacques Rueff in the discussion that followed his intervention in Rueff, J, 'La Cour et l'economie politique', in *Dix ans de jurisprudence de la cour de justice des commaunautes europeennes, Europäische Arbeitstagung* (Heymanns, 1965) 13 at 35, where he considers that the High Authority, '*est beacoup plus supranational... que la Commission C.E.E.*' For a different view, another early judge, Nicola Catalano, considered the EEC Treaty more supranational than the ECSC Treaty, *inter alia*, because the former was less detailed than the latter, containing often only the principles, not all the rules, and therefore giving more legislative latitude for the supranational institutions. See the opinion of Judge Nicola Catalano in the discussion that followed Mr Rueff's intervention at 42.

[68] See in this regard, eg, the Opinion of Advocate General Lagrange in case C-30/59 *Steenkolenmijnen v High Authority* [1961] ECR 1 in which he stated that Art. 4(c) was 'valid in itself'. See also De Wilmars, J.M., 'Aides CECA et aides CEE: aspects juridique d'une convergence économique' in Capotorti, F., Pierre, P. , *Du droit international au droit de l'intégration: liber amicorum Pierre Pescatore* (Nomos Verlagsgesellschaft, 1987) 421 at 424. For an early comparison between ECSC and EEC State aid rules by another judge of the Court of Justice, see Catalano, N., *Manuel de droit des communautés européens* (Dalloz, 1965) at 494–96. The Court would however subsequently modify its case law concerning the direct effect of Art. 4(c) as a result of the guidelines adopted by the Commission on the compatibility of aid to the coal industry. See C-390/98 *Banks* [2001] ECR I-6117 at paras 64–65: 'Although it might initially have been inferred from the judgment in De Gezamenlijke Steenkolenmijnen in Limburg v High Authority that Article 4(c) of the ECSC Treaty, in so far as it covers aid, was fully independent in its application and directly effective, that interpretation no longer holds good... Since 1965, acting on the basis of the first paragraph of Article 95 of the ECSC Treaty, the Commission has adopted successive general decisions, known as aid codes, authorising, under certain conditions and in specifically listed cases, the granting of subsidies or aid by Member States to the coal industry, which is therefore regarded as Community aid compatible with the proper functioning of the common market.'

[69] See Cases T-12/99 and T-63/99, *UK Coal plc v Commission* [2001] ECR II-2153, para. 54. See also order in Case C-111/99 *P Lech-Stahlwerke v Commission* [2001] ECR I-727, para. 41,

The ECSC approach soon proved unrealistic and national funds continued to be granted to industry alongside Community funds.[70] Indeed, through Article 95 ECSC the High Authority allowed the granting of national aids considered compatible with the objectives of the Treaty.[71] The ECSC experience thus made clear that exceptions to the prohibition of aid had to be introduced in the EEC Treaty, otherwise the EEC Treaty rules could risk being ignored as the ECSC ones. In this regard, the ECSC rules on subsidies, like those on competition, provided a precedent for the introduction of the EEC State aid rules and yet, as opposed to those on competition, the ECSC subsidy rules could not be seen as a model to be replicated by the EEC Treaty due to the experience their application demonstrated.[72]

C. The road towards the introduction of the EEC rules on subsidies

At the time of the drafting of the Rome Treaties, the founding fathers could essentially look at two sets of rules on subsidies: (i) the limited GATT system, which provided for an obligation to notify subsidies and a prohibition of export subsidies for non-primary products, and (ii) the interventionist ECSC rules which laid down an unconditional ban of national subsidies. The solution chosen was mixed: national aids were only incompatible inasmuch as they distorted or threatened to distort competition, and provided that they were liable to affect trade between Member States. Moreover, this principle of incompatibility was coupled with a large number of exceptions provided for in (then) Article 92, paragraphs 2 and 3.

In the words of an early *référendaire* of the Court and member of the Commission, the draftsmen of the EEC Treaty 'showed their realism in providing for exceptions to the general rule of incompatibility of state aids', given that State support was necessary to avoid social distress and a complete ban on aids 'would prevent such distress from being relieved with the required urgency.'[73]

and judgment in Joined Cases T-129/95, T-2/96, and T-97/96 *Neue Maxhütte Stahlwerke and Lech-Stahlwerke v Commission* [1999] ECR II-17, paras 98 and 99. The Court has however reconciled the definitions. See Case C-200/97 *Ecotrade* [1998] ECR I-7907, para. 17.

[70] See Davignon, 'Subsidies and Competition in the European Union', op. cit. at 12. See also in this regard, Scheuing, *Les aides financiers publiques*, op. cit. at 260 and footnote 11. In this context, it may be worth recalling that the subsidies to be granted by the High Authority were not stemming from State resources but from private operators.

[71] The case law of the Community courts validated this practice 'in order to deal with unforeseen situations' (see Case T-239/94 *EISA v Commission* [1997] ECR II-1839, para. 63). See also Case C-390/98 *Banks* ECR 2001 p. I-06117 at 64–65.

[72] For the role of the ECSC competition rules in the framing of the EEC ones, see Gerber, D.J., *Law and Competition in Twentieth Century Europe: Protecting Prometheus* (OUP, 1998) at 341: 'Perhaps its most important role was to provide a precedent for the inclusion of competition provisions in the Treaty of Rome and something of a model for those provisions.'

[73] Mathijsen, P., in George, K.D., and Joll, C. (eds) *Competition Policy in the UK and the EEC* (CUP, 1975) at 187.

Indeed, although the EEC Treaty provided for the institution of a system ensuring that competition in the Common Market was not distorted by Article 3, the exceptions to the general prohibition of aids laid down by then Article 92(1) EEC proved that the draftsmen were aware of the need to protect some national interests insofar as those interests would not be contrary to the common interest as interpreted by the Commission. In addition, the new Community would not provide 'Community aid', as opposed to the ECSC, making the granting of national aid more justified. Finally, the different and much broader scope of the EEC Treaty (not restricted to the coal and steel sectors) also called for a better balance between the avoidance of distortions of competition and the development of both national and community policies.

The following sections briefly describe two milestones leading to the introduction of the State aid rules in the Rome Treaties, the Spaak Report, and the *Travaux Preparatoires* of the EEC Treaty.

(1) The Spaak Report

The Report of the Heads of Delegation to the Ministers of Foreign Affairs, known as the Spaak Report, was drafted in 1956 by the so-called Spaak Committee.[74] The Report was commissioned at the Messina Conference (June 1955) and its mandate included '*l'élaboration des règles assurant un jeu non faussé de la concurrence au sein de la Communauté, qui exclut notamment toute discrimination nationale*'.[75] The Spaak Report was the main working document for the drafting of the EEC Treaty as was decided at the Conference held on Venice on 29 and 30 May 1956.[76]

The Report was clear as to the goal of the introduction of the State aid rules. The introduction to the Report stated that *in the modern world* the enlargement of markets and competition did not suffice to ensure the most rational allocation of activities and the most favourable pace for expansion. Therefore, it was necessary, on the one hand, to impose competition rules on undertakings in order to avoid agreements and practices that could have the same effect as the customs tariffs that the Treaty meant to eliminate. On the other hand, it was also required to prevent Member States from granting aids having as their *object* and *effect* the distortion of competition. Notwithstanding the foregoing, aids in the general

[74] The committee was staffed by Paul-Henri Spaak, and the six heads of delegation of the ECSC, namely, C.F. Ophuels (Germany), Baron J.C. Snoy et d'Oppuers (Belgium), F. Gaillard (France) L. Benvenuti (Italy), L. Schaus (Luxembourg), and G.M. Verrijn Stuart (the Netherlands), together with a representative of the United Kingdom, R. Bretherton, who was invited to join the discussions by M. Beyen.

[75] Trans. 'The development of rules ensuring undistorted competition within the Community, which excludes any national discrimination'. Résolution adoptée par les Ministres des Affaires Étrangères des États membres de la C.E.C.A., réunis a Messine les 1er et 2 juin 1955, Doc MAE 6/55, p. 3 (Annexe X au doc. MAE 11/55).

[76] See Communiqué de presse; doc. 125/56, p. 1 (Annexe IV au Doc. MAE 126/56).

interest and those granted with a view to expand production should not necessarily be prohibited.[77]

First, the general rule established by the Report was that State aids were incompatible with the Common Market.[78] This incompatibility was seen as an '*essential guarantee*' for the undertakings of the Community in the sense that competition would not be distorted by the States. Secondly, the notion of aid had to be broad so as to cover the support given by Member States in any form or, as the Report phrased it, '*indépendamment de la forme extérieure qu'elles revêtent*'.[79] In this regard, the Report offered the example that an exemption to a category of enterprises or to a branch of industry from the charges normally borne by them had the same effect, and therefore deserved to be analysed under the same criteria, as a traditional direct subsidy from public funds.[80]

As a result, the following principle was proposed: financial assistance, no matter in what form it is granted, is incompatible with the Common Market if it distorts competition and the distribution of economic activities by favouring certain enterprises or certain types of production. For this purpose, the Report gave the Commission the task of discerning between the permissible and non-permissible aids.[81] Member States had to notify their aid measures, yet the Commission could also investigate *ex officio* or upon information submitted by other Member States.[82] The Spaak Report also made clear that the State aid rules were complementary to the competition norms imposed on undertakings,[83] and that both sets of competition rules were complementary to the goals pursued by the fundamental freedoms.[84] Competition rules (broadly speaking) were devised as a complement to the free movement rules with a view to creating a large market from which European undertakings could profit.[85]

[77] See Report of the Heads of Delegation to the Ministers of Foreign Affairs, of 21 April 1956, Mae 120 fl56 (corrigé) (hereinafter 'Spaak Report') at 16–17.

[78] See Spaak Report at 57.

[79] Trans. 'independently of the external form they take'. Spaak Report at 57.

[80] Ibid. As discussed previously, the finding that the mitigation of charges normally borne by undertakings equates to a subsidy was made by the Brussels Sugar Convention and was restated by the US Supreme Court in the first years of the twentieth century.

[81] Ibid. '*La règle générale est que sont incompatibles avec le marché commun les aides, sous quelque forme qu'elles soient accordées, qui faussent la concurrence et la répartition des activités en favorisant certaines entreprises au certaines productions.*' (Trans. 'The general rule is that aids are incompatible with the common market in any form that they are given, which distorts competition and the distribution of activities by favoring certain undertakings or certain productions.')

[82] Spaak Report at 59.

[83] Ibid. at 57: '*Les règles de concurrence qui imposeront aux Etats viendront ainsi pour une large part faciliter ou même suppléer l'application des règles de concurrence aux entreprises.*' (Trans. 'Competition rules applicable to States will largely facilitate or even supplement the application of the competition rules to companies.')

[84] Ibid. at 55: '*Le traite devra prévoir les moyens d'éviter que des situations ou des pratiques de monopole mettent en échec les objectifs fondamentaux du marche commun*' and at 11, '*ces conditions normales de concurrence exigent des règles et des procédures en vue de redresser l'effet des interventions des États ou des situations de monopole.*' (Trans 'The treaty will provide the means to avoid that monopolies or monopolistic practices frustrate the basic objectives of the common market', and at 11, 'these normal competitive conditions require rules and procedures to redress the effects of state intervention or monopolies.')

[85] See also in this regard, Waelbroeck, M., 'Competition, Integration and Economic Efficiency in the EEC from the Point of View of the Private Firm', in *The Art of Governance: Festschrift in Honor*

Finally, the Spaak Report made an important distinction that may explain the insertion of a selectivity criterion in the notion of aid. The drafters of the Report considered aids as *artificial advantages* granted by States. Other (non-artificial) advantages, in particular those stemming from regulatory or legislative disparities between Member States, although equally distortive and '*qui formellement sont des aides ou des subventions*', could not be addressed through *ex-ante* analysis by the European Commission.[86] These non-artificial advantages would be controlled *ex post* and would ultimately be, if necessary, subject to harmonization.[87] The Report was also based on the premise that most of the general (non-selective) distortions of competition, such as social or fiscal measures, could be ultimately compensated by adjustments in the exchange rate of the national currencies.[88] With this distinction, as has been noted,[89] the drafters aimed to avoid the creation of particular niches of privilege for certain companies or sectors.[90]

(2) *The* Travaux Préparatoires *in Val Duchesse*

The Spaak Report was first discussed in Venice on 29 and 30 May 1956 by the Foreign Ministers of the six Member States of the ECSC.[91] As a result of the conference, the Report was accepted as the basis for the negotiations that were to be held at an Intergovernmental Conference on the Common Market and Euratom aimed to prepare a treaty establishing a Common Market and another treaty creating a European organization of nuclear power. The Intergovernmental Conference would be held in Brussels on 26 June 1956 under the coordination of Mr Spaak.

of Eric Stein (Nomos Verlagsgesellschaft, 1987) 1439 at 1440. See also, Hildebrand, D., *The Role of Economic Analysis in the EC Competition Rules* 3rd edn (Kluwer Law International, 2009) at 9–10.

86 Trans. 'which formally are aids or subsidies'. Spaak Report at 59.

87 See Spaak Report at 59 of French version, and at 63 of the German version. For the same view see, eg, Mederer, 'Evolution of State Aid Control', op. cit. at 27.

88 Spaak Report at 60: '*Les différences entre les charges que supportent les différentes économies, par exemple du fait des dépenses publiques ou des régimes de sécurité sociale, ne faussent pas, par elles-mêmes, les conditions de la concurrence, étant normalement compensées par les conditions générales des échanges, en particulier le taux de change.*' (Trans. 'The differences between the costs borne by individual economies, eg because of public spending or social security schemes, do not distort, by themselves, the conditions of competition as they are normally offset by the general trading conditions , in particular the exchange rate.') See, for the questioning of this assumption as no longer valid due to the evolution of the internal market by Bourgeois, J.H.J., 'State Aids, Taxation Measures and Specificity', in Dony, M., and De Walsche, A. (eds), *Mélanges en hommage à Michel Waelbroeck*, Vol. 2 (Bruylant, 1999) at 769.

89 See Di Bucci, V., member of the Legal Service of the European Commission, 'Quelques Aspects Institutionnels du Droit des Aides d'Etat' in *EC State Aid Law—Le Droit des Aides d'Etat dans la CE, Liber Amicorum Francisco Santaolalla Gadea* (Kluwer Law International, 2008) 44–45 at 43.

90 For a recent analysis of the Spaak Report in relation to the State aid rules, see the interesting work of Saydé, A., *Abuse of Union Law and Regulation of the Internal Market* (Hart, 2014).

91 The conference was held at the Cini foundation in Venice and was chaired by Christian Pineau, French Minister for Foreign Affairs. The conference was attended by Walter Hallstein (Federal Republic of Germany), Paul-Henri Spaak (Belgium), Maurice Faure (France), Gaetano Martino (Italy), Joseph Bech (Luxembourg), and Johan Willem Beyen (Netherlands).

During the discussions in Venice, the German delegation, represented by Walter Hallstein, made clear that the 'competition principle' was of the utmost importance for Germany.[92] According to the draft minutes, this principle was enunciated by Hallstein as follows '*[Des dispositions communes doivent être prises concernant] la réglementation de la concurrence de manière à empêcher toute action faussant la concurrence, qu'elle émane des autorités publiques ou de cartels ou monopoles.*'[93] Simultaneously, the French delegation, represented by Pineau, claimed that Member States had to be given large discretion in internal economic matters to deal with the 'price problems' that the evolution of the Common Market would create at national level.[94]

Under this framework, the Intergovernmental Conference for the Common Market and the Euratom started working at the Castle of Val Duchesse in Brussels. One of the Treaty negotiators underlined that the Common Market meant, first, the establishment of a large economic trade area without internal borders or artificial obstacles as a prerequisite for a subsequent eventual political union. The Common Market, he claimed, would be neither *dirigiste* nor *laissez faire*. However the Common Market had to be conducted according to the competition principle, save for exceptional circumstances, which would be dealt with in any event by Community institutions.[95] In other words, the competition principle advocated by the German delegation in Venice, and even before the Messina conference,[96] was to inform the entire Treaty.

As to the approach followed by the Member States in the EEC Treaty and how this differed from that followed by the same Member States in relation to the ECSC Treaty,

[92] See, eg, the telegram sent by Walter Hallstein to the German Foreign Ministry at the end of the Conference, on 30 May 1956 in PA AA, [s.l.]. B10 Abteilung II, Politische Abteilung. Bd. 905, Aussenministerkonferenzen-Venedig. A French version is available at: <http://www.cvce.eu/obj/telegramme_de_walter_hallstein_au_ministere_des_affaires_etrangeres_allemand_30_mai_1956-fr-434b4f9f-e271-4650-84e9-22e17b748cf4.html>.

[93] Draft minutes of the Venice Conference, Archives historiques du Conseil de l'Union européenne, Bruxelles, Rue de la Loi 175. Négociations des traités instituant la CEE et la CEEA (1955–57), CM3. Conference des ministres des affaires étrangères, Venise, 29–30 May 1956, CM3/NEGO/093; available at: <http://www.cvce.eu/en/obj/draft_minutes_of_the_venice_conference_29_and_30_may_1956-en-af6e5adf-01a5-4f22-88cd-8354a265e5db.html>.

[94] Ibid.

[95] See address given by Gaetano Martino, Italian Foreign Minister on 18 January 1957, Martino, G., 'From the ECSC to the Common Market.' Ministerio degli affari esteri (ed.). *Gaetano Martino e l'Europa, Dalla Conferenza di Messina al Parlamento europeo* (Istituto poligrafico e zecca dello stato, 1995. Translated by the CVCE) 66; available at: <http://www.cvce.eu/en/collections/unit-content/-/unit/b9fe3d6d-e79c-495e-856d-9729144d2cbd/d2545cf8-d1e3-43b2-806d-12e6e6cfdf71/Resources>: 'once the economic and social infrastructures of Western Europe are transformed by the Common Market, we shall have created the necessary conditions and instruments for united political action.'

[96] See in this regard, eg, the reference to the *German Memorandum* submitted before the Messina Conference in which the German government endorsed the broad economic integration approach (as opposed to the sector-by-sector approach) proposed by the Benelux countries and suggested the incorporation of rules preventing distortions of competition and against national discrimination in Commission of the European Communities, *The Relaunching of Europe, from the Messina Conference to the Treaties of Rome* (Office for Official Publications of the European Communities, 1985) at 18.

Mr Martino, Italian Minister of Foreign Affairs put it very clearly in 1957 'Experience of the ECSC has taught us that it is impossible to establish a federal power or achieve the political unification of Europe through the juxtaposition of a number of partial cessions of sovereignty, and we are therefore sceptical about the idea of constructing Europe by increasing the number of 'supranational authorities' with powers confined to a single sector.[97]

The decline of Monnetism was by then obvious,[98] and at the Court of Justice the less federalist approach of the EEC Treaty was noted.[99] Therefore the approach was no longer to delegate State sovereignty in full to a supranational authority but rather to ascertain *what minimum powers* had to be directed to establish a custom union, and from there to establish over time an economic and finally a political union. In other words, 'what [the draftsmen] did not want, either in Messina or at subsequent conferences, was to put the cart before the horse, political unification before economic union.'[100]

This new approach would justify a different treatment of aids and subsidies between the ECSC and the EEC contexts.[101] The delegations thus agreed on the need to prohibit State aids as means to give guarantees to private operators that competition in the market would not be distorted by State action, fully in line with the terms of the Spaak Report. The disagreements among the parties were more on the substance and on the temporary or permanent nature of the exceptions to the general prohibition,[102] and on the role that the different institutions should play in State aid control.[103]

[97] See address given by Gaetano Martino, Italian Foreign Minister on 18 January 1957, 'From the ECSC to the Common Market', op. cit.

[98] See Gillingham, J., *European Integration 1950–2003: Superstate or New Market Economy?* (CUP, 2003) at 16.

[99] See the opinion of Judge Jacques Rueff in the discussion that followed his intervention, 'La Cour et l'economie politique', in *Dix ans de jurisprudence de la Cour de justice des Communautés européennes*, op. cit. at 33: '*[le Traité de Rome] est beaucoup moins fédéral que le Traité C.E.C.A*'.

[100] See address given by Gaetano Martino, Italian Foreign Minister on 18 January 1957, 'From the ECSC to the Common Market', op. cit.

[101] Indeed, the EEC approach meant that 'aids or subsidies that a Member State may grant in any form to promote production or trade are prohibited, in that they are artificial factors introduced into the free play of competition to distort the results, save where, in exceptional cases, such aids or subsidies are authorized by the Community institutions. Such cases include aid to promote the economic development of areas where the standard of living is abnormally low and aid to facilitate the development of certain economic activities or certain economic areas, where it is not contrary to the common interest.' See address given by Gaetano Martino, Italian Foreign Minister on 18 January 1957, 'From the ECSC to the Common Market', op. cit.

[102] As regards the compatibility of aids with the Common Market, the delegations agreed that Art. 92 should include, in its second paragraph, a list of aids whose compatibility ought to constitute a '*de iure presumption*'. In addition, seemingly due to the impossibility of forecasting all '*de iure*' possible compatible aid at the time of drafting the EEC Treaty, the delegations agreed to include, as para. 3 of Art. 92, a list of possible compatible aids to be examined by the Commission. See the submission of the Italian delegation to the Common Market Group. See Neri, S. at 230 and the Note présentée le 11/9/1956 (Doc. MAE 257/56).

[103] Kusters, H.J., *Fondements de la Communauté économique européenne* (Office des publications officielles des Communautés européennes, 1990) at 248. See also for the same view, eg, Mederer, 'Evolution of State Aid Control', op. cit. at 27.

Nevertheless there were some interesting discussions that took place in relation to the concept of aid under (then to be) Article 92 EEC. A brief account of those discussions reveals that some of the conceptual issues discussed more than fifty years ago remain controversial today. In this regard, the German delegation, represented by Mr H. Von Boeckh, proposed to eliminate *for practical reasons* the wording of Article 92, paragraph 1, since the prohibition of financial assistance by Member States would be implicitly covered by the other competition rules included in the draft Treaty as part of the competition principle that transcended the Treaty.[104] The idea was that aids were forbidden and that the Commission would act upon having knowledge of the granting of an aid but not necessarily beforehand. The German delegation drew inspiration for its proposal on the original Article XVI of the GATT that, as mentioned earlier, included a mere obligation to communicate, not a presumption of incompatibility like that provided for in the final Article 92(1) EEC. The Belgian, French, Italian, and Dutch delegations opposed the German proposal on the basis that it was preferable to have this separate provision.[105] According to the Dutch delegation, the most recent drafting of Article XVI GATT also included a prohibition of subsidies such as that of Article 92(1) EEC.[106] The strong opposition forced Germany to drop its proposal.[107]

As to the actual drafting of Article 92, paragraph 1 EEC, the Belgian delegation suggested reinforcing the prohibition by adding to '*les aides accordées par les États*' the provision '*les aides accordées par les organismes dépendant de ceux-ci*.'[108] The proposal was rejected as unnecessary. However, it has been suggested that the Belgian concern explains the final formula 'granted by a Member State *or through State resources*'.[109] Therefore, the notion 'through State resources' could refer originally to public bodies belonging to the State, an interpretation that would in fact conform to the initial case law of the Court regarding State resources and the view of most commentators in the early years.[110]

Another proposal, lodged by the Dutch delegation, was also reflected in the final text. The proposal suggested prohibiting not only those aids that distort competition but also those that threatened to distort competition ('*sont de nature à fausser la concurrence*').[111] This fundamental addition has warranted a very extensive scope of application for the notion of aid since the early days as 'any impact on costs or prices' was considered as potentially distorting.[112]

[104] Ibid. and Doc.MAE/Sec. 34/56, p. 1.

[105] Ibid. and Doc.MAE/Sec. 34/56, pp. 2–3.

[106] MAE/Sec 34/56 js.

[107] Ibid. and Doc.MAE 287/56 (Art. 44, para. 1).

[108] Trans. 'aid granted by States' instead of 'aid granted by bodies dependent on them.' Ibid. and Doc.MAE/Sec. 34/56, p. 4.

[109] See Mederer, 'Evolution of State Aid Control', op. cit. at 30.

[110] See, eg, Case 173/73 *Italy v Commission* [1974] 709 at 16 or Case C-78/76 *Steinike & Weinlig v Federal Republic of Germany* [1977] ECR, p. 00595, and for the commentators see, eg, Scheuing, *Les aides financiers publiques*, op. cit. at 269–73.

[111] Doc.MAE/Sec. 34/56, pp. 2–3.

[112] Kapteyn, P.J.G., and Verloren van Themaat, P., *Introduction to the Law of the European Communities after the Accession of New Member States* (Sweet & Maxwell, 1973) at 245–47. See also

Other proposals were refused. The Dutch delegation proposed to prohibit both '*aids*' and '*subsidies*' (as in the ECSC Treaty). France, and subsequently the Groupe de Marché Commune, considered that it was unnecessary to include both terms.[113] This decision pre-dated by five years the conclusion reached by the Court of Justice in the same sense in the miners' bonus judgment,[114] decided in the ECSC Treaty context. Similarly, the German delegation proposed to consider the compatibility '*avec le marché commun*' as including both the 'establishment' and the 'functioning' of the Common Market.[115] This suggestion was not reflected in the final wording of Article 92, paragraph 1, agreed on 28 January 1957,[116] yet it forecast the evolution of the interpretation of this provision.

Finally, it may be worth recalling the interpretative declarations made in relation to Article 92 EEC at the time of adopting the Treaty, as some of the concerns expressed then remain valid today. In this sense, as regards the prohibition of aid enshrined in Article 92, paragraph 1, '*le Comité des Chef de delegation*' considered that aids to *Social Security services* were not covered by the prohibition laid down in Article 92, paragraph 1.[117] It was also reported that the Dutch Parliament had held that aid to housing could not be considered as compatible State aid because it was not State aid in the first place due to the absence of, at least, one of its constitutive elements, that is the distortion of competition. Similarly, the French delegation informed that, in its view, aids to compensate the provisions of tasks of general interest carried out by public or private companies were compatible with the Treaty.[118]

(3) Conclusions

In a nutshell, both the Spaak Report and the *Travaux Preparatoires* advocated a broad definition of State aid, a definition capable of ensuring that the elimination of obstacles to trade provided for by the fundamental freedoms would not be offset by public support to market actors. The broad definition was devised to prevent Member States from distorting the free play of competition by artificially altering the results.

The drafters of the Spaak Report and the Treaty negotiators were nonetheless conscious of the need to distinguish between acceptable and non-acceptable aids in a Treaty that was not going to be limited to two industries but instead would be open to all sectors of the economy. They were also aware of the limitations of the full delegation of sovereignty approach, especially after the defeats of the Defence and Political Communities during the 1950s, and did not want to replicate it. The

Quadri, R., Monaco, R., and Trabucchi, A. (eds), *Trattato istitutivo della C.E.E. Comentario* Vol. II (Giuffrè, 1965) at 720.

[113] Doc.MAE/Sec. 34/56.

[114] Case 30/59, *Steenkolenmijnen in Limburg v High Authority* [1961] ECR 3.

[115] Doc.MAE/Sec. 34/56.

[116] See Neri, op. cit. at 229 and Doc. MAE 343/57 (Art. 44, para. 1).

[117] See Neri, op. cit. at 233.

[118] See Neri, op. cit. at 231.

EEC Treaty had therefore to be respectful to the economic sovereignty of Member States inasmuch as this sovereignty did not impinge upon one of the fundamental objectives of the EEC Treaty. In the same vein, the Rome Treaties were not meant to replace *national aid* by *European aid*. As a result, some criteria seemed necessary, even at the level of the definition of aid, to distinguish between general measures, to be tackled *ex-post*, from selective advantages, to be tackled *ex-ante*, and even among the latter in order to exclude those measures that were not liable to distort competition or trade. Finally, both the Report and the negotiations made clear that only the Commission could be entrusted with the task of deciding on the acceptability of State aids, as this decision could not be left to the partisan will of Member States.

3. Conclusion

This chapter shows that subsidies have been granted in Europe since at least the seventeenth century chiefly for the following reasons: to (i) enhance political power, both domestic (pleasing merchants and allies) and international (increasing revenues through exports thus becoming more powerful in the international sphere); (ii) to promote particular industries (such as military and textiles); (iii) to reward individual achievements (in particular military or industrial successes); (iv) to develop State infrastructure (rail, roads, ports); and (v) to increase employment. However, negative features were identified early on, in particular: (i) the waste of scarce resources in non-productive industries; (ii) the unfair redistribution of the costs associated with subsidies between the beneficiaries (few industries or merchants), and those paying the subsidies (most industries and citizens); and (iii) the potential for conflict between subsidizing and not subsidizing nations (such as the conflict between Britain and Germany regarding subsidies to sugar in the early twentieth century).

Notwithstanding this, although some subsidy-related problems were soon identified, it was not until the twentieth century, as a part of a general trend against protectionism, that some form of multinational control of subsidies was set forth. The most remarkable precedent is the 1902 Brussels Sugar Convention that entrusted for the first time to a multinational authority the monitoring of the prohibition of subsides agreed upon by the parties. This Convention also introduced a broad notion of aid that covered both direct and indirect support.

The multinational control of subsidies would emerge again after the Second World War, fostered by the belief in 'economic peace' as a precondition for international peace and prosperity. The international regulation of subsidies materialized in the GATT after the failure of the ITO; it was however relatively weak. By contrast, the 1951 ECSC Treaty was quite radical because all national subsidies to the coal and steel sectors (the material scope of the Treaty of Paris) were forbidden and the power to grant subsidies was transferred to the High Authority. However, this supranational approach to integration was not to be replicated in the EEC Treaty after the decline of Monnet's approach. The new Treaty would be based on the attribution to the Community only of the necessary powers to achieve its goals and, primarily, the establishment of the Common Market.[119]

The new approach to integration was translated into the State aid field in a combination of a general declaration of national aid as incompatible with the Treaty, according to some criteria, followed by a long list of exceptions to this incompatibility. The exceptions would need to be interpreted by a supranational institution, the European Commission. The EEC system is thus contributory to the teachings of the previous systems because it contains: (1) a broad and undefined notion of aid; (2) a supranational monitoring system, both features present in the Brussels Sugar Convention and the ECSC Treaty in different ways; and (3) the introduction of some flexibility through a number of exemptions, a feature based on the experience of the difficult application of the total prohibition established in the ECSC Treaty.

[119] See also in this regard, Von der Groeben, H., *The European Community—The Formative Years: The Struggle to Establish the Common Market and the Political Union (1958–66)* (Office for Official Publications of the European Communities, 1987) at 23: 'Under the terms of the EEC Treaty governments were therefore expected to give up only as much sovereignty as was necessary for the Community to achieve its agreed objectives. Member States were to retain sufficient latitude to enable them to meet their overall political responsibility for the welfare of their citizens.'

3

The Evolution of European State Aid Policy

This chapter analyses the evolution of State aid policy. The focus is on the changes in the Commission's main objectives and priorities in relation to this field as the European Union (EU) proceeds down the path of further integration. The main inspiration for this chapter comes from the work of political scientists[1] who have described a number of developments affecting the evolution of the Commission's State aid policy and have divided this evolution into a number of distinct periods. As we will see, some of these periods coincide with those identified by Joseph Weiler in his inspirational 'Transformation of Europe.'[2] In our view this was to be expected because, as this chapter will show, the objectives and priorities of the State aid policy have been heavily influenced by the general political and economic developments taking place at the Community level.[3]

1. The First Period: 1958 to the Early 1970s

The first period of European integration, ranging from 1958 until the early 1970s,[4] is characterized by the Commission's focus on the elimination of barriers to trade

[1] See Lavdas, K.A., and Mendrinou, M.M., *Politics, Subsidies, and Competition: The New Politics of State Intervention in the European Union* (Edward Elgar, 1999); Doleys, T, 'Fifty Years of Moulding Article 87: The European Commission and the Development of EU State Aid Law & Policy (1958–2008)', Paper prepared for presentation at the 11th Biennial International Conference of the European Union Studies Association in Marina Del Ray, California, 23–25 April 2009; See Mederer, W., 'Evolution of State Aid Control', in Mederer, W., Pesaresi, N., and Van Hoof, M. (eds), *EU Competition Law*, Volume IV, State Aid, Book One (Leuven: Claeys & Casteels, 2008), or Blauberger, M, 'Of "Good" and "Bad" Subsidies: European State Aid Control through Soft and Hard Law' (2009) *West European Politics*, 719. See also the recent periodization of the evolution of State aids by legal scholar Tosato, G.L., 'L'evoluzione della disciplina sugli aiuti di stato', in Schepisi, C. (ed.), *La modernizzazione della disciplina sugli aiuti di Stato: il nuovo approccio della Commissione Europea e i recenti sviluppi in materia di public e private enforcement* (G. Giappichelli, 2011).

[2] See Weiler, J.H.H., 'The Transformation of Europe', *Yale Law Journal* (1990–91) 2403–83. Weiler's work has been very inspirational for this important chapter of the book.

[3] See for another periodization of the evolution of competition law largely coinciding with that of Weiler, Wesseling, R., *The Modernisation of EC Antitrust Law* (Hart, 2000) 9–74.

[4] See for this periodization, Doleys, 'Fifty Years of Moulding Article 87', op. cit. See also for this period and generally for a seminal and very influential periodization, Weiler, 'The Transformation of Europe', op. cit.

and discrimination between undertakings in different Member States.[5] These objectives were developed in the context of Member States' hostility towards State aid compliance, which contributed to selective and largely weak enforcement of these rules by the European Commission.[6]

The strong link between competition and free movement rules and the equally strong teleological enforcement that dominated this period was described graphically by an early *référendaire* of the Court of Justice and member of the Commission: 'any act or conduct which interferes or threaten to interfere with [the] free movement violates the rules on competition and it can therefore also be said that the criterion for determining whether or not a given example of market behaviour (in the broadest sense) is prohibited under these rules is to be found in the answer to the question "does this behaviour endanger the fulfilment of the objectives of the Common Market?" In other words, does it put an obstacle in the way of free trade? If the answer is "yes", then the activity under investigation violates the EEC Treaty.'[7]

In the field of State aids, the Commission's priority was to clarify the scope of application of today's Article 107 TFEU with a view to avoiding the granting of regional aid in a 'beggar-thy-neighbour' fashion,[8] and the granting of aid in some sectors that were considered particularly important at the time, namely, shipbuilding, textiles, synthetic rubber, cinema, and aircraft production.[9] The

[5] The link between the State aid rules and discrimination was emphasized in a French Report of 1959 co-authorized by then Judge at the Court of Justice and eminent French economist Jacques Rueff: '*les articles 92 et 93 du Traité de Rome tracent un cadre suffisamment souple pour permettre les interventions nécessaires à l'expansion, à condition que ces interventions ne conduisent pas à une discrimination injustifiée à l'encontre des producteurs des autres pays du Marché commun.*' (Trans. 'Articles 92 and 93 of the Treaty of Rome trace a sufficiently flexible framework to allow the interventions needed to expand, provided that these procedures do not lead to unjustified discrimination against producers in other countries of the Common Market.') See Rapport sur les obstacles à l'expansion économique présenté par le Comite institue par le Décret, No. 59-1284 du 13 novembre 1959.

[6] According to David Gerber, the Commission 'chose not to enforce vigorously the treaty provisions relating to State aids…'. Gerber, D.J., *Law and Competition in Twentieth Century Europe: Protecting Prometheus* (OUP, 1998) at 357–58. In our view, while it is true that the Commission adopted a lax approach towards the enforcement of these rules, this approach was also the result of the hostile attitude of the Council towards the enforcement of these rules, an approach quite different to that adopted in relation to the competition rules addressed to undertakings as will be explained in this chapter.

[7] Mathijsen, P., in George K.D., and Joll, C. (eds), *Competition Policy in the UK and the EEC* (CUP, 1975) at 180. This thesis was also supported by the Judgment of the Court of Justice of 13 July 1966 in Joined Cases 56 and 58/64, *Consten Grundig v Commission*, ECR 1966, 429. See also, eg, Hawk, B., 'Antitrust in the EEC—The First Decade' (1972) 41 *Fordham Law Review* 229 at 231: 'Single Market Integration, and the Elimination of Restrictive Practices which Interfere with that Integration, is the First Principle of EEC Antitrust Law', cited by Gerber, *Law and Competition in Twentieth Century Europe*, op. cit. at 347.

[8] As the Commission recognized, 'The Commission is anxious to achieve some measure of harmony among the Member States with regard to regional aid, both because of the need for balanced growth in the various regions of the Community and in an endeavour to put an end to the efforts of member countries to outbid each other and to the distortions due to excessive competition at the Community level.' Second General Report on the Activities of the Communities (European Commission, 1969) point 47, cited by Doleys, 'Fifty Years of Moulding Article 87', op. cit. at 10–11.

[9] See Doleys, 'Fifty Years of Moulding Article 87', op. cit. at 9, footnote 19. See also Von der Groeben, H., *The European Community The Formative Years: The Struggle to Establish the Common*

Commission's action in the first decade of State aid enforcement progressively moved from the exclusive pursuit of the most discriminatory measures, such as export aid, to other types of aid, such as regional or sectoral aid systems, as the Community reached the 'final phase' of integration, after the achievement of the customs union in 1968.[10]

The State aid rules were then a relatively new tool which was both quite restrictive of national liberty and unprecedented in the national laws of the founding nations. The rules, moreover, comprised a tool that had to be defined, understood, and most importantly, accepted by Member States not least as they had to trigger the monitoring system by notifying State aid projects to the Commission.[11] In this light, the limited number of decisions adopted by the Commission during this period ought not to be judged too severely,[12] not least because State aids were often discussed in political rather than legal settings, with the consequence that national legislations containing aids were eventually modified or abolished without formal decisions being taken.[13]

The Commission was therefore committed to advocate the advantages of Community action, yet it would not confront Member States directly.[14] The goal of State aid during this first phase was, according to an author of that time,[15] akin to that of the other competition rules; that is, State aid rules existed to remove any sort of discrimination between Member States and to allow the Commission to intervene when national aid harmed undertakings of other Member States without providing a benefit to the Community as a whole that could outweigh the harm caused.[16]

Market and the Political Union (1958–66) (Office for Official Publications of the European Communities, 1987) at 215, who noted that for these sensitive sectors it was convenient to take precautionary measures and to initiate sectoral investigations before specific emergencies arrived.

[10] See Scheuing, D.H., *Les aides financiers publiques aux enterprises en droit francaise et europeen* (Editions Berger-Levrault, 1974) at 321.

[11] Ibid. at 323.

[12] The number was in fact not as limited as one may think given the circumstances: in 1965 the Commissioner for Competition summarized the work carried out in the State aid until then: 450 aid schemes had been studied, thirteen had been declared incompatible with the Common Market and around sixty had been amended at the Commission request. See for this account, Dumoulin, M. (ed.), *The European Commission, 1958–72: History and Memories* (European Commission, 2007), a work undertaken on the initiative of the European Commission with contributions from former European officials, at 312.

[13] In fact, Commissioner Von der Groeben made clear that the Commission would adopt a pragmatic rather than a strict approach in these first years of the Community since, 'before a truly European answer can be found to the practical problem of competition policy a great deal of discussion is needed with the Member States and with industry.' See von der Groeben, H., Competition in the Common Market. Speech at the European Parliament. Strasbourg, 19 October 1961, at 12. See also Lavdas and Mendrinou, *Politics, Subsidies, and Competition*, op. cit. at 28–29.

[14] First Report on Competition Policy (Office for Official Publications of the European Communities, 1972) at point 134.

[15] See Walsh, A.E., and Paxton, J., *Competition Policy: European and International Trends and Practices* (Macmillan, 1975) at 43.

[16] For the relation between discriminatory aids, such as para-fiscal levies, and integration, see the early reports on competition policy of 1971, at points 181–83, of 1972, at points 108–11, or of 1973, at points 102–04.

In order to achieve these goals, and as it had done in the Antitrust field,[17] the Commission sought to lay down the implementing rules for State aid provided for in then Article 93, paragraph 3 (now 108(3) TFEU).[18] For these purposes, the European Commission undertook an inventory of 'the systems of aid in force on the territories of the Member States'[19] in order to gather knowledge about the situation, which it completed in 1964. After the completion of the inventory, the Commission proceeded in 1966 with a proposal for a draft Regulation under today's Article 109 TFEU on the application of today's Articles 107 and 108 TFEU.

The proposal was not followed by the Council. Certainly the timing was difficult, with the background of the 'empty chair' crisis and the Luxembourg Compromise in that very same year. However, the Council's approach towards State aid was very different from that depicted by Gerber with regard to the competition rules addressed to undertakings in the same period, where the Council was 'willing to allow the Commission to play the major role in shaping the competition law system'.[20] In this vein, Jordan suggested in 1975 that the different pace of policy development between the antitrust field, in which procedural rules were issued in 1962, and strict enforcement followed soon after, and the State aid policy was due to the fact that State aid cases required a political rather than an economic approach.[21] Similarly, the first Competition Commissioner recognized that although the powers of the Commission in the State aid field were fairly clearly outlined in the Treaty, the task of deciding on the admissibility or otherwise of State aids proved very difficult, since the Commission soon came into conflict with the interests of certain Member States and with previous practice.[22] Indeed, most State aid cases were negotiated and hence only few reached the Court of Justice, which explains the lack of guidance of the Court during this

[17] With the proposal for Regulation 17/62.

[18] First General Report on the Activities of the Community (European Commission, 1968) at 86. 'In this field [Aids granted by Member States], the task of the European Commission consists in controlling and preventing, in accordance with the Treaty, the grant of any direct or indirect aids by a Member State…To this effect, the European Commission will draft rules for the implementation of Article 93, paragraph 3…After this precautionary measure, the basic action in regard to existing aids will be progressively taken in hand. The Member States will be invited to report these aids in order that the procedures envisaged in Article 93 can be implemented.'

[19] Second General Report on the Activities of the Community, op. cit., 131 *et seq*. See also Third General Report on the Activities of the Community (European Commission, 1970) at 151.

[20] Gerber, *Law and Competition in Twentieth Century Europe*, op. cit. at 349, see also 351 for the contrast between the Council's attitude in the competition and State aid matters: 'In 1965, the Council further buttressed the autonomy of the Commission in competition law matters by granting it broad powers to 'legislate' without approval of the Council'.

[21] Jordan, J., 'State Aids: The Compatibility of Regional Aid Systems with the Common Market' (1976) *European Law Review* 236 at 237, quoted in Lavdas and Mendrinou, *Politics, Subsidies, and Competition*, op. cit. at 47, footnote 10.

[22] Von der Groeben, *The European Community*, op. cit. at 64. See also at 148: 'The common policy with regard to competition, whose fundamental importance to the development of the common market was continually emphasized by the Commission, was pursued energetically following the issue of Regulation 17, but the removal and prevention of subsidies contrary to the Treaty were even then proving very difficult.'

period.[23] Also, as mentioned quite realistically by an author in 1965: '*il existait certes des problèmes plus urgents que ceux posés en matière des aides*'.[24]

In 1972, the Commission submitted to the Council a second proposal to adopt a draft Regulation for the application of today's Articles 107 and 108 TFEU which was rejected.[25] This second rejection clearly showed the lack of 'willingness of Member States to place their intervention policies under Community control by agreeing to create the necessary framework of action, a State aids regulation.'[26] Indeed, the Commission acknowledged several difficulties regarding State aid enforcement in 1972.[27] Certainly, this period was a troubled one with regard to the State aid control, although some authors do not view it as necessarily wholly negative. In fact, for Dashwood, writing in 1975, the Commission had made 'very full use' of its powers in this field.[28]

To sum up, although State aid policy was formally in the Commission's power, the development of the policy during this period was relatively slow for three main reasons: (i) the absence of a clear target; that is, the lack of knowledge as to the measures that ought to be considered as pernicious State aids and hence prohibited; (ii) the absence of a strong line taken on enforcement, this due to the difficult political situation that dominated this period, the lack of cooperation and notifications by Member States (in stark contrast with the high number of agreements that were notified under Article 101 TFEU to the Commission), and the refusal of Member States to adopt procedural rules on State aids; and (iii) the selective enforcement of the Commission which focused on cases that had a clear impact on out-of-State traders, and tolerated aids which did not have a substantial effect on trade because they were not the priority for the establishment

[23] Similarly, as a former Director of DG COMP submitted, '[t]he first decade of the European Community witnessed a slow start in [State aid] policy development. There were no general guidelines and no real debate was engaged with the Member States. Protective measures (customs duties) still existed, but were progressively abolished under an accelerated timetable leading to the establishment of a true customs union in July 1968. The political difficulties of the mid-1960s slowed progress in this area. The "empty French chair" crisis, finally solved by the so-called Luxemburg Compromise, hindered the Community's decision-making affairs, and undermined the Commission's self-confidence for many years.' Ehlermann, C.D., 'State Aids under European Community Competition Law' (1994) *Fordham International Law Journal* 408 at 414.

[24] Trans. 'There were certainly more urgent problems than those posed in the field of aids.' See Ryziger, P.-F., *Discriminations et subventions, first co-report, in Dix ans de jurisprudence de la Cour de justice des Communautés européennes, Europäische Arbeitstagung* (Heymanns, 1965) 245–58 at 258.

[25] The Commission ended up withdrawing the proposal in 1976 in view of the lack of support by the Council. See reply to written question Nr. 53/78 by Mr Jahn to the Council, OJ 1978 C 150/21.

[26] Lavdas and Mendrinou, *Politics, Subsidies, and Competition*, op. cit. at 30.

[27] First Report on Competition Policy, op. cit. at points 135–38: eg (i) perfect economic rationalization cannot easily be applied to State aid due to its important social and political components, (ii) the Commission could only act under Art. 92(1) EC, 'in cases where national aid is harmful to the economic activities of other Member States'[the need to show a tangible or appreciable effect on competition and/or trade (or a De Minimis exception rule) seemed to be observed by the Commission, and also by the Court, in these early years], or (iii) the Commission recognized 'technical' difficulties to identify the 'components of aid' in some cases such as State participations or the working out of certain infrastructures.

[28] See Dashwood, A., 'Control of State Aids in the EEC: Prevention and Cure under Article 93' (1975) *Common Market Law Review* 43 at 43.

of the Common Market. Nevertheless, the European Commission made use of this period to develop a notion of aid and an enforcement system that would be ready when the time would be ripe for a more vigorous enforcement of the State aid rules. The Commission in fact 'warned' in 1963 that State aid policy would expand as the internal market developed. In the Commission's words 'the steps to be taken in this field will become increasingly important as others barriers to trade are eliminated.'[29] As we know now, this prophetic statement has proven to be accurate.

2. The Second Period: Early 1970s to Mid-1980s

The advent of the oil crisis in 1973, together with the lack of competitiveness of European companies *vis-à-vis* Japanese and US companies, prompted Member States to protect their economies to the detriment of the Common Market. Indeed, Member States responded to the oil crisis with a significant increase in the number of State aids utilized, and a clear evasion of the State aid rules that the Commission proved unable to enforce.[30] Some Member States even argued before the Court during this period that a certain measure was State aid to avoid its categorization as a violation of free movement law. In other words, the concept of State aid was sometimes raised during this period as a defence.[31] In this context, absent a State aids procedural regulation, in the presence of the oil crisis, and with Member States unwilling to cooperate, the Commission took a pragmatic, low-profile approach to State aids. The Commission considered that the national protectionist measures adopted during these early years following the oil crisis would be temporary and therefore it decided not to intervene decisively.[32]

However, by 1978 the Commission recognized that the economic problems of Member States were 'of a basic structural nature' and that they needed to be addressed for economic recovery to begin.[33] The Commission also justified the importance of State aid control for three 'undeniable reasons' which were quite

[29] Sixth General Report on the Activities of the Communities (European Commission, 1973) at 47.

[30] For the increase of State aids as a reaction to the 1973 crisis, see Caspari, M., 'The Aid Rules of the EEC Treaty and Their Application' in Schwarze, J. (ed.), *Discretionary Powers of the Member States in the Field of Economic Policies and Their Limits under the EEC Treaty* (Nomos Verlagsgesellschatft, 1988) 40 at 48. For the evasion of Community rules on State aids by the Member States see, eg, Cownie, F., 'State Aids in the Eighties' (1986) *European Law Review*, 247 at 248–49; Wulff, O., 'National Economic Policy: An Obstacle to the European Community?' in Schwarze (ed.), *Discretionary Powers of the Member States*, op. cit. 9 at 16; and Steenbergen, J., 'Trade Regulation since the Tokyo Round' in Volker, E.L.M. (ed.), *Protectionism and the European Community* (Kluwer, 1987) at 194–95.

[31] See, eg, Case 249/81 *Commission v Ireland* [1982] ECR 4005 or Case C-21/88 *Du Pont de Nemours* [1990] ECR I-889.

[32] Lavdas and Mendrinou, *Politics, Subsidies, and Competition*, op. cit. at 31.

[33] Also as to the structural problems of European industry at this time, see Kapteyn, P.J.G., 'Outgrowing the Treaty of Rome: From Market Integration to Policy Integration', in *Melanges Fernand Dehousse* (F. Nathan, 1979) at 45.

close to the justifications for this policy included in the Spaak Report.[34] The Commission thus announced in 1978 that it was going to be stricter, albeit still flexible in view of the economic situation. Advocate General Van Themaat also noted the Commission's 'harder line' in his opinion to the *Intermills* case.[35] The Commission had to be flexible as well because at this time it lacked enough leverage *vis-à-vis* Member States with regard to such a politically sensitive issue against such a febrile economic background. The aim was to work with Member States to channel aid in less damaging ways, to achieve 'co-ordination with the aim of ensuring that [aids] would not endanger interstate trade or export economic difficulties from one Member State to another.'[36]

In addition, in the early 1980s, the Commission started to exercise the formal investigation procedure provided for in today's Article 108(2) TFEU more frequently, and to remind Member States of their obligation to notify new aid measures.[37] In fact, the tendency towards non-notification in 1980 was so general that the Commission voiced the suspicion that Member States may have been attempting to circumvent the obligation to notify State aids provided for in the Treaty.[38] The increase in the Commission's toughness on State aid became even more evident under Commissioner for Competition, Frans Andriessen (1981–85). During his period of office, the Commission insisted on the duty to notify new aids, increased the number of recovery cases, and issued a communication on the accumulation of aids for different purposes where the obligation to notify was emphasized.[39] The European Parliament supported this increasingly vigorous

[34] COM(78) 221 final. Communication from the Commission to the Council. Policy on sectoral aid schemes, 221 final, 25 May 1978, available at: <http://aei.pitt.edu/3790/>. See 3.1: '(i) the customs union would be quite useless and would collapse if Member States could invalidate it by granting aids; (ii) the Common Market makes little sense unless businesses tackle the market on the strength of their own resources without any aid to distort competition between them, except where such aid is clearly justified in the general interest of the Community; and (iii) lastly, and as a corollary, a system which leaves the field open for competition and does not allow aids to interfere with the optimum distribution of production factors is essential to economic and social progress.'

[35] See opinion of AG Van Themaat in case C-323/82, *SA Intermills v Commission* [1984] ECR p. 03809: 'the Commission is less ready now than in the years from 1975 to 1978 to accept "rescue operations" such as that concerned here. An explanation of this harder line—which, as appears from the eighth recital in the preamble to the decision, was expressly supported by three Member States—is provided in the 18th recital in the preamble. It is apparent, both from that and from the 19th and 20th recitals, that the Commission regards the crisis in the paper industry as structural rather than contingent. For similar reasons the Commission is known to be pursuing a relatively severe policy in relation to aids in the steel industry.'

[36] Lavdas and Mendrinou, *Politics, Subsidies, and Competition*, op. cit. at 33. Indeed, in 1979 the Commission still accepted that flexibility had to prevail over rigidity in the enforcement of competition more generally due to 'the persistence of conditions of crisis'. See Ninth Report on Competition Policy (Office for Official Publications of the European Communities, 1980) at 9.

[37] See Commission letters (SG(77) D/122; SG (80) D/9538; SG(81) 12740; SG(83) D/13342).

[38] See Commission communication on the notification of State aid to the Commission pursuant to Art. 93(3) of the EEC Treaty: the failure of Member States to respect their obligations, OJ C 252, 30 September 1980, p. 2, quoted by Smith, M.P., 'Autonomy by the Rules: The European Commission and the Development of State Aid Policy' (1998) *Journal of Common Market Studies*, 55 at 64, footnote 6.

[39] Commission communication on the cumulation of aids for different purposes, OJ C 3, 05/01/1985 P. 2–3.

approach which was defended by the Commission.[40] More generally, from the mid-1970s to the mid-1980s the stricter stance towards State aids was part of an incipient bias towards the application of the Treaty rules to public monopolies and privileged undertakings.[41]

Despite the enforcement difficulties, the Commission started to develop some State aid policies that went beyond the mere control of illegal aid. This took the form primarily of regional aid policy and, given the economic situation, a policy for rescue and restructuring aid.[42] Initially these policies emerged out of Member States' preferences, sometimes following an express agreement between Member States in that regard, for example in regional or textile aid.[43] Subsequently, mirroring the expansion of competences undertaken by the Council, the Commission made the first steps towards some 'positive integration' measures in the *new* Community fields of environment,[44] employment,[45] Small and Medium-size Enterprises (SMEs),[46] and Research and Development (R&D).[47] Indeed, in 1980 the Commission openly demanded that State aid play a key role in industrial policy at Community, rather than national, level.[48]

Soft law instruments, such as frameworks or guidelines, were in fact the only possible instruments the Commission could adopt since the Council refused to adopt a procedural regulation on State aid. However, these turned out to be very useful instruments to insulate the Commission from external pressure in deciding State aid cases as the Commission could refer to those instruments in order to take a decision in a given case, this because the Commission must abide by its own rules.[49] It was also as this time that the Commission enunciated the 'compensatory principle' for the compatibility of State aids, according to which, 'if the Commission has to use its discretionary power not to raise objection to an aid

[40] Lavdas and Mendrinou, *Politics, Subsidies, and Competition*, op. cit. at 33, and Debates of the European Parliament (EP) 14/15.10.1981; EP Resolution 1-608/81, OJ C 287/61–62 1981; EP Resolution 1-610/81, OJ C 287/63 1981.

[41] Gardner, A., 'The Velvet Revolution: Article 90 and the Triumph of the Free Market in Europe's Regulated Sectors' (1995) *European Competition Law Review* 78 at 79.

[42] For regional aid policy measures Commission communication on general systems of regional aid, IJ 1971 C111/7; Communication of the Commission to the Council, COM (73) 1110 of 27 June 1973; Communication of the Commission to the Council, COM (75) 77 of 26.02.1975; and Communication of the Commission on general systems of regional aid, OJ 1979 C 31/9, and for rescue and restructuring aid principles, Eighth Report on Competition Policy (Office for Official Publications of the European Communities, 1979) at points 227–30. See also Mederer, 'Evolution of State Aid Control', op. cit. at 44–46.

[43] Smith, 'Autonomy by the Rules', op. cit. at 59.

[44] Community framework on State aid in environmental matters, letter to Member States S/74/30.807 of 7 November 1974.

[45] See Seventh Report on Competition Policy (Office for Official Publications of the European Communities, 1978) at points 235–36.

[46] Sixth Report on Competition Policy (Office for Official Publications of the European Communities, 1977) at point 241.

[47] Second Report on Competition Policy, op. cit. at point 121.

[48] Tenth Report on Competition Policy (Office for Official Publications of the European Communities, 1981) at 9.

[49] See, eg, in this regard Smith, 'Autonomy by the Rules', op. cit. at 62 or Blauberger, 'Of "Good" and "Bad" Subsidies', op. cit. at 726.

proposal, it must contain a compensatory justification which takes the form of a contribution by the beneficiary of aid over and above the effects of normal play of market forces to the achievement of Community objectives as contained in derogations of Article 92(3) EEC[Article 107(3)TFEU].'[50] The Court validated this important principle, which made the compatibility analysis a Community (not national) matter, in the landmark *Philip Morris* judgment.[51]

Notwithstanding all this, the most important policy development of the second period was the adoption of the Transparency Directive in June 1980,[52] which was meant to make more transparent the opaque financial relations between public undertakings and their Member States' budgets.[53] The Transparency Directive was challenged before the Court of Justice by several Member States. The Court upheld the Directive in a very important judgment for the Commission, decided in 1982.[54]

Equally important for the purposes of State aid law was the adoption of the Market Economy Investor Principle (MEIP), according to which a public investment in an undertaking in which a market operator—under normal market economy conditions—would not have invested, constitutes an advantage for the purposes of the State aid definition. The preliminary version of the MEIP was introduced for the first time by the Commission in the decision establishing Community rules for aids to the steel industry in 1981.[55] The reasoning behind the test was that the restructuring of the steel industry could not go against the principle of no discrimination between public and private operators.[56] The test

[50] Tenth Report on Competition Policy, op. cit. at point 213. For a discussion of the emergence and application of the principle see Mortelmans, K., 'The Compensatory Justification Criterion in the Practice of the Commission in Decisions on State Aids' (1984) *Common Market Law Review*, 405.

[51] C-730/79, *Philip Morris Holland BV v Commission of the European Communities*, [1980]ECR p. 02671.

[52] Commission Directive 80/723/EEC of 25 June 1980 on the transparency of financial relations between Member States and public undertakings, OJ L 195, 29/07/1980 pp. 0035–37.

[53] As Doleys has written, the Commission had noted the problems associated with the opacity of financial relations between public undertakings and Member States' budgets since the mid-1970s, although it would not be until 1980 when the Commission decided finally, confirming to the harder line adopted, to face this problem directly. See Doleys, 'Fifty Years of Moulding Article 87', op. cit. at 16. Indeed, the difficult history of the transparency directive dates back to 1976 when the Commission announced that it was working on a draft transparency directive that would, however, take four years to see the light of day. For the Commission's justification for the adoption of this Directive, see the Tenth Report on Competition Policy, op. cit. at 10.

[54] Joined Cases 188 to 190/80, *French Republic, Italian Republic and United Kingdom of Great Britain and Northern Ireland v Commission of the European Communities*, [1982] ECR 2545.

[55] Commission Decision 81/2330/ECSC of 7.8.1981. OJ 1981 L 228/14. For the references contained in this section. See Grespan, D., and Santamato, S. 'Favouring Certain Undertakings or the Production of Certain Goods: Advantage' in Mederer, Pesaresi, and Van Hoof (eds), op. cit. 273 at 307.

[56] In the Commission's words: 'When assessing aid no discrimination must be practised between undertakings, notably on account of their ownership, whether public or private. Accordingly, the rules established by this decision must also apply to any aid elements contained in financing measures taken by Member States in respect of public-sector steel undertakings. These include the provision of equity capital, the setting-off of losses, the foregoing of dividends or of normal returns on public funds or the compensation of financial burdens imposed by public authorities.' Commission Decision 81/2330/ECSC of 7 August 1981. OJ 1981 L 228/14, recital II. See also Art. 1.

was also reflected in the Shipbuilding Code, adopted by the Council in 1981 and in several Commission decisions of the early 1980s.[57] The Commission summarized the new test in the 1984 Communication concerning public holdings.[58] The MEIP was thus in keeping with the goals of the transparency directive and, notably, was supported not only by the Commission but also by the Council, anxious to make Member States' economies more competitive by reducing the heavy burden represented by inefficient public undertakings and sectors.

In sum, the second period of EU integration is more important than initially meets the eye. The Commission expanded the role and objectives of State aid law during this time. Through communications, letters, Court challenges, and with the adoption of the Transparency Directive, the MEIP, and the compensatory justification principle, the Commission set the foundations of a more ambitious State aid discipline that was no longer focused principally on the establishment of the internal market but looked also to its functioning. The State aid discipline would thus become proactive during this period. The Commission took the initiative of requesting Member States that they notify State measures systematically and clarify their dealings with public undertakings. It also started to move beyond discriminatory measures against foreign producers towards a more competition-like approach, focusing on discrimination between public and private operators and ultimately between the latter within a given Member State, not just across different Member States as previously.

3. The Third Period: Mid-1980s to Mid-1990s

During this third period,[59] the Commission profited from the increasing support to the integration process to make State aid control stricter. The famous White Paper on the Internal Market, which marked the start of this period, underlined

[57] See Council Directive No 81/363/EEC of 28 April 1981 on aid to shipbuilding. OJ L 137, 23 May 1981, and Commission decisions 82/653/EEC of 22 July 1982, OJ L 277, 29 September 1982, p. 15, and Commission decision 82/670/EEC of 2 October 1982, OJ 1982 L280/30. Even prior to this, the Commission did not object a Belgian participation in some textile undertakings because the latter were financially, industrially, and commercially viable as noted by AG Slynn. See the Opinion of Advocate General Slynn in Case 84/82 *Germany v Commission* [1984] ECR 1451 at 1500 in relation to a Commission Decision of November 1981.

[58] 'Where, applying the guidelines laid down in this paper, it is apparent that a public authority which injects capital by acquiring a holding in a company is not merely providing equity capital under normal market economy conditions, the case has to be assessed in the light of Article 92 of the EC Treaty.' See the Commission's position: Application of Arts 92 and 93 [now 87 and 88] of the EEC Treaty to public authorities' holdings, Bulletin EC 9-1984, according to which, in essence, 'there is State aid where fresh capital is contributed in circumstances that would not be acceptable to a private investor operating under normal market economy conditions'. See also Grespan and Santamato, op. cit. at 307.

[59] This period lasted until the mid- to late 1990s. See also for this periodization Lavdas and Mendrinou, *Politics, Subsidies, and Competition*, op. cit.; Doleys, 'Fifty Years of Moulding Article 87', op. cit.; Weiler, *The Transformation of Europe*, op. cit. and Gerber, *Law and Competition in Twentieth Century Europe*, op. cit.

the importance of the competition and the internal market rules for the internal market.[60] The Paper further stated that it would be 'particularly important that the Community discipline on state aids be rigorously enforced.'[61] The White Paper advanced positive integration measures by noting that the Commission would in the future seek to redirect the spending of public moneys towards competitive activities and job creation.[62] The Paper was generally welcomed and it generated a wave of optimism and trust by Member States towards the European project. Other important reports, such as the Padoa–Schioppa, the Cecchini, and the Delors Reports,[63] supported the stricter enforcement of the State aid rules with a view to the efficient functioning of the internal market.

The momentum of the 1992 project was seized by the Commission to tighten the State aid rules. The stricter approach to State aids was also part of a wider program of competition policy that targeted public distortions of competition in view of the fact that, as the Commission noted in 1990: 'at the present stage of economic integration in the Community the barriers are greatest in markets currently subject to State regulation.'[64] The 'public turn' also included the application of Article 90 EC and the application of the competition rules to State action supporting anticompetitive conduct.[65] It is also during this period that the EU grew keener on exporting its rules, not only to the European Economic Area (EEA) and the World Trade Organization (WTO) but also towards Central and Eastern European countries through the Europe Agreements.[66] All these initiatives led to

[60] 'A strong and coherent competition policy must ensure that the partitioning of the internal market is not permitted to occur as a result of protectionist state aids or restrictive practices by firms': Completing the Internal Market. White Paper from the Commission to the European Council (Milan, 28–29 June 1985). COM (85) 310 final, 14 June 1985, point 19, p. 8.

[61] Ibid. at point 158, p. 39.

[62] Ibid. at point 158, pp. 39–40. See also Brittan, L., '1992: A Bonfire of Subsidies? A Review of State Aids in the European Community' (1989) *European Access* 3 at 14: '[the Commission has changed strategy] *from merely reacting to new schemes, to a more positive one of the Commission actively selecting the important areas it should critically examine*' (emphasis added).

[63] See Commission of the EC, Efficiency, Stability and Equity: A Strategy for the Evolution of the Economic System of the European Community (the T. Padoa–Schioppa Report) (Office for Official Publications of the European Communities, 1987); Commission of the EC, The European Challenge 1992: The Benefits of a Single Market (the P. Cecchini Report) (Office for Official Publications of the European Communities, 1988); Report on Economic and Monetary Union in the European Union, Committee for the Study of Economic and Monetary Union , 17 April 1989 (the Delors Report).

[64] Twentieth Report on Competition Policy (Office for Official Publications of the European Communities, 1991) at point 53.

[65] Gerber, D.J., 'The Transformation of European Community Competition Law?' (1994) *Harvard International Law Journal*, 137. See also Gerber, *Law and Competition in Twentieth Century Europe*, op. cit. at 383. See also for an explanation of the link between the success of State aid control and the success of the internal market project the Twentieth Report on Competition Policy, op. cit. at point 169.

[66] These foreseeable accession countries were in fact asked to respect substantive State aid rules and to set up national authorities to control State aid in the same fashion that the Commission did, for otherwise the Union would enact trade protective measures against their imports. See Ehlermann, 'State Aid Control in the European Union: Success or Failure?' (1994) *Fordham International Law Journal* at 1220. See also Twenty-second Report on Competition Policy (Office for Official Publications of the European Communities, 1993) at 336. See also Twenty-sixth

some tangible results. Lavdas and Mendrinou note that although any reduction or reorientation of national subsidies may be due to changes in Member States' approaches to state intervention, since 1985 a tendency towards withdrawal or modification of aid proposals could be discerned.[67] Vogelaar further notes that the tendency to withdraw proposals could be explained because Member States anticipated a negative decision by the European Commission.[68]

In this context, the Commission reinforced its leverage in the institutional sphere, particularly *vis-à-vis* the Council.[69] The Commission was not alone in the pursuit of a tighter State aid policy during this period as the European Parliament supported the former's efforts in this direction.[70] An important fact shows the new bargaining position of the Commission *vis-à-vis* the Council, namely that during this period it would be the Council the institution asking the Commission to propose a procedural regulation. As mentioned earlier, the Council had already in 1966 and again in 1972[71] refused a Commission proposal to adopt a procedural regulation for the application of the State aid rules. However, in 1990 it asked the European Commission to submit a new draft regulation on the implementation of the State aid Treaty rules. Interestingly, this time the Commission refused.[72] The Commission had learnt to use the margin of discretion and flexibility afforded by the lack of a regulation in order to advance its own priorities in the State aid field. The Commission was therefore not interested in altering the status quo.[73]

Report on Competition Policy (Office for Official Publications of the European Communities, 1997) at 255.

[67] Ehlermann, C.D., 'The Contribution of EC Competition Policy to the Single Market' (1992) *Common Market Law Review* 257 at 275. See also the quote in Lavdas and Mendrinou, *Politics, Subsidies, and Competition*, op. cit. at 38.

[68] Ibid. and Vogelaar, FOW, 'The Impact of the Economic Recession on EEC Competition Policy, Part One: State Aids' (1985) *Swiss Review of International Competition Law* 23 at 31–32.

[69] A protagonist of the time gave the following examples: 'the Commission's more decisive approach to the exercise of its powers of implementation and control reflects its increased influence in relation to the Council and the national governments. Two examples will suffice as an illustration: first, there is the bold application of a previously little-used provision to apply the rules of competition in the member states; second, the new practice of demanding the repayment of illegally granted, which was unthinkable few years ago' See Ehlermann, C.D., 'Commission Lacks Power in 1992 Process' (1990) *European Affairs* at 70.

[70] For the support of the European Parliament see Caspari, 'The Aid Rules of the EEC Treaty and Their Application', op. cit.

[71] See COM (66) 95 of 30 March 1966, communicated to the Council on 18 April 1966 and amended by COM (66) 457 of 10 November 1966 and COM (72) 1523 of 4 December 1972.

[72] Twentieth Report on Competition Policy, op. cit. at point 170, 'The discussion was initiated by the proposal from certain Member States that the Council should play a greater role in policy formulation for State aids and in particular that the Commission should propose a Regulation under Article 94 to the Council with the aim of making aid policy more transparent. However, this view was rejected by the majority of Member States, who felt that the Commission's proposals for increasing transparency and legal certainty for Member States were sufficient.'

[73] Indeed, as Sir Leon noted, there was no need to adopt a procedural regulation since 'the objectives of juridical certainty and transparency can be best attained by continuing the well-established practice, inter alia of bilateral and multilateral dialogue and consultation in the decision-making process.' See the quote in Lavdas and Mendrinou, *Politics, Subsidies, and Competition*, op. cit. at 37–38. In a bolder way the then Director General for Competition would rephrase it: '[To submit a draft regulation to the Council] would no doubt have led to responsibility for the control of state aids being transferred to the Council, which would have been unacceptable to the Commission.'

The reinforced role of the Commission *vis-à-vis* Member States helps explain why in 1993 Italy committed to reduce its holdings in State-owned companies and to no longer cover any new debt through the so-called Andreatta–Van Miert agreement.[74] In the same year, the Commission clarified its policy on privatization and State aid.[75]

The achievement of the 1992 project led to the adoption of the Maastricht Treaty and with it the introduction of the subsidiarity principle into the Treaties. *A priori*, the principle of subsidiarity should be of no interest for the State aid discipline as this principle did not (and still does not) apply to exclusive competences of the Community such as State aids. However, the Commission linked the principle of subsidiarity to the introduction of a *de minimis* rule in the field of State aids.[76] Such a rule was introduced as part of a comprehensive program to grant favourable treatment to SMEs, an important goal that was also favoured by the European Parliament.[77] The *de minimis* rule also responded to administrative concerns as the Commission sought to reduce its workload and to concentrate on the most important State aid cases. It should be noted in this regard that between 1986 and 1992, State aid notifications had tripled in number.[78] The more efficient control of State aid was also important in light of a new feature that the Maastricht Treaty introduced, rules on Economic and Monetary Union (EMU), that a senior official of the Commission underlined could lead to more aid being granted as Member States could no longer support domestic undertakings through monetary policy.[79]

Ehlermann, 'The Contribution of EC Competition Policy to the Single Market', op. cit. at 275. See also Mederer, W., 'The Future of State Aid Control' (1996) *Competition Policy Newsletter*, 12.

[74] See for a more precise summary of the Andreatta–Van Miert Agreement, eg, the Press Release: IP/96/1197 of 18 December 1996.

[75] Twenty-third Report on Competition Policy (Office for Official Publications of the European Communities, 1994) at points 402–03.

[76] Twenty-second Report on Competition Policy, op. cit. at para. 337. 'A more far-reaching simplification of procedures has been introduced by the SME aid guidelines themselves. A de minimis facility removes altogether the obligation on Member States to notify to the Commission aid schemes which limit a firm to ECU 50 000 of aid for a particular broad class of expenditure (such as investment or training) over three years. Like the accelerated procedure, the de minimis facility is a move towards subsidiarity as well as a means of concentrating the Commission's resources on the more important cases. However, further relaxations of State aid control are not considered appropriate at present. This is an area, par excellence, where a strong central control authority is required.'

[77] Ibid. at Annex I, p. 327: 'Parliament insists that small and medium sized enterprises be given favourable treatment, and reiterates the recommendations it made in its Resolution of 13 December 1991...'.

[78] Ibid. at para. 129, table one. See also Written Question No. 2534/96 by Amadeo to the Commission. Competition rules, OJ C 060, 26/02/1997 p. 0098.

[79] As phrased by the Director of the directorate for State aid in DG IV: 'the Maastricht Treaty's rules on the economic and monetary union are probably those which will have the biggest impact on State aid inside the Community...The accomplishment of a single monetary policy will deprive Member States of one of the traditional instruments in response to cost disadvantages, devaluation,... and this may tempt them to turn to State aid. The Commission is well aware of this. It is one of the main reasons behind the tightening up of the Community's State aid policy, which you have seen taking place in the lead up to the single market and which is still going on.' See Petersen, A., 'State Aid and European Union: State Aid in the Light of Trade and Competition, Industrial and Cohesion Policies', in Harden, I. (ed.), *State Aid: Community Law and Policy* (Bundesanzeiger, 1993) 20. The Commission would link again the State aid rules to EMU in the subsequent Twenty-eighth

Finally, during this period State aid policy became more integrated with the other competition rules.[80] In this regard, the assistant to the Director General of DG Competition claimed that the State aid rules were at this point closer to the competition rules than they were to the internal market rules in that they aimed at preventing distortions of competition between competitors rather than between Member States.[81] Similarly, the Director General of DG COMP noted that State aid was no longer so much about preserving competition between Member States as between competitors in what were by then open competitive markets.[82] Consequently, the role of competitors in this field was increasingly important, not only to bring cases of non-notified aid to the Commission's attention but also to reinforce the latter's role as a neutral arbiter between States.[83] In the same vein, during this period the Commission published the first Notice on cooperation between national courts and the Commission in the State aid field,[84] thus clarifying the conditions under which competitors could challenge before national courts the failure of a Member State to notify State aid measures.

4. The Fourth Period: Mid- to Late 1990s to the Present

By the mid-1990s several authors noted that State aid policy had reached a turning point and entered a new phase.[85] The beginning of this period was marked by the joint initiative of the Commission and the Irish presidency on future prospects of State aid control of 14 November 1996. The joint initiative purported to

Report on Competition Policy (Office for Official Publications of the European Communities, 1999) at point 5. Similarly, a member of the Commission would add in 1999 that whether the Spaak report economic assumptions were valid was doubtful as macroeconomic factors no longer neutralized the effects of disparities in taxes in Member States. See Bourgeois, J.H.J., 'State Aids, Taxation Measures and Specificity. Some Thoughts', in Dony, M., and De Walsche, A. (eds), *Mélanges en hommage à Michel Waelbroeck* Vol 2 (Bruylant, 1999) at 769 and 775.

[80] See also in this regard Gerber, *Law and Competition in Twentieth Century Europe*, op. cit. at 364.

[81] Gyselen, L, 'The Emerging Interface between Competition Policy and Environmental Policy in the EC', in Cameron, J., Demaret, P., and Geradin, D. (eds), *Trade and the Environment: The Search for Balance* (Cameron, May 1994), 242 at 245: According to him, the legality standard that the Commission had to observe in both the internal market and the competition fields had to start with the following question: 'Is there a distortion of competition between national economies (Article 30 [then applies]) or between individual competitors Article 85 and 92 [then apply]?'

[82] In Ehlermann's words: 'Aid granted by a Member State is no longer controlled exclusively or principally in the interest of other Member States, but also, and perhaps even more so, in the interest of the competitors of the intended beneficiaries of the aid. The original macroeconomic approach of the authors of the EEC Treaty is being supplanted progressively by a microeconomic perspective, similar to that which has always dominated substantive and procedural antitrust law'. Ehlermann, 'State Aid Control in the European Union: Success or Failure?' op. cit. at 1219.

[83] Smith, 'Autonomy by the Rules', op. cit. at 63.

[84] Official Journal C 312, 23/11/1995 P. 0008–0013.

[85] See Mederer, 'The Future of State Aid Control', op. cit. and Lavdas and Mendrinou, *Politics, Subsidies, and Competition*, op. cit. at 44. See also Doleys, 'Fifty Years of Moulding Article 87', op. cit. at 22.

refocus priorities, increase transparency and legal certainty, and to clarify the procedural rules in the field of State aids.[86]

As 'the time seemed right for another attempt',[87] the Commission decided to submit to the Council a draft regulation under today's Article 109 TFEU, in February 1998. This proposal became the first procedural regulation for the State aid rules[88] which codified the Commission's practice and the Court's case law until that date. The Commission depicted the modernization of the State aid rules as a necessity, given the high number of aid measures notified, in order to concentrate itself 'on major cases involving large amounts of aid or new legal issues.'[89] In this regard, even before the procedural regulation, in 1998 the Commission obtained the Council's adoption of the *enabling regulation*, which allowed the Commission to exempt categories of horizontal aid from notification.[90]

One of the main policy priorities of this period was also announced by the Commission in 1998: the Commission was going to be stricter in relation to State aid measures in the form of direct business taxation.[91] For these purposes, a notice on the application of State aid law to those measures was adopted,[92] which complemented the Member States' efforts to tackle harmful taxation through the Economic and Financial Affairs Council (ECOFIN) with the adoption of a Code of Conduct on direct taxation.[93] The Commission also announced that it was going to review some

[86] See Mederer, 'The Future of State Aid Control', op. cit. at 12–13. The main reasons underpinning the initiative were: '(i) The completion of the single market, (ii) The forthcoming economic and monetary union, (iii) The ongoing liberalisation of certain sectors of the industry [including services industries such as financial and broadcasting], (iv) The enlargement of the Union, and (v) The increasing involvement of third parties in State aid procedures.'

[87] As mentioned by the Commissioner under whose mandate the proposal was made: 'The time seemed right, however, for another attempt. It should be noted that the very fact that this could be envisaged reflected the greater confidence of the Commission that Member States were generally supportive of the need for state control.' See Van Miert, K., 'Reflections on Seven Years as Commissioner Responsible for State aid', in Ehlermann, C.D., and Everson, M. (eds), *European Competition Law Annual 1999: Selected Issues in the Field of State Aids* (Hart, 2001) at 10.

[88] Council Regulation No 659/1999 of 22 March 1999 laying down detailed rules for the application of Art. 93 of the EC Treaty Official Journal L 83/1, 27 March 1999, pp. 1–9.

[89] Twenty-eighth Report on Competition Policy (Office for Official Publications of the European Communities, 1999) at point 12.

[90] Council Regulation (EC) No 994/98 of 7 May 1998 on the application of Arts 92 and 93 (now 87 and 88 respectively) of the Treaty establishing the European Community to certain categories of horizontal State aid, OJ L 142/1 (1998).

[91] Twenty-eighth Report on Competition Policy, op. cit. at point 191.

[92] Commission Notice on the application of the State aid rules to measures relating to direct business taxation OJ C 384, 10/12/1998 P. 0003–0009. This Communication also complemented the Commission's previous Communications concerning the need to tackle tax distortions after the completion of the single market, namely, the Commission communication entitled 'A package to tackle harmful tax competition in the European Union', which took 'stock of a discussion initiated by the Commission at the informal meeting of Ministers for Economic Affairs and Finance in Verona in April 1996 and given more substantial shape at the informal meeting in Mondorf-les-Bains in September 1997', and the Commission's action plan for the single market (CSE(97) 1, 4 June 1997. See in particular strategic target 2, action 1.

[93] See Conclusions of the ECOFIN Council Meeting on 1 December 1997 concerning taxation policy—Resolution of the Council and the Representatives of the Governments of the Member States, meeting within the Council of 1 December 1997 on a code of conduct for business

of its previous decisions due to '[d]evelopments in the concept of state aid over time and a stricter interpretation of Article 87 of the EC Treaty'.[94] Indeed, Regulation 659/1999 included the very interesting provision according to which a measure could be considered as aid due to the evolution of the Common Market, which admits the evolving character of the legal concept of aid that this book defends.[95] The EU courts have referred to this provision and, more recently, to the objective character of the notion of aid, to justify a change of view by the EU institutions concerning the aid character of a measure over time.[96]

Another important policy issue for the Commission during this period was the application of the State aid rules to the financing of services of general economic interest (SGEI). Although the Commission was aware from the beginning of this period that it would need to deal with the 'ongoing liberalisation of certain sectors of the industry [including services industries such as financial and broadcasting]',[97] private complainants sped up the process by forcing the Commission to take a position on this delicate issue. They have done so through complaints against incumbents of liberalized sectors and even through suits against the Commission if the latter would not act on their complaints according to their wishes.[98] The main conceptual issues were clarified at the end by the Court of Justice in the famous *Altmark* judgment that will be discussed in Chapter 4. This judgment allowed the Commission to retake the policy initiative with a package of three acts—a decision, a communication, and an amendment to the Transparency Directive adopted in 2005—that were recently replaced by a new package, mainly composed of a decision, a regulation, and a communication, adopted in 2012.

Furthermore, in 2000, the European Council held in Lisbon asked Member States to 'further their efforts to promote competition and reduce the general level of State aids, shifting the emphasis from supporting individual companies or sectors towards tackling horizontal objectives of Community interest, such as employment, regional development, environment and training or research.'[99]

taxation—Taxation of saving Official Journal C 002, 6 January 1998, P. 0001–0006. See also Council Resolution of 1 December 1997, OJ C 2/2 of 6 January 1998.

[94] Twenty-eighth Report on Competition Policy, op. cit. at point 192. The first of these decisions was the Irish corporation tax cases in which the Commission found that aid to the whole manufacturing sector (excluding services) would no longer be considered as a general measure.

[95] See Art. 1(b)(v) of Council Regulation No 659/1999 of 22 March 1999 laying down detailed rules for the application of Art. 93 of the EC Treaty, OJ L 83/1, 27 March 1999, pp. 1–9: 'aid which is deemed to be an existing aid because it can be established that at the time it was put into effect it did not constitute an aid, and subsequently became an aid due to the evolution of the common market and without having been altered by the Member State. Where certain measures become aid following the liberalisation of an activity by Community law, such measures shall not be considered as existing aid after the date fixed for liberalization.'

[96] See Case C-194/09 P, *Alcoa Trasformazioni Srl v European Commission*, ECR [2011] I-06311 and Case C-272/12 P, *Commission v Ireland and Others* ECR [2012] nyr.

[97] As mentioned earlier, see Mederer, 'The Future of State Aid Control', op. cit.

[98] The saga that led to the Chronopost case is an example of this trend. See Joined Cases C-83/01 P, C-93/01P, C-94/01/P *Chronopost* [2003] ECR p. I-6993.

[99] Presidency conclusions of the European Council in Lisbon on 24 March 2000.

State aid control was linked to the policy goals stated at the European Council Summits of Lisbon and Stockholm but also to the employment and environmental goals underlined by the Amsterdam Treaty.[100] Finally, the Commission also recognized that State aid control policy was evolving by 2001.[101] In this regard, the Lisbon agenda on State aids was taken up by Competition Commissioner Kroes in 2005 with the widely publicized 'State Aid Action Plan' (SAAP) an ambitious consultation document published in 2005 that seemed to herald a revolution in this field. Indeed, the SAAP was meant to be the first ever comprehensive reform of State aid policy,[102] and according to some authors it marked a new phase in State aid policy.[103] In essence, the SAAP called for 'less and better targeted aid',[104] and for a more *refined economic approach* in the field of compatibility of State aid, for more 'effective procedures', better enforcement, higher predictability, and enhanced transparency and partnership between the Commission and Member States in order to maintain State aid policy in a enlarged EU of then twenty-seven Member States.[105]

In addition, the SAAP not only 'recalled the reasons for controlling State aid' but also explicitly sought to reorient State aid policy towards becoming a tool for growth and jobs and facilitating the achievement of the Lisbon agenda goals.[106] The SAAP has inspired a substantive reform of the existing guidelines and block exemptions. The reorientation of State aid policy has led to the desirability of more aid being directed towards the so-called horizontal objectives in the first years of the SAAP application or rather 'inspiration' as the SAAP is not a legislative document[107] It remains to be seen whether some part of the horizontal aid

[100] See the Ninth Survey on State Aid in the European Union, Brussels, 18 July 2001 COM (2001) 403 final, at 1–13.

[101] Ibid. at 43.

[102] See 'The State Aid Action Plan', in Mederer, Pesaresi, and Van Hoof (eds), op. cit. at 65.

[103] Mederer, 'Evolution of State Aid Control', op. cit. at 23. We have decided to include the SAAP within the fourth period as we believe that it shares many tenets with the modernization initiative that initiated this period and with that currently unfolding: State Aid Modernisation (SAM).

[104] COM (2005) 107 final of 7 July 2005; State Aid Action Plan. Less and Better Targeted State Aid: A Roadmap for State Aid Reform 2005–2009 (Consultation document); SEC(2005) 795.

[105] For a comprehensive review of the SAAP, see Kleiner, T., 'The State Aid Action Plan', in Mederer, Pesaresi, and Van Hoof (eds), op. cit. 65. For a less enthusiastic view on the SAAP see, eg, Buendia Sierra, J.L., and Smulders, B., 'The Limited Role of the "Refined Economic Approach" in Achieving the Objectives of State Aid Control: Time for Some Realism', in Di Bucci, V., Buendia Sierra, J.L., Smulders, B., et al. (eds), *EC State Aid Law—Le Droit des Aides d'État dans la CE, Liber Amicorum Francisco Santaolalla Gadea* (Kluwer Law International, 2008) 18, or Buendia Sierra, J.L., 'Not like this: Some Sceptical Remarks on the "Refined Economic Approach" in State Aid', in Proceedings of 4th Experts' Forum on New Developments in European State Aid Law, 18 and 19 May 2006, European State Aid Law Institute (Lexxion, 2006) 59.

[106] Ibid. at 70–71.

[107] As the Commission has noted recently, aid to horizontal objectives (ie aid that is not granted to specific sectors) represents more than 80 per cent of State aid to industry and services, *excluding crisis measures*. In fact, if the measures adopted in light of the extraordinary financial crisis measures were considered just the opposite, results would (logically) hold true: 'If the corresponding aid volumes were included in the total of the sectoral aid for 2009, the share of horizontal objectives in relation to total aid to industry and services would amount to approximately 12%. Around 88% would be sectoral aid, of which the financial crisis measures represent the largest part (more than 96%).' See Commission Staff Working Document, Facts and figures on State aid in the Member

granted (eg R&D aid) does not include some 'classic' sectoral aid. This phenomenon would not be new as Member States have in the past 'dressed' State aid in the way that they considered would be most favoured by the Commission.[108]

In any event, the application of the SAAP reform has been shadowed over the last few years by the 2008 financial crisis and the massive aids that have been granted to try to overcome it. However, as opposed to what has happened in previous crises, the maturity of the enforcement system and the flexible and proactive approach adopted by the European Commission has avoided a total abandonment of the discipline. Indeed, since the very beginning of the crisis Member States called on the Commission to intervene and they welcomed its proposals in this field.[109] The Commission has been quite flexible in relation to crisis-related measures, approving provisionally virtually all cases of financial aid granted to banks.[110] The Commission's approach to address the financial crisis was in fact exceptional. It invoked today's Article 107(3)(b), that allows for aid to be granted to remedy a serious disturbance of the economy, and on this basis the Commission assessed the aids granted to banks at the start of this crisis. Finally, for our purposes, the use of this exceptional legal basis has allowed the Commission to focus the exceptional measures on the compatibility arena, leaving the definitional part of Article 107(1) TFEU in principle unaffected, although, as will be discussed in Part III of this book, the definition of aid has also been influenced by the Commission's response to the financial crisis.

More recently, the SAAP's momentum is being replaced by another initiative, the SAM (State Aid Modernisation), announced by the then Commissioner for Competition, Mr Joaquín Almunia, at the beginning of 2012, and which has been the subject of a number of communications and is practically completed.[111] There are three main objectives of the SAM, which is linked to the Europe 2020

States Accompanying the Report from the Commission State Aid Scoreboard—Autumn 2010 Update—COM(2010) 701 final, at 20.

[108] 'intensification in the Commission's monitoring function in one issue area may be effective in changing national tendencies on subsidies in that area while at the same time driving private firms (under the risk of repayment) to reformulate their demands (eg, to turn to R&D projects) and/or diversify their lobbing strategies'. See Lavdas and Mendrinou, *Politics, Subsidies, and Competition*, op. cit. at 42.

[109] See Council Conclusions—Ecofin Council of 7 October 2008: 'legitimate interest of competitors must be protected, in particular through the state aids rules [and] [w]e welcome the Commission's continued commitment to act quickly and apply flexibility in state aid decisions, within the framework of the single market and state aid regime. The Council welcomes the Commission's commitment to shortly issue guidance setting out the broad framework within which the state aid compatibility of recapitalisation and guarantee schemes, and cases of application of such schemes, could be rapidly assessed.'

[110] See in this regard, Ahlborn, C., and Piccinin, D., 'The Great Recession and Other Mishaps: the Commission's Policy of Restructuring in a Time of Crisis', in Szyszczak, E. (ed.), *Research Handbook on State Aid* (Edward Elgar, 2011) 124 at 151: 'So far, the Commission has approved financial crisis aid to banks in all cases except one'.

[111] See, eg, Communication from the Commission to the European Parliament, the Council, the European Economic and Social Committee and the Committee of the Regions, EU State Aid Modernisation (SAM), Brussels, 8 May 2012, COM (2012) 209 final.

strategy for growth:[112] (i) to foster growth in a strengthened, dynamic, and competitive internal market; (ii) to focus enforcement on cases with the biggest impact on the internal market; and (iii) to streamline rules and decisions.[113] The Communication mainly focuses, as did the SAAP, on the compatibility analysis as it establishes some criteria for what has to be considered as growth-enhancing good aid, although it includes revision of the *de minimis* regulation and of some block exemptions that could affect measures currently falling within the obligation to notify new aid. The Communication also states that the notion of aid will be clarified with a view to contributing to easier implementation.[114] Positively, in our view, a focus on cohesion and equality of possibilities seems to be included in the new strategy. In the words of Commissioner Almunia, 'in a period when the spending capacity of EU countries is so uneven, State aid control must focus more than ever on its primary role of ensuring a level playing field in the Single Market.'[115]

Finally, the European Commission has very recently adopted a number of decisions,[116] coinciding with the last months of Commissioner Almunia in office, related to tax rulings in Ireland, the Netherlands, and Luxembourg, concerning the income tax to be paid by certain multinationals, and this could signal a new and important goal in the Commission's policy agenda: the fight against tax evasion. Politically speaking, the *momentum* is propitious to carry out these *ex-officio* investigations. As the financial crisis abates, and following years of budgetary cuts and social protest, which have been dramatic in some Member States, the Commission's initiative will probably be welcome by many, including several Member States that can now see how their tax bases are significantly reduced due to the hard-line tax planning of some multinationals. In this regard, it should be noted that some recent initiatives have been taken, not only at the EU level, but also at the Organisation for Economic Co-operation and Development (OECD) and the G20 levels, precisely designed to curb corporate tax avoidance (eg the Base Erosion and Profit Shifting (BEPS) project). Similarly, some Member States, starting with the United Kingdom, have adopted national measures to limit tax evasion by multinational companies (the so-called Google tax). It appears that

[112] Commission Communication 'Europe 2020—A Strategy for Smart, Sustainable and Inclusive Growth', COM (2010) 2020 final, 3 March 2010.

[113] Ibid. at 8.

[114] A draft Communication on the notion of aid was published by the Commission for consultation at the beginning of 2014. The draft is a very useful and well-prepared document that summarizes the main jurisprudence of the EU Courts concerning the notion of aid. The draft also includes many references to the decisional practice of the Commission which, while being useful, may not be taken as binding unless backed by the Community Courts given that only the Court of Justice is competent to interpret the boundaries of this notion under the Treaties. See for the notice and the replies of interested parties: <http://ec.europa.eu/competition/consultations/2014_state_aid_notion/index_en.html>.

[115] Presenting the State aid modernization initiative EP workshop: State Aid Modernisation Brussels 25 September 2012, Reference: SPEECH/12/657.

[116] See State aid SA.38373 (Ireland Alleged aid to Apple), State aid SA.38375 (Luxembourg Alleged aid to FFT), State aid SA.38374 (Netherlands Alleged aid to Starbucks), and State aid SA.38944 (Luxembourg Alleged aid to Amazon).

this new goal will remain high on the Commission's agenda, as can be inferred from the Mission letter to the new Competition Commissioner, Mrs Margrethe Vestager, by the new President of the Commission.[117]

5. Conclusion

The brief analysis of the evolution of the Commission's policy in State aid shows how dynamic the development of this policy has been. It also shows how the evolution of this policy has been connected with the main economic and political events that have affected the Community, now the Union. In this regard, the account is in line with the historical review of subsidies and subsidy control where it was noted that subsidy policies have traditionally been heavily influenced by the broader political and economic context in which they have been adopted.

This account contrasts with the well-established and apparently static jurisprudence concerning the notion of aid. Indeed, judgments on State aid, including the most recent ones, usually refer to formulas and definitions laid down by the Court of Justice in the 1960s and 1970s as if such notions were not affected by any of the multiple developments identified earlier. Against this view, the following chapters will discuss how policy and enforcement considerations have also transcended into the definition of aid, and how they have done so in a remarkably coherent fashion with the course of developments described in this chapter.

[117] Mission Letter to new Commissioner for Competition, Mrs Vestager, Brussels, 10 September 2014 by Mr Juncker: 'During our mandate, I would like you to focus on the following: Mobilising competition policy tools and market expertise so that they contribute, as appropriate, to our jobs and growth agenda, including in areas such as the digital single market, energy policy, financial services, industrial policy *and the fight against tax evasion*' (emphasis added).

PART II

4

The Notion of Advantage

Part II of the book applies the analytical framework described in Part I to the main judgments related to the concept of aid for our purposes, those judgments in which for the first time the Court forged a number of formulas that have since become the standards used to depict this concept. In this regard, Part I looked at the origin of subsidy control, the legislative history of today's Article 107 TFEU, and the evolution of State aid policy, with particular emphasis on the evolution of the aims that the State aid rules have pursued in different periods of the development of the internal market. The following chapters will use the analysis carried out to discuss the main formulas concerning the concept of aid.

This chapter will deal with the main formulas related to the notion of advantage under Article 107(1) TFEU. We start, however, by discussing a case decided under the ECSC Treaty. This is because in this judgment the Court laid down a general definition of aid that is still referred to as a valid definition of this concept, also in the context of the TFEU. The analysis of this case will help the reader appreciate the understanding of the notion of aid and that of advantage by the Court of Justice at the very beginning of the European integration process. This case is also important because as early as in 1963 the European Commission applied the concept of aid established by the Court in this case to the concept of aid under Article 107(1) TFEU, and so did the Court of Justice some years later.[1]

1. The *De Gezamenlijke Steenkolenmijnen* Case (C-30/59)

A. Introduction and background to the case

Any discussion of the advantage criterion under Article 107(1) TFEU usually includes a reference to the definition of 'aid' laid down by the Court of Justice in

[1] See reply to parliamentary question No. 48 of Mr Burgbacher, OJ C125, 17 August 1963. See also the opinion of Advocate General Warner in case 173/73, *Italy v Commission* [1974] ECR at 723. For one of the first explicit references to this definition, see the judgment of the Court of 15 March 1994, Case C-387/92 *Banco Exterior de España SA v Ayuntamiento de Valencia* [1994] ECR p. I-00877 at 13.

the famous *De Gezamenlijke Steenkolenmijnen* judgment (hereinafter also referred to as the *miners' bonus* case).[2] That judgment gives a very broad notion of aid which encompasses an equally wide notion of advantage.[3]

The origins of this case go back to February 1956, when the Federal Minister for Economic Affairs informed the High Authority that the German Government intended, among other initiatives concerning the coal sector, to grant to all who worked underground in the mines a tax-free shift bonus, to be paid by the coal undertakings through a reduction of tax paid on wages. The German government held that this measure was necessary to avoid the departure of mineworkers to other industries. The aim of the measure, the government argued, was therefore social and hence compatible with the goals of the European Coal and Steel Community Treaty.

Following an exchange of communications between the High Authority and the German government, the former declared that the shift bonus would not be incompatible with the Treaty so long as Germany respected some conditions, and in particular, acknowledged the need to compensate the effect of this measure on the German undertakings by abolishing the public payment of part of the employers' contributions to miners' pension insurance, thus eliminating the advantage offered to the coal undertakings by this measure—although the criterion of advantage as such was not mentioned in the notion of aid under the ECSC Treaty. This letter was challenged before the Court by the Dutch industry association, *De Gezamenlijke Steenkolenmijnen*. The Court, however, held that the letter was not a *decision* for the purposes of the Treaty.[4] After this judgment, the association asked the High Authority to record by a decision that in financing the miners' bonus out of public funds, Germany had failed to fulfil its obligations under the Treaty. The High Authority replied confirming that to the contrary, it would not take such decision. It was this final communication, the decision of rejection, which led to case 30/59.

Before moving to a discussion on the legal dispute it may be interesting to note, for the purposes of understanding the context of the case, some of the arguments put forward by the applicant related to the effects of the measure under review.[5] In essence, the applicant underlined that Dutch prices for coal were based on German prices, that there was scarcity of labour, and that the bonus for miners had tempted many Dutch miners to emigrate to Germany.

[2] C-30/59 *Steenkolenmijnen v High Authority* [1961] ECR 1.

[3] C-30/59 *Steenkolenmijnen v High Authority* [1961] ECR 1 at 39.

[4] See C-17/57, *De Gezamenlijke Steenkolenmijnen in Limburg v High Authority of the European Coal and Steel Community* [1959] ECR 9.

[5] These arguments were noted not only by the Court but also by the Advocate General in the case and by a contemporary author, early attaché (later *référendaire*) at the Court of Justice. See also Chevallier, R.M., 'L'Arrêt 30-59 de la Cour de Justice des Communautés Européennes' (1962), *Revue Générale de Droit International Public* 546.

(1) The policy context

The origins of this case go back to 1956, before the adoption of the European Economic Community Treaty, and concerned the High Authority, not yet the European Commission. As discussed in Chapter 2, the ECSC Treaty was quite interventionist given that its intention was to replace national aid to the coal and steel industries with aid granted at Community level.[6] The policy was thus to ensure that Member States did not exercise jurisdiction over the coal and steel industries by granting subsidies. However, the ambitious task assigned to the High Authority proved politically impossible, as Member States, like Germany in this case, managed to grant bonuses and even to paralyse the action of the High Authority. The intervention of the Court, as we will see, did little to solve this situation.

(2) Judgment of the Court of Justice

The Court embarked on the issue of first defining the terms 'subsidy' and 'aid', something that was not really necessary as all parties agreed that the bonus was a subsidy, the question being whether the subsidy was compensated. This was not an easy task since there was no national definition of subsidy that the Court could use at that time.[7] In the same vein, Advocate General Lagrange had noted that the three parties involved in the case, as well as himself, found it difficult to give a precise and unchallengeable definition of the word 'subsidy'.[8]

The Court, as suggested by the AG, interpreted the notions of aid or subsidy in accordance with the fundamental (also called 'philosophical') articles laid down by the ECSC Treaty,[9] namely, Articles 2, 3, 4, and, to a lesser extent, Article 5 ECSC.[10] The Court held that '[s]ince these definitions [definition of aid and subsidy] are not contained in the Treaty, they are acceptable only if they are substantially borne out by the provisions of the Treaty or by the objects which it pursues.'[11] In this regard, the general scheme provided for in the Treaty aimed

[6] See Stuyck, J., Abraham, F., and Goemans, C. (eds), *Subsidies and Competition in the European Union: Generale Bank Lectures 1994–1995* (Leuven University Press, 1996) 11–13. See also Luengo Hernandez de Madrid, G.E., *Regulation of Subsidies and State Aids in WTO and EC Law—Conflicts in International Trade Law* (Kluwer Law International, 2007) 292.

[7] See Chevallier, 'L'arrêt 30-59 de la Cour de justice des Communautés européennes', op. cit. at 568–69.

[8] See Opinion of Advocate General Lagrange, C-30/59 *Steenkolenmijnen v High Authority* [1961] ECR 1, delivered on 5 November 1960.

[9] See Rueff, J. 'La Cour et l'Economie Politique', in *Dix ans de jurisprudence de la Cour de justice des Commaunautes europeennes, Europäische Arbeitstagung* (Heymanns, 1965) at 15; available at: <http://babordplus.univ-bordeaux.fr/notice.php?q=%22Communaut%C3%A9s%20europ%C3%A9ennes%2C%20Cour%20de%20justice%20-%20Jurisprudence%20-%20Actes%20de%20congr%C3%A8s%22&spec_expand=&sort_define=score&sort_order=1&rows=10&start=0>.

[10] See also in this regard the note to this judgment made by the contemporary author Boulois, J., 'Jurisprudence de la Cour de Justice des Communautés Européennes' (1961) *Annuaire français de droit international*, 267.

[11] C-30/59 *Steenkolenmijnen v High Authority* [1961] ECR 1 at 19.

at ensuring the most rational distribution of production at the highest level of productivity (Article 2 ECSC), and this had been interpreted by the Court even before this judgment as the the distribution resulting from the intrinsic characteristics of the different undertakings in the market place, absent any type of distortion, either private (such as cartels) or public (such as subsidies or special charges).[12] It is within this framework that the Court laid down its famous definitions of aid and subsidy: 'A subsidy is normally defined as a payment in cash or in kind made in support of an undertaking other than the payment by the purchaser or consumer for the goods or services which it produces. An aid is a very similar concept, which, however, places emphasis on its purpose and seems especially devised for a particular objective which cannot normally be achieved without outside help. *The concept of aid is nevertheless wider than that of a subsidy because it embraces not only positive benefits, such as subsidies themselves, but also interventions which, in various forms, mitigate the charges which are normally included in the budget of an undertaking and which, without, therefore, being subsidies in the strict meaning of the word, are similar in character and have the same effect*'[13] (emphasis added).

In light of this, the Court, noting that the measure under review, financed by public funds, mitigated the production costs of the coal undertakings, found that 'viewed in isolation', the measure was a subsidy and hence ought to be considered incompatible with the Common Market. The question was, then, whether this *prima facie* subsidy or aid could be still considered as a prohibited measure if the effects of it were eliminated. In this regard, the High Authority had argued before the Court that the alleged effects of the *bonus* were in any event compensated by the withdrawal of the public contribution to the pension fund that undertakings had to pay, and this prevented the measure from qualifying as a subsidy or aid. The Court however avoided deciding the matter, although it implicitly admitted that such a defence was possible by noting that the compensation procedure, which the Court considered vague and ill-defined, did not constitute, in all cases, a repayment equivalent to the amount of expenditure to be reimbursed. Based on this rejection of the compensation argument, a former judge and current Advocate General of the Court of Justice has held that, in case of doubt, the Court will opt for the consideration that a certain measure amounts to aid,[14] and this seems not to conform completely with the rules on the burden of proof that clearly place on the Commission the burden to show the concurrence of all the criteria of aid.[15]

[12] Joined Cases 7/57 and 9/54, *Groupement des industries sidérurgiques Luxembourgeoises v ECSC High Authority* [1954–56] ECR 175.

[13] C-30/59 *Steenkolenmijnen v High Authority* [1961] ECR 3.

[14] See also Wathelet, M., and Partsch, P.E. 'Delimitation des contours de la notion d'aide d'état en droit communautaire', in *Les aides d'état en droit communautaire et en droit national* (Bruylant, 1999) 1 at 14.

[15] See, eg, C-159/01 *Netherlands/Commission* [2004] Rec. p. I-4461 at 43.

(3) Assessment

The ECSC Treaty did not provide for any definition of 'aid' or 'subsidy' (both terms being cited in Article 4(c)). The same was true for many other technical terms that were included in the Treaty but nowhere defined. Consequently, it was for the Court of Justice to define those concepts. In this regard, as Jacques Rueff, an early judge of the Court of Justice and an economist by training stated in 1965, the Court was given great discretion to define the numerous technical terms provided for in the ECSC and EEC Treaties. In this context, and with a view to avoid turning this discretion into arbitrariness, the Court decided to interpret these technical terms in accordance with some fundamental, also called '*philosophical*', articles laid down by the ECSC Treaty,[16] namely, Articles 2, 3, 4, and, to a lesser extent, Article 5 ECSC. Any article of the Treaty would be interpreted in accordance with the general scheme represented by those four articles. With this crucial decision, already stated in its first judgment,[17] the Court of Justice initiated its famous teleological interpretation of the Treaty provisions.

The general scheme designed by those articles, as interpreted by the Court, aimed at ensuring the most rational distribution of production at the highest level of productivity, an aim that was explicitly mention in Article 2 ECSC. This formula, continuously repeated by the Court over the years,[18] was further clarified by the Court: the most rational distribution of production was the one that resulted *par la nature des choses*; that is, the distribution that resulted from the intrinsic characteristics of the different undertakings in the market place absent any type of distortion, either private (such as cartels) or public (such as subsidies or special charges).[19] For the Court, the Common Market had to act like a theatre where the natural conditions of production would determine the behaviour and performance of the different economic operators.[20]

[16] See Rueff, 'La Cour et l'economie politique', op. cit. at 15.

[17] See C-1/54 *France v ECSC High Authority* [1954–56] ECR p. 1: 'Articles 2, 3 and 4 of the Treaty...constitute fundamental provisions establishing the Common Market and the common objectives of the Community.' The Court was even more explicit soon after: 'Articles 2, 4 and 5 which, together with Article 3, must always be observed because they establish the fundamental objectives of the Community. Those provisions are binding and must be read together if they are to be properly applied. These provisions can stand by themselves and accordingly, in so far as they have not been adopted in any other provision of the Treaty, they are directly applicable. If they have been adopted or are governed by other provisions of the Treaty words relating to the same provision must be considered as a whole and applied together.' See C-8/57 *Groupement des hauts fourneaux et aciéries belges/ECSC High Authority* [1957–58] ECR p. 245.

[18] See, eg, Joined Cases 7/57 and 9/54, *Groupement des industries sidérurgiques Luxembourgeoises v ECSC High Authority* [1954–56] ECR 175, or C-30/59 *Steenkolenmijnen v High Authority* [1961] ECR 3.

[19] As the Court stated in an early judgment, 'The most rational distribution of production in accordance with Article 2 is that which is based in particular upon the composition of production costs resulting from output, that is, from the physical and technical conditions particular to the various producers.' Joined Cases 7/57 and 9/54, *Groupement des industries sidérurgiques Luxembourgeoises v ECSC High Authority* [1954–56] ECR 175.

[20] As Judge Jacques Rueff phrased it: '*dans la jurisprudences de la Cour, le Marché Commun apparaissait essentiellement comme un theater sur lequel les conditions naturelles de la production devaient déterminer le comportement des acteurs économiques*'. (Trans. 'in the case law of the Court,

With this background in mind, as Judge Rueff noted, it was not so surprising that the Court defined in a very similar way three different terms: special charge,[21] subsidy,[22] and discrimination.[23] These were viewed as artificial distortions to the most rational/natural distribution of production in that they altered the production costs of the affected economic operators in ways unrelated to the actual productivity/competitiveness of those operators. Similarly, AG Lagrange stated in his opinion that Article 4 (c) concerned direct interventions in the functioning of the Common Market that were considered 'to be in themselves contrary to the very conditions on which that common market was established.'[24] Therefore, they did not need to interfere with the conditions of competition in the market but rather,

the Common Market mainly appeared as a theatre where the natural conditions of production would determine the behavior of economic actors'). See Rueff, 'La Cour et l'economie politique', op. cit. at 20. See also, eg, the opinion of AG Lagrange in case C-30/59 *Steenkolenmijnen v High Authority* [1961] ECR 3 at p. 41: 'the cases referred to in Article 4 (c) involve direct interventions in the functioning of the common market which are considered to be in themselves contrary to the very conditions on which that common market was established. Because of this they are deemed to be incompatible with it without the need to establish or even to consider whether there is, in actual fact, any interference with the conditions of competition or it is liable to occur; its existence is presumed solely from the purpose of the measure. This is the same principle as that applied, for example, to customs duties: no one asks whether they are a form of protection or are merely fiscal: there is no common market if there are national customs duties. In the same way there is no real common market in an industry straddling several countries if one of those countries subsidizes its own industry; the rules of competition should be evolved only by adapting each industry to the natural conditions, except of course for any necessary transitional measures taken to enable adaptation to be effected without exceptional difficulty, which, as stated in its first paragraph, is the purpose of the Convention on the Transitional Provisions.'

[21] See Joined Cases 7/57 and 9/54, *Groupement des industries sidérurgiques Luxembourgeoises v ECSC High Authority* [1954–56] ECR 175: 'a charge may be presumed to be special and therefore abolished and prohibited by the Treaty if, by affecting unequally the production costs of comparably placed producers, it introduces into the distribution of production distortions which do not result from changes in productivity.'

[22] See C-30/59 *Steenkolenmijnen v High Authority* [1961] ECR 3: 'Among the declared aims of the Community, in article 2 of the Treaty, is that it "shall progressively bring about conditions which will of themselves ensure the most rational distribution of production at the highest possible level of productivity, while safeguarding continuity of employment and taking care not to provoke fundamental and persistent disturbances in the economies of member states". A subsidy or aid, within the meaning of the definition given above in itself constitutes an obstacle to the most rational distribution of production at the highest possible level of productivity inasmuch as, being a payment made by someone other than the purchaser or consumer, it makes it possible to fix or maintain selling prices which are not directly related to production costs and thereby to establish, maintain and develop economic activity which does not represent the most rational distribution of production at the highest possible level of productivity.'

[23] See Joined Cases C-32/58 and C-33/58 *Snupat v ECSC High Authority* [1958] ECR 1959 p. 127: 'On the basis of the abovementioned provisions there may be considered as discriminatory in principle and, accordingly, prohibited by the Treaty, inter alia, measures or interventions, even those emanating from the High Authority, which are calculated, by substantially increasing differences in production costs otherwise than through changes in productivity, to give rise to an appreciable disequilibrium in the competitive position of the undertakings concerned. In other words, any intervention attempting to distort or actually distorting competition artificially and significantly must be regarded as discriminatory and incompatible with the Treaty, whilst measures which take into account the internal organization of an undertaking and the use by it of its own resources cannot be regarded as discriminatory.'

[24] See Opinion of Advocate General Lagrange, C-30/59 *Steenkolenmijnen v High Authority* [1961] ECR 3 at p.41.

they were presumed to interfere with those conditions 'solely from the purpose of the measure'.[25] A second important remark made by AG Lagrange was that 'everything affecting the common market', including interventions to guide that market if necessary, had been transferred to the ECSC institutions: 'The States have lost jurisdiction'.[26]

In any event, the notion of aid and of advantage given in the *miners' bonus* case placed explicit emphasis both on the *purpose* and on the *effect* of a given public measure, although subsequent case law has only underlined the effect part.[27] The definition also placed emphasis in the *real object* of the measure, whether it is social or economic, as suggested by the Advocate General in his opinion. In fact, after considering that the shift bonus appeared to amount to a subsidy or aid under the definition just given, the Court still looked at whether the shift bonus satisfied the requirements of Article 2 of the treaty; namely, to safeguard continuity of employment and to avoid creating fundamental and persistent disturbances in the economies of Member States. The fact that the alleged justification could invalidate the definition of the measure as a subsidy is, in my view, supported by the Court statement in the sense that '[f]or the foregoing reasons, viewed in itself, the miner's bonus, financed out of public funds, constitutes a subsidy or aid granted by the Government of the Federal Republic to the German coal-mining industry and there is no valid reason, based on the treaty, which could invalidate this description.'[28] This was also the view of Chevallier, who held that for the measure to qualify as a subsidy the Court looked for the *intention* of the German government for granting the bonus at issue.[29]

Such a broad notion was coherent with the goal of removing all national support, *in any form whatsoever*, to the coal and steel industries. Specifically, it was consistent with the full delegation of sovereignty to the High Authority that Member States had made for the coal and steel sectors. It was also in line with the ECSC Treaty intention, noted by the Court,[30] to replace all national aid to the coal and steel industries with aid granted at Community level. This broad definition was also consistent with the lack of limitations or qualifications of Article 4(c) ECSC, which promoted the recognition of its immediate application

[25] In this regard, AG Lagrange equated subsidies and aids to custom duties: 'no one asks whether they are a form of protection or are merely fiscal, there is no common market if there are national customs duties. In the same way there is no real common market in an industry straddling several countries if one of those countries subsidizes its own industry'. Ibid.

[26] Ibid. at 42. See also for the necessary distortive effects of either subsidies or aids, see Cases 27–29/58, *Hans Fourneux et Fonderies de Givors v High Authority* [1960] ECR 241 p. 254.

[27] See, eg, Plender, R., 'Definition of Aid', in Biondi, A., Eeckhout, P., and Flynn, J., (eds) *The Law of State Aid in the European Union* (OUP, 2004) 3 at 6.

[28] C-30/59 *Steenkolenmijnen v High Authority* [1961] ECR 3.

[29] See Chevallier, 'L'Arrêt 30-59 de la Cour de justice des Communautés européennes', op. cit. at 578.

[30] In the Court of Justice's own terms, '[the ECSC Treaty] intends to reserve to the Community institutions and withhold from the states the right to grant, within the community, subsidies or aids and to impose special charges in any form whatsoever. The strict wording of article 4 itself emphasizes the exclusive character of the community's jurisdiction within the Community.' C-30/59 *Steenkolenmijnen v High Authority* [1961] ECR 3, para. 22.

by the Court, the forerunner of the notion of direct effect.[31] Indeed, the notion of subsidy or aid provided for in the ECSC Treaty did not require any sort of distortion of competition or selectivity criteria,[32] and did not contain any *de minimis* rule,[33] as opposed, it was argued, to the EEC Treaty which required a 'tangible' effect on competition and trade.[34]

Finally, the *miners' bonus* judgment also shows the lack of political commitment towards the enforcement of the prohibition of subsidies in the first years of European integration. In this regard, the judgment was brought about by an application lodged by a Dutch association of undertakings, *De Gezamenlijke Steenkolenmijnen*, in view of the refusal by the High Authority to take action on the complaint that the association had made to it in 1959. At first, the High Authority considered it a *de facto* subsidy and hence forbade it. Subsequently, it decided to give the German government more time because the Council of Ministers decided that incentives for the recruitment and productivity of miners might be necessary, probably because at that time there was a serious scarcity of coal in the Community.[35]

However, after the judgment was rendered, and although it expressly urged the High Authority to adopt the necessary steps towards the cancellation of the forbidden subsidy, the High Authority did not show any intention of acting in that respect.[36] One year later, the High Authority adopted formal measures to constrain Germany to comply with the judgment. In any event, these measures were subsequently suspended in order to treat them in the framework of a '*mixed*

[31] See De Wilmars, J.M., 'Aides CECA et aides CEE: aspects juridique d'une convergence economique', in Capotorti, F. et al. *Du droit International au droit de l'intégration: liber Amicorum Pierre Pescatore* (Nomos Verlagsgesellschaft, 1987) at 424. See also for an early comparison between ECSC and EEC State aid rules by another judge of the Court of Justice, Catalano, N., *Manuel de droit des Communautés Européennes* (Dalloz, 1965) at 494–96.

[32] 'Article 4(c) of the [ECSC] Treaty lays down such a general, strict and unconditional prohibition on aid that it is unnecessary to examine whether, in point of fact, there is interference or potential interference with the conditions of competition in order to be able to declare aid incompatible with the common market. That prohibition does not presuppose that the aid is such as to distort or threaten to distort competition by favouring certain undertakings or the production of certain goods.' See Cases T-12/99 and T-63/99, *UK Coal plc v Commission* [2001] ECR II-2153, para. 54. See also order in Case C-111/99 P *Lech-Stahlwerke v Commission* [2001] ECR I-727, para. 41, and judgment in Joined Cases T-129/95, T-2/96, and T-97/96 *Neue Maxhütte Stahlwerke and Lech-Stahlwerke v Commission* [1999] ECR II-17, paras 98 and 99. The Court has, however, reconciled the definitions. See Case C-200/97 *Ecotrade* [1998] ECR I-7907, para. 17.

[33] See Cases T-12/99 and T-63/99, *UK Coal plc v Commission* [2001] ECR II-2153, para. 55. See also order in Case C-111/99 P *Lech-Stahlwerke v Commission* [2001] ECR I-727, para. 41, and judgment in Joined Cases T-129/95, T-2/96, and T-97/96 *Neue Maxhütte Stahlwerke and Lech-Stahlwerke v Commission* [1999] ECR II-17, para. 147.

[34] Note regarding the parties' argument concerning trade and competition, 'The applicant's arguments are somewhat similar to those of the defendant. It emphasizes that the Treaty establishing the European Coal and Steel Community, in contrast to that establishing the European Economic Community, prohibits subsidies regardless of whether they have a tangible effect on the common market.'

[35] Haas, E., *The Uniting of Europe: Political, Social, and Economic Forces, 1950–1957* (Stanford University Press, 1958) at 85, and Rueff, 'La Cour et l'economie politique', op. cit. at 18.

[36] Spierenburg, D., and Poidevin,R,. *Histoire de la Haute Autorité de la Communauté du Charbon et de l'Acier: Un expérience supranationale* (Bruylant, 1993) 656.

committee'.[37] As a former Director General of DG Competition, Claus-Dieter Ehlermann noted, the absolute prohibition of aids contained in Article 4(c) was totally disregarded.[38]

To conclude, the definition of aid was a product of the Court which, in view of the absence of definitions in either Community or national laws for subsidy or aid, laid down a broad definition, including taxes or social charges, that was consistent with the fact that Member States had lost jurisdiction to intervene by any and all means (regulation or subsidies *stricto sensu*) in the market for the coal and steel sectors. The Court ruled against the High Authority, which had defended the possibility of compensating the effects of an aid through other means affecting the overall burden of the undertakings. In this regard, while not ruling out completely the possibility of looking at the possible compensation, and therefore the possible neutralization of the effects of an aid, the Court held that a reduction of the production costs of an undertaking was an aid in itself, and that the ECSC Treaty, as opposed to the EEC Treaty, did not require any tangible effect on competition or trade for a measure to be aid (there were no criteria in Article 4(c)). Therefore, both the definition and the judgment were closely related to the nature of ECSC, something that the Commission would disregard when it translated the Court's definition of aid to the EEC context.

2. The *Meura* Case (C-234/84)

A. Introduction and background to the case

The *Meura* judgment is known for being the first case in which the Court of Justice explicitly approved the Market Economy Investor Principle test ('MEIP').[39] According to the MEIP, a public investment in an undertaking in which a market operator would not have invested under normal market economy conditions constitutes an advantage under Article 107(1) TFEU. This test was thus different from that previously upheld by the Court in relation to the concept of advantage, a test that was based on the mitigation of the costs that should normally be borne by an undertaking in the sense of the miners' bonus case or others laid down by the Court during the first period of evolution of the State aid policy, such as Italian textiles or para-fiscal levies, discussed in the next chapters.

The origins of this case date back to 1982, when the Belgian government, through a regional public holding company, made a subscription in the capital

[37] Ibid. See also footnotes 16 and 17.

[38] Ehlermann, C.D., 'State Aid Control in the European Union: Success or Failure?' (1994) *Fordham International Law Journal* at 1216.

[39] C-234/84 *Belgium v Commission* ('Meura') [1986] ECR 2263. In two previous cases the Court had endorsed the reasoning of the Commission concerning the MEIP (See Case 323/82 *Intermills v Commission* [1984] ECR 3809 and Joined Cases 296 and 318/82 *Netherlands and Leeuwarder Papierwarenfabriek v Commission* [1985] ECR 809) yet it was in the Meura judgment where the Court explicitly adopted it and even complemented it.

of an undertaking which specialized in manufacturing equipment for the food industry (Meura), and granted a loan to the same undertaking. Belgium did not notify the Commission of these measures, and the latter contacted the Belgian government '*after hearing of the decision to grant the aid*' and opened the formal investigation procedure under Article 108 TFEU.

At the end of the investigation the Commission adopted a decision by which it held that a private financial group would not have made such an investment in view of the financial situation of the undertaking in question.[40] The Belgian government appealed the decision before the Court.

B. The policy context

The decision was taken during the second period of evolution of the State aid policy which was discussed in Chapter 3. Towards the end of this period, thus by the time of adopting the decision under review, the Commission toughened the enforcement of the State aid rules because it realized that the flexible approach that it held during the 1970s was not bringing about the desired results.

A key concern for the Commission at this time was the impact of the public sector on the economies of most Member States. Out of this concern, as discussed in Chapter 3, the Commission adopted the Transparency Directive in June 1980, decided to apply the MEIP test systematically and to tackle other concerns related to the action of public undertakings through the internal market rules, in particular by the application of the Treaty rules to public monopolies and privileged undertakings under Articles 37 EC and 30 EC.[41]

C. The judgment of the Court of Justice

The judgment of the Court in *Meura* was particularly laconic. The Court held that '[a]n appropriate way of establishing whether a [loan and a subscription of capital] is a State aid is to apply the criterion which was mentioned in the Commission's decision and, moreover, was not contested by the Belgian Government, of determining to what extent the undertaking would be able to obtain the sums in question on the private capital markets. In the case of an undertaking whose capital is held by the public authorities, the test is, in particular, whether in similar

[40] Commission Decision of 17 April 1984 on aid which the Belgian Government has granted to an undertaking at Tournai manufacturing equipment for the food industry, OJ L 276, 19 October 1984 p. 0034–36 at 35: 'In the present case, the company's financial situation was a handicap which makes it very unlikely that it could have raised the finance it needed to survive on the private capital market. Considering its history of repeated serious financial difficulties, the injection of Bfrs 145 million in the company by SRIW constituted aid within the meaning of Article 92 (1) and not a subscription of risk capital according to normal practice in the market sector.' In fact, the company at stake had been making losses for many years and even the banks with whom the company had a long commercial relationship had rejected to loan any more money to it.

[41] Gardner, A, 'The Velvet Revolution: Article 90 and the Triumph of the Free Market in Europe's Regulated Sectors' (1995) *European Competition Law Review*, 78 at 79.

circumstances a private shareholder, having regard to the foreseeability of obtaining a return and leaving aside all social, regional-policy and sectoral considerations, would have subscribed the capital in question.'[42] Belgium had in fact not contested the MEIP, its main argument being instead based on the principle of neutrality enshrined today in Article 345 TFEU.

The reference in the passage just quoted to all social, regional policy, and sectoral considerations, which did not appear in the Commission decision, may perhaps be explained by reference to the opinion of the Advocate General in this case. AG Lenz had in fact argued that the aim of a measure had to be taken into consideration in order to distinguish between State aids and grants to public undertakings by the State in its capacity as a private operator. In the AG's words:

> In order to differentiate between State aid and grants to public undertakings by the State in its capacity as a private operator, the aims of the action must be taken into consideration, at least as evidence. The aim may determine in which category a particular advantage given to public undertakings falls in so far as if the reason is one of economic policy—for example, social or structural policy—this may make it appear to be an aid, whereas a viable investment which is intended to produce a return is less likely to be viewed as an aid.[43]

D. Assessment

In this case, the Court supported a *new* test for the concept of advantage. The test was, however, anything *but* new; the Commission had envisaged it as early as in 1963,[44] and even applied it in one or two cases during the early 1970s.[45] What

[42] C-234/84, *Belgium v Commission* ('Meura') [1986] ECR p. 02285–85 at para. 14. See also para. 12.

[43] Opinion of AG Lenz in case 234/84 *Belgium v Commission* ('Meura') [1986] ECR 2263 at p. 02271.

[44] See the Reply to Parliamentary Question No. 48 of Mr Burgbecher, 30.July.1963, OJ 2235/63: '*Au cas où la puissance publique renonce, en tout ou en partie, a la rémunération du capital propre d'une entreprise d'État ou de toute autre entreprise publique, un telle renociation pourrait, le cas échéant, être considérée comme une aide d'État. De l'avis de la Commission, ceci pourrait se concevoir dans la mesure ou un propriétaire ou actionnaire privé se trouvant dans une situation comparable et agissant en vertu de considérations d'ordre économique, ne renoncerait pas—ou ne renoncerait que dans un mesure limitée—á la rémunération de son capital propre; autrement dit, la renonciation a laquelle consentirait la puissance publique résulterait en l'occurrence non pas considérations d'ordre économique, mais de motifs d'ordre politique.*'

[45] Second Report on Competition Policy (Office for Official Publications of the European Communities, 1973) at point 124: 'In certain cases (establishment by a central government of new undertakings, acquisition of non-precarious holdings in firms already existing or to be set up in association with private interests), the central government normally assumes the role of entrepreneur or venture capital investor. Although the official measure is normally dictated by exigencies going beyond the profit motive, this factor is inherent in the public ownership, the existence and the special nature of which is confirmed by Article 222, and it could not be used alone to justify the bringing into play of the Treaty rules on aids. This is not the case, however, where the central authority, through financial agencies it sets up at its initiative and with its financial support, confines itself to the acquisition in certain firms of holdings which by their special nature (e.g. duration, purpose, terms) show clearly what the aim of the acquisition is to help the firms until such time as they will have overcome temporary difficulties.'

was new was the Commission's determination to apply this test systematically, as shown by the opening of an *ex officio* investigation in *Meura*, and the Council's support of its application, as it is clear from the introduction of the test in the Shipbuilding Code adopted by the Council in 1981, and this may explain why Belgium did not contest the test before the Court.

The MEIP test was indeed a product of the Commission supported by the Council. Both institutions shared the objective of liberalizing the economy and reducing the size of public debt and the public sector in the more neoliberal context that dominated the early 1980s, both within the Commission and within the Council. The Court backed both institutions by holding the MEIP test valid to differentiate between legitimate public economic interventions under the principle of neutrality from State aids.

The MEIP marked a change in the understanding of the State aid rules. If those rules had until then been applied to preserve the conditions of competition in the common market by preventing Member States from altering the production costs of—principally—private undertakings, after the MEIP the focus was more on creating, not preserving, the conditions of competition by targeting inefficient public undertakings that remained afloat only because of public support. In the same vein, before the introduction of the MEIP the State aid rules were largely reactive and focused on inter-jurisdictional competition (undertakings or rather industries from different Member States, as in the *miners' bonus* or the *Italian textiles* cases), while through the MEIP they became proactive, a tool to discipline the public sector and to allow private undertakings to compete with public ones, even within one and the same national market (intra-jurisdictional competition). Indeed, the MEIP test had no precedent in the historical efforts to define and control subsidies reviewed in Part I of this work, from the nineteenth century to the GATT or the ECSC. The MEIP has therefore to be understood as a product of the evolution of the internal market, as steered by the European Commission when it considered, jointly with the Council, the time ripe for disciplining the behaviour of public undertakings and for limiting public participation in failing undertakings.

Indeed, the Commission welcomed this judgement in the Sixteenth Competition Report,[46] and, according to the Commission's agent in this case, by constraining public undertakings to adjust their behaviour to market rules and to face competition from private operators on equal footing, the Commission, supported by the case law of the Court, paved the way to the privatization process that took place between the mid-1980s and mid-1990s.[47] The test was in fact

[46] See Sixteenth Report on Competition Policy (Office for Official Publications of the European Communities, 1987) at point 313.

[47] Abate, A., 'Privatisations et déréglementations en droit communautaire', in *EC State Aid Law—Le Droit des Aides d'État dans la CE, Liber Amicorum Francisco Santaolalla Gadea* (Kluwer Law International, 2008) at 247.

mostly applied to rescue and restructuring cases in its first years of application.[48] In this regard, the Commission and the General Court noted in 2003 in a case involving several German banks that the MEIP was being applied innovatively to profitable undertakings, as until that time that principle had been mainly applied in cases where the State had injected capital into undertakings which were suffering losses or which required restructuring.[49]

3. The *SFEI* Case (C-39/94)

A. Introduction and background

This case is known for being the first in which the Court of Justice coined the more recent definition of aid, namely: 'that in order to determine whether a State measure constitutes aid, it is necessary to establish whether the recipient undertaking receives an economic advantage which it would not have obtained under normal market conditions.'[50]

The origins of this case, decided in 1996, may be traced back to December 1990,[51] when the Commission received a State aid complaint lodged by competitors of the French Post Office, La Poste. The complaint referred to aid allegedly granted by the French State through the public undertaking La Poste to its subsidiaries, which provided express delivery services in a market open to competition. The Commission decided to take no action on the complaint in March 1992. The decision rejecting the complaint was appealed before the Court of Justice. Following this appeal, the Commission decided to withdraw the decision of rejection and to continue analysing the complaint in July 1992.[52]

However, the competitors of La Poste did not wait for the Commission's new decision and lodged appeals before a national court (Tribunal de Commerce de Paris), claiming the violation of today's Article 108(3) TFEU, as the alleged State aid measures had never been notified to the Commission. The national Court reviewing this new challenge made a preliminary reference to the Court of Justice, asking, *inter alia*, whether the provision of logistical and commercial assistance by

[48] See Council Directive 81/363/EEC of 28 April 1981 L 137/39, and Commission decisions 82/653/EEC of 22 July 1982, OJ L 277, 29 September 1982, p. 15 and Commission decision 82/670/EEC of 2 October 1982, OJ 1982 L280/30.

[49] See Joined Cases T-228/99 and T-233/99, T-228/99, Westdeutsche Landesbank Girozentrale v Commission ECR [2003] II-00435 at 205 and 213.

[50] C-39/94 *SFEI v La Poste* [1996] ECR I-3547 at para. 60.

[51] The background of this case is explained in the Opinion of Advocate General Tizzano in Joined Cases C-83/01 P, C-93/01P, C-94/01/P *Chronopost* [2003] ECR p. I-6993.

[52] Ibid. at footnote 5: 'by letter of 10 March 1992 the Commission notified SFEI of its decision to take no action on the complaint under Article 92 of the Treaty. On 16 May 1992 SFEI together with other undertakings lodged an action with the Court of Justice for annulment of that decision. The Court ruled that it was not necessary to proceed to judgment (order of 18 November 1992 in Case C-222/92 *SFEI and Others v Commission*, not published in the ECR) in the light of the Commission Decision of 9 July 1992 to withdraw the decision of 10 March 1992'.

a public undertaking to its subsidiaries without asking for the normal payment in return for its services should be regarded as State aid. This preliminary ruling is the judgment under review.

B. The policy context

The years between the beginning of the Commission's procedure concerning this case (1990) and the Court's judgment (1996) fall within the third period of evolution of the State aid policy discussed in Chapter 3. This time was very important for the development of this policy because the Commission gradually prepared to deploy to the full its Treaty powers in this field and Member States finally became willing to cooperate with the Commission as part of the 1992 programme and, subsequently, on the way towards the Economic Monetary Union.

During this period State aid policy became more closely integrated with the other competition rules (addressed to undertakings).[53] Indeed, by the year of adoption of the judgment under review, the role of competitors, who were non-state actors, in the State aid field had become very important and useful for the Commission as they drew to the Commission's attention many cases of non-notified State aid. They also indirectly reinforced the Commission's role as a neutral arbiter between States as the Commission could claim that it was forced to carry out an investigation due to the complaint.[54] For these reasons, competitors have often being allies of the European Commission's enforcement of the State aid rules, and yet, as we will see in this case, they have also placed significant demands on the European Commission if the latter failed to act on their complaints.

C. The judgment of the Court of Justice

The Court, referring to the traditional case law on advantage, concluded that the concept of aid included not only positive benefits but also interventions which mitigate the charges which are normally included in the budget of an undertaking.[55] The Court also found that the supply of goods or services on preferential terms is capable of constituting State aid.[56] It laid down the standard test for aid and advantage: 'Accordingly, in order to determine whether a State

[53] See in this regard and as mentioned earlier, Ehlermann, 'State Aid Control in the European Union: Success or Failure?' op. cit. at 1219. In Ehlermann's words, 'Aid granted by a Member State is no longer controlled exclusively or principally in the interest of other Member States, but also, and perhaps even more so, in the interest of the competitors of the intended beneficiaries of the aid. The original macroeconomic approach of the authors of the EEC Treaty is being supplanted progressively by a microeconomic perspective, similar to that which has always dominated substantive and procedural antitrust law.'

[54] Smith, M.P., 'Autonomy by the Rules: The European Commission and the Development of State Aid Policy' (1998) *Journal of Common Market Studies* at 63.

[55] Ibid. at para. 58.

[56] Joined Cases 67/85, 68/85, and 70/85 *Van der Kooy and Others v Commission* [1988] ECR 219, para. 28, and Case C-56/93 *Belgium v Commission* [1996] ECR 1-723 para. 10.

measure constitutes aid, it is necessary to establish whether the recipient undertaking receives an economic advantage which it would not have obtained under normal market conditions'.[57]

Finally, the Court upheld that the determination of whether the measures under review in *La Poste* amounted to an economic advantage had to be carried out pursuant to 'an economic analysis taking into account all the factors which an undertaking acting under normal market conditions should have taken into consideration when fixing the remuneration for the services provided.'[58] This analysis, so the Court concluded, was for the national judge to carry out, and the Court of Justice did not provide any further criteria on how one might do so.

D. Assessment

This case could be seen as yet another application of the MEIP test. There is more to it than that, however.

The analysis shows a Commission unwilling to take a decision on a subject which was quite sensitive and for which it did not yet have a clear policy line. In fact, the Commission was engaged in a broader exercise when it received the complaint that led to the judgment reviewed in 1990. The Commission was drafting the Green Paper on the development of the single market for postal services. This document made reference to the liberalization of express delivery services, achieved as a result to the Commission's intervention,[59] yet the document did not address the issue of possible cross-subsidization by vertical undertakings acting in reserved and non-reserved areas such as La Poste. La Poste's competitors forced the Commission, through national and European proceedings, to adopt a position on this matter. Indeed, the case shows that the Commission was no longer able to set the pace of State aid policy. Third parties, usual allies of the Commission against Member States in this field, now turned into enemies, forcing the Commission to take up a position in a matter where the Commission seemingly preferred not to do so.

The Court of Justice was thus bound to take a decision on a case that had been avoided by the Commission, a case that was delicate because it involved a new issue: that of determining the concept of advantage in a partially liberalized sector. The Court's answer was quite orthodox: it cited the main case law on the advantage criterion, from the *miners' bonus* to the *Meura* case. However, it did in fact leave the answer to the national court by deferring to it the actual analysis that had to be carried out in order to determine whether there was an advantage; that is, to ascertain whether the remuneration for the services provided by La Poste was lower than that which a normal undertaking acting under normal market conditions would have paid. The Court's deferral may perhaps be justified by

[57] C-39/94 *SFEI v La Poste* [1996] ECR I-3547 at para. 60. [58] Ibid. at para. 61.

[59] See Green Paper on the Development of the Single Market for Postal Services. COM (91) 476 final, 11 June 1991 [EU Commission—COM Document] at 56.

the fact that the case reached it as a preliminary reference. On the other hand, this deferral led to a saga of cases that lasted almost two decades.

In this regard, after this judgment, delivered on 1 October 1997, the Commission finally adopted the decision that it had refused to adopt prior to 1992. The Commission concluded that the logistical and commercial assistance provided by La Poste did not amount to State aid as the subsidiaries paid 'full-cost prices' for it—that is, La Poste's total costs plus a remuneration for the equity capital investment. This decision was challenged before the Court of First Instance (CFI) which considered that the decision was not consistent with the ruling of the Court of Justice because the decision should have analysed the remuneration that a private investor, which was not operating in a reserved sector (therefore not like La Poste), would have requested.[60] On appeal, the Court of Justice quashed the CFI judgment. The Court of Justice held, in essence, that the CFI was wrong in considering that the Commission should have taken into consideration not the situation of La Poste, but instead that of a private undertaking acting under normal conditions. Indeed, so the Court held, given that La Poste was entrusted with a service of general economic interest, for which purposes it had acquired (or was afforded) the postal network, La Poste was not acting as a normal market operator and therefore 'normal market conditions' had to be interpreted in this case as those objective and verifiable elements, such as the La Poste's actual costs in providing the services at stake, available to the Commission and the Court.[61] Notwithstanding all this, in a subsequent judgment the CFI annulled again the Commission's 1997 decision for its alleged defective motivation and, once more, the case was brought back to the ECJ which yet again quashed the CFI's judgment, thus finally closing this saga eighteen years after the complaint was lodged before the Commission.[62]

It should be noted that the European Commission did not participate in the litigation that emerged from the CFI ruling annulling its decision. Therefore, the Commission clearly left to the Court the decision as to what standard had to be applied to undertakings such as La Poste: a 'pure' market economy standard, based on the costs of a 'normal undertaking acting under normal market conditions', as defended by the CFI, or a more 'realistic' standard, taking into account the actual costs of an undertaking such as La Poste, which was performing a service of general economic interest.[63] It goes without saying that the standard chosen substantially affected the position of the incumbents in reserved sectors, given that if the 'pure' market economy standard would have been adopted, as defended by the CFI, they would have had to show that their costs were the most efficient.

[60] See Case T-613/97 *Ufex and Others v Commission* [2000] ECR II-4055.

[61] Joined Cases C-83/01P, C-93/01P, and C-94/01P *Chronopost I* [2003] ECR I-6993.

[62] See T-613/97 *Ufex II* [2006] ECR 1531. Joined Cases C-341/06 P and C-342/06 P *Chronopost SA and La Poste v Union francaise de l'express (UFEX) and Others* [2008] ECR I-4777 (Grand Chamber).

[63] See AG Tizzano in Joined Cases C-83/01P, C-93/01P, and C-94/01P *Chronopost I* [2003] ECR I-6993 at p. 20: 'The Commission on the other hand did not respond and, is therefore not a party in the present cases.'

The adoption by the Court of the realistic approach can be seen as deferring to the Member States' power to organize their own public sector, even at the expense of inefficiencies and to the detriment of the most orthodox application of the MEIP. The normal application of this test would have probably called for a comparison such as the one proposed by the Court of First Instance—a comparison based on the costs of a normal operator under normal market conditions. The deferential approach of the Court has been noted by academics[64] and recognized by a judge of the Court, who has held that in deciding the *Chronopost* case, the Court adopted an approach which balanced the strict application of the State aid rules and ensuring workable conditions for public services:

'the opposing aims of the prohibition of any state aid in Article 107(1) TFEU and the necessity of ensuring workable conditions for public services according to Article 106(2) and Article 14 TFEU have to guide our reflections. The basic idea is to keep the prohibition of state aid effective, even if aid is granted by way of cross-subsidization. This purpose may, of course, not endanger the good functioning of public service operations, which enjoy a particular recognition in Union law. To me it seems quite inappropriate to strive for a hierarchical understanding of both values in terms of Union law. The challenge is rather to achieve practical solutions designed for an equivalent realization of both objectives. To my mind, the rationale of the jurisprudence in Chronopost seems to be rightly based on this balancing approach.'[65]

In our view, the judgement under review in *SFEI* can be described as balanced. On the one hand, the Court established the principle according to which all public action, not only public capital injections but also transactions of public undertakings such as those reviewed in this case, had to be analysed under the MEIP test, that is, under the prism of normal market conditions. In this regard, as discussed in *Meura*, subjecting the action of public authorities and undertakings to the market favoured the liberalization and privatization processes that were taking place in the European Union during the 1990s. On the other, the Court mitigated the consequences of this finding in SFEI the case at hand by taking the actual costs of La Poste as the relevant ones for the analysis of the advantage criterion, and therefore, avoiding to conclude that public undertakings had to be conducted under efficiency standards without any articulation of how this might be done by European institutions and particularly by the Commission.

Indeed, the Court's solution may have also been motivated by the lack of a clear proposal by the European Commission. Not only did the Commission avoid taking a decision on the complaint for a long time but also, when it finally did, it refused to defend it before the Court of Justice after its decision was annulled by the CFI. In other words, the Commission was not proposing the Court to apply the MEIP test strictly. In fact, the Commission's focus until that moment was

64 Slot, P.J., 'A View from the Mountain: 40 Years of Developments in EC Competition Law' (2004) *Common Market Law Review*, 443 at 458.

65 von Danwitz, T., 'The Concept of State Aid in Liberalized Sectors', in Cremona, M. (ed.), *Market Integration and Public Services in the European Union* (OUP, 2011) 103 at 114.

on increasing transparency in the dealings between public operators and the States, and between the former and their subsidiaries in non-reserved sectors (preventing cross-subsidization). The efficiency of the public sector was not a priority for the Commission at that time.[66] In the absence of the Commission's support, it would have been for the Court, and the Court alone, to oppose Member States in such a delicate issue as the efficiency of incumbent operators in reserved sectors, and this at a time when the Commission and the Council were engaged in discussing the appropriate role of services of general economic interest in the Single Market.[67]

4. The *Altmark* Case (C-280/00)

A. Introduction and background

The *Altmark* judgment is known for having resolved the question of whether compensation for the costs of performing a Service of General Economic Interest (SGEI) confers an advantage to the recipient undertakings in the sense of Article 107(1) TFEU.[68]

The 'history' of the litigation that preceded this case is well known and will not be restated here at length.[69] In essence, the Court of Justice, together with the Commission and the Council,[70] first considered in 1983 that compensation for the provision of public services did not comprise State aid. The question arose again in 1997. This time it was put to the General Court and the latter concluded that it was indeed aid, though justified.[71] This approach was tacitly approved by the Court of Justice by dismissing the appeal lodged by the original plaintiffs, not the Commission, against the decision.[72] Three years later, the General Court rejected the Commission's submission

[66] Indeed, as the Commission had made clear before the Court of First Instance in a parallel case related to La Poste: 'the aim of Article 92 of the Treaty is not to limit the absolute level of public service costs but to prevent resources from being transferred to competitive activities [thus] as regards the complaint that it did not base its calculations on minimum costs rather than on actual costs, the Commission replies that its role is not to improve the efficiency of the public postal service in France.' See T-106/95 *FFSA and Others v Commission* [1997] ECR II-00229 at 85–86. The case had also been initiated by a complaint in 1990 that the Commission refused to consider for several years until it was brought before the European courts.

[67] See, eg, the first and second Communications on 'Services of General Interest in Europe', issued between the Commission decision and the CFI judgment on this case: Communication from the Commission—Services of general interest in Europe COM/2000/0580 final OJ C 281/3 of 26 September 1996 and European Commission, Services of General Interest in Europe, COM(2000) 580, final of 20 September 2000, Brussels.

[68] C-280/00 *Altmark* [2003] ECR I-7747

[69] For a complete summary of the different answers that to this question have offered the Community courts, see Santamato, S., 'Advantage in the Context of Services of General Economic Interest under Altmark', in Mederer, W., Pesaresi, N., and Van Hoof, M. (eds), *EU Competition Law*, Volume IV, State Aid, Book One (Claeys & Casteels, 2008) 369 at 369–72.

[70] As inserted in the Council Directive 75/439/EEC of 16 June 1975 on the disposal of waste oils. OJ L 194, 25 July 1975 P. 0023–0025.

[71] Case T-106/95 *FFSA v Commission* [1997] ECR II-229 at paras 143–47.

[72] Order of 25 March 1998, C-174/97 P *FFSA and others/Commission* ECR 1998, p. I-1303. However, and against the most extended view, it is submitted that the General Court in this case

that the measure at stake—public service compensation paid to the Portuguese TV broadcaster RTP—was not aid because it was intended merely to offset the additional costs of the public service tasks entrusted to RTP without there being any 'over-compensation'.[73] The issue reached the Court of Justice again in *Ferring* in 2001. The Court, quoting the *ABDHU* case, considered that 'provided there is the necessary equivalence between the exemption and the additional costs incurred', there was no real advantage.[74]

At that point the *Altmark* case arrived to the Court of Justice. The question was presented to the Court in the form (again) of a preliminary ruling, as in *ABDHU* and *Ferring*, which in itself showed that the Commission was not particularly active in the matter (evidenced by the lack of Commission decisions) and that there was a growing uncertainty as to the appropriate legal standard at the national level.[75] As noted by the Advocate General assigned to the case, the question posed by the national court in *Altmark* concerned not the advantage criterion but that on the effect on trade.[76] The Court was, however, expected to give a definitive answer to the question of compensation of SGEI in light of the advantage criterion of then Article 107(1) TFEU in view of the number of conflicting Court cases and AGs' opinions on the matter.

On the Court's table were three possibilities: to declare public compensation always as an advantage (supported by the General Court and, since recently, by the Commission); to declare it as mere compensation (and therefore not advantage) if it was intended only to offset the costs of discharging the SGEI (supported by some Member States and the previous case law of the Court in *ABDHU* and *Ferring*); or, the more sophisticated approach advanced by AG Jacobs in the pending GEMO case, to declare public compensation as not comprising aid if there is a direct and manifest link between the State financing and the public service obligations (the *quid pro quo* approach).

Underlying the three possibilities was one fundamental issue of procedural nature: the control of State aids by the European Commission through the obligation to notify new aids provided for in Article 108(3) TFEU. With the no-aid approach this control would largely disappear as Member States would not need to notify the compensation measures, consequently incompatible aid could be

did not necessarily support the 'aid approach' in the case of compensation for the performance of an SGEI. Rather, the General Court was analysing the Commission's argument according to which the compensation was not State aid by virtue of Art. 90(2). See case T-106/95 *FFSA v Commission* [1997] ECR II-229 at para. 163, and at paras 195–97.

[73] T-46/97 *SIC v Commission* [2000] ECR II-02125.

[74] C-53/00 *Ferring v ACOSS* [2001] ECR I-9067 at para. 27. Advocate General Tizzano had supported the same view in his opinion to the case, also noting that the General Court had erred in considering that because of the effects-based case law on the notion of aid a measure intended to offset the cost of a public obligation was necessarily an aid. See Opinion of AG Tizzano in C-53/00 *Ferring v ACOSS* [2001] ECR I-9067 at para. 61.

[75] The above was also supported by the fact that another preliminary ruling on the same matter was pending before the Court at the same time; the GEMO case C-126/01 *GEMO* [2003] ECR I-13769.

[76] First opinion of Advocate General Léger in C-280/00 *Altmark* [2003] ECR I-7747 at para. 56.

granted without the Commission ever being informed; conversely, with the always-aid approach, this control risked paralysing the functioning of essential public services, such as ambulances services for example, if they had to await Commission approval.

B. The policy context

This case was decided during the fourth period of evolution of the State aid policy. As discussed in Chapter 3, during this period the Commission and the Council agreed on the need to modernize and make more efficient the enforcement of the State aid rules, also in view of the increasing number of State aid complaints and notifications brought before the European Commission. Both institutions were also in agreement as to the need to fight harmful taxation through the State aid rules in what became one of the most important policy initiatives of this period. Less clear, however, was the position of the Commission and the Council as regards the issue under review in this case, namely, the compatibility of public service compensation with the State aid rules.

As noted by AGs Léger and Tizzano,[77] for many years the Commission considered that financial compensation for the performance of public service obligations did not comprise State aid. The Commission made that position clear in the *ABDHU* case as well as in several publications, including guidelines from 1997.[78] Similarly, the Council was originally of the 'no-aid' view, as was shown by Council Directive 75/439/EEC of 16 June 1975 on the disposal of waste oils[79] and by the Council submissions in *ABDHU*.[80] However, this position was no longer clear as shown by the Laeken Presidency conclusions of the European Council asking for a policy framework for aid to public services, and also by the division of Member States before the Court in *Altmark*.[81]

[77] First Opinion of Advocate General Léger in Case C-280/00 *Altmark* [2003] ECR I-7747 at para. 64, and Opinion of Advocate General Tizzano in Case C-53/00 *Ferring SA v Agence centrale des organismos de sécurité sociale* [2001] ECR I-9067 at para. 27. Ferring case, para. 56.

[78] See, as noted by AG Tizzano, 'Community guidelines on State aid to maritime transport', OJ 1997 C 205, p. 5 at point 9, or European Commission, *Droit de la Concurrence dans les Communautés Européennes, Volume IIB, Explication des Règles Applicables aux Aides d'État* (Office for Official Publications of the European Community, 1997) at 7, where the Commission clearly stated that '*une contribution étatique dont l'effet se limiterait strictement à compenser un désavantage objectif mis à charge de l'entreprise bénéficiaire, ne tombe pas sous le coup de l'article 92.*' (Trans. 'a State contribution whose effect would be limited strictly to offset an objective disadvantage charged to the beneficiary, do not fall within the scope of Article 92'.)

[79] OJ 1975 L 194, p. 23.

[80] C-240/83 *ADBHU* [1985] ECR 531 at para. 18: 'The commission and the council, in their observations, rightly argue that the indemnities do not constitute aid within the meaning of articles 92 et seq of the EEC Treaty, but rather consideration for the services performed by the collection or disposal undertakings.'

[81] As noted by AG Léger (Second Opinion of Advocate General Léger in Case C-280/00 *Altmark* [2003] ECR I-7747 at para. 72) the European Council had expressed its will to have a policy framework for aid to public services in the Laeken Presidency conclusions. Also, before the Court in this case the German and Spanish governments supported the no-aid approach while the Danish, French, Netherlands, and UK governments supported the *quid pro quo* approach.

In this context, since the publication of the first Commission communication on SGEI in 1996,[82] where the Commission did not consider it necessary to modify its traditional no-aid approach to the issue of compensation, a number of developments had taken place in the Community which might explain the change in the Commission's viewpoint. Some of them were recorded by the Commission in its second communication on the issue of SGEI, published in 2001 at the explicit request of the European Council of Lisbon, which included:[83] (i) the adoption of the Treaty of Amsterdam, that introduced a provision (new Article 16 EC) on SGEI '*Without prejudice to Articles 77, 90 and 92*'; (ii) further liberalization at Community level;[84] (iii) the General Court judgments in FFSA and SIC against the Commission 'no-aid' view; and (iv) the 2000 changes in the Transparency Directive to include that 'whenever the compensation is fixed for an appropriate period following an open, transparent and non-discriminating procedure, there is the presumption that such aid is compatible with the State aid rules of the Treaty.'[85]

On these bases, and at the request of the European Council, the Commission once again analysed the issue of compensation for public service obligations under the State aid rules and ultimately concluded that 'financial compensation granted to the provider of a service of general interest constitutes an economic advantage within the meaning of Article 87(1) EC. However, such compensation may qualify for an exemption under Article 87(2) and (3) EC or it may qualify for a derogation under Articles 73 and 86(2) EC.'[86]

In this context, AG Léger noted that all the policy efforts would be pointless if the Court would uphold the no-aid approach suggested by the Sixth Chamber of the Court in *Ferring*. In the words of the AG, 'By ruling that aid intended to offset the cost of public service obligations does not come within the Treaty rules governing State aids, the Sixth Chamber of the Court would appear to have rendered pointless the efforts taken by the competent authorities to define Community policy in the area of public sector financing. I would therefore ask the Court to review the interpretation given in Ferring.'[87]

[82] Commission Communication 96/C 281/03 on services of general interest in Europe (OJ 1996 C 281, p. 3).

[83] Communication 2001/C 17/04 of the Commission on public interest service in Europe (OJ 2001 C 17, p. 4).

[84] Ibid. at 2–6: 'As the internal market deepened, new issues have arisen relating to the delimitation of certain services that were previously supplied primarily on a non-competitive basis, but which now elicit, or may elicit, competitors…Competing providers in the private sector…claim that existing arrangements give an unfair advantage to the organisation entrusted by the public authorities with the provision of such services and infringe Community law.'

[85] Ibid. and at 26.

[86] Report presented by the Commission to the Laeken European Council of 17 October 2001 on services of general interest, COM (2001) 598 final at paras 14–15. See also First Opinion of Advocate General Léger in Case C-280/00 *Altmark* [2003] ECR I-7747 at para. 96.

[87] First Opinion of Advocate General Léger in Case C-280/00 *Altmark* [2003] ECR I-7747 at paras 97–98.

C. Judgment of the Court of Justice

As is now well known, the Court decided that for compensation to the provision of SGEI to escape the classification of State aid, a number of conditions must be satisfied. In particular, the Court listed four conditions:

(i) First, the recipient undertaking must actually have public service obligations to discharge, and the obligations must be clearly defined... Second, the parameters on the basis of which the compensation is calculated must be established in advance in an objective and transparent manner, to avoid it conferring an economic advantage which may favour the recipient undertaking over competing undertakings... Third, the compensation cannot exceed what is necessary to cover all or part of the costs incurred in the discharge of public service obligations, taking into account the relevant receipts and a reasonable profit for discharging those obligations... and Fourth, where the undertaking which is to discharge public service obligations, in a specific case, is not chosen pursuant to a public procurement procedure which would allow for the selection of the tenderer capable of providing those services at the least cost to the community, the level of compensation needed must be determined on the basis of an analysis of the costs which a typical undertaking, well run and adequately provided with means of transport so as to be able to meet the necessary public service requirements, would have incurred in discharging those obligations, taking into account the relevant receipts and a reasonable profit for discharging the obligations.[88]

D. Assessment

To this author's knowledge, this case was the first in which the Court laid down procedural requirements in order for a measure to escape the definition of advantage within the meaning of Article 107(1) TFEU. The Court made a compromise between the different approaches put forward by the parties and AGs, opting for a more refined version of the *quid pro quo* approach. By following a sophisticated *quid pro quo* approach, the Court (in Grand Chamber formation) also modified its previous case law. Indeed, after two rejections (in the *ABDHU* and *Ferring* cases), the Court admitted that compensation for the provision of public services could amount to State aid. Similarly, the efficiency requirement that the Court had avoided in the *Chronopost* judgment was included in the fourth condition of the *Altmark* ruling which made clear that the Court would consider as an advantage any compensation given to an undertaking entrusted with an SGEI covering costs higher than the minimum ('the least to the community').

The Court, as it had done in previous occasions, did not explain how to reconcile the new decision with its previous case law.[89] In this regard, it has been held that the *Altmark* and the *Chronopost* rulings are inconsistent and the former

[88] Case C-280/00 *Altmark* [2003] ECR I-7747 at paras 89–93.

[89] In this regard, it might be noted that explicit recognition of modifications or adjustments in the case law of the Luxembourg Court are rare, the most famous of course being the Keck judgment, C-267/91, and C-268/91 *Keck and Mithouard* [1993] ECR I-6097.

should prevail.[90] This view would be supported by the fact that the *Altmark* decision was rendered after the *Chronopost* one and by the Court's Grand Chamber formation, and also because the *Altmark* case allowed the Court to address the issue of compensation for the provision of public services squarely whereas the *Chronopost* case did not as it was highly dependent on the facts of the case (cross-subsidization between an incumbent and its subsidiaries). A way of reconciling these two judgments would, however, be to leave *Chronopost* to cases where it is impossible to find a benchmark against which to assess the costs of a normal operator under market conditions, as was the case of La Poste according to the Court of Justice in the *Chronopost* case.

The judgment of the Court seems to conform with the evolution of the advantage criterion since the *Meura* case, confirmed by the SFEI casee, as it made the conduct of public undertakings, or in this case undertakings entrusted with the provision of SGEI, subject to market discipline. At the same time the judgment also allowed Member States discretion to define and organize their public services,[91] while providing legal certainty and guidance to national courts which also have to interpret the notion of aid, as had been requested by AG Léger.[92] Therefore, this judgment seems to be a balanced one between different interests, namely the orthodox application of the State aid rules, the powers of Member States to define and organize their public services and the special role that these services are recognized to have in the Community since the Amsterdam Treaty, and the interests of private parties and national courts to be able to know the conditions of compensations of the provision of SGEI to verify whether aid is being given and thus Article 108(3) may be violated.[93]

Finally, it is remarkable that the European Commission, just as in the *Chronopost* case, refused to submit observations. Instead, the Commission made clear before this ruling that it was expecting guidance from the Court to propose a policy line to Member States.[94] Indeed, the Commission *'clarified'* the policy

[90] See in this regard also Buendia Sierra, J.L., 'Finding the Right Balance: State Aid and Services of General Economic Interest', in Di Bucci, V., Buendia Sierra, J.L., Smulders, B., et al. *EC State Aid Llaw—-Le Droit des Aides d'État dans la CE, Liber Amicorum Francisco Santaolalla Gadea* (Kluwer Law International, 2008) 191 at 200.

[91] See in this regard, eg, Biondi, A., 'Justifying State Aid: The Financing of Services of General Economic Interest', in Tridimas, T., and Nebbia, P. (eds), *European Union Law for the Twenty-First Century, Volume II* (Hart Publishing, 2004). See also Buendia Sierra, 'Finding the Right Balance: State Aid and Services of General Economic Interest', op. cit. See also Slot, 'A View from the Mountain: 40 Years of Developments in EC Competition Law', op. cit. at 458.

[92] Second opinion of Advocate General Léger in Case C-280/00 *Altmark* [2003] ECR I-7747 at paras 85–88.

[93] See also for the conclusion that the application of the State aid rules to SGEI is being balanced with the existance of specific legal provisions that recognize the importance of SGEI for EU law, and, he also adds, by the principle of solidarity, De Cecco, F., *State Aid and the European Economic Constitution* (Hart, 2013) at, eg, 164–65.

[94] Report from the Commission on the state of play in the work on the guidelines for state aid and SGEI, COM/2002/0636 final at p. 2: In the Commission's words, 'pending the Court's judgments in the aforementioned cases [Altmark and GEMO], the Commission takes the view that it is not possible to finalise a text on public service compensation that would provide the legal certainty expected by the Member States and undertakings performing SGEIs.' The Commission considered, in the same text, that regardless of the classification, '[t]he compensation that certain undertakings

implications of this judgment in a 'package' comprising three acts, a decision, a communication, and an amendment to the Transparency Directive adopted in 2005. As in *Chronopost*, the Commission thus left to the Court the thorny issue of reconciling the economic criterion of advantage with the political issue of the provision of public services (SGEI).

5. The *EDF* Case (C-124/10 P)

A. Introduction and background

This case is known for being the first in which the Court of Justice, in Grand Chamber formation, held that the MEIP test can be applied to fiscal measures.[95] In this regard, the judgment qualifies both the *Meura* and the *SFEI* judgments discussed above by broadening the scope of the measures that can be reviewed under this test.

The origin of this case goes back to 2001 when the Commission requested France to provide information concerning some measures related to the company Electricité de France (EDF)—which at the relevant time was a public undertaking—that could involve State aid. At the end of its investigation the Commission considered that the French State had granted an aid to EDF by waiving a tax claim valued at €888.89 million. This amount corresponded to the corporation tax owed by EDF to the French State. Including interest, the Commission calculated that the aid granted to EDF would amount to €1217 million. France contended during the administrative procedure that the waiving of a tax to EDF could be regarded as a capital injection of an amount equivalent to the partial tax exemption. In other words, according to the French government, the State measure under review was not an aid but an investment made by EDF's shareholder, the State. The Commission refused to examine the validity of this argument, claiming, in essence, that the MEIP 'can be applied only in the context of the pursuit of an economic activity, not in the context of the exercise of regulatory powers.'[96]

EDF, supported by France, challenged this decision before the General Court. This Court annulled the Commission's decision on the basis that the Commission should have examined whether the French State had acted as a private investor.

rightly receive for providing SGEIs must not constitute advantages that enable them to compete unfairly in the most profitable liberalised sectors.'

[95] Case C-124/10 P *European Commission v Électricité de France (EDF) and Others* [2012] ECR nyr at para. 92. In the Court's terms, 'in view of the objectives underlying Article 87(1) EC and the private investor test, an economic advantage must—even where it has been granted through fiscal means—be assessed inter alia in the light of the private investor test, if, on conclusion of the global assessment that may be required, it appears that, notwithstanding the fact that the means used were instruments of State power, the Member State concerned conferred that advantage in its capacity as shareholder of the undertaking belonging to it.'

[96] Commission Decision 2005/145/EC of 16 December 2003 on the State aid granted by France to EDF and the electricity and gas industries (OJ L 2005 49, p. 9) at para. 96.

In other words, it was inappropriate for the Commission to focus on the form (fiscal legislation) to exclude the applicability of the MEIP test. The Commission should have also taken into account the nature and the economic objectives pursued by the contested State measure.[97] The Commission brought an appeal before the Court of Justice against the General Court's judgment. According to the Commission, the Market Economy Investor Test was not applicable in the case of fiscal measures. The Commission's position was supported by a competitor of EDF (Iberdrola) and by the European Free Trade Association (EFTA) Surveillance Authority. This is the judgment that we will review.

B. The policy context

This case was initiated by the Commission in 2001. It thus corresponds to the fourth period identified by political scientists, a period characterized by a number of initiatives purporting to make State aid control more efficient and transparent through the adoption of legal procedural rules, and increased focus on a number of goals, so-called horizontal goals (Lisbon Agenda goals), such as research and development (R&D) or environmental protection towards which State aid should be channelled. The period is also characterized by the Commission's and the Council's determination to address harmful taxation measures through the State aid rules, a goal that was supported by the issuing of a communication on State aids and direct business taxation in 1998.

The period is also characterized by an increase in the number of notifications and complaints brought before the European Commission and the substantial improvement in the enforcement of the State aid rules when compared with the previous periods. In this context, the enormous amount of aid allegedly granted made it a very important case for France, and the fact that the case was initiated by the Commission *ex officio* are revealing factors of the Commission's confidence in its strong enforcement line during this phase.

C. Judgment of the Court of Justice

The Court first noted, in agreement with the applicant and the GC, that the MEIP test is only applicable if the Member State concerned has conferred 'in its capacity as shareholder and not in its capacity as public authority, an economic advantage on an undertaking belonging to it'.[98] In this regard, the Court supported the General Court by holding that the objective pursued by the State should be taken into consideration in order to distinguish whether the State had acted in its capacity as shareholder, in which case the MEIP test is applicable, or

[97] See T-156/04 *EDF v Commission* [2009] ECR II 4503.

[98] Case C-124/10 P *European Commission v Électricité de France (EDF) and Others* [2012] ECR nyr at para. 81.

whether it had acted as a public authority. As discussed earlier, this had already been held many years before by Advocate General Lenz in the *Meura* case.[99]

Similarly, the Court also held that tax measures could be subject to the MEIP:

> As regards the question whether the applicability of the private investor test could be ruled out in the present case simply because the means employed by the French State were fiscal, it should be recalled that, under Article 87(1) EC, any aid granted through State resources—in any form whatsoever—which, in terms of its effects, distorts or threatens to distort competition is incompatible with the common market in so far as it affects trade between Member States.[100]

The Court also held that the intention underlying Article 87(1) EC and the private investor test is thus to prevent the recipient public undertaking from being placed, by means of State resources, in a more favourable position than that of its competitors.[101] In this vein the Court held that:

> it follows from all of the foregoing that, in view of the objectives underlying Article 87(1) EC and the private investor test, an economic advantage must—even where it has been granted through fiscal means—be assessed inter alia in the light of the private investor test, if, on conclusion of the global assessment that may be required, it appears that, notwithstanding the fact that the means used were instruments of State power, the Member State concerned conferred that advantage in its capacity as shareholder of the undertaking belonging to it.[102]

In this regard the Court noted that the application of the MEIP would have made it possible to determine 'whether, in similar circumstances, a private shareholder would have subscribed, to an undertaking in a situation comparable with that of EDF, an amount equal to the tax due.'[103] In other words, the Court held that even though the investment at stake was very high, only through the carrying out of the MEIP analysis could the Commission conclude that a private investor would not have made that transaction. In this regard the Court held that the GC had not violated the principle of equal treatment or the objective pursued by the private investor test.

As to whether it was necessary to define a reference investor, the Court held that, contrary to the situation in *Chronopost*, it was not impossible to compare the situation of EDF with that of a private undertaking operating in sectors identical to those in which EDF operates.[104] The Court concluded that the rules of

[99] Opinion of AG Lenz in case 234/84 *Belgium v Commission ('Meura')* [1986] ECR 2263 In the AG's words, 'In order to differentiate between State aid and grants to public undertakings by the State in its capacity as a private operator, the aims of the action must be taken into consideration, at least as evidence. The aim may determine in which category a particular advantage given to public undertakings falls in so far as if the reason is one of economic policy—for example, social or structural policy—this may make it appear to be an aid, whereas a viable investment which is intended to produce a return is less likely to be viewed as an aid.'

[100] Case C-124/10 P *European Commission v Électricité de France (EDF) and Others* [2012] ECR nyr at para. 88.

[101] Ibid. at para. 90. [102] Ibid. at para. 92. [103] Ibid. at para. 95.

[104] Ibid. at paras 101–02.

the burden of proof had not been reversed and therefore the Commission was required to take into account the possible applicability of the MEIP test. In the Court's words:

> Consequently, where it appears that the private investor test could be applicable, the Commission is under a duty to ask the Member State concerned to provide it with all relevant information enabling it to determine whether the conditions governing the applicability and the application of that test are met, and it cannot refuse to examine that information unless the evidence produced has been established after the adoption of the decision to make the investment in question.[105]

In addition, the Court included some findings in paragraphs 81–86 related to the evidence that Member States pleading the MEIP must be able to show. In particular, the Court held that:

> for the purposes of showing that, before or at the same time as conferring the advantage, the Member State took that decision as a shareholder, it is not enough to rely on economic evaluations made after the advantage was conferred, on a retrospective finding that the investment made by the Member State concerned was actually profitable, or on subsequent justifications of the course of action actually chosen.[106]

D. Assessment

The basis for the Court's decision in this case is ultimately the effects-based formula applicable to the concept of aid; that is that the concept of State aid does not distinguish between State intervention measures by reference to their aims or form but defines them in relation to their effects.[107] Applied to the facts of the case, the Court concluded that the Commission should have analysed whether the same alleged advantage to EDF would have been provided by a private investor under normal market conditions. In other words, the Court favoured the effects of a State measure over its form. Finally, the Court added that when a Member State aims to rely on the MEIP, it must be able to produce evidence that the measure implemented was analysed under market conditions; that is, the Member State must be able to show evidence concerning its decision to make the investment at stake from before or the same time as the alleged advantage was conceded.

[105] Ibid. at para. 104.

[106] Case C-124/10 P *European Commission v Électricité de France (EDF) and Others* [2012] ECR nyr at para. 85.

[107] See in this regard, eg, the following passage of the judgment: 'However, the financial situation of the recipient public undertaking depends not on the means used to place it at an advantage, however that may have been effected, but on the amount that the undertaking ultimately receives. Consequently, when considering whether the private investor test was applicable, the General Court did not err in law by focusing its analysis, not on the fiscal nature of the means employed by the French State, but on the improvement—with a view to the opening up of the electricity market—in EDF's financial situation and on *the effects of the measure in question on competition*' (emphasis added). Ibid. at para. 91.

In our view, this decision is problematic and inconsistent with the goals pursued by the MEIP test. As AG Darmon summarized in an early opinion: 'Article 92 applies where costs which normally fall on undertakings are borne by the State, thus favouring such undertakings in relation to others.'[108] The contested measure, a tax debt, is clearly one of those costs that normally fall on undertakings. Therefore, the relief of this cost should have been considered, it is submitted, as an aid. This case is also inconsistent with the main reasons for which both the MEIP and the effects-based formula were introduced. As to the MEIP, this test was introduced to ensure that Member States would not treat public undertakings more favourably than private ones, as the Advocate General, the Commission, and the EFTA Surveillance Authority underlined in this case. The MEIP test was also a complement to the Transparency Directive, introduced in parallel to the MEIP, to bring clarity to the dealings between public undertakings and Member States. Indeed, the MEIP was applied since the early 1980s to monitor closely State intervention in the economy as the latter started to be seen as the last barrier to trade that had to be removed in order to achieve the internal market. The MEIP test was, thus, ultimately based on the principle of non-discrimination between public and private operators and on the need for transparency in the dealings between public undertakings and Member States.

The decision of the Court in this case is at odds with the reasons underpinning the introduction of the MEIP. It makes the dealings between a public undertaking (as EDF was at the relevant time) and the State less transparent, and it also makes possible favouring public undertakings over private ones, as usually the former have more dealings with the State that could eventually be settled through the waiving of taxes. Indeed, Member States will be under no obligation to notify measures such as the contested tax waiving in this case, which provided according to the Commission an aid amount of over €1 billion to EDF, if they consider that the transaction was overall market conforming.

In this regard, the Court included in paragraphs 81–86 of the judgment a number of *dicta* concerning the evidence that Member States must be able to produce, if they are so requested, in order to benefit from the application of the MEIP. The introduction of these criteria reminds one of the Court's judgment in *Altmark* where, also in Grand Chamber formation, the Court established some procedural criteria concerning the notion of advantage. Indeed, both sets of criteria could be considered in principle as addressed to national judges in order to provide them with a checklist for the application of the State aid rules in two sensitive contexts for Member States: (i) the legitimate provision by Member States of so-called public services in *Altmark*, and (ii) the also legitimate role of Member States as shareholders.

In this regard, the judgment would form part of the trend towards simplification and clarification of the State aid rules that can be observed in the case law of the Court since the 2000s with cases such as *Altmark* or *Preussen Elektra*.

[108] See opinion of AG Darmon in case 248/84 *Germany v Commission* [1987] ECR, 4013 at 4027.

However, in contrast with the situation in *Altmark*, the Court seems to depart in this case from the (flawed) assumption that the Commission will regularly review measures such as the contested one. Indeed, the Court says in paragraph 82 of the judgment that 'if a Member State relies on that test *during the administrative procedure*, it must, where there is doubt…'. Similarly, in paragraph 86 the Court States that '[i]f the Member State concerned provides the Commission with the requisite evidence…'. Therefore, more than addressed to national jurisdictions, the criteria in this case seems to be addressed primarily to the European Commission. However, as stated earlier, there is no reason for a Member State to notify a measure that is not State aid because the MEIP test applies and is passed. Consequently, the *administrative procedure* will not be initiated, save for in the case of a complaint lodged before the Commission or an *ex officio* investigation launched by the latter.

Therefore, the case seems to be also at odds with the tendency towards the clarification of the State aid rules for national jurisdictions and private applicants. Indeed, the judgment conveys a criticism of the Commission's refusal to analyse the applicability of a test so well enshrined in the case law, only because the form adopted to confer the advantage was fiscal legislation.[109] The outcome of this criticism, the Court's judgment in this case, may however affect the enforcement of the State aid rules, not only for the Commission but also for national courts, as the latter will face the argument that a certain tax concession was justified on profit-making grounds, and for those purposes they will have to apply some criteria that seem to be addressed primarily to the Commission. Furthermore, these criteria are also far less clear than that established in the *Altmark* case.

Finally, the judgment is also at odds with the traditional understanding and the objectives pursued by the effects-based formula. As will be reviewed in the next chapter, the formula favouring the assessment of the effects of a public measure over its form or aim for the purposes of the State aid analysis was introduced by the Court to avoid the possibility that the national categorization of a measure as, for example, social or monetary, could trump the competence of the European Commission under the State aid rules. The formula, as applied in this case, risks actually yielding the result that it aimed to avoid because Member States will be able to avoid notification by defining a tax exemption as market conforming. It is therefore suggested that a classic reading of the effects-based formula would not have supported the outcome reached in this case either. It is also submitted that the form in this case—tax legislation—does matter as the case law of the Court has even developed a specific test to deal with selective tax advantages (the derogation test discussed below), the application of which will also be compromised in

[109] The Court of Justice seems in fact to have joined the General Court in its criticism to the Commission when the latter refuses categorically to carry out the Market Economy Investor Principle. See in this regard, among others, the case T-196/04 *Commission v Ryanair* [2008] ECR II-3643, or the more recent Joined Cases T-29/10 and T-33/10 *The Netherlands and ING Groep NV v European Commission* [2012] ECR nyr. See also in this regard Köhler, M., 'New Trends Concerning the Application of the Private Investor Test' (2011) *European State Aid Law Quarterly*, 21.

practice if Member States avoid the notification of tax exemptions where there are some commercial dealings with the alleged aid beneficiary.

6. Conclusion

During the first period of evolution of the State aid policy identified in Chapter 3, the Court did not give any definition of advantage under Article 107(1) TFEU. Indeed, this concept seems to have been encapsulated in the more general concept of aid as no particular discussion related to it appeared in the judgments of the Court during this period. Similarly, the concept of advantage had not been defined either in previous definitions of bounties or subsidies reviewed in the historial part such as the Brussels Sugar Convention under which 'all advantages derived directly or indirectly, by the several categories of producers, from State fiscal legislation' were forbidden, without considering it necessary to define the term advantage.

This concept was first defined in relation to the ECSC Treaty in the *miners' bonus* case. The definition given by the Court in that context is, however, relevant for our purposes as it has been accepted by the Court as applicable to the notion of aid provided under Article 107(1) TFEU.[110] Moreover, the definition of advantage that can be inferred from the *miners' bonus* judgment is also similar to that which can be deduced from the early judgments of the Court in the EEC context, such as *exports rediscount rate* or *Italian textiles*, discussed in the next chapter, both concerned with aid conferred through the mitigation of charges.[111]

This early notion of advantage, including 'not only positive assistance in money or kind but also any measure that relieves an undertaking of a burden it would otherwise have to bear',[112] was originally based on the assumption that any alteration of the production costs of the economic operators active in the ECSC Market, either private or public, was prohibited, as the competence to intervene in that market had been granted to the High Authority. This notion was also economically sound as both positive benefits and the mitigation of charges had a similar effect on the beneficiary (the reduction of production costs), and this was equally relevant for the EEC context. The difference in the latter context was that not any advantage was automatically prohibited but only those that could distort competition and had an effect on trade, both criteria being more meaningful during the first period than they are today for the reasons that will be discussed in Chapter 7.

110 See reply to parliamentary question No. 48 of Mr Burgbacher, OJ C125, 17 August 1963. See also for one of the first explicit references to this definition, the judgment of the Court of 15 March 1994, Case C-387/92, *Banco Exterior de España SA v Ayuntamiento de Valencia*, [1994] ECR p. I-00877 at 13.

111 In fact Advocate General Warner referred to the concept of aid under the ECSC Treaty as applicable in the EEC context. See opinion of AG Warner in case 173/73, ECR 1974 at 723.

112 Ibid.

In a nutshell, the notion of advantage that can be discerned from the *miners' bonus* case and the early cases of aid in the EEC context was very broad: any measure reducing the production costs of the beneficiary undertaking in the Common Market would be considered as advantage. This notion did not require any quantitative analysis; it sufficed that the measure reduced the production costs of undertakings for it to be an advantage. In this regard, the notion of advantage was judged from the undertaking's perspective, that is, whether a particular measure improved the particular situation of a given undertaking. However, as mentioned above, due to the need in the EEC context to distort competition and affect trade, the Commission would restrict the application of this notion to State measures affecting an entire industry, such as the textiles industry, or even many industries, as in the French exports rediscount rate.

The concept of aid was not defined either in the EEC context during this period.[113] The lack of definitions is characteristic of the early jurisprudence of the Court under the EEC Treaty as the Court was originally more focused on institutional than on substantive issues. Indeed, Judge Koopmans referred to the case law of the period comprising the 1950s and 1960s as *institutional*, a term that we have borrowed for our analysis.[114] In the same vein, Gerber has referred to the first period of European integration (from 1958 to 1973 also in his account) as one in which the Court reinforced the prerogatives of the Commission to the detriment of those of Member States,[115] and laid down broad teleological principles that could guide the Commission's future enforcement, two features that appear in the early cases on State aid mentioned earlier (*exports rediscount rate* and *Italian textiles*). Indeed, the Court followed a notion of advantage similar to that laid down in the *miners' bonus* case, a broad and flexible notion that allowed the Commission to subject monetary and fiscal measures (retained fields of Member States under the EEC Treaty) to the State aid rules.

During the second period of evolution of the State aid policy, a new test for the notion of advantage was incorporated, a test that was fully in line with the Commission's priorities during this period, the MEIP. This test was not the result of a new trend in economic thinking, a new form of State intervention in the market, or a new understanding of the notion of aid or that of advantage. Instead, the

[113] In the same vein, for example, the Commission did not suggest a definition of the concept of aid in the 1971 guidelines concerning aids to the textile industry. Commission communication to the Member States on the Community framework on aid to the textile industry (SEC (71) 363 final—July 1971).

[114] Koopmans, T., 'The Role of Law in the Next Stage of European Integration' (1986) *International and Comparative Law Quarterly*, 925 at 926–27: 'The institutions are, in this view, the centrepiece of the European construction. This institutional trend can also be traced in the early case law of the Court of Justice. The things that mattered in the 1950s and the early 1960s were subjects like the autonomy of the High Authority vis-a-vis the Member States, the Community legal system as a legal order in its own right, the priority of this legal order over national law, and the effect of Treaty obligations on the rights of citizens—the line of authority of Van Gend & Loos and Costa/ENEL, in a way'.

[115] Gerber, D., *Law and Competition in Twentieth Century Europe: Protecting Prometheus* (OUP, 1998) at 351–53.

new test was the outcome of the change of focus and priorities of the European Commission, supported this time by the Council,[116] towards the application of the State aid rules in a way that contributed to the restructuring of the public sector and the reduction of the heavy burden that it represented for Member States' budgets.[117]

This test marked also the beginning of a new tendency, namely, the application of the State aid rules to situations that concerned undertakings resident in a single Member State and not, as in the first period, within different Member States. The State aid rules were thus becoming applicable to cases of intra-jurisdictional competition and not, as before, exclusively to cases of inter-jurisdictional competition as the main obstacles to the internal market were removed. Furthermore, the Commission's initiative to apply this test also shows that it was becoming proactive in the State aid field and that these rules were becoming a more integrated part of the competition rules, applicable not only, as in the past, to create the Common Market through the elimination of trade barriers but also to ensure the functioning of that market by eliminating distortions created by public undertakings.

Indeed, the MEIP test was not a 'discovery' of the 1980s. The Commission had outlined this test almost literally in 1963,[118] and even applied it during the early 1970s.[119] What explains the emergence of the MEIP in the case law of the Court

[116] See for another instance of partnership between the Commission and Member States despite the a priori conflicting interests Thatcher, M., 'The Commission and National Governments as Partners: EC Regulatory Expansion in Telecommunications 1979–2000' (2001) *Journal of European Public Policy* 558.

[117] According to the agent of the Commission, a former head of the State aid team at the legal service of the Commission, in one of the first applications of the MEIP before the Court (the *Meura* case) by constraining public undertakings to adjust their behaviour to market rules, and to face competition from private operators on equal footing, the Commission, supported by the case law of the Court, paved the way to the privatization process that took place between the mid-1980s and mid-1990s. See Abate, 'Privatisations et Déréglementations en Droit Communautaire', op. cit. at 247.

[118] Second Report on Competition Policy, op. cit. at point 124: 'In certain cases (establishment by a central government of new undertakings, acquisition of non-precarious holdings in firms already existing or to be set up in association with private interests), the central government normally assumes the role of entrepreneur or venture capital investor. Although the official measure is normally dictated by exigencies going beyond the profit motive, this factor is inherent in the public ownership, the existence and the special nature of which is confirmed by Article 222, and it could not be used alone to justify the bringing into play of the Treaty rules on aids. This is not the case, however, where the central authority, through financial agencies it sets up at its initiative and with its financial support, confines itself to the acquisition in certain firms of holdings which by their special nature (e.g. duration, purpose, terms) show clearly what the aim of the acquisition is to help the firms until such time as they will have overcome temporary difficulties.'

[119] The Commission held in 1963: '*Au cas où la puissance publique renonce, en tout ou en partie, a la rémunération du capital propre d'une entreprise d'État ou de toute autre entreprise publique, un telle renociation pourrait, le cas échéant, être considérée comme une aide d'État. De l'avis de la Commission, ceci pourrait se concevoir dans la mesure ou un propriétaire ou actionnaire privé se trouvant dans une situation comparable et agissant en vertu de considérations d'ordre économique, ne renoncerait pas—ou ne renoncerait que dans un mesure limitée—á la rémunération de son capital propre; autrement dit, la renonciation a laquelle consentirait la puissance publique résulterait en l'occurrence non pas considérations d'ordre économique, mais de motifs d'ordre politique.*' Reply to Parliamentary Question n°48 of Mr Burgbecher, 30 July 1963, OJ 2235/63.

is the Commission's (and Council's) determination to prevent the granting of aid to inefficient undertakings, many of them public. The introduction of the MEIP in fact coincided with another Commission's initiative, the 1980 Transparency Directive, which clarified the dealings between Member States and public undertakings, a necessary step towards the application of the State aid rules to these previously opaque financial relations.

Finally, the Court's support of the new test was also coherent, as in the first period, with other developments taking place in European law at the same time, such as the Court's general support to the Commission during the second period of integration, support that led Judge Koopmans to name the period comprising the 1970s (thus largely overlapping our second period) as *instrumental* to the Community's ends. Similarly, other authors have noted the deferential approach of the Court to legislative measures adopted by the European institutions[120] and to the Commission's position in antitrust cases during this period.[121]

Conversely, during the third period, the main development of the concept of aid was not the result of a Commission's proposal followed by the Court's endorsement. The development, established in the *SFEI* case, consisted in coining a new definition of aid based on an extension of the MEIP test to any transaction involving public authorities or undertakings.[122] This formula was driven by the new actors in the enforcement of the State aid rules, that is private applicants and national courts.

Indeed, after the formal achievement of the internal market and in the context of the liberalization of formerly reserved sectors, private actors started to lodge State aid complaints in a more systematic fashion against incumbents such as La Poste in the *SFEI* case. This case also shows that when dissatisfied with the Commission's inaction on their complaints, the same private actors would also now lodge appeals at the national level under Article 108(3) TFEU (in case of lack of notification of the contested measure), and at the European level against the Commission's failure to act. The *SFEI* case shows in fact that the Commission was no longer able to dictate the pace of State aid policy and to try to shape the concept of aid accordingly. Third parties, former allies of the Commission against the unwilling Member States, turned in some instances into enemies, forcing the Commission to take a position in matters where the Commission did not yet intend to do so.

In this context, the definition of aid coined by the Court in *SFEI* (an extension of the MEIP test) was coherent with the evolution of the State aid rules

[120] For the general support of the Court to Community legislation in the internal market context, see Maduro, M.P. *We the Court, The European Court of Justice and the European Economic Constitution* (Hart Publishing, 1998) at 77.

[121] Gerber, D., *Law and Competition in Twentieth Century Europe: Protecting Prometheus* (OUP, 1998) at 360.

[122] Case C-39/94 *Syndicat français de l'Express international (SFEI) and others v La Poste and others* [1996] ECR p. I-03547 at 60: 'in order to determine whether a State measure constitutes aid, it is necessary to establish whether the recipient undertaking receives an economic advantage which it would not have obtained under normal market conditions'.

discussed in the previous period, an evolution towards an application of these rules in a intra-jurisdictional fashion and in cases involving single undertakings as beneficiaries, and not industries as in the early cases such as French exports rediscount rate, para-fiscal levies, or Italian textiles to be discussed in Chapters 5 and 7. This definition was therefore rather logical in the context of the internal market in the mid-1990s. In fact, the Commission, and even the French State, agreed with it. The delicate issue of the case, and presumably the reason for which the Commission avoided to take a decision in the case for a long time, was that of applying the State aid rules to an undertaking entrusted with a service of general economic interest in a context of partial liberalization, a politically sensitive issue that, it seems, the Commission preferred to leave the Court of Justice to solve. In fact, even the Court left the final analysis to the national court which led to litigation that lasted almost two decades.

Finally, during the fourth period, the concept of advantage has been refined in the context of the compensation for the provision of SGEI. The main authority of this period, the *Altmark* judgment, includes a mix of procedural and substantive criteria to identify whether an advantage has been conferred. The Court of Justice has been the protagonist of the definition of advantage in this last period.

This mix is the result of a balancing exercise made by the Court between the interests of private applicants and national judges to have legal certainty, to whom the Court provided a checklist to evaluate whether a given compensation for the provision of public services should have been notified to the European Commission, the interests of Member States to define and organize their public services, to which the Court allowed a considerable margin of discretion, and the effective application of the State aid rules, that would have warranted—as explained by Advocate General Léger in his opinions to the *Altmark* case—a finding of aid in most cases.

Following the path initiated in the third period with the *SFEI* case, the Commission did not provide significant guidance to the Court, and it even avoided submitting pleadings in some important cases such as *Chronopost* and *Altmark*. This ambivalent attitude coincided with the introduction in the Treaty of Amsterdam of a provision that called for the respect of the role of services of general economic interest in the Community. In this regard, the Commission may have thought that it was for the Court to reconcile the different Treaty articles. After the *Altmark* judgment the Commission regained the policy initiative by adopting a number of measures,[123] which have been subsequently updated.[124]

The other significant novelty regarding the concept of advantage during this period has been concerned with the applicability of the MEIP test to fiscal measures in the *EDF* case. As discussed earlier, this development was not sought by

[123] A decision, a communication, and an amendment to the Transparency Directive adopted in 2005.

[124] For information on the new package the Communication from the Commission on the application of the European Union State aid rules to compensation granted for the provision of services of general economic interest, see text with EEA relevance, OJ C 8, 11 January 2012, p. 4–14.

the European Commission, which strongly opposed it before the Court, and it is in our view inconsistent with the reasons underpinning the introduction of the MEIP test. Indeed, the Grand Chamber of the Court might have been influenced by its recent case law concerning selectivity in the Gibraltar case, and, in particular, by the 'end of formalism' approach followed in that case. The Court may have also been influenced by another Grand Chamber decision, *Altmark*, as it also includes guidance concerning the evidence that Member States have to show in the context of the application of the MEIP test to fiscal measures. However, in our view this case will bring more obscurity than clarity to the dealings between public undertakings and Member States, a reason justifing the introduction of the MEIP test in the 1980s, and should therefore have been resolved in the opposite direction.

Finally, the case law of the Court during this period is also coherent with the evolution of the case law of the Court since the Amsterdam Treaty, an evolution that has been referred to by Judge Everling as balanced,[125] and that we have also referred to in the State aid context as one of balanced instrumentalism. The Court still remains largely supportive of the European Commission yet it is so in a more compromising manner. Indeed, we find in the two judgments reviewed (*Altmark* and *EDF*) an attempt by the Court to balance the application of the State aid rules with other objectives now included in the Treaties, such as the role of public services in the Community after the Amsterdam Treaty and the interests of private applicants and national courts in having legal certainty for the purposes of applying Article 108(3) TFEU at national level. The balanced approach of the Court in the State aid field in the last years has been noted recently, among others,[126] by Judge Von Danwitz with reference precisely to the *Altmark* and *Chronopost* judgments discussed in this chapter.[127]

[125] See Everling, U., 'On the Judge-made Law of the European Community's Courts', in O'Keeffe, D. (ed.), *Judicial Review in European Union Law: Liber Amicorum in Honor of Lord Slynn of Hadley* (Kluwer, 2000) 36 at 39.

[126] Gian Luigi Tosato defines the post-Amsterdam period as a '*riequilibrio della disciplina*' (rebalancing of the discipline) that includes a '*riequilibrio nei rapport tra regole di mercato ed interessi generali*'. (Trans. 'rebalancing the relationship between market rules and general interests'). See Tosato, G.L., 'L'Evoluzione della Disciplina sugli aiuti di Stato', in Schepisi, C. (ed.), *La modernizzazione della disciplina sugli aiuti di Stato: il nuovo approccio della Commissione europea e i recenti sviluppi in materia di public e private enforcement* (Turin: G. Giappichelli, 2011) at 8.

[127] See Von Danwitz, T., 'The Concept of State Aid in Liberalized Sectors', op. cit.

5

The Notion of Selectivity

This chapter is devoted to the selectivity requirement. We will apply the analytical framework described in the previous chapters to the judgments in which for the first time the Court forged a number of formulas related to the notion of selectivity.

1. The *French Exports Rediscount Rate* Case (C-6/69 and 11/69)

A. Introduction and background of the case

The French exports rediscount rate case[1] was one of the first judgments laid down by the Court in relation to the notion of selectivity. The Court supported in this case a broad notion of selectivity that covered a measure open to all undertakings that exported products in France. Indeed, this case is often cited as the first one in which the Court laid down the concept of *de facto* selectivity; that is, a measure *prima facie* open to all undertakings in a Member State yet in fact it only benefits a certain group (even many, but not all) of them. The case is also important because it was one of the first in which the Commission and the Advocate General gave a definition to the notion of selectivity provided for in Article 107(1) TFEU.

The origins of this case go back to 1964 when the Commission asked the French government to abolish a number of measures, including a preferential rate for exports, which it considered amounted to State aid. The French government refused to follow the Commission's advice, arguing, in essence, that rediscount rates formed part of monetary policy, which was not harmonized at Community level, and were not devised to grant aids. The Commission then warned France with opening the procedure of investigation provided by Article 93, to no avail.

After some years, and in view of the arrival of the customs union by July 1968, the French government committed to study the possibility of abolishing the special re-discount rate. Notwithstanding, in June 1968 at the request of France, the Commission authorized the temporary introduction of some measures to counter the difficult financial situation that the French economy was undergoing. Among

[1] Joined Cases C-6/69 and C-11/69 *Commission v France* [1969] ECR 523.

those measures, the Commission authorized the temporary maintenance of a preferential rediscount rate on the export of domestic products. The difference between the preferential rate and the general rate could not exceed more than 1.5 points as from 1 November of the same year and, in any event, had to be abolished on 31 January 1969 at the latest.

However, France maintained a difference of more 1.5 per cent between the preferential and the general rate after 1 November which, together with the entering into force of the customs union in 1968,[2] made the Commission open an infringement proceeding and to bring a lawsuit against France before the Court for failure to fulfil its obligations under the Treaty.

B. The policy context

The long-running dispute that resulted in the judgment under review occurred during the first phase of evolution of the State aid policy. This phase is generally characterized by the elimination of the most prominent obstacles to trade, particularly in goods. State aid rules were not an exception. The initial focus of the Commission was to tackle those measures that were clearly discriminatory.[3] Indeed, the goal of State aid during this first phase was akin to that of the other competition rules; that is, to remove any sort of discrimination between Member States and to allow the Commission to intervene when national aid harmed nationals of other Member States without providing a benefit to the Community as a whole that could outweigh the harm caused.[4]

By the same token, some restrictions to competition and trade were tolerated, provided that they did not entail discrimination. Indeed, as described in Chapter 3, discriminatory measures such as export aid and para-fiscal levies benefitting national industry at the expense of foreign competitors were the main target of competition rules applicable to Member States in the first years of European integration. Nevertheless, although the Commission was committed to voice the advantages of Community action it would hesitate, as in this case, to confront Member States directly until the customs union entered into force.[5]

[2] See as referred by AG Roemer in Joined Cases 6/69 and 11/69 *Commission v France* [1969] ECR from p. 546 at p. 546: 'In view of the establishment of the customs union on 1 July 1968 it appeared to the Commission particularly desirable that the preferential rediscount rates should be abolished by the latest on this date.'

[3] The Commission is referred to in this section as if it had a single voice and yet, internally, the Commission has many voices, often contradictory and opposed, between the different Directorates General and the Legal Service as to the definition and eventual compatibility of a measure with the State aid rules. See in this regard, eg, Blauberger, M., 'Of "Good" and "Bad" Subsidies: European State Aid Control through Soft and Hard Law' (2009) *West European Politics* 719.

[4] See Walsh, A.E., and Paxton, J., *Competition Policy: European and International Trends and Practices* (Macmillan, 1975) 43.

[5] First Report on Competition Policy (Office for Official Publications of the European Communities, 1972) at point 134.

C. The judgment of the Court of Justice

The Court's judgment was cryptic. In essence, the Court, mentioning the duty of loyalty (then) embodied in article 5 EEC, held that the exercise of reserved powers by Member States could not allow for the unilateral adoption of measures prohibited by the Treaty.

In this case, the prohibited measure was the granting of aid, considered in principle incompatible with the Treaty under Article 107(1) TFEU. In this regard, the Court noted that 'under [today's] article [107] the member states have agreed that any aid granted by them in any form whatsoever which distorts or threatens to distort competition is incompatible with the common market.' The Court then found that 'a preferential rediscount rate for exports, granted by a state in favour *only of national products exported and for the purpose of helping them to compete in other member states with products originating in the latter*, constitutes an aid within the meaning of article 92, the observance of which it is the Commission's task to ensure'[6] (emphasis added).

Finally, the Court concluded that '[n]either the fact that the preferential rate in question is applicable to all national products exported and only to them nor the fact that in establishing it the French government may have resolved to approximate the rate to those applied in the other member countries can remove from the measure in question the *character of an aid* which is prohibited except in the cases and procedures provided for by the Treaty'[7] (emphasis added).

D. Assessment

Both the Commission and the Advocate General in this case (Roemer) considered the measure selective by focusing on the undertakings; that is, the measure was selective because only exporting undertakings were favoured to the detriment of those that produced mainly for the domestic market. This broad view of the concept of selectivity was shared by many authors at the time of the judgment.[8] The Court agreed with the outcome sought by the Commission and the Advocate General yet it focused on the products ('aid to national products exported'), not on the undertakings, and gave to the judgment a broader meaning, a teleological one, emphasizing the consequences that the granting of aid could have for the establishment of the internal market.

[6] Joined Cases 6/69 and 11/69 *Commission v France* [1969] ECR 546 at para. 20.

[7] Ibid. at para. 21.

[8] According to these authors 'economic measures which apply equally to all investors in a given country (not within a given area in a country), wherever they invest, are not prohibited by Article 92 (1), since they benefit to all investors and not certain investors.' See Schrans, G., 'National and Regional Aid to Industry under the EEC Treaty' (1973) *Common Market Law Review*, 174 at 176. See also the references cited by Mathijsen, p., *A Guide to European Community Law* (1972) 99; Verloren Van Themaat, P. *Inleiding tot het recht van de Europese Gemeenschappen* (Deventer, 1970) 258; and Megret, J., Waelbroeck, M., Vignes, D., *Le droit de la Communauté Economique Europeen* (Vol. 4, Concurrence, 1972) 381.

In fact, the Court did not deem it necessary to elaborate at any length the finding of selectivity in this case. For the Court the measure was selective because *all national products exported and only they* benefitted from it. No reference to the export undertakings as a separate group within all the undertakings resident in France was deemed necessary. Indeed, the second part of the sentence in which the Court justified the selective character of the measure under review (namely, 'and for the purpose of helping them to compete in other member states with products originating in the latter') might have been mainly related to justify the requirements of distortion of competition and effect on trade given its similarity to the opinion of the AG as to the fulfilment of the requirement of effect on trade in this case.[9]

In any event, the lack of detail concerning the different criteria of the notion of aid shows that the Court appeared interested in sending a strong message of principle: any unilateral measure aimed at affecting the conditions of competition in the internal market would be sanctioned after the achievement of the customs union. This was in fact not far from the original notion of aid under the European Coal and Steel Community (ECSC) Treaty reviewed in the previous chapter because, in that context, any measure affecting the productions costs of undertakings, and thus the conditions of competition, was considered prohibited.

The Court's broad notion of selectivity (but also of advantage, distortion of competition, or effect on trade) can be understood when seen from the perspective of the teleological interpretation that dominated the early case law of the Court. Indeed, according to this interpretation, these provisions of the Treaty had to be read in the light of the other provisions of the Treaty and of the Treaty as a whole.[10] From this perspective, unilateral measures that discriminated between imported and domestic products with the effect of altering the price of the imported products were the main target of the early case law.[11] In this context, the measure under

[9] AG Roemer in Joined Cases 6/69 and 11/69 *Commission v France* [1969] ECR from p. 546 at pp. 552–53: 'Finally, it appears also significant, and this is an ultimate criterion, that export subsidies may "affect trade between Member States". For this the deciding factor is the intention to promote exports and that trade relations would develop differently without this influence. Actual trade figures as given by the French Government are not therefore decisive.' See in this regard a recent judgment of the General Court in which it is considered that the reference to products originating in other Member States was related to the distortion of competition and effect on trade criteria and not to the notion of selectivity: Case T-219/10, *Autogrill España, SA v European Commission* [2014] nyr. At 73–74.

[10] For this approach see the account of one of the first *référendaires* at the Court of Justice Chevallier, R.M., 'Methods and Reasoning of European Court in its Interpretation of Community Law' (1964) *Common Market Law Review*, 21.

[11] For a good example of the early teleological approach, see the Judgment in Case C-2/62 *Commission/Luxembourg and Belgium* [1962] ECR p. 825 at 432: 'In order to see whether a charge has an equivalent effect to a customs duty, it is important to consider this effect in connexion with the objectives of the Treaty, notably in that Part, Title and Chapter containing Articles 9 and 12, that is in relation to the free movement of goods, and still more generally the objectives of Article 3 which are aimed at preventing the distortion of competition…It follows from all these factors that a charge having equivalent effect within the meaning of Articles 9 and 12, whatever it is called and whatever its mode of application, may be regarded as a duty imposed unilaterally either at the time of importation or subsequently, and which, if imposed specifically upon a product imported from

review (the export aid) was also a unilateral measure that discriminated between domestic products and products exported (not imported), altering the price of the latter and thus creating a distortion in the free movement of goods that was going to be felt in other Member States. Indeed, the explicit message of the Court in this case was that the measure amounted to an aid because France purposefully aimed to support (alter the price of) French products exported, hence, to the detriment of the products commercialized in other Member States. In this vein, even before this judgement (in 1965) a former judge of the Court, Nicola Catalano, had held that a rebate given to exports (*a ristourne a l'exportation*) would qualify as State aid because '*en général, toutes facilites discriminatoires consenties dans le but de favoriser des entreprises ou des produits déterminés pourraient avoir un caractère d'aide.*'[12]

The Court thus focused on the purpose ('*le but*') of the measure at stake—'*for the purpose of helping them to compete* in other member states with products originating in the latter' to find out the '*aid character*' of the measure. In other words, the Court found that the measure did comprise aid because its purpose was to distort trade between Member States by favouring domestic products exported over those produced in other Member States. This subjective view of the notion of aid was noted by a contemporary annotation to this judgment.[13] Similarly, one of the judges of the Court in this case, Pescatore, used it as an example of the application of Article 5 of the Treaty, the message of the judgment being that Article 5 enshrined a 'duty of solidarity underlying the obligations of the Member States in the financial sphere indeed in the Community as a whole. This obligation prohibits Member States from taking unilateral measures.'[14]

a Member State to the exclusion of a similar domestic product, has, by altering its price, the same effect upon the free movement of products as a customs duty.'

[12] Catalano, N., *Manuel de droit des communautés européennes* (Paris: Dalloz, 1965) at 495 (trans. 'in general, all discriminatory facilities granted in order to promote businesses or products could have an aid character'). Judge Catalano was also of the opinion that the prohibition of aid would only apply if the free movement of goods was affected: '*Il semble évident que... l'interdiction n'opère que dans la mesure ou la libre circulation des marchandises peut être troublée.*'

[13] See Brinkhorst, L.J., and Verougstraete, I.M., 'Annotation in Joined Cases C-6/69 and C-11/69, *Commission v France*, [1969] ECR 523', (1970) *Common Market Law Review* 483 at 487. 'The Court found simply that the purpose of the preferential discount rate for exports only was to assist French products in their competition on the markets of the member States with national products of the latter. It constituted therefore a state aid, authorization for the retention of which had to be granted by the Commission beforehand. It should be noted that the Court used in this respect a *subjective formula* ("granted... with a view to") thus emphasizing the intent of the measure, *rather than an objective formula, considering its effect*' (emphasis added).

[14] Pescatore, P., *The Law of Integration: Emergence of a New Phenomenon* (A.W. Sijhoff, 1974) at 39–40. In this vein, the bold terms employed by the Court of Justice in this case may have also been influenced by the fact that France for years blatantly ignored the Commission's requests to reduce or eliminate the rediscount rate in question. Indeed, the French attitude was criticized even by some contemporary commentators and businesses in France as a conflict that could have been avoided. Lemaitre, P., 'Un conflit qui aurait pu être évité—Devant la Cour de Luxembourg la Commissione reproche à la France le maintien d'un taux de réescompte favorable à ses exportations' (1969) *Revue du Marché Commun* 57–59: '*l'avantage économique résultant pour l'industrie francaise du maintien d'un loyer de l'argent avantageux pour ses exportations n'est pas suffisant pour mériter de s'opposer de façon si spectaculaire au décisions de Bruxelles.*' (Trans. 'the economic benefit arising for the French industry of maintaining a rent of the money to benefit its exports is not enough to merit opposing so dramatically the Brussels decisions.')

Finally, the subjective formula used by the Court in this case to define aid necessarily contrasts with the formula that the Court has repeatedly emphasized since the *Italian textiles* case in the sense that a State aid measure must be analysed through its '*effects*' rather than through its *aims or causes*,[15] and that the notion of State aid is an objective one.[16] However, placed in their context, both formulas, the subjective and the objective, can be understood better. As to the subjective formula used in this case, because it is precisely targeted at favouring national products over foreign products in the Common Market, export aid was considered prohibited because it was clearly contrary to the main goal of the early years of European integration which was the creation of the Common Market. In this regard, borrowing an expression that AG Lagrange used for the concept of aid under the ECSC Treaty, these kinds of aids were prohibited 'solely from the purpose of the measure'.[17] Export aid has indeed been considered since the early days as particularly pernicious.[18] This not only applies to intra-community but also to international trade.[19]

However, as will be discussed later, the effects-based formula was not meant to exclude any role for the objectives of a State measure under the concept of aid but rather to avoid that the mere national categorization of a measure as social or fiscal

[15] See, eg, C-173/73 *Italy v Commission* [1974] ECR 709 para. 27; C-56/93 *Belgium v Commission* [1996] ECR I-723 para. 79; C-241/94 *France v Commission* [1996] ECR I-4551, para. 20; C-75/97, *Belgium v Commission* [1999] ECR I-3671, para. 25; and C-409/00 *Spain v Commission* [2003] ECR I-10901, para. 46.

[16] C-487/06 P *British Aggregates v Commission* [2008] ECR I-10515 paras 111–14 and 185–86; T-98/00, *Linde AG v Commission* [2002] ECR. II-3961 para. 33, see also Final Decision at 166.

[17] In this regard, AG Lagrange equated subsidies and aids to custom duties 'no one asks whether they are a form of protection or are merely fiscal, there is no common market if there are national customs duties. In the same way there is no real common market in an industry straddling several countries if one of those countries subsidizes its own industry.' Ibid.

[18] Kapteyn, P.J.G., and Verloren van Themaat, P., *Introduction to the Law of the European Communities after the Accession of New Member States* (Sweet & Maxwell, 1973) at 246: 'It is obvious that Article 92 again forms an essential complement of the four freedoms. Thus, abolition of customs duties would produce unacceptable results if the industry where to be faced in its domestic market with competition from foreign undertakings distorted by export subsidies.'

[19] The Commission has underlined the exceptionality of aids to exports *vis-à-vis* domestic subsidies in the context of trade holding that 'Governments have always used financial intervention as an essential tool of economic and social policy. So long as the impact of such interventions is general, they do not distort competition at the national level. Thus measures normally regarded as being in the public interest, for instance to improve a country's infrastructure or its education, health or transport services, do not have a distorting effect. For there to be distortion of competition, the advantages must be conferred selectively; in the case of export subsidies, on goods for export but not goods for the domestic market or, in the case of domestic subsidies, with the aim of helping specific firms.' See 85/233/EEC: Commission Decision of 16 April 1985 terminating the anti-subsidy proceeding concerning imports of soya meal originating in Brazil, OJ L 106, 18/04/1985 P. 0019–0027. Indeed, by 1975 commentators underlined that export aid was prohibited because it clearly affected intra-community trade and the principles of the Common Market after the customs union. These authors underlined that the Commission had a consistent policy against this kind of aid. See Walsh and Paxton, *Competition Policy*, op. cit. at 44: 'it is more especially incompatible with the free movement of goods and services when a member State artificially develops its sales to partner countries while exempting its domestic market from the effects of the aid granted. Such aid cannot benefit from any exception whatever and this applies to any form of aid, including its intensity, its reasons or ultimate objectives.'

would negate completely the Commission's competence. To conclude, after this judgment, and with express reference to it, the Commission initiated proceedings against State measures supporting exports.[20]

2. The *Italian Textiles* Case (C-173/73)

A. Introduction and background of the case

In the *Italian textiles* case,[21] the Court laid down a number of fundamental formulas that are relevant for the notion of selectivity, namely that (i) Article 92 EEC (107 TFEU) does not distinguish between measures of state intervention concerned by reference to their causes or their aims but defines them in relation to their effects; (ii) a *prima facie* selective advantage may be justified by the nature or general system in which it is included; and that (iii) an aid to an entire sector has to be considered as selective.

The origins of this case go back to 1969, when the Italian government notified to the European Commission a draft law on the restructuring, reorganization, and conversion of the textile industry. The Commission considered that some provisions of that draft legislation infringed the State aid rules and asked Italy to abolish them. Italy formally complied with the Commission's request. However, the legislation finally published by the Italian government included a provision, Article 20, which had not previously been submitted to the Commission. This provision, which became the object of the decision adopted by the Commission, provided for a reduction in the social charges concerning family allowances (from 15 per cent to 10 per cent) to the textile and garment-making industry and small crafts for a period of three years. The Commission decision was challenged by Italy before the Court only after the Council refused, as Italy had formally requested, to declare the measure compatible under Article 93(2) paragraph three.

B. The policy context

This case was initiated at the end of the first period of evolution of the State aid policy identified in Chapter 3 and decided at the beginning of the second period, in 1974. The first period, when the Commission decision was adopted, was characterized, as discussed earlier, by the Commission's focus on the elimination of barriers to trade and discrimination between undertakings in different Member States in a context of Member States' reluctance to comply with the State aid provisions included in the Treaty, which led to a very weak enforcement regime that continued until the late 1970s.

[20] The first of them started in 1970 against Italy concerning a preferential rate for the financing of medium-term credits for intra-Community trade. See Fourth General Report on the Activities of the Communities (European Commission, 1971) 33 at point 37.

[21] C-173/73, *Italy v Commission* [1974] ECR 709.

With regard, in particular, to the textiles sector, between the notification of the draft law at issue in this case (1969) and the entering into force of the contested measure in 1971, the Commission published its first guidelines on State aids for the textile industry.[22] The main reason behind these guidelines was the crisis of the European textile industry, with low demand growth, few technical improvements, and increasing competition from outside the Community. This crisis had exacerbated the risk of a subsidy race among the Community Member States and the Commission attempted to reduce this risk by introducing some principles that Member States should follow.[23]

Indeed, the textiles industry was one of the few sectors on which the Commission focused in the early years of European integration in the field of State aids. Pursuant to these guidelines, aids could only be justified if they were suitable to improve the structure of the textile industry. By contrast, the guidelines underlined that State aids to the textile industry could not lead to capacity increases.[24] Aid could also not directly affect price formation, which was considered likely to affect trade and competition in an appreciable way. Consequently, all aid to production and operation was forbidden.[25]

The Commission noted, in fact, that the contested provision contravened the principles laid down by these guidelines which, interestingly, did not define the notion of aid or its criteria; they just referred to 'aids'.[26] It is therefore not difficult to speculate about why the Commission investigated and adopted a decision in this case: it was a case pertaining to one of the most problematic sectors at the time, the Commission had adopted guidelines on aid to this sector that had been ignored, and the Italian government had even concealed the aid measure from the notification of the relevant legislation.

[22] Commission communication to the Member States on the Community framework on aid to the textile industry (SEC(71) 363 final—July 1971).

[23] Ehlermann, C.D., 'State Aids under European Community Competition Law' (1994) *Fordham International Law Journal*, 408 at 416: 'The origin of this initiative was the crisis caused by slow adjustment to technological change, slow growth of domestic demand, and cheap imports from developing countries. The approach followed resembled the one adopted regarding regional aid schemes: coordination with Member States to avoid escalation of aid from countries seeking to protect their own industries, leading to "beggar thy neighbour" spirals.'

[24] See in this regard, eg, Commission Decision of 8 March 1989, on the French Government's aid proposal in favour of Caulliez Frères, cotton yarn producer located in Prouvy, France (89/456/EEC): 'In the 1971 guidelines the Commission points out that aids in the textile and clothing sector, which is marked by a very high degree of competition at Community level, involve a risk of causing distortion of competition which is unacceptable to competitors who do not benefit from such measures. Aids, which generally have very marked repercussions in this sector of industry, may under these guidelines be justified if they improve the structure of the textile industry. Such aids must be understood, according to the guidelines, to refer to aids to textile undertakings intended, inter alia, to facilitate the elimination of surplus capacity in the branches or sub-branches where it exists and to encourage the conversion of marginal activities to activities other than those of the textile sector. Aids of this nature must, however, meet certain conditions specified in the Guidelines of 1971, in particular they must not load to increases in capacity.'

[25] First Report on Competition Policy, op. cit. at point 172.

[26] Commission Decision of 25 July 1973 on Art. 20 of Italian Law No. 1101 of 1 December 1971 on the restructuring, reorganization, and conversion of the textile industry, Official Journal L 254, 11/09/1973 P. 0014–0015.

C. The judgment of the Court of Justice

This judgment contains important clarifications concerning all the criteria of today's Article 107(1) TFEU. We will concentrate on the effects-based formula, relevant to all the criteria of the notion of aid, and to the paragraphs more specifically related to the notion of selectivity.

The Court, and incidentally the same Court that nine days later would deliver the famously broad Dassonville formula on the notion of measure having an equivalent effect to a quantitative restriction,[27] considered it necessary to adopt an equally broad formula for the notion of aid, namely that 'Article 92 does not distinguish between the measures of State intervention concerned by reference to their causes or aims but defines them in relation to their effects. Consequently, the alleged fiscal nature or social aim of the measure in issue cannot suffice to shield it from the application of Article 92.'[28] The effect of this formula, as in the internal market context, was to bring within the scope of the Treaty many State measures independently of their categorization at the national level.

Subsequently, the Court analysed the main argument put forward by Italy that the charges concerning family allowances entailed a disadvantage for the textile sector that was corrected by the introduction of the contested measure. The Court refused this argument, which had been partially admitted by the European Commission, holding that 'the partial reduction of social charges pertaining to family allowances devolving upon employers in the textile sector is a measure intended partially to exempt undertakings of a particular industrial sector from the financial charges arising from the normal application of the general social security system'.[29]

Finally, the Court added to the foregoing paragraph *in fine* the famous sentence '*without there being any justification for this exemption on the basis of the nature or general scheme of this system*'[30] (emphasis added).

D. Assessment

This judgment is mostly cited for two reasons: (i) for the emphasis on the effects of a measure, as opposed to its form, for the State aid analysis, and (ii) for the possibility of justifying a measure by the general system of which it forms part. The analysis of the policy context casts more light on these two formulas.

As to the first formula, its breadth may be understood against the background of the Court's case law during the 1970s, particularly during the first half of this decade, a period in which the Court laid down broad principles that help achieve objectives set by the European Commission. Indeed, a judge of the Court described this period as instrumental 'where the law serves to promote the Community's end',[31] a phrase that we will borrow for our analysis. In the

[27] Case 8/74 *Danssonville* [1974] ECR 837.

[28] Case 173/73 *Italy v Commission* [1974] ECR 709 at 13.

[29] Ibid. at 15.

[30] Ibid.

[31] Koopmans, T. 'The Role of Law in the Next Stage of European Integration' (1986) *International and Comparative Law Quarterly* 925 at 927.

same vein, Judge Everling and others[32] have noted that during this period the Court laid down broad principles that could in the future be narrowed down. As in this case, the principles laid down by the Court during this period reinforced the prerogatives of the Commission to the detriment of those of Member States and guided the Commission's future enforcement.[33] In the case under review, this principle allowed the Commission to review a measure pertaining to the social field, a field that was the competence of Member States. The Court could in fact have referred to its previous case law regarding fiscal (*parafiscal levies* case C-47/69) or monetary measures (*French exports* C-6&11/69) which made clear that Member States could not invoke 'retained powers' to circumvent the State aid rules. The Court could have even declared the appeal inadmissible for the deliberate omission of the contested provision by Italy in the notified instrument or, as a contemporary author to the case phrased it, for the '*manquement délibéré a l'ocasion de la procedure de l'information*.'[34] Instead, as in other occasions in these formative years, the Court decided to declare the case admissible and to make a clear statement on the importance of the State aid rules and their pre-eminence *vis-à-vis* retained powers in light of the general spirit of the time. In other words, the Court made clear that Member States could not evade the State aid rules simply by referring to a social, fiscal, or monetary goal or regulation.[35]

The Court did not say, though, that the social goals pursued by the measure were completely irrelevant for the analysis of the concept of aid. Instead, the Court simply found that the contested measure was not justified by the alleged aim put forward by Italy, as the family allowances system in Italy did not provide for a disadvantage to the textiles undertakings that had to be corrected through the measure under review. Indeed, as summarized in a contemporary annotation to this case, the Court just concluded that the measure under review amounted to an exception to the social system and was granted to support certain undertakings. Therefore, the measure was not truly social.[36]

This brings us to the second famous formula, the justification of the *prima facie* selective measure by the general system applicable in Italy. It is clear from

[32] See Everling, U., 'The Court of Justice as a Decision Making Authority', in *Michigan Law Review*; Stein, E. (ed.), *The Art of Governance: Festschrift in Honor of Eric Stein* (Nomos Verlagsgesellschaft, 1987) 156 at 162–63 at referred by Maduro, M.P., in Maduro, M.P., *We the Court, The European Court of Justice and the European Economic Constitution* (Hart Publishing, 1998) at 26.

[33] Gerber, D.J., *Law and Competition in Twentieth Century Europe: Protecting Prometheus* (OUP, 1998) at 351–53: 'The Court frequently enunciated broad principles and values rather than limiting itself to ruling on the facts of individual cases. It looked to the future and aimed at guiding the Commission in its development of competition policy.'

[34] Trans. 'deliberate breach of the information procedure'. Ibid.

[35] For a similar understanding of this formula, see Bacon, K., 'State Aids and General Measures', EUI Thesis at 91–92.

[36] See Krsjak, P., 'Annotation Case C-173/73' (1975) *Gazette du Palais*, 481. See in this regard, eg, '*la Cour conclut que ce dégrevement partiel des charges sociales est une mesure d'exception arrêtée au profit des enterprises et non une charge sociale telle que l'avance le Gouvernement italien*' at 482 (trans. 'the Court concluded that partial reduction of social charges is an exceptional measure adopted for the benefit of businesses and not a social charge as held by the Italian Government').

the arguments submitted before the Court that this test was fully created by the Court: neither the Commission nor the Advocate General had made any specific reference to it. However, it is submitted that the Court did not attempt to create the test that is used to limit the selectivity criterion in the field of social or fiscal measures today. Instead, the Court was just reacting to the specific argument put forward by Italy: that the measure was intended to restore a special handicap of the social system specifically affecting the textile sector within the Italian industry.

The Italian government had in fact argued that if the national legislature had been aware of the specific situation of the textile industry at the time of adopting the first legislation on family allowances, it would have provided for this reduction earlier.[37] What the Court did was study whether the measure was in fact restoring fair conditions of competition and making up for a specific disadvantage or not (thus to study the real purpose of the measure). The Court concluded that the measure at stake was an aid because it made an exemption to a general system that, contrary to what Italy had claimed, did not entail any disadvantage for the textile industry when compared with others (so there was no justification for a compensation).

Other elements support the conclusion that the Court was not creating a specific test of selectivity for social measures or, more generally, for aids granted through general legislation (eg, tax legislation). For instance, the Commission did not make any reference to this exception in its comment to the case included in the Fourth Report on Competition Policy,[38] nor did it made any reference to this exception two years later when referring to this case in another Report on Competition Policy. Similarly, no reference to the justification test was made in a contemporary annotation of this case, even though there was a reference to the exceptional character of the measure under review was (but not to the fact that the exception could not be justified).[39] In fact, even three years later, in 1977, there was no trace of the limitation concerning the nature or general scheme in the Commission's words concerning the derogation test: 'The Commission's view, confirmed by the judgment of the Court of Justice in Case 173/73, has always been that exoneration from a compulsory general charge imposed by the State, whether or not of a fiscal nature, constitutes an aid within the meaning of Article 92 et seq. of the EEC Treaty.'[40] Similarly, it even seems that the case was not considered particularly innovative at the time when it was delivered as no article or annotation was written about it in any of the main European law journals.[41] More importantly, the Court and its Advocate Generals took twenty

[37] However, also in this case the measure would have been selective if limited to the textile industry, but not if the general system would have distinguished between male and female contributions to the family allowances.

[38] See Fourth Report on competition policy (Office for Official Publications of the European Communities, 1975) at points 156 and 157.

[39] See Krsjak, 'Annotation Case C-173/73' (1975), op. cit. 481 at 482.

[40] See Fourth Report on competition policy (Office for Official Publications of the European Communities, 1977) at point 252.

[41] See, eg, in this regard, the Court's '*Notes aux arrêts de la Cour de justice*', where two commentaries, in an Italian and a French review, both two-pages long, are mentioned in relation to this case.

years to refer to this justification again, in 1993, at a time when the Court limited the Commission's powers in a number of fields, including State aids.[42] Finally, to this author's knowledge, the Court only repeated the formula laid down in case C-173/73 as a justification of a *prima facie* selective measure in the *Maribel* bis/ter case (1999) after the Commission had published the Notice on the application of the State aid rules to measures relating to direct business taxation (the 'Notice')[43] in 1998 which included that justification (with reference to the Italian textiles case) as one of its main novelties.[44]

In fact, the original ambiguity of case C-173/73, where it is not clear whether Italy was referring to the selectivity or the advantage criteria in its pleading is reflected in the Commission's Notice on direct business taxation and State aids. In this regard, according to the Notice, an advantage accrues when the measure at stake mitigates the charges normally borne by the recipient, unless the relief is justified 'by the nature or general scheme of the system', and the Notice quotes for this the *Italian textiles* case.[45] However, in order to identify whether a tax measure is selective the Notice also mentions the justification by the nature or general scheme of the system test, and reference is made again to the same part of this judgment.[46]

To conclude, this judgment shows that the Court was willing to go beyond the Commission's submissions at this time of the European integration process. In this regard, the Commission had admitted in its pleading that the family allowances system entailed a disadvantage for the Italian textiles sector.[47] However, the Court rejected that finding in its judgment, as discussed. Similarly, the Commission had also admitted that the situation in other Member States could be taken into consideration to assess whether the Italian system conferred an advantage. In fact, even the Spaak Report suggested that a comparison with the situation prevailing

[42] Joined Cases C-72/91 and C-73/91*Sloman Neptun* [1993] ECR I-887, para. 21. For the lack of intermediate references see, eg, C-159/01, Netherlands/Commission [2004] ECR I-4461 at para. 42. Even in the *Sloman* case the Court made no explicit reference to the justification by the nature or general system.

[43] OJ C 384, 10 December 1998.

[44] Case C-75/97 *Belgium v Commission* [1999] ECR I-3671, para. 32.

[45] Case 173/73 *Italy v Commission* [1974] ECR 709 at 15: 'it must be concluded that the partial reduction of social charges pertaining to family allowances devolving upon employers in the textile sector is a measure intended partially to exempt undertakings of a particular industrial sector from the financial charges arising from the normal application of the general social security system, *without there being any justification for this exemption on the basis of the nature or general scheme of this system*' (emphasis added).

[46] See Notice, footnote 8. This problematic overlap has been criticized; see, eg, Rossi-Maccanico, P. 'State Aid Review of Business Tax Measures Proposals for State Aid Control of Direct Business Tax Measures' (2007) *European State Aid Law Quarterly*, 215 at 218: 'pursuant to the fiscal aid Notice specificity may only be justified by the inherent logic of the tax system and the Member State has to provide proof of it. As a result, fiscal specificity has become unreasonably narrow, to the point where it overlaps with the notion of tax advantage or derogation.'

[47] The Commission's argument in this regard was that other sectors were also at a disadvantage because of the employment of women preponderantly yet the contested measure only concerned the textile sector and for this reason it was selective.

in other Member States could be relevant for the advantage analysis.[48] However, the Court also rejected that finding.[49] In this regard, as AG Warner had held, the availability of such a defence (the existence of similar advantages in other Member States) could make the enforcement of the State aid provisions a 'dead letter'.[50]

3. The *France v Commission (FNE)* Case (C-241/94)

A. Introduction and background of the case

This case has been chosen as it adds to the previous case law a definition of selectivity—'a measure is selective if it entails advantages accruing exclusively to certain undertakings or certain sectors'—and it broadens this notion by holding that a measure open to all undertakings in a given Member State should be considered selective if the administration enjoyed discretion as to the granting of it.

Regarding the background of the case, in 1993, Kimberly Clark Sopalin (Kimberly Clark), a company established in France, decided to lay off 207 of its 465 employees. Pursuant to French social legislation, Kimberly Clark had to draw up and implement a 'social plan' whose purpose was mainly to avoid or reduce redundancies, and to facilitate the re-employment of some of the employees that had to be laid off. Kimberly Clark adopted a social plan which the French State partially financed through the Fonds National de L'Emploi (FNE).

On June 1994, after receiving a complaint from a competitor of Kimberly Clark, the Commission adopted a decision classifying as State aid the financial participation of the State in the 'social plan' approved by Kimberly Clark. The main reason underlying the Commission's decision was that the discretional character of the FNE intervention made the financial compensation selective. In the Commission's words 'FNE may on a purely discretionary basis decide whether it wishes to contribute to the social plan and what the amount of its contribution will be.'[51] France challenged this decision before the Court of Justice.

[48] See the Spaak Report, Report of the Heads of Delegation to the Ministers of Foreign Affairs, of 21 April 1956, 62, French version : '*Il apparait cependant qu'une industrie apparemment désavantagée cesse de l'être si la même surcharge relative existe dans même industrie des autres pays. Au contraire, ce désavantage se maintient si cette surcharge n'existe pas ailleurs, et s'accroit si la même industrie est relativement déchargée dans l'autre pays considère.*'

[49] In fact, the Court had already refused a similar argument in the past: see Joined Cases C-6/69 and 11/69, *Commission v France*, [1969] ECR 523 at para. 21.

[50] See the opinion of Advocate General Warner in case 173/73 *Italy v Commission* [1974] ECR 709 at 727. For a similar finding of the Court during the 1970s, this time concerning the notion of distortion of competition, see Case C-78/76 *Steinike & Weinlig v Federal Republic of Germany* [1977] ECR 595 at para. 24: 'Any breach by a Member State of an obligation under the Treaty in connexion with the prohibition laid down in Article 92 cannot be justified by the fact that other Member States are also failing to fulfil this obligation. The effects of more than one distortion of competition on trade between Member States do not cancel one another out but accumulate and the damaging consequences to the common market are increased.'

[51] Twenty-fourth Report on Competition Policy, op. cit. at 518, Annex II.

B. The policy context

This case pertains to the third phase of evolution of the State aid policy. The period between the beginning of the Commission's procedure concerning this case (1994) and the Court's judgment (1996) was highly relevant for the development of the State aid policy. After decades of scant enforcement due to the lack of notifications by Member States, the Commission was finally able to deploy its Treaty powers in the field of State aids. Indeed, the context was ripe for this development given the general confidence and support that the 1992 project had garnered. In fact, the stricter approach to State aids was only part of a wider programme, namely, the '*public turn*' of competition policy since, as the Commission noted in 1990, 'at the present stage of economic integration in the Community the barriers are greatest in markets currently subject to State regulation.'[52] The turn also included the application of then little-used Article 90 EC or the application of the competition rules to State action supporting anticompetitive conduct.[53]

Indeed, the idea that State aid policy had to help preserve competitive markets, particularly after the elimination of most barriers to trade in 1992, seems to have been quite apparent inside the Commission's directorate for competition during this time. Similarly, and in line with a conception of the State aid rules as being further integrated with the general competition policy, competitors started to have an increasingly important role in the development of the State aid policy. Indeed, by bringing complaints they have drawn the Commission's attention to non-notified State aid, which has allowed the Commission to adopt decisions in this field even in the absence of notifications by Member States. In this fashion they have reinforced the Commission's role as a neutral arbiter between States particularly.[54] For these reasons competitors have often being allies of the European Commission. In this regard, for example, the Commission was alerted to the aid to Kimberly Clark in this case by one of that company's competitors.

C. The Court's judgment

The Court's judgment was very succinct. The judgment first stated, in accordance with the *Italian textiles* case, that Article 92(1) does not distinguish between measures of State intervention by reference to their causes or aims but defines them in relation to their effects in order , as in that case, to make clear that only because the contested measure had a social character it could not be excluded *a limine* from the scope of Article 92 of the Treaty.

Once this preliminary (jurisdictional) point was made, the Court entered into the analysis of the particular characteristics of the measure at stake. The measure

[52] Twentieth Report on Competition Policy, op. cit. at point 53.

[53] Gerber, D.J. 'The Transformation of European Community Competition Law?' (1994) *Harvard International Law Journal* 137.

[54] Smith, M.P., 'Autonomy by the Rules: The European Commission and the Development of State Aid Policy' (1998) *Journal of Common Market Studies* at 63.

was indeed not limited 'sectorially or territorially or by reference to a restricted category of undertakings'.[55] However, by virtue of the degree of discretion enjoyed by the French authorities, the Court found that the contested system was 'liable to place certain undertakings in a more favourable situation than others and thus to meet the conditions for classification as aid within the meaning of Article 92(1) of the Treaty.'[56]

D. Assessment

The selectivity test in the two instances previously reviewed, the *French exports rediscount rate* and the *Italian textiles* cases, was developed in a context of damage to intra-community trade and to out-of-State traders: the preferential rediscount rate favoured French products (and producers) at the expense of products/producers from other Member States.[57] Similarly, sectorial aid given to the Italian textile industry clearly damaged the textile industry of other Member States (while favouring that of Italy).

However, the aid given to Kimberley Clark in this case was not necessarily or primarily against the interests of out-of-State undertakings. Instead, it may well be that the competitor that lodged the complaint against Kimberly Clark was a French company or a foreign company established in France. Indeed, the rationale of prohibiting the aid to Kimberley Clark was simply that France could 'place certain undertakings in a more favourable situation than others' under its jurisdiction.

This judgment reveals a transformation of the role of State aid that we have also witnessed in the previous chapter in relation to the notion of advantage: a trend towards the application of the State aid rules incresingly in a context of intra-jurisdictional competition and thus not necessarily in a context of inter-jurisdictional competition as was the case previously. This evolution had also been experienced in the internal market context where increasingly since the 1980s many measures and regulations were 'challenged in the Court by nationals of the State in question, not other EU nationals or importers.'[58]

Similarly, the judgment reveals that the role of the prohibition of aid is no longer exclusively to help establish the internal market, which to a large extent had already been established after 1993, but to ensure the proper functioning of that market. In this regard, the notion of selectivity in this case encapsulates

[55] Case C-241/94 *France v Commission* [1996] ECR I-4551, para. 24. [56] Ibid.

[57] See in this regard the original conception included in the First Report on Competition Policy, op. cit. at point 133: 'State aid generally means a conflict of interests between the recipient economic agents and their competitors in other Member States who find themselves placed in a less favourable position on the Community markets than that which they would have held in the absence of such aid.'

[58] See supra Maduro, *We the Court*, op. cit. at 63 where he cites the following cases as examples of this trend: Case 286/81, *Oosthoek's* [1982] ECR 4575; Case 126/82, *Smit* [1983] ECR 73; Case 237/82 *Jongeneel Kaas* [1984] ECR 483; Joined Cases 80 and 159/85 *Edah* [1986] ECR 3359; and Case C-241/89 *SARPP* [1990] ECR I-4695.

an obligation on the State to set up objective and non-discriminatory criteria to intervene in the market financially, even with regard to a public authority acting for social reasons, for otherwise the State intervention would be considered State aid. This notion of selectivity brings about a sort of due process obligation for the State to treat undertakings fairly. In this regard, after this judgment several Advocate Generals started to underline the relation between the principle of no discrimination and equal treatment and the requirement of selectivity in the field of State aids.[59] Moreover, the evolving role of the selectivity criterion developed in parallel to that experienced by the advantage one with the Market Economy Investor Principle. Both tests looked at the situation in a given Member State and both referred to the principle of no discrimination, that is, the MEIP to the prohibition of discrimination between public and private undertakings, and the selectivity criterion to the prohibition of discrimination between all businesses under the same Member State.

In this regard, the relationship between the notion of discrimination and the selectivity requirement can be traced back to the first survey on State aids in the European Community, published by the Commission in 1988. In that survey, after announcing that the Commission would apply stricter criteria in the State aid field in view of the evolution of the internal market project and in the advent of its completion in 1992,[60] the Commission made clear that State aids were not only prohibited in the interests of out-of-State competitors but also in the interests of those undertakings that ultimately subsidized the aid at stake at the national level directly or indirectly.[61] It is also in this survey, originally only accessible to Member States, where the Commission gave an economic explanation of the selectivity requirement based on the alleged more harmful effects of selective measures compared to general ones because the latter's distorting effects are 'diluted across the whole spectrum of economic activity'.[62] After this survey, and

[59] See, eg, AG Cosmas in C-353/95P *Tiercé Ladbroke v Commission* [1997] ECR I-7007, para. 30, AG Stick-Hackl in C-66/02 *Italy v Commission* [2005] ECR I-109010, p. 75, or AG La Pergola in C-75/97 *Belgium v Commission ('Maribel')* [1999] ECR I-3671, p. 8.

[60] SEC(88) 1981, 13 December 1988 at p. 2: 'In fact, as the integration process progresses, the distortions of competition caused by state aids are felt more acutely by competitors not receiving aids. Therefore, the Commission will apply stricter criteria in its aid disciplines, otherwise the positive benefits that should be fostered by this market Integration will not be fully realised.'

[61] Ibid. at p. 7: 'The Commission has always considered that aids have a direct and immediate impact on competition because by the definition of their specificity they are targeted at certain objectives often in a selective and discriminatory way. In order to favour the aided enterprise, taxes must be levied on the rest of the economy. Thus not only are enterprises in other Member States put at a competitive disadvantage by the aid because the aided enterprises are favoured in a way outside the normal fiscal or social security systems that contribute to the equilibrium between Member States, but also enterprises not receiving aid in the same Member State are disadvantaged and pay higher taxes directly or indirectly.'

[62] SEC(88) 1981, 13 December 1988 at pp. 6–7: 'The Treaty's relatively strict approach towards aids and the Commission's policy in this field has been based on the economic view that aids have a more direct and Immediate Impact on the conditions of competition between Member States than general measures. By concentrating state resources on certain enterprises or sectors, and by giving them benefits which are in addition to the normal system applied in a Member State, the favoured enterprises or sectors are for the reasons explained below put at a clear advantage not only vis-à-vis competitors In the same Member States, but also vis-à-vis competitors In other Member

before the judgment under review, the Commission had already held that a State measure could be selective by reason of the discretion enjoyed by the authorities in its application equating the term 'selection' with that of 'discrimination'.[63]

Finally, the adoption of a discrimination-like language for the notion of selectivity may have also conformed with the goal of making the State aid rules more accessible to private applicants that were by this time an important ally of the European Commission in bringing these rules closer to the other competition rules, as Gerber has noted.[64] In this regard, in the year of adoption of the Commission decision in this case, the assistant to the Director General of DG Competition claimed that the State aid rules were closer to the competition than to the internal market rules in that they aimed at preventing distortions of competition between competitors rather than between Member States.[65] Similarly, the Director General of DG Competition himself held in the same year that the

states. This prima facie distortive effect of aids must be contrasted with measures applied generally and in a non-discriminatory way across the whole economy. However, this is not to say that general measures may not distort competition. If they do, they fall under Articles 101/2. Nevertheless, it is widely held that the direct effect of most general measures is likely to be diluted across the whole spectrum of economic activity, be compensated or counteracted by other general measures, or be neutralised to a large extent by exchange rate changes. The rationale for the distinction between aids and general measures in the Treaty, and the greater willingness to tolerate the latter, is furthermore based on a recognition to-date by the Commission that it is not the aim of competition policy to try to remove fundamental differences between Member States' cost structures which contribute to the wider economic and social framework within which firms operate in each Member State. Indeed, to do so would undermine the basis for mutually beneficial trade. Where there are differences in the role of the state in the economy and the provisions of public goods, there will also be differences in the overall level of taxation. Even in countries where the general burden of taxation is similar, for historical and political reasons there may be significant differences in the structure of the taxation system.'

[63] See Twenty-third Report on Competition Policy (Office for Official Publications of the European Communities, 1994) at 246, point 390. As the Commission phrased it: 'For a scheme that subsidizes firms for particular activities to fall within Article 92(1), it must "favour", i.e. particularly benefit, certain firms or industries. In other words, there must be an element of *selection or discrimination* in relation to the beneficiaries. This favoured group needs not be specified in the rules of the scheme or be readily identifiable. It is sufficient that the scheme could benefit certain firms particularly, though these are not identifiable in advance, and this is especially so if the authorities applying it have a degree of discretion in selecting beneficiaries or setting the level of subsidy' (emphasis added). On this basis, the Commission had considered as State aid a number of job-creation schemes adopted by Denmark and had also asked Member States to inform in their notifications of new whether the aid was given discretionarily. Ibid. at points 441–42. See also Annex II in which the Commission includes a notification form for new aids where Member States had to explain, 'For each aid instrument, a precise description of its rules and conditions of application should be given, including in particular its intensity, its tax treatment and whether the aid is granted automatically once certain objective criteria are fulfilled or whether there is an element of discretion for the competent authorities.'

[64] See Gerber, *Law and Competition in Twentieth Century Europe: Protecting Prometheus*, op. cit. at 364 where he notes that during the period from mid 1980s to mid 1990s the State aid rules became integrated in the general competition policy.

[65] Gyselen, L, 'The emerging interface between competition policy and environmental policy in the EC' (OUP, 1998) at 245. According to him, the legality standard that the Commission had to observe in both the internal market and the competition fields had to start with the following question: 'Is there a distortion of competition between national economies (Article 30 [then applies]) or between individual competitors (Article 85 and 92 [then apply])?'

control of aid was no longer exclusively in the interest of Member States but perhaps even more so in the interest of the competitors of the intended beneficiaries of the aid.[66]

4. The *Maribel bis/ter* Case (C-75/97)

A. Introduction and background of the case

This case is known for being the first in which the Court stated that a measure applicable to a high number of undertakings or even sectors can still be selective.[67] The importance of this case is, however, not limited to the adoption of this formula. It initiated the analytical framework that has led to the current standard test for selectivity, namely, that a measure is selective if it is 'such as to "favour certain undertakings or the production of certain goods" in comparison with other undertakings which are in a legal and factual situation that is comparable in the light of the objective pursued by the measure in question'.[68]

As to the background of this case, the measure under review consisted in a reduction of social charges introduced by Belgium to some sectors that were particularly exposed to international competition. The measure at stake benefitted certain sectors of the Belgian economy explicitly listed by legislation. Hence, the sectorial selectivity of the contested measure was quite obvious. Two companies referred the case to the Commission: one of them claimed that support for the sectors most exposed to international competition was incompatible with the State aid rules. The other claimed that this support was discriminatory (against undertakings in Belgium not benefitting from the aid) and demanded to be afforded equal treatment. The discrimination-like test proposed by the Commission in the late 1980s and early 1990s proved indeed to be attractive for competitors yet, at odds with the State aid discipline, some of them demanded that aid also be given to them to end the discrimination.

B. The policy context

Several authors consider that State aid policy reached a turning point and entered a new phase by the mid-1990s, the time of the entering into force of the contested

[66] Ehlermann, C.D., 'State Aid Control in the European Union: Success or Failure?' (1994) *Fordham International Law Journal* at 1219

[67] Case C-75/97 *Belgium v Commission* ('Maribel') [1999] ECR I-3671, para. 32.

[68] This second formula was in fact coined in a subsequent case, *Adria–Wien*, yet the Court referred in that case to the Maribel judgment for the relevant test See, eg, C-143/99 *Adria–Wien Pipeline and Wietersdorfer & Peggauer Zementwerke* [2001] ECR I-8365, para. 41; subsequently repeated in many judgments, including Grand Chamber judgments, eg, Case C-409/00 *Spain v Commission* [2003] ECR I-1487, para. 47; Case C-88/03 *Portugal v Commission* (Azores) [2006] ECR I-7115, para. 54; C-172/03 *Heiser* [2005] ECR I-1627, para. 40; and Joined Cases C-428/06 to C-434/06 *UGT–Rioja and Others* [2008] ECR I-06747, para. 46.

national law in this case. The new phase would start with the joint initiative of the Commission and the Irish presidency on future prospects of State aid control of 14 November 1996, the adoption of the procedural regulations, the Council's Code of Conduct for direct business taxation, and the adoption by the Commission of its important notice on the application of the state aid rules to measures relating to direct business taxation on 11 November 1998. The main aims of the new period have been to refocus priorities, increase transparency and legal certainty, and to clarify the procedural rules in the field of State aids.[69] The most significant policy initiative has been the use of the State aid rules to combat harmful business taxation.[70]

Furthermore, as discussed in the previous case, with the advent of the completion of the internal market the Commission was willing to apply the State aid rules more strictly than before. The Commission did in fact review many social measures, such as employment aid, introduced by Member States to counter the difficult economic situation affecting many European economies during the early 1990s. In this regard, although the Commission stated that it positively valued the adoption of measures to foster employment, it also made clear that it would not allow those measures to be granted in a discriminatory way.[71] In this context, the Commission received a complaint concerning the social measures introduced by Belgium with the reform of the Maribel scheme.

C. Judgment of the Court of Justice

The Court of Justice coincided with the Commission in that the measure was selective because it was restricted to certain sectors of the Belgian economy. In this regard, the Court noted that 'Neither the high number of benefitting undertakings nor the diversity and importance of the industrial sectors to which those undertakings belong warrant the conclusion that the Maribel bis/ter scheme constitutes a general measure of economic policy, as the Belgian Government claims.'[72]

However, the Court did not stop the analysis at that point. Instead, the Court analysed whether the exclusion of some sectors from the application of the measure was compatible with its alleged objective (promotion of employment of manual workers). In this regard, the Court noted that the objectives of the measure at stake were compatible with the general social system in force in Belgium. The

[69] See Mederer, W., 'The Future of State Aid Control' (1996) *Competition Policy Newsletter* 12, and Lavdas, K.A., and Mendrinou, M.M., *Politics, Subsidies, and Competition: The New Politics of State Intervention in the European Union* (Edward Elgar, 1999) at 44. See also Doleys, T., 'Fifty Years of Moulding Article 87: The European Commission and the Development of EU State Aid Law & Policy (1958–2008)', Paper prepared for presentation at the 11th Biennial International Conference of the European Union Studies Association in Marina Del Ray, California, 23–25 April 2009 at 22.

[70] Commission notice 98/C 384/03 in Official Journal C 384 of 10 December 1998, 3.

[71] See, eg, Twenty-third Report on Competition Policy, op. cit. at points 439–42.

[72] C-75/97 *Belgium v Commission* ('Maribel') [1999] ECR I-3671, para. 32.

Court also noted that Member States retained important powers in the field of social security systems and that they could, through the redistribution of social charges, pursue, among others, the objectives advanced by the Belgian authorities, namely, the maintenance of a high level of employment amongst manual workers and the maintenance of an industrial sector in order to balance the Belgian economy. However, the achievement of those objectives did not justify reducing the scope of application of the measure at stake to the undertakings chosen by the measure, which excluded some industrial sectors where manual labour rates were high (therefore sectors in an objectively similar position in the sense of the argument put forward by Belgium) and included other non-industrial sectors such as horticulture and forestry in which manual labour rates were low.[73]

D. Assessment

The most cited formula stemming from this judgment—the one concerning the potentially selective character of a measure applying to many undertakings and sectors—can be explained by reference to the criteria for general measures laid down by the Commission since the late 1980s, and particularly in the early 1990s. According to these criteria Article [107] of the Treaty does not apply to general measures applicable to all undertakings of a Member State where those measures meet objective, non-discriminatory, and non-discretionary requirements.[74]

The Belgian government submitted that the Maribel bis/ter scheme was a general measure under that definition and that 'by 'all undertakings' it had to be understood those which were in an objectively similar position',[75] and not 'all undertakings' in a given Member State, the reason for this probably being that otherwise it would be very difficult to adopt social, fiscal, or economic policy measures, as they hardly apply simultaneously to all undertakings in a given Member State. In this regard, the Belgian government noted that even the Commission had conceded in a Communication on the monitoring of State aid and reduction of labour costs that measures favouring certain categories of workers, therefore benefitting only those undertakings employing those categories of workers, did not constitute State aid if they applied automatically and 'without discrimination.'[76] In fact, the Commission had explicitly referred to 'companies which are in the same objective position' in a 1996 decision: 'To differentiate between State aid and general measures the Treaty provides the Commission only with the criterion of specificity, aid being defined in Article 92 of the Treaty as measures "favouring certain

[73] In fact the Commission had shown in the decision that the only 47 per cent of manual workers were employed in the sectors benefitting from the measure whereas 53 per cent of them were working in sectors excluded from the measure. See Commission decision of 4 December 1996 concerning aid granted by Belgium under the *Maribel bis/ter* scheme (97/239/EC) OJ L 95/25.

[74] See Twenty-fourth Report on Competition Policy (Office for Official Publications of the European Communities, 1995) at 347.

[75] C-75/97 *Belgium v Commission* ('Maribel') [1999] ECR I-3671, para. 17.

[76] Communication 97/C 1/05 on the monitoring of State aid and reduction of labour costs (OJ 1997 C 1, p. 10).

undertakings or the production of certain goods"'. A comparison should therefore be made, within one and the same Member State, between the treatment of companies benefitting from the measure in question and the general system applied to *companies which are in the same objective position.*[77]

The Court accepted this interpretation of the concept of 'all undertakings' by analysing whether the undertakings employing manual workers, thus those in a comparable situation or 'in an objectively similar position' benefitted from the contested measure.[78] The Court, after finding that some of the sectors excluded from the contested measures (as the tertiary or the building sector) were in a comparable situation to those sectors benefitting from the contested measures, concluded that the measure was *prima facie* selective. It is in this context that the Court held 'that neither the high number of benefitting undertakings nor the diversity and importance of the industrial sectors to which those undertakings belong warrant the conclusion that the Maribel bis/ter scheme constitutes a general measure of economic policy'. In other words, the Maribel bis/ter scheme could not be a general measure, even if it applied to many undertakings in many sectors, because it discriminated between undertakings that were in a comparable situation as defined by the objective of the measure (the fostering of employment of manual workers).

Once this *prima facie* selectivity was established, the Court analysed whether the contested scheme could be justified by the nature or general scheme of the Belgian social security system. In this regard, the Commission emphasized in its pleadings that the 'justification for the measures to reduce the burden of social security costs adopted under the Maribel bis/ter scheme should be sought in the internal logic of the general social welfare system existing in Belgium and not in the specific purpose of the scheme.'[79] The Commission's position was in fact consistent with the test that it had included in its notice on direct business taxation and State aid, published while this case was pending.[80] The Court, however, while admitting that the measure could only be justified by the general social security system applicable in Belgium (and not by the Maribel scheme), took into account the objectives pursued by the general social security system, rather than its internal logic, as requested by the Commission. Furthermore, the Court noted that the objectives of the general social security system were very close to the objectives

[77] See Commission Decision of 13 March 1996 concerning fiscal aid given to German airlines in the form of a depreciation facility (96/369/EC).

[78] Advocate General La Pergola had held in point 8 of its opinion to this case that 'it is obviously necessary to take account of the persons to whom the measures are addressed and to analyze whether the Maribel bis/ter scheme is directed at a category of undertaking [those employing manual workers] considered in its entirety without introducing exemptions from any general scheme which would otherwise apply to those undertakings.'

[79] C-75/97 *Belgium v Commission* ('Maribel') [1999] ECR I-3671, para. 18.

[80] Commission Notice on the application of the State aid rules to measures relating to direct business taxation, OJ C 384, 10/12/1998 p. 0003–0009 at point 26: 'A distinction must be made between, on the one hand, the external objectives assigned to a particular tax scheme (in particular, social or regional objectives) and, on the other, the objectives which are inherent in the tax system itself. The whole purpose of the tax system is to collect revenue to finance State expenditure....'

pursued by the contested scheme,[81] and that Member States retained the power to organize their social security systems and to promote objectives of employment policy, such as those pursued by both the Maribel bis/ter scheme and the general social security system applicable in Belgium.[82] Nevertheless, the Court concluded that those objectives could not justify the selective character of the advantage under review.[83]

In light of all this, the Court supported the Commission in this important case concerning a social measure applicable to many undertakings and sectors. The Court also implicitly supported the selectivity test contained in the notice on direct business taxation and State aids published while this judgment was pending by following the derogation justification analysis proposed in that notice. However, the victory for the Commission in this case was a Pyrrhic one. The Court also introduced some important qualifications to the discrimination-like test for selectivity defended by the Commission since the early 1990s by concluding that the concept 'all undertakings' referred to those in a comparable position by reference to the objective pursued by the measure, and not to all undertakings in a given Member State, as the Commission had traditionally claimed. In the words used by a former senior Commission official, 'According to the Commission the term of comparison or the benchmark [for the selectivity test] is the treatment of all enterprises or the production of all goods in the Member State applying the measure.'[84] Contrary to the Commission's submissions, also included in the notice on direct business taxation and State aids, the judgment seems to take into consideration the social objectives pursued by the contested measure at the level of the justification of the measure by the general system and not, or at least not only, the internal logic of the general social welfare system.

Therefore, the judgment appears to us as a balanced one between the application of the State aid rules and the social objectives pursued by the measure under review. In this regard, one can only speculate if, for these reasons, the Commission did not include the substantive test for selectivity carried out by the Court in this case in its account of the judgment included in the 1999 competition report. Instead, the Commission only referred in the competition report to the formula that has become the best known of this judgment: that '[n]either the high number of benefitting undertakings nor the diversity and importance of the industrial sectors to which those undertakings belong warrant the conclusion that the Maribel bis/ter scheme constitutes a general measure of economic policy'.[85]

[81] C-75/97 *Belgium v Commission* ('Maribel') [1999] ECR I-3671, para. 36: 'It is true that an increased reduction of social security contributions, concerning only a limited category of employers owing to their belonging to certain industrial sectors, thus relieving them of certain social security charges, does not at first sight appear to derogate from the nature and scheme of the general system of social protection.'

[82] Ibid. at para. 37.

[83] Ibid. at 38–39.

[84] Bourgeois, J.H.J., 'State Aids, Taxation Measures and Specificity. Some Thoughts', in Dony, M., and De Walsche, A., *Mélanges en hommage à Michel Waelbroeck*, Vol 2 (Bruylant, 1999) at 767.

[85] Twenty-ninth Report on Competition Policy (Office for Official Publications of the European Communities, 2000) at point 241.

5. The *Adria–Wien* Case (C-143/99)

A. Introduction and background

This judgment is usually referred to as the one in which the Court laid down the current formula for selectivity.[86] As discussed above, the Court did coin that formula for the first time in this case although it did so building on the analysis carried out by the Court in the *Maribel bis/ter* judgement and with reference to it.

The Court's judgment was a preliminary ruling requested by the Austrian Constitutional Court which submitted two questions concerning energy taxes on the consumption of electricity and natural gas. In particular, Austria adopted, under tax reforms within the framework of the Strukturanpassungsgesetz (Structural Adjustment Law) of 1996, three laws; namely, a law on the tax on electricity, a law on the tax on natural gas, and a law on the rebate of energy taxes. The first two laws imposed taxes on the supply and consumption of electricity and natural gas. The third, in contrast, provided for a rebate of the energy taxes levied on supplies of natural gas and electricity; those taxes had to be reimbursed, on application, inasmuch as they exceeded 0.35 per cent of net production value. The laws at stake had not been notified to the European Commission under today's Article 108(3) TFEU.

The proceedings that led to the preliminary reference were initiated by several undertakings active in the services sector, such as Adria–Wien Pipeline GmbH, whose principal activity was the construction and operation of oil pipelines. This company had been refused a tax rebate on energy tax because their main activity was not primarily related to the manufacture of goods. The main question before the Court was thus whether a tax rebate granted only to undertakings whose activity is shown to consist primarily in the manufacture of goods was to be considered as selective under then Article 87(1) EC (today 107(1) TFEU). Finally, the case was also interesting as it concerned the first preliminary ruling ever requested by a Constitutional Court, opening a path that has been followed by other constitutional courts in recent years.[87]

[86] 'such as to "favour certain undertakings or the production of certain goods" in comparison with other undertakings which are in a legal and factual situation that is comparable in the light of the objective pursued by the measure in question' See, eg, C-143/99 *Adria–Wien Pipeline and Wietersdorfer & Peggauer Zementwerke* [2001] ECR I-8365, para. 41; subsequently repeated in many judgments, including Grand Chamber judgments, eg, C-409/00 *Spain v Commission* [2003] ECR I-1487, para. 47; Case C-88/03, *Portugal v Commission* (Azores) [2006] ECR I-7115, para. 54; C-172/03 *Heiser* [2005] ECR I-1627, para. 40; and Joined Cases C-428/06 to C-434/06 *UGT–Rioja and Others* [2008] ECR I-6747, para. 46.

[87] See the Opinion of Advocate General Kokott in Case C-169/08 *Presidente del Consiglio die Ministri v Regione autonoma della Sardegna*, [2009] ECR 2009 I-10821, footnote 13.

B. The policy context

This case was decided during the fourth period of evolution of the State aid policy discussed in Chapter 3. Reference is made to the context described in *Maribel bis/ter* as that case was also decided during the fourth period, characterized by a number of initiatives purporting to make State aid control more efficient and transparent, more focus on a number of so-called horizontal goals, such as research and development or environmental protection, towards which State aid should be channelled, and it also focused on the systematic application of the State aid rules to harmful taxation measures.

C. The judgment of the Court of Justice

The Court of Justice dealt first with the second question that had been referred by the Austrian Constitutional Court, namely, whether a tax rebate such as that included in the contested measure open to all undertakings in the national territory regardless of their activity could be qualified as aid. The answer of the Court was, quite logically, negative: 'As is apparent from the terms of Article [107(1)] of the Treaty, an economic benefit granted by a Member State constitutes State aid only if, by displaying a degree of selectivity, it is such as to favour "certain undertakings or the production of certain goods". A State measure which benefits all undertakings in national territory, without distinction, cannot therefore constitute State aid.'[88]

The Court then moved to the first question, that is, whether a tax rebate open to the whole primary and secondary sectors (manufacturing sector), can be considered as 'displaying a degree of selectivity', sufficient to make the measure fall within the purview of Article 107(1) EC. In this regard, after noting that the supply of energy on preferential terms to manufacturing undertakings could amount to State aid based on previous case law, the Court stated that '[t]he only question to be determined is whether, under a particular statutory scheme, a State measure is such as to favour "certain undertakings or the production of certain goods" within the meaning of Article 92(1) of the Treaty in comparison with other undertakings which are in a legal and factual situation that is comparable in the light of the objective pursued by the measure in question.'[89] The Court finally held, based on the *Italian textiles* and the *Maribel bis/ter* case law, that a *prima facie* selective measure could still be justified by the nature or general scheme of the system of which it is part.

Applying these principles, the Court found the Austrian scheme selective. Indeed, the Court stated that the advantage (in the form of the tax rebate) granted to undertakings whose activity consisted primarily in the production of goods was not justified 'by the nature or general scheme' of the taxation system at stake, the

[88] C-143/99 *Adria–Wien Pipeline* [2001] ECR I-8365 at paras 34–35.
[89] Ibid. at para. 41.

Strukturanpassungsgesetz of 1996. The main argument supporting this conclusion was that 'undertakings supplying services may, just like undertakings manufacturing goods, be major consumers of energy and incur energy taxes above 0.35% of their net production value—the threshold above which undertakings manufacturing principally goods are eligible for the energy tax rebate.'[90] Similarly, the Court held that 'the ecological considerations underlying the national legislation at issue do not justify treating the consumption of natural gas or electricity by undertakings supplying services differently than the consumption of such energy by undertakings manufacturing goods. Energy consumption by each of those sectors is equally damaging to the environment.'[91]

D. Assessment

This case can be seen as a translation into the fiscal field of the *Maribel bis/ter* test, which had been developed in the social field. There is however a feature that makes the *Adria* judgment more difficult to interpret: that the Court considered the energy taxation system introduced by Austria as the relevant framework for the purposes of the analysis of the selectivity criterion, including the justification by the nature or general system. The rebate had therefore to be analysed against the 'internal logic' of the Strukturanpassungsgesetz (Structural Adjustment Law) of which it formed part.

The contested measure in this case (the rebate) reduced the burden for energy taxation of some companies, those incurring energy taxes above 0.35 per cent of their net production value. However, it seems that the Court, following the *Maribel bis/ter* logic, did not consider the measure selective for that reason but rather because not all undertakings meeting that requirement (to pay taxes above 0.35 per cent of their net production value) could benefit from the reduction. Finally, as in *Maribel*, the Court looked for the possibility of justifying the measure under the general system which, in this case, was the energy taxation itself. The Court found that the rebate could not be justified by the ecological considerations underlying that system introduced by the Strukturanpassungsgesetz (Structural Adjustment Law) and therefore held that the measure was selective.

The transposition of the *Maribel* judgment into the fiscal domain may have not been the desired outcome of this case for the European Commission, especially because the Court had given in that case considerable weight to the social goals pursued by the *Maribel bis/ter* scheme under the justification analysis by the nature or general social security system.[92] Against this background, the Commission was

[90] Ibid. at para. 50. [91] Ibid. at para. 52.

[92] In fact the Court had almost equated the goals pursued by both the contested measure and the Belgian general social security system and had even pointed to the case law recognizing the retained powers of Member States to organize their social security systems. See Case C-75/97 *Belgium v Commission* ('*Maribel*')[1999] ECR I-3671, para. 37: 'as Community law stands at present, the Member States retain their powers to organise their social security systems (Case C-238/94 *Garcia and Others* [1996] ECR 1-1673, para. 15). They may therefore pursue objectives of employment policy, such as those relied on by the Kingdom of Belgium, amongst which are, in particular, the

defending at this time a restrictive justification test for fiscal measures: derogatory fiscal measures could only be justified if they were necessary for the smooth functioning of the fiscal system, that is, for its internal logic.[93]

Indeed, neither from the opinion of the Advocate General nor from the Court's judgment does it appear that the Commission cited the test laid down by the Court in the *Maribel bis/ter* case. Indeed, just as in the 1999 report,[94] the only part of that case that the Commission seems to have raised is the formula concerning the potential selective character of a measure, even if the latter is open to many undertakings and sectors.[95] The foregoing would be corroborated by the fact that the Commission did consider the measure under review, even if open to all sectors, selective and not justified by the general system in a subsequent decision.[96] Indeed, following this judgment, 'Austria broadened the measure to include undertakings from all sectors. In its assessment of the amended scheme, however, the Commission found that the measure was still selective, because even if formally speaking the rebate was open to all undertakings, in practice the only undertakings that would benefit would be those with a high energy consumption in relation to their net production value'.[97] In this regard, the Commission concluded that the measure was not consistent with the internal logic of the tax and even represented a clear deviation from the overall structure and functioning of the tax system as 'any exemption from an energy tax for energy-intensive users, which by definition are also polluters, cannot be in the nature and logic of the system.'[98] The Court would support this Commission's view in a subsequent judgment (*Transalpine*).[99]

maintenance of a high level of employment amongst manual workers and the maintenance of an industrial sector in order to balance the Belgian economy…'.

[93] As the Commission had held in a decision of 1996, 'In terms of taxation the Commission takes the view that measures derogating from the general rule do not qualify as State aid where they are economically justified in respect of the efficiency of the system. This is usually reflected in the fact that such measures are not applied solely to specific sectors, are based on objective and horizontal criteria or conditions, and are not limited in time.' Later in the same decision the Commission held that the measures were not justified because '[t]hey are not based on objective criteria and seem to be in no way indispensable to the smooth functioning of the German tax system.' See Commission Decision of 13 March 1996 concerning fiscal aid given to German airlines in the form of a depreciation facility (96/369/EC).

[94] Twenty-ninth Report on Competition Policy (Office for Official Publications of the European Communities, 2000) at point 241.

[95] The Commission seems in fact to have referred in that case to the C-6/97 *Italy v Commission* [1999] ECR I-2981 in support of the selectivity of the measure, and to the formula from the *Maribel bis/ter* case. See, eg, the Opinion of Advocate General Mischo in case C-143/99 *Adria–Wien Pipeline* [2001] ECR I-8365 at paras 35 and 47.

[96] Commission Decision of 9 March 2004 on an aid scheme implemented by Austria for a refund from the energy taxes on natural gas and electricity in 2002 and 2003, OJ L 190, 22 July 2005, p. 13.

[97] See Commission Decision of 8 March 2011 on State aid measure C 24/09 (ex N 446/08)—State aid for energy-intensive businesses under the Green Electricity Act in Austria (notified under document C(2011) 1363) OJ L 235, 10 September 2011, pp. 42–62 at para. 96.

[98] Commission Decision of 9 March 2004 on an aid scheme implemented by Austria for a refund from the energy taxes on natural gas and electricity in 2002 and 2003, OJ L 190, 22 July 2005, p. 13 at para. 53.

[99] C-368/04 *Transalpine Ölleitung in Österreich* [2006] ECR I-I-09957.

Therefore, in this judgment, as in the *Maribel bis/ter* case, the Court limited the notion of 'all undertakings' for the purposes of the selectivity test to those in a comparable position by reference to the objective pursued by the contested measure, in this case an environmental one. This case, however, shows that the practical effect of such limitation might be very restricted as in the end, even when the contested measure was open to all sectors the Court considered it selective.[100] In this regard, it is submitted that the breadth of the notion of selectivity developed by the Court is justified because, in the end, the objectives pursued by a given measure (environmental or any other) should not allow that measure to escape the concept of aid as these are national objectives and the Court has held since the *Philip Morris* case that national objectives cannot make an aid compatible with the Treaty. Consequently, they should not be able, either, to avoid the qualification of a measure as State aid. The following cases points to this interpretation.

6. The *Azores* Case (C-88/03)

A. Introduction and background

This case is known for being the first in which the Court of Justice accepted that the reference framework for assessing the existence of selectivity does not need to be national. That framework can be, according to the Court, regional or otherwise infra-national if some conditions are met. The case is also noted here as the first in which the Court of Justice clarified that only the intrinsic (technical) principles of a fiscal system, and not the extrinsic objectives that such system pursues, can justify a *prima facie* selective measure.[101]

As to the background to this case, it started with a request for information sent by the Commission to the Portuguese authorities after the former had learnt from the media that the Portuguese government had adopted a scheme adapting the national tax system to the specific characteristics of the Autonomous Region of the Azores.[102] After receiving explanations from the Portuguese authorities concerning the newly adopted scheme, the European Commission opened a State aid investigation. In the framework of this investigation, the Portuguese government, supported by the Regional Government of the Åland Islands, held that the Azores region was an autonomous region which enjoyed administrative and financial autonomy recognized by the Portuguese Constitution. Therefore, insofar as the measures under review were approved by the Azores region under its own powers, the tax reductions at stake ought to be seen as a general measure of tax policy and not as a selective measure.

[100] Ibid. [101] Case 88/03, *Portugal v Commission*, [2006] I-07115 at para. 81.

[102] See Commission Decision of 11 December 2002 on the part of the scheme adapting the national tax system to the specific characteristics of the Autonomous Region of the Azores which concerns reductions in the rates of income and corporation tax, OJ 18 June 2003 L 150/52.

The Commission, however, concluded that measures adopted by regional authorities could amount to State aid if the criteria of Article 107(1) TFEU were met, as it was the case since the tax measures under review entailed reduced rates of income and corporation tax for natural and legal persons established in the Azores. The Commission also added that this conclusion was in line with the classic understanding of the concept of aid as an objective one, based on the effects of the measure and not on its form. Therefore, to allow for a distinction based on the body that adopts the measure at stake would remove the effectiveness from Article 107(1). The Portuguese government appealed this decision to the Court of Justice.

B. The policy context

This case was initiated by the Commission in January 2000. It therefore corresponds to the fourth period identified in Chapter 3. Reference is thus made to the policy context described in the two previous cases, also delivered during this period. One only needs reminding at this point that the main aims of the new period have been to refocus priorities, increase transparency and legal certainty, and to clarify the procedural rules in the field of State aids.[103] The clarification was partly due to the number of cases that the Commission currently reviews, significantly higher than in previous periods. Finally, the most significant policy initiative has been the use of the State aid rules to combat harmful business taxation[104] and, since the mid-2000s, the reorientation of the State aid rules towards the achievement of a number of Community goals usually referred to as Lisbon Agenda goals, pursuant to the Commission's State Aid Action Plan (SAAP).[105]

C. The judgment of the Court of Justice

The Court, in Grand Chamber formation, cited the *Adria–Wien* formula as the relevant test for selectivity.[106] The Court then went on to affirm that the reference framework for the application of this assessment did not need to 'be defined within the limits of the Member State concerned, so that a measure conferring an advantage in only one part of the national territory is not selective on that ground alone for the purposes of Article 87(1) EC.'[107]

The Court laid down the circumstances under which a measure adopted by a infra-national body could escape the concept of aid: 'in order that a decision taken in such circumstances [a decision adopted by a regional or local authority

[103] See Mederer, 'The Future of State Aid Control', op. cit., and Lavdas, K.A., and Mendrinou, *Politics, Subsidies, and Competition*, op. cit. at 44. See also Doleys, 'Fifty Years of Moulding Article 87', op. cit. at 22.

[104] Commission notice 98/C 384/03 in Official Journal C 384 of 10/12/1998 p. 3.

[105] COM (2005) 107 final of 7 July 2005; State Aid Action Plan. Less and Better Targeted State Aid: A Roadmap for State Aid Reform 2005–2009 (Consultation document); SEC(2005) 795.

[106] Case 88/03 *Portugal v Commission* [2006] I-07115 at para. 54.

[107] Ibid. at para. 57.

in the exercise of sufficiently autonomous powers in relation to the central power approving a tax rate lower than the national rate and which is applicable only to undertakings present in the territory within its competence] can be regarded as having been adopted in the exercise of sufficiently autonomous powers, that decision must, first of all, have been taken by a regional or local authority which has, from a constitutional point of view, a political and administrative status separate from that of the central government. Next, it must have been adopted without the central government being able to directly intervene as regards its content. Finally, the financial consequences of a reduction of the national tax rate for undertakings in the region must not be offset by aid or subsidies from other regions or central government.'

Applying this test the Court found, in essence, that the Azores region failed to be economically autonomous and therefore that the reference framework for the assessment of the measures under review had to be national. Analysed under that context the contested measures were selective.

Finally, the Court adopted the second formula mentioned in the introduction to this judgment, that '[a] measure which creates an exception to the application of the general tax system may be justified by the nature and overall structure of the tax system if the Member State concerned can show that that measure results directly from the basic or guiding principles of its tax system. In that connection, a distinction must be made between, on the one hand, the objectives attributed to a particular tax scheme which are extrinsic to it and, on the other, the mechanisms inherent in the tax system itself which are necessary for the achievement of such objectives.'[108] Applying this formula, the Court concluded that the regional development or social cohesion policy objectives allegedly pursued by the contested scheme were not sufficient to justify it under the general scheme of the Portuguese tax system, based, *inter alia*, in the principle of the ability to pay of the different categories of tax payers.

D. Assessment

This case is representative of a clash between two dynamics that have been taking place in the EU since the 1990s, namely, the increasing enforcement of the State aid rules and the equally increasing recognition of the constitutional identity of Member States as a potential limit to the application of European Union law.

As to the first dynamic, it is submitted that the stricter enforcement of the State aid rules that have taken place since the mid-1980s and particularly during the 1990s has led to the adoption of the second formula discussed above. In essence, the Commission has, in the way towards the completion of the internal market but also afterwards, attained the support of Member States in the enforcement of the State aid rules. This has allowed the Commission to review more cases following notifications and to see its proposals for procedural regulations adopted.

[108] Ibid. at para. 81.

In addition, in the particular application of the State aid rules to direct business taxation, the Commission received the support of the Economic and Financial Affairs Council (ECOFIN) and the Code of Conduct concerning harmful taxation. A product of this dynamic is thus the final recognition by the Court that only technical or intrinsic principles or objectives are available for the justification by the nature or general scheme test. This conclusion, already included in the Commission notice on the application of State aid to business direct taxation,[109] and proposed even before in a 1996 Commission decision,[110] seems to have been resisted to some extent by the Court in cases such as *Maribel* and *Adria–Wien* as already discussed, and makes the scope of the justification test very limited in practice. With this finding, the Court, in Grand Chamber formation, thus bestowed a strong support to the Commission's policy concerning harmful business taxation. In this regard, as it has been argued in the assessment to the previous case, we believe that the Court's approach is justified also in line with the traditional case law on the compatibility of State aid since the *Philip Morris* judgment, according to which only community and not national objectives can be accepted to declare a State aid measure compatible under Article 107 TFEU.

As to the second dynamic, since the adoption of the Maastricht Treaty there is an increasing recognition of the constitutional identity of Member States as a potential limit to the application of EU Law. The Maastricht Treaty stipulated in Article 6(3) that '[t]he Union shall respect the national Identities of its Member States.' That Treaty also introduced the principle of subsidiarity and the recognition of the role of regions in the process of European integration. Examples of the latter were the introduction of the Committee of the Regions and the possibility for a Member State to be represented by a member of a regional government in the Council. After the Maastricht Treaty, and before the judgment under review, the (unratified) Treaty establishing a Constitution for Europe, which included a provision ensuring the respect for national constitutional identities,[111] had been signed by all Member States in 2004, and also in that year the Court had allowed in the *Omega* judgment a national court to protect human dignity as recognized by the German Constitution in detriment of a strict interpretation of the free movement rules.[112]

This second dynamic, it is submitted, led to the adoption of the first formula laid down by the Court in this judgment, that is, the possibility of infra-national reference frameworks for the analysis of selectivity. The formula

[109] Commission Notice on the application of the State aid rules to measures relating to direct business taxation (OJ 1998 C 384, p. 3).

[110] See Commission Decision of 13 March 1996 concerning fiscal aid given to German airlines in the form of a depreciation facility (96/369/EC).

[111] Article I-5: The Union shall respect the equality of Member States before the Constitution as well as their national identities, inherent in their fundamental structures, political and constitutional, inclusive of regional and local self-government. It shall respect their essential State functions, including ensuring the territorial integrity of the State, maintaining law and order and safeguarding national security.

[112] C-36/02 *Omega* [2004] ECR I-9609.

is also balanced because the division of powers enshrined in the Constitution of a given Member State will not be enough to qualify a measure as general and not selective. The economic situation of the region granting the aid will also be considered to avoid the granting of aids by regions that cannot bear the financial consequences of that granting. In fact, in the case under review, the Azores region was institutionally (constitutionally) and even procedurally autonomous yet it was not economically self-sufficient. The solution chosen by the Court is, however, more deferential to national identity than to the orthodox application of the State aid rules.[113]

The tendency towards the respect of the national constitutional identity has been strengthened after the entry into force of the Lisbon Treaty which provides, under Article 4(2) TEU that '[t]he Union shall respect the equality of Member States before the Treaties as well as their national identities, inherent in their fundamental structures, political and constitutional, inclusive of regional and local self-government…Indeed, even before the entry into force of the Lisbon Treaty some Advocate Generals had referred to this provision,[114] one of them in a State aid case UGT–Rioja.[115] In this latter case, which concerned the alleged general character of a number of measures adopted by the infra-national authorities of the Basque region in Spain, the Court followed the approach laid down in the *Azores* case. The decision of the Court in the *UGT–Rioja* case, which was a preliminary ruling, was followed by national proceedings that have ultimately found the measures adopted by the infra-national authorities as non-selective in the sense of the *Azores* jurisprudence.[116] Importantly, the Judge-Rapporteur of the *Azores* and *UGT–Rioja* cases, Judge Rosas, has referred to the EU Court's judgments as an example of the increasing recognition of the role of regions and of the national constitutional identity of Member States.[117]

[113] In fact, it has been cited as an instance of observance by the Court of Justice of a particular constitutional arrangement in order to justify an exception or distinction in the application of EU Law which otherwise would not have applied. See Besselink, L.F.M., 'National and Constitutional Identity Before and After Lisbon' (2010) *Utrecht Law Review* 36.

[114] See opinion of Advocate General Poiares Maduro in case C-213/07 *Michaniki* [2008] I-09999 at para. 31.

[115] See opinion of Advocate General Kokott in Joined Cases C-428/06 to 434/06 *UGT–Rioja* [2008] I-06747 at para. 54.

[116] See *inter alia* the Spanish Supreme Court judgment of April 3 2012 (Rec. 1336/2010).

[117] See Rosas, A., and Armati, L., *EU Constitutional Law: An Introduction* (Hart, 2012) at 108: 'the status autonomous regions enjoy under the national constitution may affect the way in which Union Law will apply to them. The clearest example of such an effect concerns state aid law, where the ECJ has departed somewhat from the traditional Union/Member State dichotomy, looking beyond this distinction to the actual power of regional bodies to determine the applicable legal and economic framework for action'. Judge Rosas refers in this regard to Article 4 (TEU) of the Lisbon Treaty (also included in the unratified Constitutional Treaty) and the *Azores* (C-88/03, *Portugal v Commission (Azores)* [2006] ECR I-7115) and *UGT–Rioja* (C-428/06 to C-434/06 *UGT–Rioja and Others* [2008] ECR I-06747) judgments. I would like to thank Judge Rosas for kindly agreeing to meet me at the Court of Justice and for his very useful comments regarding my Ph.D. thesis on which this book is based.

7. The *British Aggregates* Case (C-487/06P)

A. Introduction and background

This case is referred to as the first in which the Court of Justice found that 'Article 87(1) EC defines State interventions on the basis of their effects, *and thus independently of the techniques used by the Member States to implement their interventions*'[118] (emphasis added). This addition, it is submitted, has heralded a new line of cases in which the Court challenges the national characterization of a fiscal system as general by holding that the measure is in fact selective despite the appearance of its being general given by the regulatory technique that has been used to put it into effect.

The origin of this case lies back in September 2001 when a complaint was lodged before the European Commission concerning a levy, the AGL, on aggregates adopted by the United Kingdom. Aggregates are materials used for construction. They can be divided, for the purposes of our work, into *virgin aggregates*, which are those extracted from nature, and *recycled aggregates*, which are those that have been used at least once. The AGL affected only virgin aggregates. The aim of the levy was to discourage the use of virgin aggregates (consequently encouraging the use of recycled ones) for environmental reasons. The United Kingdom notified the AGL to the Commission,[119] which concluded, without opening the formal investigation procedure, that the AGL was not State aid because its *prima facie* selective character was justified by the logic and nature of the tax system, save for an exception for Northern Ireland, that was nevertheless declared compatible.[120]

The Commission decision was challenged before the then Court of First Instance by the British Aggregates Association (BAA). The CFI dismissed the action and fully confirmed the Commission's decision, in essence holding[121] that the Commission had rightly concluded that AGL was not selective even if it did not apply to activities similar to those which were taxed under it and which had a comparable impact on the environment, due to the Member States prerogatives to set priorities concerning environmental protection. BAA lodged an appeal against

[118] See for references, eg, Case C-279/08 P *Commission v Netherlands* [2011] nyr, para. 51. See also the Grand Chamber judgment in C-106/09 P and C-107/09 P *Government of Gibraltar v Commission* [2011] ECR nyr, para. 87.

[119] In fact, the UK notified the scheme to the Commission with the title 'phased introduction of the aggregates levy in Northern Ireland', probably arguing that only the phased introduction of the scheme and not the latter itself could contain elements of aid. See C-487/06 P, *British Aggregates v Commission* [2008] ECR I-10515, para. 2 (point 14).

[120] The part declared compatible by the Commission was an exception providing for a phased introduction of the AGL in Northern Ireland. Another exception was that exports of virgin aggregate were exempted from the levy. The Commission also considered that this exemption was justified by the logic and nature of the tax system. See Commission Decision C (2002) 1478 final of 24 April 2002 on State aid file N 863/01—United Kingdom/Aggregates Levy.

[121] See Case T-210/02 *British Aggregates v Commission* [2006] ECR II-2789.

the CFI's judgment before the Court of Justice. This appeal is the subject of our discussion.

B. The policy context

This judgment was also delivered during the fourth period of evolution of the State aid policy discussed in Chapter 3, therefore reference is made to that chapter and to the three previous cases discussed in this chapter for the policy context. As summarized above, the main aims of the new period have been to refocus priorities, increase transparency and legal certainty, and to clarify the procedural rules in the field of State aids,[122] motivated in part by the increased in the number of cases that the Commission currently reviews. The most significant policy initiative of this period has been the use of the State aid rules to combat harmful business taxation,[123] and, since the mid-2000s, the reorientation of the State aid rules towards the achievement of a number of Community goals usually referred to as Lisbon Agenda goals, among which—for the purposes of this case—figures the protection of the environment, pursuant to the Commission's State Aid Action Plan (SAAP).[124]

C. The judgment of the Court of Justice

The Court of Justice, recalling the *Italian textiles* and *Adria–Wien* judgments, held that the General Court had erred in holding that Member States could decide to exclude some products from taxation that had a similar impact on the environment by virtue of their competences in that field. In the Court's terms, 'the Court of First Instance disregarded Article 87(1)EC, as interpreted by the Court of Justice, by holding, in paragraph 115 of the judgment under appeal, that Member States are free, in balancing the various interests involved, to set their priorities as regards the protection of the environment and, as a result, to determine which goods or services they decide to subject to an environmental levy, with the result that the fact that such a levy does not apply to all similar activities which have a comparable impact on the environment does not mean that similar activities, which are not subject to the levy, benefit from a selective advantage.'[125]

The Court also concluded that '[t]he Court of First Instance also erred in distinguishing, in paragraphs 120 and 121 of the judgment under appeal, the present case from the facts which gave rise to the judgment in Adria–Wien Pipeline and Wietersdorfer & Peggauer Zementwerke on the ground that the latter concerned,

[122] See Mederer, 'The Future of State Aid Control', op. cit., and Lavdas and Mendrinou, *Politics, Subsidies, and Competition*, op. cit. at 44. See also Doleys, 'Fifty Years of Moulding Article 87', op. cit. at 22.

[123] Commission notice 98/C 384/03 in Official Journal C 384 of 10/12/1998, p. 3.

[124] COM (2005) 107 final of 7.07.2005; State Aid Action Plan. Less and better targeted State aid: a roadmap for State aid reform 2005–2009 (Consultation document); SEC(2005) 795.

[125] C-487/06 P *British Aggregates v Commission* [2008] ECR I-10515, para. 86.

not the definition of the material scope of an environmental levy, as in the present case, but the partial exemption from payment of such a levy which was granted to a certain category of undertakings. Article 87(1) EC defines State interventions on the basis of their effects, *and thus independently of the techniques used*'[126] (emphasis added).

Finally, also in line with the opinion of Advocate General Mengozzi, the Court found that any difference in the treatment of comparable undertakings for environmental reasons should have been dealt with under the compatibility analysis of aid (Article 87(2) and (3) EC) and not in the analysis of the concept of aid.[127]

D. Assessment

The main development this case offered with regard to the concept of aid consists in the addition of a reference to *the techniques used* by Member States to the effects-based formula concerning the definition of aid laid down by the Court in the *Italian textiles* case,[128] and in the clarification of the limited role that national objectives should play within that definition. As explained earlier, the effects-based formula has consistently been applied to avoid the fact that the national categorization of a measure as social, monetary, or fiscal, automatically excludes the competence of the Commission to review the measure in question under the State aid rules.[129] In the Court's words, the (for example) social character of a given State measure 'is not therefore sufficient to exclude it outright from being categorized as aid for the purposes of Article 92 of the Treaty.'[130]

It is submitted here that the *rationale* of the Court's addition to the classic formula remains the same. Indeed, the Member State concerned in this case (UK) did not claim that the measure in question could not be reviewed by the European Commission because the protection of the environment remained largely a national competence. Instead, the argument was that the AGL was not selective, and hence the scheme not an aid, because the definition of its material scope had been made in accordance with some environmental priorities that Member States could make in view of their powers in this domain in the absence of Union's harmonization. The General Court accepted this line of argument but the Court of Justice did not. For the latter, Member States may not avoid the application of Article 107 TFEU by providing selective advantages through the definition of the material scope of a tax (leaving outside some undertakings that should have been taxed in light of the objective pursued by the measure) rather than through derogations of a general tax.

[126] Ibid. at 89. [127] Ibid. at 92.

[128] The traditional formula states that 'Article 92 does not distinguish between the measures of State intervention concerned by reference to their causes or aims but defines them in relation to their effects'.

[129] See in this regard, eg, Case C-342/96 *Spain v Commission* [1999] ECR 2459, para. 23.

[130] See, eg, Case C-241/94 *France v Commission* [1996] ECR I-4551, para. 21.

Indeed, this case confirms and clarifies the *Maribel* and the *Adria–Wien* judgments as to the definition of *prima facie* selectivity, and the *Azores* judgment in relation to the justification analysis of *prima facie* selective measures. It is now clear that the references to 'measures applicable to all undertakings' made by the Commission in the early 1990s to define general measures have to be understood as all undertakings in an objectively similar position as regards the objective pursued by the fiscal or social measure under review. Similarly, as to the justification analysis, it is also now clear that the justification will have to be made by reference to the technical principles that make the fiscal system function, such as the 'ability to pay' principle, and not by the environmental or other objectives alleged by the Member State. This view is confirmed by the judgment of the General Court on referral from the Court of Justice on this case as the former has followed the formula laid down by the Court of Justice in the *Azores* case for the analysis of the justification of a *prima facie* selective measure by the nature or general scheme.[131]

To sum up, Member States can therefore introduce modifications in their fiscal system that may result in the granting of an advantage to some tax payers to the detriment of others provided that those modulations are based on the guiding principles of the fiscal system. Conversely, Member States may not pursue policy goals, even as important as the preservation of the environment, through selective fiscal measures without the Commission's blessing under the compatibility rules.

The very narrow scope of the justification by the nature or general scheme defended by the Court is coherent, in our view, with the principle of incompatibility of State aids with the internal market and with the fact that, as discussed earlier, in this area the Treaty removes from Member States the possibility of justifying a measure on national grounds such as, for example, the protection of the environment before national or European courts. Only the Commission can make that assessment on the basis of Community objectives as the Court found in the *Philip Morris* judgment (discussed below). It would therefore be at odds with the logic of the Treaty that Member States (or national or European courts) could do at the definitional stage what they cannot do at the compatibility level. It is for these reasons coherent that the justification by the nature or logic of the system be more limited than the proportionality test or the justifications that Member States can invoke in the internal market context. This interpretation of the judgment makes it also coherent with the recognition by the Court in two judgments delivered in the same year (2008) of the cohesion of the tax system as an *overriding reason in the public interest* capable of justifying a restriction to the free movement rules.[132]

[131] Case T-210/02 RENV *British Aggregates Association v European Commission* [2012] ECR nyr. at para. 84: 'It will be recalled in that regard that, for the purposes of that assessment [Justification on the basis of the nature or general scheme of the AGL], a distinction must be made between, on the one hand, the objectives attributed to a particular tax regime and which are extrinsic to it and, on the other, the mechanisms inherent in the tax system itself which are necessary for the achievement of such objectives, since, as basic or guiding principles of the tax system in question, those objectives and mechanisms could support such justification, which it is for the Member State to demonstrate.'

[132] See Lenaerts, K., 'State Aid and Direct Taxation', in Kanninen, H., Korjus, N., and Rosas, A. (eds), *EU Competition Law in Context, Essays in Honour of Virpi Tiili* (Hart Publishing, 2009)

Finally, the Court's judgment in this case was contrary not only to a Member State's position but also to that of the Commission and the General Court. It could therefore be said, borrowing the expression of Judge Pescatore,[133] that the Court seems to have '*une certaine idée des aides*', independent from that of the Commission and the General Court, based on an understanding of these rules within the Treaty architecture. Given its privileged position, the Court of Justice may take into account more than other Community bodies or institutions the number and complexity of the values and interests now included in the Treaties, specially given the special and exclusive relation that the Court has with national judges under the preliminary ruling procedure. This relation continually brings to the Court new issues related to those values and interests that it has to address in a coherent way with its already very extensive case law.

8. The *Gibraltar* Case (Joined Cases C-106/09P and C-107/09P)

A. Introduction and background

This case is the first that the author is aware of in which the Court of Justice has concluded that for a tax measure to be selective, 'the criteria forming the basis of assessment which are adopted by a tax system [must] be such as to characterise the recipient undertakings, by virtue of the properties which are specific to them, as a privileged category, thus permitting such a regime to be described as favouring "certain" undertakings or the production of 'certain' goods within the meaning of Article 87(1) EC.'[134] The case is also the first in which the Court explicitly concludes that a whole fiscal system is intrinsically selective, that it has been specifically devised to favour certain undertakings or the production of certain goods that the legislator had in mind. The tax system had in fact been introduced by Gibraltar 'as a response to the State aid investigations against the Gibraltar exempt and qualifying offshore regimes as well as the criticisms formulated by both the Code of conduct group and the OECD.'[135]

As to the background of the case, the European Commission opened a State aid formal investigation procedure in relation to two measures applicable in Gibraltar in 2001, namely tax measures concerning 'exempt companies' and 'qualifying companies', which, according to the Commission, benefitted offshore

291 at 305–06. I would like to thank Judge Lenaerts for kindly agreeing to meet me at the Court of Justice and for his very useful comments regarding my Ph.D. thesis on which this book is based.

[133] Pescatore, P., 'The Doctrine of "Direct Effect": An Infant Disease of Community Law' (1983) *European Law Review* 155.

[134] Joined Cases C-106/09 P and C-107/09 P *Government of Gibraltar v Commission* [2011] ECR nyr at 104.

[135] See Van de Casteele, K., and Hocine, M., 'Favouring certain undertakings or the production of certain goods:Selectivity' in Mederer, W., Pesaresi, N., and Van Hoof, M. (eds), *EU Competition Law*, Volume IV, State Aid, Book One (Claeys & Casteels, 2008) 247 at 268.

companies.[136] A year later, Gibraltar repealed all its corporate tax measures, including those under investigation, and replaced them with a new entire corporate tax system, which was notified to the Commission and is ultimately the subject of the case under review.

The new corporate tax system, applicable to all companies established in Gibraltar, departed from the traditional corporate tax in that it was not based on profits but rather consisted of a payroll tax, a Business Property Occupation Tax (BPOT) and a registration fee. Companies would only pay the payroll and the BPOT taxes if they made a profit, and, in any case, they would not pay taxes exceeding 15 per cent of profits. Finally, certain activities, namely financial services and utilities, were subject to additional charges (a top-up or penalty tax) on profits that could be allocated to those activities.

The Commission considered that the reform of the corporate tax system was intrinsically selective because the combined effect of the various criteria (particularly of the payroll tax and the BPOT) was to set a different level of taxation for different sectors of the economy. Indeed, the result of the combination of the different criteria was that some companies, in particular offshore companies which by definition had neither employees nor property, did not pay taxes at all, perpetuating in this manner the system that had been previously criticized by the Code of Conduct, the Commission, and the OECD.[137] The Commission also considered that the system at issue was regionally selective. However, since the Court of Justice did not enter into that discussion we will not deal with the issue of regional selectivity.

The Commission decision was appealed before the then CFI by both the governments of Gibraltar and the UK. The CFI annulled the Commission's decision. In essence, the General Court held that the Commission could not lawfully classify a tax measure as selective without first identifying the 'normal' tax regime, and only then show that the measure amounted to a derogation from that general scheme. Finally, as a third step, the CFI held that the Commission should have assessed whether the derogation from the normal regime was justified by the nature or general scheme of the system of charges to which it belonged. Therefore, given that the Commission had not followed that path, the General Court concluded that the Commission could not lawfully declare the corporate system as selective, because that would be tantamount for the Commission to substitute the role of Member States in determining their normal tax system.[138] The judgment of the CFI was

[136] See OJ 2002 C 26, p. 13 and OJ 2002 C 26, p. 9. The opening decisions were challenged by Gibraltar and the UK before the General Court (see Joined Cases T-195/01 and T-207/01 *Government of Gibraltar v Commission* [2002] ECR II-2309).

[137] Commission Decision 2005/261/EC of 30 March 2004 on the aid scheme which the UK is planning to implement as regards the Government of Gibraltar Corporation Tax Reform (OJ 2005 L 85, p. 1). The OECD concluded in 2000 that Gibraltar was a tax haven in light of the criteria set out by the OECD Report: Harmful Tax Competition: An Emerging Global Issues, Paris (1998).

[138] Joined Cases T-195/01 and T-207/01 *Government of Gibraltar v Commission* [2002] ECR p. II-02309, in particular paras 143–46 and 171–74.

appealed to the European Court of Justice by the Commission and the Kingdom of Spain. This judgment is the subject of our analysis.

B. The policy context

The case was decided during the fourth period of evolution of the State aid policy discussed in Chapter 3. In addition, the following will describe briefly the particular policy background of the case under review.

The policy background to this case goes back to the initiative that Mario Monti, then Commissioner for Internal Market and Taxation, adopted to increase coordination between Member States on direct business taxation. This initiative was followed, as it is well known, by the ECOFIN adoption of a Code of Conduct on direct taxation,[139] and by the commitment 'in parallel' by the Commission 'to adopt in 1998 guidelines for this type of aid and to review the tax arrangements in force in the Member States.'[140] As the Commission stated in those guidelines, '[f]ollowing the completion of the single market and the liberalisation of capital movements, it has also become apparent that there is a need to examine the particular effects of aid granted in the form of tax measures and to spell out the consequences as regards assessment of the aid's compatibility with the common market.'[141]

Following the adoption of the Code of Conduct, a working group was created with a view to assess the tax measures that might fall within the Code. Among the measures scrutinized, the working group identified sixty-six tax measures with harmful features, three of them in Gibraltar.[142] The Commission decision in this case analysed and then sanctioned two of the three measures of the Code concerning Gibraltar, and it was adopted, perhaps not surprisingly, with Mario Monti as Commissioner for Competition, thus closing the circle that had begin in 1996 with him as Commissioner for Internal Market and Taxation.

C. The judgment of the Court of Justice

The Court started by restating two of the traditional formulas of selectivity mentioned earlier. First, the one originated with the Opinion of AG Roemer in the

[139] Council Resolution of 1 December 1997, OJ C 2/2 of 6 January 1998.

[140] Twenty-seventh Report on Competition Policy (Office for Official Publications of the European Communities, 1998) at 69, point 231.

[141] Commission Notice on the application of the State aid rules to measures relating to direct business taxation, Official Journal C 384, 10/12/1998 P. 0003–0009. The Commission included this action within the action plan for the single market, CSE(97) 1, 4 June 1997, strategic target 2, action 1, which provided that with a view to remove tax distortions the Commission would 'clarify the scope and improve the coherence of the application of Community competition rules, including rules on state aids.'

[142] See Report from the Code of Conduct Group (Business Taxation) to the ECOFIN Council on 29 November 1999.

French exports rediscount rate case, according to which 'advantages resulting from a general measure applicable without distinction to all economic operators do not constitute State aid within the meaning of Article 87 EC'.[143] Second, the *Maribel–Adria* formula discussed above.[144] Within this framework, the Court held that the requirement to make a profit and the capping of tax at 15 per cent of profits were not selective measures but rather 'measures applicable without distinction to all economic operators',[145] from which any advantage that could accrue to some companies would only be incidental or random. Therefore, the Court agreed with the General Court as regards these two alleged elements of selectivity identified by the Commission.

However, the Court differed with the General Court and the Advocate General in relation to the most important point of the case: the (lack of) taxation of offshore companies. Both the General Court and the Advocate General had found that by failing to observe the analytical framework set out in the 1998 Notice to distinguish selective from general measures, the Commission could not lawfully conclude that offshore companies (which have neither employees nor physical presence in Gibraltar) enjoyed a selective advantage. The Court of Justice rejected this conclusion as follows:

First, the Court recalled that 'Article 87(1) EC does not distinguish between measures of State intervention by reference to their causes or their aims but defines them in relation to their effects, *and thus independently of the techniques used*' (emphasis added). The part of the test here emphasized had been developed by the Court, as discussed, in the *British Aggregates* case. The test, with the 'new' wording, had also been followed by the Court in another recent case in which, as in *British Aggregates*, the Court overruled a General Court judgment that had considered a State measure as not selective and therefore as no-aid.[146] In this case, the reference to the technique allowed the Court to censure the approach followed by the General Court.[147]

The Court then moved on to re-interpret its own (Grand Chamber) case law, according to which 'the very existence of an advantage may be established only when compared with 'normal' taxation',[148] and did so by holding that the notion

[143] Joined Cases C-106/09 P and C-107/09 P *Government of Gibraltar v Commission* [2011] ECR nyr, para. 73 and case law cited therein.

[144] According to which, 'Article 87(1) EC requires assessment of whether, under a particular legal regime, a national measure is such as to favour "certain undertakings or the production of certain goods" in comparison with others which, in the light of the objective pursued by that regime, are in a comparable factual and legal situation.' Ibid. para. 75 and case law cited therein.

[145] Ibid. para. 80.

[146] Case C-279/08 P *Commission v Netherlands* [2011] nyr, para. 51.

[147] Ibid. at 88, that 'The General Court's approach, based solely on a regard for the regulatory technique used by the proposed tax reform, does not allow the effects of the tax measure in question to be considered and excludes from the outset any possibility that the fact that no tax liability is incurred by offshore companies may be classified as a "selective advantage". That approach is therefore at variance with the case-law cited in para. 87 above [the aims versus effects test as phrased in this and the two previous judgments mentioned by the Court].'

[148] Case C-88/03 *Portugal v Commission* (Azores) [2006] ECR I-7115, para. 56.

of selectivity may not be dependent on the use of a certain regulatory technique if the measure at stake produces the same effects in law and or in fact as State aid.[149] On those bases, the Court found that the Gibraltar tax reform, by the combination of the criteria used, led to the same result than the derogation from the normal taxation system would have produced. Therefore, the General Court had erred in demanding the Commission to identify in the contested decision a reference framework for establishing the existence of a selective advantage for offshore companies. The General Court had also erred by not analysing the factors that the Commission took into account to conclude that the tax system benefitted offshore companies.[150]

However, according to the Court, and tellingly at odds with the case law since *Adria–Wien*, this is not sufficient to conclude that the measure at stake was *prima facie* selective. The Court added a new criterion, namely that 'the criteria forming the basis of assessment which are adopted by a tax system... be such as to characterise the recipient undertakings, by virtue of the properties which are specific to them, as a privileged category'.[151] Therefore, the Court found that the criteria of the Gibraltar tax regime were generally applicable, and yet, it discriminated between undertakings which were in a comparable situation and that the criteria employed was able to characterize the beneficiaries (offshore companies) as a privileged category by virtue of the properties which were specific to them labour and property, since offshore companies 'by their nature have no employees and do not occupy business premises'.[152]

[149] Joined Cases C-106/09 P and C-107/09 P *Government of Gibraltar v Commission* [2011] ECR nyr, paras 91–92. The Court held that '[the Azores case-law referring to the notion of normal taxation] does not make the classification of a tax system as "selective" conditional upon that system being designed in such a way that undertakings which might enjoy a selective advantage are, in general, liable to the same tax burden as other undertakings but benefit from derogating provisions, so that the selective advantage may be identified as being the difference between the normal tax burden and that borne by those former undertakings... Such an interpretation of the selectivity criterion would require, contrary to the case-law cited in paragraph 87 above [*British Aggregates* development concerning the *techniques used*], that in order for a tax system to be classifiable as "selective" it must be designed in accordance with a certain regulatory technique; the consequence of this would be that national tax rules fall from the outset outside the scope of control of State aid merely because they were adopted under a different regulatory technique although they produce the same effects in law and/or in fact.'

[150] In that regard, the Court found that 'it is apparent that the regime at issue, by combining those bases, even though they are founded on criteria that are in themselves of a general nature, in practice discriminates between companies which are in a comparable situation with regard to the objective of the proposed tax reform, namely to introduce a general system of taxation for all companies established in Gibraltar.' See Joined Cases C-106/09 P and C-107/09 P *Government of Gibraltar v Commission* [2011] ECR nyr, para. 101.

[151] Ibid. at 104. The Court justified this additional requirement on the basis of the case law which states that 'a different tax burden resulting from the application of a "general" tax regime is not sufficient on its own to establish the selectivity of taxation for the purposes of Article 87(1) EC.' Ibid. at 103.

[152] Ibid. at 106.

D. Assessment

This case could be seen as either being one of fiscal sovereignty or one of State aid circumvention. There are powerful arguments on both sides. The Court opted for the latter, rightly in our view. The Court refused to accept the 'competence' argument alone. Looking backwards, the Court has never accepted a 'naked' argument based on the exclusive competence of the Member States for a measure to escape the notion of aid. This is true for tax policy (eg, *miners' bonus* case), monetary policy (*French exports rediscount rate* case), or social policy (*Italian textiles, FNE, Maribel bis/ter* cases). It is also true for cases where the national exclusive competence (such as environment) is raised in order to allow for discrimination between undertakings that are in a comparable factual and legal situation (*Adria–Wien, British Aggregates, NOx*).

This case was however more difficult than previous ones because the *national* authority had deliberately decided to exclude some companies from taxation but not through a derogation from the normal tax regime, as in the previous cases, but as a (necessary) result of the application of the normal tax system. This 'technique', in the eye of the Court, forced the latter to issue a new criterion, namely, that the national ('general') criteria be such as to characterize the recipient undertakings by virtue of the properties which are specific to them as a privileged category. In other words, the Court, bound by the specific facts of the case, not to say unique facts of the case given that there are not so many - tax heavens declared by the Organisation for Economic Co-operation and Development within the EU, moved away from the formalism that has characterized this area of EU law in recent years and very close to substance: offshore companies receive aid as a result of the technique devised by *Gibraltar*, precisely to circumvent the OECD, the Code of Conduct working group, and the Commission's State aid critics. To some extent, the Court's conclusion recalls the *real purpose* test proposed by Advocate General Lagrange fifty years ago: it is necessary to ascertain whether the real object, the real purpose of the measure in question is, for example, fiscal, or whether the real object is other 'and consists either in imposing charges on undertakings which would not normally be placed upon them or, on the other hand, of exempting them from a charge which they would normally have to bear, in that case.'[153]

The reference to technique in the wording of the effects-based approach of State aids is consistent with the traditional role that the Court had given to that test to preclude the fact that the categorization of the measure by the State as, for example, social, fiscal, or monetary could make it escape from the notion of aid laid down in Article 107(1). In this case, as in *British Aggregates* and *NOx*, it was no longer the national definition of the character of the measure (social, fiscal, monetary, etc) but the technique employed by the public authority which, according

[153] See Opinion of Advocate General Lagrange, C-30/59 *Steenkolenmijnen v High Authority* [1961] ECR 3 at [1960] ECR p. 43.

to the Court, pursued the same aim: to exclude the measure in question from the notion of aid. The Commission had surely noted this case law, as can be inferred from its pleading: 'the [CFI's] approach gives decisive weight to fiscal technique over an assessment in the light of a measure's effects.'[154]

Therefore, this case is in line with the latest judgments of the Court since *British Aggregates* in which the Court seems to have perceived a trend towards the creation of *ad hoc* general systems based on the criteria introduced by the notice on direct business taxation and State aids (the derogation justification test) that has been confirmed by the Court since the *Maribel* case. This approach, that particularly in this case could be referred to as an 'end of formalism' approach, may have yielded the correct result in this difficult and extreme case yet it may prove problematic in others as we have seen above in the context of the advantage criterion in the *EDF* judgment.

9. Conclusion

During the first period of evolution of the State aid policy the Court did not coin any definition of selectivity. Unsurprisingly, no definition of this concept could be found in previous Treaties that were selective by nature such as the Brussels Sugar Convention, that dealt with a single product, or the ECSC Treaty, that dealt with two sectors (as discussed the GATT did not define subsidy). The Court, as discussed in relation to the advantage criterion, was generally during this period more interested in institutional issues, in laying down the foundations of the Treaty system, than in substantive issues, in explaining in detail the content of the Treaty rules. In this regard, as Judge Koopmans explained in relation to a period that he coined as *institutional*, issues such as the direct effect of the Treaty provisions were the main concern of the early case law of the Court, and this could also be seen in the State aid field, in which the Court found that today's Article 108 TFEU did not have direct effect, save for its third paragraph and that Article 107 did not have that effect either as only the Commission, and not national courts, could assess the compatibility of an aid with the Common Market, a finding that the Commission had requested from the Court in order, presumably to safeguard its prerogatives under the compatibility analysis.[155]

The Court did however make some findings related to the notion of aid in *French exports rediscount rate*,[156] a case that was mostly concerned with the notion of selectivity yet the Court interpreted it more broadly. Indeed, as discussed earlier

[154] Joined Cases C-106/09 P and C-107/09 P *Government of Gibraltar v Commission* [2011] ECR nyr, para. 54. See also the reference to this Commission's argument in the opinion of AG Jaaskinen: 'In short, the General Court's approach gives decisive weight to fiscal technique over substance, whereas, according to settled case-law, State aid must be assessed in the light of its effects.'

[155] See Case 6/64 *Flaminio Costa v E.N.E.L.* [1964] ECR P. I-0114. See also Case C-77/72, *Capolongo v Maya* [1973] ECR 611 at para. 6.

[156] See Joined Cases C-6/69 and 11/69 *Commission v France* [1969] ECR 523.

in this chapter, the Court upheld the Commission's decision in this case yet it focused its reasoning on products ('aid to national products exported') not on undertakings, and gave to the judgment a teleological meaning, emphasizing the consequences that the granting of this kind of aid (export aid) could have for the establishment of the internal market. The message sent by the Court in this case, that any unilateral measure aimed at affecting the conditions of competition in the internal market would be sanctioned after the achievement of the customs union, was in fact related to the duty of loyalty enshrined in then Article 5 EEC.[157] Indeed, the formula adopted by the Court in this case to find the aid character of the French measure under review was subjective, based on the intent, the purpose of the measure, and not objective, based on the effects.[158] This can be explained by the context, strongly influenced by the teleological objective of creating the Common Market, and the measure under review, export aid, clearly contrary to the Common Market as it favoured national products over products originating in other Member States. The measure distorted the conditions of competition and trade in the Common Market, as the Court retained, solely from its own purpose.

During the second period of evolution of the State aid policy the Court introduced a number of important clarifications to the concept of aid and to that of selectivity in the *Italian textiles* case.

First, the Court found that the concept of aid had to be defined by reference to the effects of the measure under review and not by reference to its purpose or aim. This effects-based formula was tellingly at odds with the subjective formula laid down in the previous *French exports rediscount rate* case. However, the new formula was more coherent with the evolution of the case law of the Court in the context of the internal market, where the measures were analysed by reference to their effect, and to the Commission's preference for the effect of national measures as the relevant benchmark, as it allowed for the review of all types of national measures under Community law, even if those measures were adopted in fields for which Member States remained formally competent. The Commission had made this preference explicit in cases such as the famous *Dassonville*,[159] decided only nine days after the *Italian textiles* case, in the internal market context and even earlier in the State aid field.[160] In this regard, as has been noted by several authors,

[157] Pescatore, *The Law of Integration*, op. cit. at 39–40.

[158] See Brinkhorst, L.J., and Verougstraete, I.M., 'Annotation in Joined Cases C-6/69 and C-11/69, *Commission v France*, [1969] ECR 523', op. cit. at 487: '("granted...with a view to") thus emphasizing the intent of the measure, rather than an objective formula, considering its effect.'

[159] See argument of the Commission in Dassonville as referred in the Court's judgment: 'According to the Commission, any measure, whatever its nature or content may, by reason of its effect on the free movement of goods, constitute a measure having equivalent effect, provided that it is not covered by another provision of the Treaty.' Case 8/74 *Dassonville* [1974] ECR 837 at 846.

[160] See the reference in Doleys, 'Fifty Years of Moulding Article 87', op. cit. at 9, footnote 19, to the following Commission's statement made in 1963: 'Included among the modalities that the Commission understood to fall within the meaning of Article [107(1)] were: "tax exemptions, preferential interest rates, guarantees of loans on especially favorable terms, acquisition of land or buildings either gratuitously or on favorable terms, provisions of goods and services on preferential terms, indemnities against losses *and other measures having equivalent effect*"' (emphasis added).

the Court was during this period very supportive of the European Commission and, more generally, was ready to interpret the law in the way that best served the interests of European integration, making Judge Koopmans refer to this period as instrumental for that integration. In this context, the effects-based formula of the concept of aid might be considered as an example of the new trend in interpretation. Finally, as it has also been submitted, the effects-based formula was not meant to exclude any role for the objectives of a State measure under the concept of aid but rather to avoid that the mere national categorization of a measure as social or fiscal would negate completely the Commission's competence.

It was also in this case where the Court coined the formula known as the justification by the general system of *prima facie* selective measures. In this regard, it has been submitted that the Court did not attempt to limit the selectivity criterion in the field of social measures. Instead, the Court was just reacting to the specific argument put forward by Italy: that the measure was intended to restore a special handicap of the social system affecting specifically the textile sector within the Italian industry. Indeed, it would seem incoherent with the period in which this judgment was laid down the proposal by the Court of a formula that limits a concept that was at the time very little used due to the weak enforcement of the State aid rules. This interpretation is supported by the lack of references to the justification test in the Commission's competition reports and decisions or in the Court case law until the 1990s.[161] This interpretation might also be supported by the fact that, far from limiting the concept of aid, the Court went in this case even beyond the submissions of the European Commission in order to make the concept of aid more easily applicable.[162]

To conclude, the concept of selectivity that emerges from the *Italian textiles* case, the sectorial selectivity—aid given to an entire national industry—was not challenged by the affected State as it was a notion that could be traced back

[161] To this author's knowledge, the Court only repeated the formula laid down in this case as a justification of a *prima facie* selective measure in the Maribel bis/ter case (C-75/97 *Belgium v Commission* ('*Maribel*') [1999] ECR I-3671), after the Commission had published the Notice on the application of the State aid rules to measures relating to direct business taxation in 1998 which included that justification as one of its main novelties.

[162] In this regard, for example, the Commission had admitted in that case that the employment of a majority of women entailed a disadvantage on the basic family allowance system in Italy. The Commission had also accepted that some sort of comparison between the situation in Italy and that prevailing in other Member States should be used for the finding of an advantage, an argument that could in fact be found in the Spaak Report. See the Spaak Report, 62 of the French version : '*Il apparait cependant qu'une industrie apparemment désavantagée cesse de l'être si la même surcharge relative existe dans même industrie des autres pays. Au contraire, ce désavantage se maintient si cette surcharge n existe pas ailleurs, et s'accroit si la même industrie est relativement déchargée dans l'autre pays considère.*' However, the Court refused both submissions in the final judgment. The Court had in fact already refused a similar argument in the Joined Cases C-6/69 and 11/69, *Commission v France* [1969] ECR 523 at para. 21. In this regard, as underlined by AG Warner, the availability of such a defense (the existence of similar advantages in other Member States) could make the enforcement of the State aid provisions a 'dead letter'. See Opinion of Advocate General Warner in case 173/73, *Italy v Commission* [1974] ECR at 727. See also for a similar finding of the Court during the 1970s, this time concerning the notion of distortion of competition, Case C-78/76 *Steinike & Weinlig v Federal Republic of Germany* [1977] ECR p. 00595 at para. 24.

directly to the Treaty (that refers to aid to certain undertakings *or productions*). The notion of selectivity in this case was thus coherent with the understanding of the State aid rules within the internal market logic that predominated in the Court's during the late 1960s and 1970s; that is, as measures that prevent the introduction of artificial distortions of competition and trade between national industries.

During the third period, that could be referred to as *definitional*, the Commission introduced, for the first time, some criteria to distinguish between general and selective measures, both in the first survey on State aids (addressed in principle to Member States) and in the competition reports of the early 1990s.[163] According to these criteria, 'Article [107] of the Treaty does not apply to general measures applicable to all undertakings of a Member State where those measures meet objective, non-discriminatory and non-discretionary requirements'.[164] The Commission may have felt it necessary to clarify the State aid rules as these were becoming more operational due to the increasing number of notifications and private complaints fostered by the 1992 programme spirit. The criteria proposed by the Commission to distinguish between general and selective measures were ultimately based on the notion of equal treatment and, it is submitted, this had a significant impact in the Court's definition of the selectivity criterion since the 1990s.

In this regard, in the main case concerning selectivity during this period analysed above, the *FNE* case, the Court found that a measure was selective because the national authorities enjoyed discretion in the application of the measure and this was liable to place some undertakings in a more favourable position than others. Importantly, the references to discrimination between undertakings were made in a context of intra-jurisdictional competition, that is, on competition between undertakings in a single Member State and not, as before, between undertakings active in different Member States or rather between national industries or products as the Court had retained in the previous cases.

Indeed, although the selectivity analysis has always been carried out taking into consideration the situation of undertakings within a single Member State,[165] the focus of the early cases, and particularly of the *French exports rediscount rate* case, had been in the distortive effect that an aid could have in the situation of undertakings active in different Member States, and this because the early applications of the State aid rules were concerned with sectoral aid and with aid to several national productions. Also, early cases such as the *para-fiscal levies* case (discussed in Chapter 7) were concerned with discriminatory aid measures against the interests of out-of-State traders. However, in this case, the discrimination was not

[163] See SEC(88) 1981, European Commission,13 December 1988 at p. 7. See also, eg, Twenty-third Report on Competition Policy, op. cit. at 246, point 390.

[164] See Twenty-fourth Report on Competition Policy, op. cit. at 347.

[165] See in this regard, eg, the opinion of AG Roemer in Joined Cases 6/69 and 11/69 *Commission v France* [1969] ECR 546 where he compares the situation of exporting undertakings with that of those undertakings that do not export for the finding of selectivity.

necessarily against the interests of out-of-State traders but against undertakings placed in the same Member State and probably having the same 'nationality'. This judgment in fact reveals a transformation of the role of State aid that we have also witnessed in the previous chapter in relation to the notion of advantage: a trend towards the application of the State aid rules more and more in a context of intra-jurisdictional competition and thus not necessarily in a context of inter-jurisdictional competition as before.[166]

Furthermore the case also reveals a changing role of the prohibition of aid as no longer exclusively aimed at establishing the internal market by removing obstacles to trade. This prohibition was also now applied to ensure the proper functioning of that market. This case also reveals an increasing interest of competitors and not only States in the application of these rules. As Ehlerman phrased it, there was a move from a macroeconomic to a microeconomic conception of these rules, that were also becoming more integrated with the rest of the competition rules.[167] These rules were thus no longer applied exclusively to prevent distortions of competition between national industries but more and more to prevent those distortions within individual national markets.[168]

Finally, the adoption of a discrimination-like language for the notion of selectivity may have also been in line with the Commission's goal of making the State aid rules more accessible to private applicants, who could easily perceive whether they had been discriminated against by not receiving an aid given to a competitor. Indeed, the main cases on selectivity that followed this one were brought before the Commission by undertakings or associations claiming unequal treatment in favour of their competitors (*FNE, Maribel bis/ter, Adria–Wien*), asking in some cases even (such as in *Adria–Wien*) to be given aid as well.

During the fourth period, the Court, although generally supportive of the Commission, has adopted a number of formulas concerning selectivity that reflect a balanced or compromising approach. For these reasons we also refer to the fourth period, particularly towards the end of the 1990s onwards, as one in which the Court adopted an approach of *balanced instrumentalism*. The Court has gained significant protagonism in relation to the definition of aid during this period, as also observed in the previous chapter concerning advantage.

[166] As explained earlier, this evolution had also been experienced in the internal market context where increasingly since the 1980s many measures and regulations were 'challenged in the Court by nationals of the State in question, not other EU nationals or importers.' See supra Maduro, *We the Court*, op. cit. at 63 where he cites the following cases as examples of this trend: Case 286/81, *Oosthoek's* [1982] ECR 4575; Case 126/82, *Smit* [1983] ECR 73; Case 237/82, *Jongeneel Kaas* [1984] ECR 483; Joined Cases 80 and 159/85, *Edah* [1986] ECR 3359; and Case C-241/89, *SARPP* [1990] ECR I-4695.

[167] Ehlermann, 'State Aid Control in the European Union', op. cit. at 1219.

[168] Gyselen, 'The Emerging Interface between Competition Policy and Environmental Policy in the EC', op. cit. at 245: According to him, the legality standard that the Commission had to observe in both the internal market and the competition fields had to start with the following question: 'Is there a distortion of competition between national economies (Article 30 [then applies]) or between individual competitors (Article 85 and 92 [then apply])?'

In this regard, in the *Maribel bis/ter* and *Adria–Wien* judgments the Court endorsed the Commission's position as to the outcome of the case while limiting the notion of 'all undertakings' for the purposes of the selectivity test to those in an objective comparable position by reference to the objective pursued by the contested measure. Similarly, in both instances the Court, while supporting the derogation-justification test proposed by the Commission in the notice on direct business taxation, gave in our view some weight to the social and environmental objectives pursued by the measure in question, and thus it did not simply analysed whether both measures were justified by the intrinsic (technical) features of respectively the general social or environmental system in which they were inserted as suggested in the notice and required by the Commission in both instances.

By contrast, in the *Azores* case the Court finally supported the position that only technical or intrinsic principles or objectives are available for the justification by the nature or general scheme test. In this regard, it has been submitted that the narrow scope of the justification by the nature or general scheme defended by the Court in this case is coherent with the principle of incompatibility of State aids with the internal market and with the fact that, in this area, the Treaty removes from Member States the possibility of justifying a measure on national grounds such as, for example, the protection of the environment, before national or European courts. Only the Commission can make that assessment on the basis of Community objectives as the Court found in the *Philip Morris* judgment (discussed below). It would therefore be at odds with the logic of the Treaty that Member States (or national or European courts) could do at the definitional stage what they cannot do at the compatibility level. It is for these reasons coherent that the justification by the nature or logic of the system be more limited than the proportionality test or the justifications that Member States can invoke in the internal market context.[169] Conversely, the Court disagreed with the Commission in relation to the so-called regional selectivity; that is, that advantages granted by infra-national bodies cannot be considered as general measures. The Court did so, it has been submitted, as an example of the increasing recognition of the role of regions and of the national constitutional identity of Member States.[170] Thus, in

[169] This interpretation of the judgment makes it also coherent with the recognition by the Court in two judgments delivered in the same year (2008) of the cohesion of the tax system as an overriding reason in the public interest capable of justifying a restriction to the free movement rules. See Lenaerts, K., 'State Aid and Direct taxation', in Kanninen, Korjus, Rosas (eds), op. cit. 291 at 305–06.

[170] As noted by the Judge-Rapporteur of the *Azores* and *UGT–Rioja* cases, Judge Rosas. See Rosas and Armati, *EU Constitutional Law*, op. cit. at 108: 'the status autonomus regions enjoy under the national constitution may affect the way in which Union Law will apply to them. The clearest example of such an effect concerns state aid law, where the ECJ has departed somewhat from the traditional Union/Member State dichotomy, looking beyond this distinction to the actual power of regional bodies to determine the applicable legal and economic framework for action'. Judge Rosas refers in this regard to Art. 4 (TEU) of the Lisbon Treaty (also included in the unratified Constitutional Treaty) and the *Azores* (C-88/03, *Portugal v Commission (Azores)* [2006] ECR I-7115) and *UGT–Rioja* (C-428/06 to C-434/06 UGT–Rioja and Others [2008] ECR I-06747) judgments. I would like to thank Judge Rosas for kindly agreeing to meet me at the Court of Justice and for his very useful comments regarding my Ph.D. thesis on which this book is based.

keeping with the balanced approach that characterizes the case law of the Court since the Amsterdam Treaty, the Court made a balance between two rules now included in the Treaty: Article 107 TFEU and Article 4 TEU.

Finally, in the last two judgments reviewed, *British Aggregates* and *Gibraltar*—but also in the *NOx* case—the Court has applied the *Azores* formula concerning justification of a *prima facie* selective measure by the intrinsic principles of the general fiscal system to three cases in which, it is submitted, the Court has perceived a will to circumvent the State aid rules by creating *ad hoc* general systems and not exceptions to them or, in the Court's words, by using a 'certain regulatory technique'. The last example of the new trend towards the avoidance of circumvention is the *Gibraltar* case that represents what we have termed an 'end of formalism' approach, and that has also influenced the case law of the Court concerning other criteria of the concept of aid.

6

The Notion of Aid Granted by the State or through State Resources

In this section we will apply the analytical framework followed in the previous two chapters to the main formulas that have appeared in the case law of the Court in relation to the notion of aid granted by the State or through State resources.

1. The *Steinike and Weinlig* Case (C-78/76)

A. Introduction and background of the case

This case is known as the first in which the Court affirmed that the term 'State resources', included in the concept of aid under Article 107, refers to both aid granted directly by the State or by public or private bodies established or appointed by it to administer the aid. In other words, there is no difference between aid granted by the State or through 'State resources'.[1]

The case arrived at the Court in the form of a preliminary ruling. In the main proceedings the plaintiff, a German company which imported citrus concentrates from Italy and other countries into the German market, had challenged the imposition by German law of a compulsory contribution to a fund. The money raised by the fund in question was subsequently spent by an agency created for market research and advertising of the German food industries. The plaintiff claimed that the contribution which it was required to pay was illegal on the ground that this contribution financed a State aid prohibited under article 107(1).

In the part of the preliminary reference related to the criterion under review, the German court asked whether the phrase 'any aid granted through State resources' was satisfied if the State agency itself received aid from the State or private undertakings. Related to this, the national court also asked whether there was aid in

[1] Case C-78/76 *Steinike & Weinlig v Federal Republic of Germany* [1977] ECR p. 595. The case is also foundational in other aspect as the Court held for the first time that Art. 107 TFEU applies to all private and public undertakings and all their production.

the sense of granting a *gratuitous advantage* if the recipient of aid is not a private undertaking but a State agency.[2]

B. The policy context

This case was brought and decided during the second period of evolution of the State aid rules discussed in Chapter 3. During this period, the Commission continued to focus on the elimination of barriers to trade and discrimination between undertakings in different Member States in a context of protectionism. In fact the protectionism emerging from the oil crisis led to an increase in aids and also to a pragmatic and low-profile enforcement approach by the European Commission.

Indeed, the State measure in question in this case had been notified to the Commission which had raised no objections, probably due to the lack of discrimination against out of State traders. In this regard, the Commission also rejected the idea that the measure under review could amount to a charge having an equivalent effect to a quantitative restriction, as it was not clear whether the measure in question benefitted German products exclusively.[3] The Commission's inaction in this case was also in line with the general permissive approach just described.

C. Judgment of the Court of Justice

In relation to the question posed by the general Court concerning the criterion under review, namely whether there were 'State resources' involved, the Court held that:

> [t]he prohibition contained in Article 92 (1) covers all aid granted by a Member State or through State resources without its being necessary to make a distinction whether the aid is granted directly by the State or by public or private bodies established or appointed by it to administer the aid. In applying Article 92 regard must primarily be had to the effects of the aid on the undertakings or producers favoured and not the status of the institutions entrusted with the distribution and administration of the aid.[4]

Therefore, the Court interpreted the term 'State resources' as referring to public or private distributors of State aid.

As to the question concerning the origin of the funds used to finance the aid at stake in this case, the Court also held that '[a] measure adopted by the public authority and favouring certain undertakings or products does not lose the

[2] As referred by Advocate General Warner in his joined opinion of cases C-74/76 *Ianelli & Volpi v Meroni*, and Case C-78/76 *Steinike & Weinlig v Federal Republic of Germany* [1977] ECR at p. 00583.

[3] 'The Commission doubts whether it is a case of charges having an effect equivalent to customs duties. It is not sufficiently well established that the contribution in question exclusively benefits German products and it is doubtful whether there is sufficient identity between, on the one hand, the domestic and imported products subject to the contribution, and on the other hand, the domestic products benefitting from the activities of the Fund.' Case C-78/76 *Steinike & Weinlig v Federal Republic of Germany* [1977] ECR at p. 602.

[4] Case C-78/76 *Steinike & Weinlig v Federal Republic of Germany* [1977] ECR 595 at para. 21.

character of a gratuitous advantage by the fact that it is wholly or partially financed by contributions imposed by the public authority and levied on the undertakings concerned.'[5] Therefore, the Court found that the origin of the funds, whether private or public, was not ultimately relevant, the important element being that the funds are the result of action by a public authority.

D. Assessment

The question raised by the national Court concerned the term 'State resources'. In particular, the main question of this case was whether there could be State resources even if the 'aid' was partly or totally financed by private undertakings. The Court's positive reply to this question was consistent with the opinion of academics at the time of the judgment, who explained the reference 'through State resources' in Article 107 as meaning public or private bodies distributing the aid instead of the State, and consistent too with the discussions held in Val Duchesse discussed in Chapter 2 in relation to this criterion.[6]

The Court's conclusion was also consistent with that followed in the *parafiscal levies* case discussed in the next chapter (C-47/69), where the Court had held that parafiscal charges, which are also financed by private contributions, could be qualified as aid and also declared incompatible with the Treaty. The Commission had in fact by the time of adopting this judgment a well-established practice on para-fiscal charges because they usually—though not in this case—led to discrimination between the undertakings that pay the levy (usually both foreign and domestic) and those that benefit from the proceeds of the levy (only domestic).[7]

The Court, following the Commission's submissions and its previous judgment in *Italian textiles*, held that State resources had to be interpreted from the point of view of the recipient of the aid and not on the basis of the status of the grant authority; that is, what is relevant is the effect of the measure, not the form it adopts, the origin of the funds that finance the aid, or the status of its distributor.

To conclude, in this case the Court followed a functional interpretation of the concept of aid to find that not only public bodies but also private ones could be considered as State resources under Article 107(1), the relevant criteria being the presence of State action/compulsion and the effect of the measure on the recipient undertaking. Similarly, the Court applied the same *effet utile* logic to the question of the origin of the funds, whether public or private. The judgment was thus consistent with the early judgments of the Court described in the previous chapters in which the Court laid down broad principles that allowed for a flexible interpretation of this provision by the Commission.

[5] Ibid. at para. 22.

[6] See, eg, Scheuing, D.H., *Les aides financiers publiques aux enterprises en droit francaise et europeen* (Editions Berger-Levrault, 1974) at 269–73.

[7] See, eg, Fourth General Report on the Activities of the Communities (European Commission, 1971) 34.

2. The *Van Tiggele* Case (C-82/77)

A. Introduction and background of the case

This case is usually referred to as the first in which the Court established that the notion of State aid must necessarily entail a financial burden for the State. The case arrived at the Court in the form of a preliminary ruling only a year after the *Steinike and Weinlig* judgment. This time, the question referred by the national Court was whether the fixing of minimum prices for the retail sale of alcoholic beverages by a State authority, which has the effect of benefitting certain categories of undertakings, could be regarded as 'aid granted by the State'. The national Court also asked whether the same price-fixing measure amounted to a prohibited quantitative restriction on imports or a measure having equivalent effect under then Article 30 EEC.

B. The policy context

Reference is made to the policy context described in *Steinike and Weinlig* since it is essentially the same, so only some references to the precise year of this judgment will be made here. By 1978 the Commission had recognized that the economic problems affecting Member States in the post-oil-crisis era were not temporary or directly linked to the oil crisis but rather they were of a structural nature and needed to be tackled if economic progress was to be initiated.[8] The Commission thus announced in 1978 that it was going to be stricter, albeit still flexible in view of the economic situation. The Commission had to be flexible as well since, at this time, it lacked sufficient leverage *vis-à-vis* Member States; evidence of this is the lack of notifications of new aid in spite of the high number of aids being granted after 1973.

C. Judgment of the Court of Justice

In the relevant part of the judgment the Court concluded that '[w]hatever definition must be placed upon the concept of an 'aid' within the meaning of that article it is clear from the wording thereof that a measure characterized by the fixing of minimum retail prices with the objective of favouring distributors of a product at the exclusive expense of consumers cannot constitute an aid within the meaning of Article 92.' Secondly, the Court added that '[t]he advantages which such an intervention in the formation of prices entails for the distributors of the product are not granted, directly or indirectly, through State resources within the meaning of Article 92.'[9]

[8] As to the structural problems of European industry at this time, see Kapteyn, P.J.G., 'Outgrowing the Treaty of Rome: From Market Integration to Policy Integration', *in Melanges Fernand Dehousse* (Labor, 1979) 45.

[9] Case 82/77 *Van Tiggele* [1978] ECR 25 at paras 24–25.

D. Assessment

As mentioned, this case is usually referred to as the first in which the Court concluded that the concept of aid must entail a financial burden for the State. However, the term 'State resources' included in the last sentence of the passage quoted above could be interpreted in two different ways: (i) as referring to 'public or private bodies established or appointed by the State to administer the aid' in the sense of the *Steinike and Weinlig* judgment, or (ii) as State funds, in other words, as State money as it has been understood since the adoption of this judgment.

In favour of the first interpretation it could be argued that the *Steinike and Weinlig* judgment, in which the Court had interpreted the term 'State resources', had been delivered only a year before and was therefore still good law, and because in the case at hand there was no intermediary appointed by the State to administer the advantage conferred by the contested measure. However, in our view the correct interpretation of this case is the second for a number of reasons. First, because the question posed by the national Court was whether the price-fixing measure under review could be considered as and 'aid granted by the State' (not as an aid granted 'through State resources'). Therefore, the Court's answer was that an aid granted by the State must entail a financial loss, that is, financial resources, which unfortunately the Court described as 'State resources'. Secondly, the Court concluded that the measure under review favoured distributors 'at the *exclusive expense of consumers*', an expression that had been used by the Advocate General in his opinion to make precisely the point that the measure did not entail a financial loss for the State or for public undertakings. Thirdly, the view that the concept of aid required a financial charge for the State or its intermediaries was widespread among commentators and judges of the Court at the time when the *Van Tiggele* decision was rendered.[10] Similarly, the European Commission and several Advocates General had reached the same conclusion before this judgment.[11] In

[10] See Scheuing, *Les aides financiers publiques aux enterprises en droit francaise et europeen*, op. cit. at 268, who referred to the need of financial character of a measure for it to be State aid. In a similar vein, Judges Catalano, Trabucchi, and Monaco implicitly demand a financial charge as they only give examples of State aid measures either direct as subsidies or indirect as tax reliefs. See Catalano, N., *Manuel de droit des Communautes europeennes* (Dalloz, 1965) at 495, or Quadri, R., Monaco, R., and Trabucchi, A. (eds), *Trattato istitutivo della C.E.E. Comentario*, Vol. II (Giuffrè, 1965) at 720.

[11] See, eg, the view of the Commission and the Advocate General in the Judgment of 6 October 1970, 9/70, *Franz Grad v Finanzamt Traunstein* [1970] ECR 00825 at 835. AG Roemer shared the Commission's view of the no-aid character of taxes on competitors. The Court did not rule on this issue in the final judgment: '[The Commission and the German Government] claim that [Article 92] only refers to cases in which an undertaking receives payments financed out of public funds without giving consideration in return or else in which it is exempted from a charge', as referred by the Court at p. 835. Similarly, as to the opinion of AG Roemer: 'The concept of aid requires, as has already been stated in other cases, for example, in the judgment in Case 30/59 (Rec. 1961, pp. 38 and 39), a contribution at the expense of public funds or the reduction of charges which an undertaking normally has to bear', at 853. See also the then Commissioner for Competition, Von der Groeben, H., *The European Community—The Formative Years: The Struggle to Establish the Common Market and the Political Union (1958–66)* (Office for Official Publications of the European Communities, 1987) at 64: 'Distortion of competition by direct or indirect aid from *public funds* has to be prevented to ensure the same conditions for all those engaging in competition' (emphasis added).

the same vein, some of the contemporary annotations written in relation to this judgment did not even deal with the question of the notion of aid, as they probably assumed that the Court had not said anything new,[12] and one of them was even critical with the Court's judgment precisely for having confirmed that the notion of aid entailed a financial charge to the State.[13] Fourthly, this interpretation of the notion of aid was consistent with the first definitions of aid discussed in Chapter 1 such as the Brussels Sugar Convention definition that referred to measures granted by 'State *fiscal* legislation'. Finally, and more importantly, this interpretation is also coherent with the judgments of the Court in the famous *Sloman Neptun* and *Preussen Elektra* cases discussed below.

Having said that, a contemporary reader of State aid law may find it surprising that the Commission submitted in this case that the notion of aid necessarily entailed some sort of financial burden for the State,[14] as in this way the Commission was seemingly defending a limitation of the notion of aid, and thus a limitation of its exclusive competence concerning the control of aid. However, a combination of factors may justify the Commission's position, which in fact reinforced rather than weakened its exclusive competence in the State aid field. This is so because a broad notion of 'aid granted by the State' could jeopardize the Commission's exclusive competence to declare aids compatible with the Treaty, given that it could be confused with the rules concerning the free movement of goods, in particular with Article 30 EEC, which prohibited quantitative restrictions on imports and measures having an equivalent effect.

Indeed, as the Commission had pleaded before the Court only two years before this judgment, the *Guardian of the Treaties* was interested in a clear-cut distinction between the scope of then Articles 30 and 92 because a conflation of the two scopes could lead to national judges supplanting the exclusive discretionary powers that the Treaty conferred on the Commission in the field of State aid. In the Commission's words:

[12] See Akyürek-Kievits, H.E., 'Case 82/77, Openbaar Ministerie (Public Prosecutor) of the Kingdom of the Netherlands v. Jacobus Philippus van Tiggele. Preliminary ruling of 24 January 1978 at the request of the Gerechtshof, Amsterdam (1978) E.C.R. 26', (1979) *Common Mark`et Law Review* 139. This second note makes this brief reference to the question of State aid in a footnote: 'A second question posed by the Gerechtschof was whether Articles 92 and 94 must be interpreted as meaning that price-control rules such as those in issue could constitute a state aid. The Court responded in the negative. Whatever definition were to be placed upon the concept of an "aid" within the meaning of Article 92, it was clear that it could not apply to the fixing of minimum retail prices, since any advantages accruing to the distributors of the product in question were not granted, directly or indirectly, from the resources of the State.'

[13] Focsaneanu, L., 'Réglementations nationales de prix et droit communautaire—jurisprudence de la Cour de justice des Communautés européennes—Prix de Produits Industriels' (1986) *Revue du Marché Commun*, 281 at 288.

[14] See, as referred in the arguments of the judgment: 'The Commission considers that the rules in dispute do not constitute an aid within the meaning of Articles 92 to 94 since they entail neither the provision by the public authorities, directly, indirectly or a posteriori, of a benefit in cash or in kind, nor the renunciation by the authorities of the imposition of taxation or other benefits in cash or in kind owed to them.' See Case 82/77 *Openbaar Ministerie v Van Tiggele* [1978] ECR 25 at 37.

The Commission takes the view that subsidies fall within Article 92 and not Article 30. Although almost all systems of aid have an effect on trade and are for this reason capable of influencing it, their compatibility with the provisions of the Treaty should nevertheless be considered as a whole in relation to Article 92 and with due regard to the absolute discretionary power which Article 93 confers on the Commission. *The effect of including aids within the area of application of Article 30 would be to modify adversely the scope of this provision, to replace the Commission's discretion by that of the Court and to grant private individuals full rights in an area in which they can take no legal action because Article 92 does not have direct effect*'[15] (emphasis added).

In this regard, the Commission, the AG, and the Court found that the minimum price fixed constituted a measure having an effect equivalent to a quantitative restriction on imports prohibited under Article 30 EEC. Therefore, it is submitted that the Commission did not have any particular interest to defend a broad notion of aid in this case as the national measure was nevertheless contrary to the Treaty.

Finally, another novelty of this case has to do with the effects-based formula applied to the concept of aid since the *Italian textiles* case. As discussed above, the Court had previously held, also in the *Steinike and Weinlig* judgment, that the concept of aid had to be assessed from the point of view of the beneficiaries of the State measure, a point that had also been raised by the plaintiff.[16] However, the Court looked at whether the contested measure entailed a financial charge to the State or to public or private distributors of aid on behalf of the State. The *rationale* for this departure, it is submitted, has to be found in the Commission's request for a concept of aid limited to financial measures, made in a period (the 1970s) in which the Court was sympathetic to Commission's submissions, and in the general architecture of the Treaty that subjects State regulatory and legislative measures to the free movement rules. In addition, the application of the free movement rules in this case allowed not only the Court but also national courts, due to the direct effect of Article 30 EEC, to review

[15] As referred by the Court's judgment of 22 March 1977 in Case 74/76 *Ianelli and Volpi v Meroni* [1977] ECR 557 at p. 562. For the relationship between State aids and free movement provisions, a relationship which is more constitutional (as a division of competences: aids are entrusted to the Commission and free movement provisions directly to individuals) than functional (as they share the main goal). For other authors who had defended the difference between Arts 30 and 92 in order to avoid the blurring of the distinction of these two articles, see the references included in Slotboom, M., 'State Aid in Community Law: A Broad or Narrow Definition?' (1995) *European Law Review* 289 at 298, footnote 39. See also Biondi, A., and Farley, M. 'The Relationship between State Aid and the Single Market' in Szyszczak, E. (ed.) *Research Handbook on State Aid* (Edward Elgar, 2011) 277. See also in this regard the opinion of AG Mancini in case 177/78, *Pigs and Bacon Commission* [1979] ECR 02161, 2207: 'Article 30 of the Treaty forbidding, as between Member States, quantitative restrictions on imports and all measures having equivalent effect could not be interpreted so widely as to extend to obstacles to trade which, as such, were covered by Articles 92 and 93. In reaching that conclusion the Court had regard to the circumstance that *otherwise the provisions of Articles 92 to 94 would be rendered largely inoperative*' (emphasis added).

[16] As referred by the Court in Case 82/77 *Van Tiggele* [1978] ECR 25 at p. 36: 'According to the case-law of the Court, namely the judgment of 2 July 1974 in Case 173/73 *Italy v Commission* [1974] ECR 709); judgment of 22 March 1977 in Case 78/76 *Steinike and Weinlig v Germany* [1977] ECR 595), Article 92 does not draw any distinction on the basis of the causes or objectives of the measures in question; it considers them solely in terms of their consequences.'

these measures directly and even to validate their restriction in some instances by reference to the justifications provided for in the Treaty, features alien to the State aid field.

3. The *Poor Farmers* Case (C-290/83)

A. Introduction and background of the case

This case is the first in which the Court of Justice held that under Article 107(1) TFEU 'aid need not necessarily be financed from State resources to be classified as State aid'. This has been considered to be in conflict with the finding of the Court in the *Van Tiggele* judgment which established that the concept of aid requires a financial burden for the State.

As to the background, in 1981 France had notified a number of measures to the Commission under Article 108(3) TFEU. Among those measures there was a grant made by a public body (the Caisse nationale de Crédit Agricole) to farmers undergoing difficult economic circumstances. This so-called solidarity grant was intended to subsidize the poorest farmers and included a budget of *circa* 1.5 thousand million francs. Given that France had notified the measure under Article 108, it was in principle clear that the measure was *a priori* State aid. The Commission thus initiated the State aid formal investigation procedure. However the Commission stopped this procedure after receiving the following information from France: (i) the State representatives were a minority in the governing board of the public body that adopted the decision to pay the grant at stake, and (ii) the grant was paid with a surplus generated by the management of private funds 'and not of State resources'. In light of this information, the Commission held that the measure was not aid under Article 107 but 'a measure having an effect equivalent to State aid'. The Commission thus discontinued the State aid procedure under Article 108(2) and initiated the standard infringement procedure provided for then in Article 169 of the Treaty, claiming that France had failed to fulfil its obligations under the Treaty. As a result of this procedure, and in view of the French disregard to the Commission's requests, the Commission brought an action against France before the Court.

B. The policy context

The judgment of this case was delivered during the second period of evolution of the State aid policy discussed in Chapter 3. Towards the end of this period, the Commission adopted a stricter enforcement line than it had taken previously and started to focus more on cases involving public undertakings. Indeed, as it clearly emerges from the competition reports of the early 1980s, a key concern for the Commission at this time was the increasing burden of the public sector on the economy. Out of this concern the Commission adopted the Transparency Directive in June 1980. With the approval of this Directive the Commission aimed to obtain information about the financial relations between public undertakings and Member States that would also prove useful for the MEIP test that the Commission started to apply systematically by this time.

C. Judgment of the Court of Justice

The Court held that '[b]y virtue of the generality of the terms employed in [Article 107(1)] any State measure, in so far as it has the effect of according aid in any form whatsoever, may be assessed on the basis of [that article] for its compatibility with the common market.' In addition the Court stated that '[a]s is clear from the actual wording of Article [107 (1)], aid need not necessarily be financed from State resources to be classified as State aid.'[17]

The Court did not mention the previous *Van Tiggele* case but rather the *Steinike and Weinlig* judgment in support of this conclusion: 'the prohibition contained in Article [107 (1)] covers all aid granted by a Member State or through State resources and there is no necessity to draw any distinction according to whether the aid is granted directly by the State or by public or private bodies established or appointed by it to administer the aid.'[18] Indeed, the Court found that the measure in question amounted to State aid and that such concept left no scope for measures equivalent to aid.

Therefore the Commission should have continued the procedure under Article 108(2) because the measure was clearly an aid, as the French Government had conceded by notifying it to the Commission under the State aid provisions of the Treaty.

D. Assessment

In our view, the alleged tension between this judgment and the *Van Tiggele* decision, to which Advocate Generals have referred,[19] does not exist. The Court required a financial burden also in this case although it clarified that such burden could be financed by an intermediary in the sense of the *Steinike and Weinlig* judgment and therefore that it was not necessary for the burden to be financed by the State directly. This interpretation also emanates from a natural reading of the following passage of the judgment in this case: 'It follows that Article 92 of the Treaty covers aid which, like the solidarity grant in question, was decided *and financed* by a public body and the implementation of which is subject to the approval of the public authorities, the detailed rules for the grant of which correspond to those for ordinary State aid and which, moreover, was put forward by the Government as forming part of a body of measures in favour of farmers

[17] C-290/83 *Commission v France* [1985] ECR 439 at para. 14. [18] Ibid.

[19] See the opinion of AG Mengozzi in Joined Cases C-399/10 P and C-401/10 P, *Bouygues and Bouygues Télécom v Commission and Others*, nyp at 38.

which were all notified to the Commission in pursuance of Article 93 (3)' (emphasis added).[20] This view is also confirmed by another judgment laid down by the Court between the *Van Tiggele* and this decision in which a financial burden on the State was required,[21] and also by the famous *Philip Morris* judgment in which the Court referred to 'State *financial* aid' in its most significant paragraph.[22]

The Commission insisted again in requiring a financial burden for the State as a condition for the application of today's Article 107(1) TFEU. A justification for this position, that as discussed above limited the measures that the Commission could review under the State aid rules, might be that the Court had already established the need for a financial burden for the State in *Van Tiggele* (at the Commission's request). Another answer, compatible with the first, might be that the Commission still preferred to limit the concept of aid to financial measures in order to avoid conflation with the internal market rules, yet the applicability of Article 30 EEC in this case was less obvious than in *Van Tiggele*. The combination of the two answers may perhaps explain why the Commission proposed a new concept that would allow scrutinizing the measure under review without broadening formally the concept of aid under Article 107.

In any event, the solution found by the Commission to achieve these ends was not orthodox as there was no reference in the Treaty for a notion of measures having an effect equivalent to aid. It was therefore rejected by the Court in bold terms. It should be noted, in this regard, that several authors, including judges of the Court, have observed that the Court became stricter *vis-à-vis* Commission decisions in the early and mid-1980s, requiring more solid legal basis and annulling Commission decisions.[23] This case could thus be an example of the Court's stricter approach.

[20] See C-290/83 *Commission v France* [1985] ECR 439 at para. 15. The Court reached the same conclusion in a subsequent case in which it made clear that what mattered was not that the funds of the Greek Central Bank were public but that the latter was under the direct control of the State. See Case 57/86, *Greece v Commission* [1988] ECR 2855 at paras 12 and 13: 'The Court has consistently held (see in particular the judgment of 30 January 1985 in Case 290/83 *Commission v France* [1985] ECR 439) that an aid need not necessarily be financed from State resources to be classified as a State aid. Article 92 covers all aid granted by States or through State resources and there is no necessity to draw any distinction according to whether the aid is granted directly by the State or by public or private bodies established or appointed by it to administer the aid. In the present case it need merely be pointed out that the repayment of interest was introduced by the Hellenic Republic through the Bank of Greece which, for that purpose, acted under direct State control and that the banks reimburse the interest or send documents evidencing the purchase of foreign currency to the Bank of Greece, which then makes the payment.'

[21] Joined Cases 213/81 to 215/81 *Norddeutsches Vieh—und Fleischkontor Will and Others* [1982] ECR 3583, para. 22. See particularly the last sentence: 'Although the term "aid granted through State resources" is wider than the term "State aid", the first term still presupposes that the resources from which the aid is granted come from the Member State.'

[22] Case 730/79 *Philip Morris* [1980] ECR I-2671, para. 11: 'when state financial aid strengthens the position of an undertaking compared with other undertakings competing in intra-community trade the latter must be regarded as affected by that aid.'

[23] Koopmans, T. 'The Role of Law in the Next Stage of European Integration' (1986) *International and Comparative Law Quarterly* 925 at 931. See also Goyder, D.G., *EEC Competition Law* (OUP, 1988) at 383–84, or Ross, M., 'A Review of Developments in State Aids 1987–88'(1989) *Common Market Law Review* 167 at 178, who speaks of a 'wrist-slapping' by the Court around 1983.

4. The *Van der Kooy* Case (C-67/85)

A. Introduction and background of the case

This case is known for being the first in which the Court concluded that for a measure adopted by a public or private body to constitute State aid, the measure at stake has to be attributable to the State.[24] This finding thus added the need to trace the adoption of the measure back to the action of the State to the notion of aid. In other words, that State aids must be imputable to the State.

The origins of the case go back to 1981 when the Commission found that the Netherlands granted State aid to horticultural growers in the form of a preferential price for gas.[25] The Commission started the State aid procedure after making a study of distortions of competition in glasshouse horticulture.[26] What is surprising is that the study in question was carried out in 1968, a full twelve years before the initiation of the case. The new approach toward public intervention of the early 1980s, together with the arrival of a more liberal Commissioner and the adoption of the Transparency Directive may help explain the 'sudden' action after a decade of passivity. This decision was challenged before the Court of Justice. However, since a new tariff was negotiated following the decision, the Commission repealed that decision and, therefore, the challenges against it were also dropped. It is this new preferential tariff, introduced in 1984, which led to a new decision and ultimately to the judgment under discussion.

The tariff was negotiated between three parties: (i) Gasunie—a private-law company in which the Netherlands Government held, directly and indirectly, 50 per cent of the capital and the remainder was held by two private companies—(ii) a public body representing agricultural undertakings, and (iii) an association of local gas-distribution companies. The Commission concluded, in essence, that the tariff charged by Gasunie deliberately forwent certain revenues in order to provide a financial advantage for all Netherlands growers who use natural gas to heat their glasshouses, and that this advantage was not justified on commercial grounds.[27]

In particular, the decision stated that a preferential tariff is caught by the prohibition in Article 107(1) of the Treaty when the following three factors are met: '(i) when the tariff favours certain undertakings or the production of certain goods competing with the undertakings or production of other Member States, and the products in question are traded within the Community, (ii) when the tariff has been imposed by a public authority, (iii) when the tariff results in compensation

[24] Joined Cases 67, 68, and 70/85 *Van der Kooy and others* [1988] ECR, p. 219. See for a subsequent reference to this case Case C-482/99 *France v Commission* ('Stardust Marine') [2002] ECR I-4397 at para. 24.

[25] Decision 82/73 of 15 December 1981 (Official Journal 1982, L 37, p. 29).

[26] Ibid. at II.

[27] Commission Decision of 13 February 1985 on the preferential tariff charged to glasshouse growers for natural gas in the Netherlands (OJ L 97, 4 April 1985, pp. 49–56).

from the State being paid to the distribution company or to the State receiving less revenue.' Therefore, the Commission required both (i) State intervention, that is, the requirement that the tariff be imposed by a public authority (second criterion), and (ii) State funds, that is loss of revenue for the State (third criterion).

The decision was challenged by several growers benefitting from the preferential tariff, by the association of growers that took part in the agreements concluded by Gasunie (the Landbouwschap), and by the Netherlands Government.

B. The policy context

The decision that led to the judgment under discussion was adopted in 1985, two years after the decision adopted in the French case discussed above. Therefore the policy context remained broadly the same described in relation to the previous case—new stricter approach towards State aids as part of a stricter approach towards public intervention in the economy. Perhaps the main novelty that took place between 1983 and 1985 was the confirmation of the Market Economy Investor Principle (MEIP) test in the Commission's practice, supported by the Court in several judgments, including the landmark *Meura* case.[28]

C. Judgment of the Court of Justice

The way in which the Court phrased the issue under examination in this case did resemble the MEIP test:

> It should be observed at the outset that this case raises the question whether the fixing of the tariff charged for a source of energy at a level lower than that which would normally have been chosen may be regarded as "aid" when it is attributable to action by the Member State concerned and the other conditions laid down by Article 92 are satisfied. In such circumstances the State, or the entity on which it exerts influence, does not apply the tariff as an ordinary economic agent but uses it to confer a pecuniary advantage on energy consumers, in the same way as it grants aid to certain undertakings, forgoing the profit which it could normally realize.[29]

Moreover, in line with previous cases, the Court did not analyse whether the origin of the funds allegedly granted was or not public in order to reach the conclusion that the aid was granted by the State or through State resources. Instead, the Court dealt with the criterion under review under the heading 'Whether the fixing of the contested tariff was the result of action by the Netherlands State', and concluded that 'the fixing of the contested tariff is the result of action by the

[28] C-234/84 *Belgium v Commission* ('Meura') [1986] ECR 2263. In two previous cases the Court had endorsed the reasoning of the Commission concerning the MEIP (see Case 323/82 *Intermills v Commission* [1984] ECR 3809, and Joined Cases 296 and 318/82 *Netherlands and Leeuwarder Papierwarenfabriek v Commission* [1985] ECR 809), yet it was in the *Meura* judgment where the Court explicitly adopted it and even complemented it, as we will discuss.

[29] Joined Cases 67, 68, and 70/85 *Van der Kooy and others* [1988] ECR 219 at para. 28.

Netherlands State and thus falls within the meaning of the phrase "aid granted by a Member State" under Article 92 of the Treaty.'[30]

D. Assessment

In our view, this judgment adds little to the *Steinike and Weinlig* and *Poor Farmers* decisions discussed earlier. It confirms that the concept of aid granted by the State or through State resources includes a financial transfer (in this case, as the AG had held in his opinion to this case, the loss of revenue arising from the preferential tariff) under the control of the State.[31] Whether the origin of the funds transferred is public (as in *Poor Farmers*) or private (as in *Steinike and Weinlig*) is not relevant; what matters is that the State retains control over the financial transfer.

As to the issue of imputability, in our view the Court dealt with this notion specifically because several parties, including the Netherlands State, had rejected that the conduct of Gasunie could be *attributed to the State*. In other words, they negated that Gasunie could be considered as 'State resources' in the sense of the *Steinike and Weinlig* judgment; that is, as a public or private authority instituted by the State to grant the aid.

Indeed, the notion of imputability seems a reaffirmation of the same idea: The granting of the preferential tariff has to be attributable to the action of the State for otherwise the funds of the undertaking distributing the aid could not be considered as granted through 'State resources' in the sense just mentioned. By exclusion the same conclusion can be reached: the alleged aid was not granted directly by the State as a matter of fact. The question therefore was whether Gasunie, through which the aid had been granted, could be seen as a 'State resource' under the meaning of Article 107. In this regard, as AG Slynn had submitted, a selective benefit can be granted other than directly by the State in certain circumstances: 'Indeed, if it were not so, it would be too easy to avoid the intention of Articles 92 and 93 of the Treaty.'[32]

Having said that, the notion of imputability was also justified in the 1980s context by reference to the principle of neutrality between public and private undertakings, a principle that had been emphasized several times during that decade, including in the Transparency Directive and the MEIP test. This is so because it would seem contrary to that principle that any financial transaction adopted by a company in which the State had some influence would necessarily be subject

[30] Ibid. at para. 38.

[31] AG Slynn concluded that there were State resources in this case because the advantage granted by Gasunie through the preferential tariff was not justified by commercial reasons. In other words, the measure was aid because the MEIP test was not satisfied and thus because there was a loss to the State. See the Opinion of AG Gordon Slynn in Joined Cases 67, 68, and 70/85, *Van der Kooy and others* [1988] ECR at p. 219 at 251.

[32] See the Opinion of AG Gordon Slynn in Joined Cases 67, 68, and 70/85 *Van der Kooy and others* [1988] ECR, p. 219 at 249.

to State aid scrutiny. It therefore seems more appropriate to require first that the transaction at stake is the result of State action.

5. The *Sloman Neptun* Case (Joined Cases C-72/91 and C-73/91)

A. Introduction and background of the case

This case is usually referred to as the first in which the Court clearly stated that the notion of State resources included in Article 107(1) TFEU has to be understood as State funds. It should be remembered at this point that the judgment in *Van Tiggele* was concerned with the notion of 'aid granted by the State', and 'State resources' could be understood as referring to the public or private bodies distributing the aid (in the sense of the *Steinike and Weinlig* case) or as State funds, although it has been suggested that the second interpretation is the correct one.

As with most cases related to the notion of State resources, this case also arrived to the Court in the form of a preliminary ruling. An explanation for this could be the lack of Commission's decisions supporting an expansive understanding of this notion, an understanding that would presumably had been challenged before the Court. This explanation would be in line with the argument defended in this chapter concerning the Commission's preference for the application of internal market rules (instead of the State aid ones) to borderline cases until the beginning of the 1990s. For our purposes, the relevant question asked by the national Court was whether the non-application of German employment and social security law (to non-EU seafarers) should be regarded as State aid to German shipowners.

B. The policy context

This case falls within the third period of evolution of the State aid policy discussed in Chapter 3. In the period immediately leading to this judgment (delivered in 1993) the Commission had profited from the momentum of the 1992 internal market programme to tighten the State aid rules and to secure a more rigorous enforcement. In fact, the stricter approach to State aids was only part of a wider programme, namely, the '*public turn*' of competition policy,[33] that aimed at abolishing State distortive measures as, at the Commission held in 1991, 'at the present stage of economic integration in the Community the barriers are greatest in markets currently subject to State regulation.'[34] In this context, the

[33] See for this expression Gerber, D.J. 'The Transformation of European Community Competition Law?' (1994) *Harvard International Law Journal* 137. See also Gerber, *Law and Competition in Twentieth Century Europe*, op. cit. at 383. For an explanation of the link between the success of State aid control and the success of the internal market project see the Twentieth Report on Competition Policy (Office for Official Publications of the European Communities, 1991) at point 169.

[34] Twentieth Report on Competition Policy, op. cit. at point 53.

Commission reinforced its role in the institutional sphere, and particularly *vis-à-vis* the Council.[35] In a nutshell, State aid control became an instrument for economic change and for the long-desired restructuring of European industry that would result from the 1992 project.

C. Judgment of the Court of Justice

The Court stated that '[t]he distinction between aid granted by the State and aid granted through State resources serves to bring within the definition of aid not only aid granted directly by the State, but also aid granted by public or private bodies designated or established by the State.'[36] Therefore, the Court confirmed the *Steinike and Weinlig* finding.

Then the Court continued by holding that:

> [t]he system at issue does not seek, through its object and general structure, to create an advantage which would constitute an additional burden for the State or the abovementioned bodies, but only to alter in favour of shipping undertakings the framework within which contractual relations are formed between those undertakings and their employees. The consequences arising from this, in so far as they relate to the difference in the basis for the calculation of social security contributions, mentioned by the national court, and to the potential loss of tax revenue because of the low rates of pay, referred to by the Commission, are inherent in the system and are not a means of granting a particular advantage to the undertakings concerned.[37]

Thus the Court confirmed that a financial burden is necessary and that it can fall either on the State or on public or private distributors of aid as discussed in the *Poor Farmers* and *Van der Kooy* cases.

D. Assessment

The Court thus concluded that the concept of aid entails a financial burden. The Court also clarified that the reference to 'State resources' in the *Van Tiggele* case had to be understood as State funds. Furthermore, the Court also confirmed that the financial burden may fall directly on the State or indirectly on public or private bodies designated or established by the State. Finally, the Court admitted that the measure under review could entail a potential loss to the State yet this loss would be inherent in the system under review and therefore was 'not a means of granting a particular advantage to the undertakings concerned.'[38]

The judgment of the Court in this case was soon perceived by some commentators as a restrictive turn to the notion of aid at odds with the previous case law of the Court. In particular, they noted the Court's shift away from the *action by*

[35] See Ehlermann, C.D., 'Commission Lacks Power in 1992 Process' (1990) *European Affairs* 65 at 70.

[36] Joined Cases C-72/91 and C-73/91 *Sloman Neptun* [1993] ECR I-887 at para. 19.

[37] Ibid. at para. 21. [38] Ibid.

the State as the main requirement, regardless of the origin of the funds, towards the primordial importance of the latter.[39] Other authors considered, by contrast, that the decision was a confirmation of the previous jurisprudence and, in particular, of *Van Tiggele*.[40] In our view the latter view is more accurate. This case can be seen as a confirmation of *Van Tiggele* in the sense that in both cases there were advantages to some undertakings derived from State legislation without any direct financial charge to the State or to public or private intermediaries of the State. Therefore, rather than restricting its previous case law, this judgment can be depicted as one by which the Court refused to expand its previous case law.

This judgment represented the first serious disagreement as to the concept of aid between the Commission and the Court of Justice. In this regard, in *Van Tiggele* the Commission had considered that the measure at stake was not State aid because there was no financial loss for the State and the Court followed. Instead, in this case the Commission defended the position that any measure of whatever nature which entails a specific advantage was a State aid even if not financed from public funds,[41] and the Court did not follow.

The change in the Commission's position regarding the financial nature of the concept of aid can be explained as part of the stricter approach towards State aids that this institution adopted in the context of the 1992 programme. Indeed, as already discussed, the Commission had in the past preferred to apply the fundamental freedoms to cases such as this in order to avoid conflation between the scope of the fundamental freedoms and that of State aids (to safeguard its discretionary powers in the latter field) and to ensure the abolition of discriminatory measures in the most effective way, given the relative weakness of the State aid regime before the mid-1980s when compared with the free movement rules. However, the time was now ripe for the enforcement of the State aid rules even to the detriment of the scope of application of the free movement rules, as the internal market had formally been achieved in 1992 and the need for the strong application of, for example, Article 30 EEC had diminished. In addition, the Commission had in the meantime developed a number of soft-law instruments concerning the compatibility of aid measures that could be applied to measures such as the contested one in this case. Indeed, the broadening of the notion of aid defended by the Commission in this case can also be seen as an attempt to enforce the specific compatibility rules that it had set out for the shipping industry.[42]

[39] Rodríguez Curiel, J.W., 'Giro jurisprudencial restrictivo del concepto de ayuda de Estado (sentencia del Tribunal de Justicia de las CC.EE. de 17-3-93)' (1993) *Gaceta Jurídica de la C.E. y de la Competencia* 5 at 9.

[40] Slot, P.J., 'Joined Cases C-72/91 and C-73/91, Sloman Neptun Schiffahrts A. G. v. Seebetriebsrat Bodo Ziesemer der Sloman Neptun Schiffahrts A.G., Judgment of 17 March 1993' (1994) *Common Market Law Review* 137.

[41] See as referred by the Court in the judgment under review Joined Cases C-72/91 and C-73/91 *Sloman Neptun* [1993] ECR I-887 at para. 17.

[42] See, eg, the guidelines for the assessment of State aid to shipping SEC (89) 921 final of 3 August 1989. See also the Report for the hearing in this case at pp. ECR 1993 I-889–90.

Finally, although it is always difficult to speculate about the reasons that made the Court refuse a broadening of the concept of aid, one reason for the Court's answer in this case might have been legal certainty. This reason would make the *Sloman Neptun* judgment consistent with a series of cases, also decided in 1993, in which the Court seemed to favour legal certainty and formalism over the effectiveness (*effet utile*) of Community law. The most famous of these cases is of course *Keck*, decided a few months after *Sloman Neptun*.[43] Some authors have in fact linked the Court's decisions in *Keck* and *Sloman Neptun* as both cases referred to the issue of further broadening a Community provision that had already been expanded by the Court (Articles 30 and 92) after the Court's experience of having a sweeping notion of Article 30 in the Sunday trading saga.[44]

In the same vein, other authors have also underlined the 'lighter touch' of the Court in relation to the regulation of the market that surrounded the period when the *Sloman Neptun* judgment was laid down.[45] Similarly, Maduro and others have noticed that the Court has traditionally accepted a cautious approach in censuring State regulations directly in light of competition values.[46] Finally, the Court may have preferred to be especially prudent in this case as it concerned a social measure adopted by Germany and defended by its government before the Court in a context of increasing criticism coming from Germany in the autumn of 1992 against the Court for certain judgments that benefited, as in this case, non-Community migrants. The 'dismay of the Court' created by this criticism was recognized by Judge Mancini.[47]

In any event, subsequent case law on State aid has confirmed this view, that is the Court's reluctance to assess State legislation and/or regulation under the State aid rules.[48] Indeed, as suggested earlier in relation to the *Van Tiggele* judgment, from the Court's case law seems to emerge the principle that it is not for the Commission, under the compatibility of aid rules, but for the national judges—and eventually for the Court through the preliminary reference procedure—to asses

[43] Joined Cases C-267 and C-268/91 *Keck and Mithouard* [1993] ECR I-6097.

[44] See, eg, Davies, P., 'Market Integration and Social Policy in the Court of Justice' (1995) *Industrial Law Journal*, 49 at 59–62.

[45] See Ross, M., 'State Aids: Maturing into a Constitutional Problem' (1995) *Yearbook of European Law* 79 at 82. See also the references mentioned by Ross in footnote 14 of that page.

[46] See Poiares Maduro, M., *We the Court, The European Court of Justice and the European Economic Constitution* (Hart Publishing, 1998) at 75. See also the references cited therein: Triantafyllou, D. 'Les règles de la concurrence et l'activité étatique y compris les marchés publics' (1996) *RTDE* 32 at 68; and Mengozzi, P., 'Il Principio dell'Investitore in una Economia di Mercato e i Valori del Diritto Comunitario' (1995) *Rivista di Diritto Europeo* 19 at 24.

[47] See Mancini G.F., and Keeling, D.T., 'Language, Culture and Politics in the Life of the European Court of Justice' (1994–95) *Columbia Journal of European Law* 397 at 408. Judge Mancini recognized 'the dismay of the Court, first, when the German press began, in the autumn of 1992, to vehemently criticize some judgments benefitting Italian and non-Community migrant workers and, later, when it learnt that those protests were inspired or shared by the Minister of Social Affairs, Norbert Bliim, and even by Chancellor Kohl.'

[48] See Case C-189/91 *Kirsammer-Hack* [1993] ECR 1-6185, para. 16; Joined Cases C-52/97, C-53/97, and C-54/97 *Viscido* [1998] ECR I-2629, para. 13; Case C-200/97 *Ecotrade* [1998] ECR I-7907, para. 35; Case C-295/97 *Piaggio* [1999] ECR I-3735, para. 35.

under the free movement rules the legality of State regulation or legislation under the Treaty, beyond of course fiscal or social measures entailing a direct financial charge for the State or for public or private bodies designated or established by the State, 'State fiscal legislation' in the sense of the Brussels Sugar Convention, that fall under the State aid rules.

6. The *Preussen Elektra* Case (C-379/98)

A. Introduction and background

This case is usually referred to as the first in which the Court has concluded that aid must be granted by the State and through State resources (thus reading the two requirements cumulatively). In other words, the Court has confirmed in this case that the term 'State resources' must necessarily entail a financial burden.

The case arrived to the Court also in the form of a preliminary ruling. A regional German court asked the Court of Justice three questions concerning the interpretation of Articles 30, 92, and 93(3). In essence, the national Court asked whether a legislation that required private electricity supply undertakings to purchase electricity from renewable energy sources at minimum prices higher than the real economic value of that type of electricity, and to distribute the financial burden resulting from that obligation between those electricity supply undertakings and upstream private electricity network operators constituted State aid within the meaning of Article 107(1), and whether the same statutory provisions could be considered as a measure having an equivalent effect to a quantitative restriction. In this case, however, as opposed to *Van Tiggele*, the first question was whether the measure at stake was State aid and whether it amounted to a violation of the free movement rules.

It should be noted that the German legislation at stake was not new to the European Commission. In fact, the Commission had reviewed it under the State aid rules, although it had not come to a decision given that 'important legislative changes at Community level were expected in the near future in connection with the implementation of the electricity directive and proposals for harmonised rules on electricity from renewable sources'. The Commission had therefore decided to wait until the German government established a report on the operation of the contested measure.[49]

B. The policy context

This case has been decided during the fourth period of evolution of the State aid policy discussed in Chapter 3. This period was initiated by the joint initiative of the Commission and the Irish presidency on future prospects of State aid control

[49] Opinion of AG Jacobs in case C-379/98 *Preussen Elektra* [2001] ECR I-2099 at para. 38.

of 14 November 1996, which purported to refocus priorities, increase transparency and legal certainty, and to clarify the procedural rules in the field of State aids.[50] This clarification and modernization was needed due to the increase in the number of notifications and complaints brought before the Commission since the mid- to late 1990s and even more so after the 2004 enlargement.

The more systematic application of the State aid rules has also led to an expansion in the number of policy instruments concerning the compatibility of State aid measures with the internal market. In this regard, and relevant for the purposes of this case, by the mid-1990s the Commission started adopting Community guidelines on State aid for environmental protection,[51] and preparing a block exemption regulation for environmental aid by 1998,[52] the year of adoption of the contested measure. In addition, by the end of 2000, the Commission adopted new environment State aid guidelines which established a ceiling to the amount of aid that Member States could give to cover the cost of producing energy from renewable sources.[53]

C. The judgment of the Court of Justice

The Court of Justice established very clearly that State resources equated to State funds and that they were required for a finding of aid by holding that:

> [t]he case-law of the Court of Justice shows that only advantages granted directly or indirectly through State resources are to be considered aid within the meaning of Article 92(1). The distinction made in that provision between 'aid granted by a Member State' and aid granted 'through State resources' does not signify that all advantages granted by a State, whether financed through State resources or not, constitute aid but is intended merely to bring within that definition both advantages which are granted directly by the State and those granted by a public or private body designated or established by the State.[54]

The Court added that in the case at hand the obligation imposed on private electricity supply undertakings did not involve any direct or indirect transfer of State resources to undertakings which produce renewable energy electricity. Furthermore, as in *Sloman Neptun*, the Court held that the fact that the

[50] See Mederer, W., 'The Future of State Aid Control' (1996) *Competition Policy Newsletter* 12, and Lavdas and Mendrinou, *Politics, Subsidies, and Competition: The New Politics of State Intervention in the European Union*, op. cit. at 44. See also Doleys, T, 'Fifty Years of Moulding Article 87: The European Commission and the Development of EU State Aid Law & Policy (1958–2008)' (Edward Elgar, 1999) at 22.

[51] OJ 1994 C 72, p. 3.

[52] Twenty-eighth Report on Competition Policy (Office for Official Publications of the European Communities, 1999) at point 185

[53] Thirtieth Report on Competition Policy (Office for Official Publications of the European Communities, 2001) at point 301: 'Regarding renewable energy sources, which are given a high priority, Member States will in future be able to grant inter alia aid to cover the difference between the cost of producing energy from renewable sources and the market price of that energy up to the amount required for the depreciation on the installations in question'.

[54] C-379/98 *Preussen Elektra* [2001] ECR I-2099 at para. 58.

undertakings obliged to buy electricity would have worse economic results for that reason and hence would pay less in taxes was an inherent feature of the system, and could not be considered as an advantage under Article 107(1). The Court also rejected, as in *Poor Farmers*, a final argument of the Commission according to which if the measure at stake could not be considered as aid it should be considered as a measure having an equivalent effect to an aid.

D. Assessment

The Court's refusal to broaden the scope of the concept of aid in this case contrasted drastically with the opinion of the European Commission, which had claimed, in essence, that the effects-based approach to the concept of aid and the *effet utile* of this provision called for an aid finding. The Commission's position was thus coherent with that maintained since the achievement of the internal market, the systematic application of the State aid rules, and the development of a body of soft law concerning compatibility that, as in this case, was relevant (environmental aid guidelines).

The Court's judgment is in our view consistent with the previous case law for the reasons discussed in the review of *Van Tiggele* and *Sloman Neptun*. The solution given by the Court in this case has also been praised by reasons of legal certainty in the context of increasing intervention of national courts in the application of the State aid rules.[55] In addition, Advocate General Jacobs has noted that this decision may be coherent with the need to avoid subjecting to the Commission and the Court under the State aid rules many national legislative and regulatory measures.[56] AG Maduro has also underlined the problem that would entail broadening the application of the State aid rules to cover most national legislative measures, as Member States are entitled to adopt general measures to regulate economic activities.[57]

[55] Vesterndorf, B., 'A Further Comment on the New State Aid Concept as this Concept Continues to be Reshaped—Pearle—A Further Piece of the State Aid Puzzle?' (2005) *European State Aid Law Quarterly* 393 at 399. See also Biondi, A., 'Some Reflections on the Notion of "State Resources" in European Community State Aid Law' (2007) *Fordham International Law Journal* 1426 at 1140.

[56] See, eg, Opinion of Advocate General Jacobs in Joined Cases C-52/97, C-53/97, and C-54/97 *Viscido* [1998] ECR I-2629 at para. 16: 'to investigate all such regimes would entail an inquiry on the basis of the Treaty alone into the entire social and economic life of a Member State.'

[57] See the Opinion of Advocate General Poiares Maduro in case C-237/04 *Enirisorse SpA v Sotacarbo SpA* [2006] ECR I-2843 at para. 45. In his strong opinion, AG Maduro suggested that the Court should use the selectivity rather than the State resources criterion to distinguish 'between distortions resulting from the adoption of measures to regulate economic activities and those caused by a transfer of public resources to certain undertakings'. Similarly, AG Darmon concluded that the *ratio legis* of the concept of aid was to subject to joint supervision intervention by the State which goes beyond the general legislative framework of economic activities. See Opinion of Advocate General Darmon in case Joined Cases C-72/91 and C-73/91 *Sloman Neptun* [1993] ECR I-887, para. 55. See also in this regard the Opinion of Advocate General Jaaskinen in Joined Cases C-106/09 P and C-107/09 P *Government of Gibraltar v Commission* [2011] ECR nyr, para. 189. More generally, AG Kokkot has reminded that Member States may adopt 'legislation which pursues an aim in the public interest—for example, health protection, environmental protection

In this context, AG Jacobs suggested in his opinion to the *Preussen Elektra* case that other rules, such as the internal market rules, may be available to deal with situations excluded from the notion of aid. In fact, in *Preussen Elektra* the internal market rules were found applicable and so too in the more recent *UTECA* case.[58] Indeed, the internal market rules apply precisely to legislative and regulatory measures. They are also more protective to the interests of Member States than the State aid rules as Member States can invoke under the internal market rules reasons of national interest (both as justifications for a restriction or as mandatory requirements) while in the case of State aids, following the *Philip Morris* judgment, the justifications in this field have to be of a Community, not a national, interest as interpreted by the European Commission.

Therefore, the application of the internal market rules to situations where there is no financial burden for the State or for public or private bodies instituted by the State to grant aid would seem to us in line with the general approach of the Treaty regarding national legislative and regulatory measures. Having said that, it is submitted that if this pattern becomes a generalized practice to avoid the application of the State aid rules, as the referring Court in this case had warned,[59] the Court may, in the spirit of the recent judgments concerning selectivity, consider such practice an unacceptable circumvention of the State aid rules based on a 'regulatory technique' and thus conclude that there is State aid, a solution that we would support.[60] Indeed, recent judgments of both the Court of Justice and the General Court seem to point in this direction.[61] The proposed solution would also be in line with that found in the World Trade Organization context, where a specific provision has been adopted under the agreement on subsidies and countervailing duties (SCM Agreement) to cover the situation where a government entrusts or directs a private body to, *inter alia*, provide a transfer of funds to an undertaking.[62] The rationale of this provision is precisely to prevent governments

or road safety—to which both public and private establishments are subject.' Opinion of Advocate General Kokott in Case C-222/07 *UTECA* [2009] ECR I-1407 at para. 135. See also para. 137.

[58] Case C-222/07 *UTECA* [2009] ECR I-1407.

[59] As referred by AG Jacobs the national court had held that 'such a narrow interpretation of the concept of State aid would allow Member States easily to circumvent the control mechanisms of Article 93 of the Treaty with potentially grave consequences for competition.' See opinion of AG Jacobs in case C-379/98 *Preussen Elektra* [2001] ECR p. I-2099 at para. 58. On the possibilities that this judgment may have open for circumvention see Jaeger, T., 'Goodbye Old Friend: Article 107's Double Control Criterion' (2012) *European State Aid Law Quarterly* 535, or Rubini, L, 'The Elusive Frontier: Regulation under State Aid Rules' (2009) *European State Aid Law Quarterly* 277.

[60] For a recent case in which the Grand Chamber of the Court has made reference to the regulatory technique used by the Member State to back the finding that the measure was State aid under 107(1) TFEU, see Joined Cases C-106/09 P and C-107/09 P Government of Gibraltar v Commission [2011] ECR nyr at para 50.

[61] See in this regard the judgments of the Court of Justice in C-206/06 Essent Netwerk Noord and Others [2008] ECR I-05497 and particularly C-262/12 Vent De Colère and Others [2013] nyr.; Regarding the General Court see the judgment in case T-251/11 Austria v Commission [2014] ECR nyr.

[62] WTO Agreement on subsidies and countervailing duties at Art. 1.1a(1)(iv).

from circumventing the SCM agreement by using the private body as a 'proxy' to make the financial contribution.[63]

7. The *France Télécom (Bouygues)* Case (Joined Cases C-399/10 P and C-401/10 P)

A. Introduction and background

This Grand Chamber judgment is known for having clarified that it is not necessary under Article 107(1) TFEU for a public measure to place an inmediate burden on the budget of the State in order to be qualified as State resources. The Court concluded that a sufficiently concrete risk of imposing an additional burden on the State in the future suffices to meet that criterion of the notion of aid.[64] This judgment represents the most important clarification of the notion of State resources since the *Preussen Elektra* judgment.

The main facts of the case can be summarized as follows. France Télécom (FT) was in 2002 a public limited company over which the French State retained more than half the shares. FT published in 2002 its accounts for 2001, which showed a poor financial situation which became worse in the following months. Several credit rate agencies downgraded FT's rating significantly. This trend was reversed in July 2002 when the French authorities stated that the French State would, if necessary, take steps to prevent FT from being faced with any financing difficulties. These statements were subsequently repeated several times during the following months and in December of the same year the French government announced its commitment to subscribe in proportion to its shareholding to a €15 billion recapitalization operation. In the same month a French public entity sent FT a signed draft shareholder loan contract ('the shareholder loan offer') in the amount of €9 billion. FT did not sign the offer as it was no longer necessary due to its improved financial situation. Consequently, the shareholder loan was never implemented.

France notified the Commission, among other measures, of the shareholder loan offer. Two private applicants lodged complainants before the Commission considering as State aid both the public declarations made by the French authorities in favour of FT and the announcement of the shareholder loan offer in the amount of €9 billion. The Commission finally considered the shareholder loan

[63] See in this regard Bagwell, K.W., Bermann, G.A., and Mavroidis, P.C. (eds), *Law and Economics of Contingent Protection in International Trade* (CUP, 2009) at 22, and the Appellate Body Report, United States—Countervailing duty investigation on dynamic random access memory semiconductors (DRAMS) from Korea (WT/DS296/AB/R, adopted on July 20, 2005), paras 108, 115, 116.

[64] See in this regard the Draft Commission Notice on the notion of State aid pursuant to Article 107(1) TFEU at points 53 and 84, with reference to this judgment: 'The creation of a sufficiently concrete risk of imposing an additional burden on the State in the future, by a guarantee or by a contractual offer, is sufficient for the purposes of Article 107(1)'.

offer, in the context of the reiteretated official statements in favour of FT, as State aid in a 2004 decision.[65] The Commission however found that it did not have sufficient information to show that the public statements in favour of FT were sufficient to commit State resources.

The Commission decision was challenged by both France and FT and by the private complainants who claimed that the Commission should have also considered as aid the public declarations in support of FT. The General Court concluded, in essence, that the Commission had failed to show that the shareholder loan offer, when placed in the context of the declarations from July 2002, conferred an advantage to FT granted through State resources.[66]

In particular, the General Court held that the public statements in favour of FT amounted to an advantage under Article 107(1) TFEU. However, according to this Court, this advantage was not followed by a corresponding charge to the State budget. The alleged transfer of public resources (the €9 billion shareholder loan offer) in this case did not follow the identified advantage (the public statements) but rather a separate and additional advantage that was not as such established in the Commission's decision. This judgment was appealed before the Court, that reversed it in agreement with its Advocate General.

B. The policy context

This case was initiated in 2002 when France notified the Commission of a number of measures including the shareholder loan offer. It thus corresponds to the fourth period identified by political scientists, characterized by a number of initiatives purporting to make State aid control more efficient and transparent through the adoption of legal procedural rules and an increased focus on a number of so-called horizontal goals (Lisbon Agenda goals). The period is also characterized by the Commission's and the Council's determination to address harmful taxation measures through the State aid rules, a goal that was supported by the issuing of a communication on State aids and direct business taxation in 1998. Indeed, one of the measures in favour of FT considered aid by the Commission in the contested decision was granted through a preferential business tax treatment.

The period is also characterized by an increase in the number of notifications and complaints brought before the European Commission and by the substantial improvement in the enforcement of the State aid rules when compared with the previous periods. In this regard, France notified the shareholder loan offer even if it was not used by France Télécom, something very unlikely only a few years earlier. In the same vein, two private actors lodged complaints to the Commission and many interested parties participated in the administrative procedure once the

[65] Commission Decision 2006/621/EC of 2 August 2004 on the State Aid implemented by France for France Télécom (OJ 2006 L 257, p. 11).

[66] Joined Cases T-425/04, T-444/04, T-450/04, and T-456/04 *France and Others v Commission* [2010] ECR II-2099.

Commission opened the formal investigation procedure. In addition, the case also shows the Commission's determination to deal with very sensitive cases involving a great amount of State aid and to do so using novel theories. Indeed the Commission recognized in the contested decision that it was the first time that it had used public statements in order to qualify as aid a shareholder loan offer that, in isolation, probably would not have qualified as State aid.[67] Finally, the Commission hired economic experts to decide this difficult case in a way preceding the friendlier approach towards the use of economics in this field of the State Aid Action Plan, that would be published a year after the adoption of this decision.

C. Judgment of the Court of Justice

The Court first recalled the *Sloman Neptum* and *Preussen Elektra* case law according to which '[t]he very wording of [Article 107(1) TFEU] and the procedural rules laid down in Article 108 TFEU show that advantages granted from resources other than those of the State do not fall within the scope of the provisions in question.'[68] Secondly, the Court referred to the case law according to which 'it is not necessary to establish in every case that there has been a transfer of State resources for the advantage granted to one or more undertakings to be capable of being regarded as a State aid within the meaning of Article 107(1) TFEU',[69] case law that has been used in the past to underline that tax exemption measures were also covered by the notion of aid.[70] Thirdly, citing the *EDF* case, it underlined that Article 107(1) TFEU defines measures of State intervention in relation to their effects.[71] Consequently, '[a]s State interventions take various forms and have to be assessed in relation to their effects, it cannot be excluded, as the Bouygues companies and the Commission rightly argued, that several consecutive measures of State intervention must, for the purposes of Article 107(1) TFEU, be regarded as a single intervention.'[72] Therefore, the Court concluded that by excluding the consideration of the different State measures in this case as a single intervention the General Court erred in law. The Court then recalled that the Commission must establish a sufficiently direct link between, on the one hand, the advantage given to the beneficiary and, on the other, a reduction of the State budget or a sufficiently concrete economic risk of burdens on that budget.[73] 'However, contrary to what the General Court found, it is not necessary that such a reduction,

[67] Commission Decision 2006/621/EC of 2 August 2004 on the State Aid implemented by France for France Télécom (OJ 2006 L 257, p. 11) at point 263.

[68] Joined Cases C-399/10 P and C-401/10 P, *Bouygues and Bouygues Télécom v Commission and Others*, nyp at 99.

[69] Ibid. at 100.

[70] See in this regard the next paragraph of the judgment: 'In particular, measures which, in various forms, mitigate the burdens normally included in the budget of an undertaking, and which therefore, without being subsidies in the strict meaning of the word, are similar in character and have the same effect, are considered to be aid.' Ibid. at 101.

[71] Ibid. at 102. [72] Ibid. at 103. [73] Ibid. at 109.

or even such a risk, should correspond or be equivalent to that advantage, or that the advantage has as its counterpoint such a reduction or such a risk, or that it is of the same nature as the commitment of State resources from which it derives.'[74] In light of the foregoing, the judgment of the General Court under appeal was set aside.

D. Assesment

The Court criticizes the decision of the General Court for two main reasons. First, for having adopted an excessively formalist approach by refusing to consider several State measures as a single intervention. In other words, refusing to analyse globally all the elements of the file, as the Commission had done and the private competitors demanded. Secondly, on a more substantive level, the General Court was criticized for demanding a close correspondence between the advantage and the reduction of the State budget.

The Court's judgment in this case confirms the less formalist approach followed by this Court, and particularly by its Grand Chamber, in recent years.[75] The Court cited the *EDF* decision to underline the view that Article 107(1) TFEU defines measures of State intervention in relation to their effects, something perhaps not surprising as the Judge Rapporteur in this case was also rapporteur in the *EDF* Grand Chamber judgment. Indeed, as the AG had observed in his robust opinion, the GC's decision was 'marred by excessive formalism, a characteristic which is difficult to reconcile with the principle of applying the concept of aid by reference to the effects of the measure at issue.'[76]

On the more substantive level, the rejection of the close connection requirement between the advantage and the charge to the State budget is also revealing of the Court's desire to simplify the case law by avoiding new rules in the application of the main criteria of the notion of aid. Related to the foregoing, the Court's judgment also confirms that the *Sloman Neptun* and *Preussen Elektra* case law should not be extended by requiring not only a charge to the State budget but also a corresponding one to the advantage identified. That case law, which the Court restated in the commented decision, remains therefore fully valid but strictly limited to its essential meaning, namely that legislation or regulation that result in an economic advantage to some undertakings without public resources involved is not State aid. The *Sloman Neptun* and *Preussen Elektra* jurisprudence is consequently more and more isolated and, in the absence of additional constitutional justifications for it in the case law (as those advanced above in the commentary to that judgment), is becoming increasingly difficult to justify in light of

[74] Ibid. at 110.

[75] See also in this regard Biondi, A., 'State Aid is Falling Down, Falling Down: An Analysis of the Case Law on the Notion of Aid' (2013) 50 *Common Market Law Review* Issue 6, 1719–43 at 1726.

[76] Opinion of AG Mengozzi in Joined Cases C-399/10 P and C-401/10 P, *Bouygues and Bouygues Télécom v Commission and Others*, nyp at 78.

the effects-based rule so present now in the recent decisions of the Grand Chamber of the Court.

Finally, the case shows how a pragmatic Commission, reinforced by the momentum of the fourth phase of State aid policy, regained protagonism in relation to the concept of aid by proposing a controlled enlargement of the criterion of State resources, controlled because it refused to adhere to the thesis of the complaints, who defended that the mere public statements amounted to State aid, and instead opted for an expansion that was not revolutionary in light of the case law and practice concerning State guarantees. This controlled expansion was nonetheless very important from a precedent value perspective, as it has been shown during the financial crisis where the principle introduced in this decision has been applied.[77]

8. Conclusion

During the first period of evolution of the State aid policy the Court did not lay down any definition or formula of the concept of aid granted by the State or through State resources. No leading judgment concerning this criterion has therefore been included during this period. Nevertheless, from cases decided during this period, reviewed earlier under other criteria, two key elements emerged: the notion of aid was of a financial nature and the benefit granted to some undertakings had to be the result of State conduct. As to the financial nature of the concept of aid, this view was widespread among commentators and judges of the Court,[78] and was in line with the concept of 'State fiscal legislation' included in the definition of subsidy of the 1902 Brussels Surgar Convention. Similarly, the European Commission and several Advocates Generals had reached the same conclusion before the *Van Tiggele* decision,[79] and so seems to have found the Court in a case decided during this period.[80] As to the requirement of action by the State, early cases show that the origin, private or public, of the funds that ultimately finance the aid seemed irrelevant, as it was also irrelevant the status, private or public, of the entity administering the aid, what matter was that the aid was granted as the result of action by the public authorities.[81]

[77] See, eg, Commission Decision NN 25/2008 of 30 April 2008 WestLB risk shield, paras 37–38.

[78] See Scheuing, *Les aides financiers publiques aux enterprises en droit francaise et europeen*, op. cit. at 268, who referred to the need of financial character of a measure for it to be State aid. In a similar vein, Judges Catalano, Trabucchi, and Monaco implicitly demand a financial charge as they only give examples of State aid measures either direct as subsidies or indirect as tax reliefs. See Catalano, N., *Manuel de droit des Communautes europeennes*, op. cit. at 495, or Quadri, Monaco, and Trabucchi (eds), *Trattato Istitutivo della C.E.E. Comentario*, op. cit. at 720.

[79] See, eg, the view of the Commission and the Advocate General in the Judgment of 6 October 1970, C-9/70 *Franz Grad v Finanzamt Traunstein* [1970] 825 at p. 835. See footnote 11.

[80] Case 47/69 *Government of the French Republic v Commission* [1970] ECR 487 at 4: 'This provision [Article 108(2)], by thus taking into account the connexion which may exist between the aid granted by a Member State and the method by which it is financed through the resources of that State…'.

[81] This can be seen for example in the *Italian textiles* case decided at the very beginning of the second period. See Case 173/73 *Italy v Commission* [1974] ECR-710 at 16: 'As the funds in question

Finally, this broad and flexible concept, together with the absence of a precise definition, was in line with the *institutional* approach of the case law of the Court during this period, an approach that has also been depicted in previous chapters as teleological as it allowed the Community institutions to subject to the Treaty rules almost any financial measure that could create an obstacle to trade. In this regard, the notion of aid granted by the State or through State resources during this period was in line with those of the two previous criteria examined (advantage and selectivity) in that it permitted tackling discriminatory measures against foreign traders, such as parafiscal levies, that were charged on all undertakings active in a given market yet the proceeds of the charge imposed only benefitted domestic undertakings.[82]

During the second period, the functional interpretation of the Treaty led the Court to confirm that not only public but also private bodies instituted by the State to administer aid could be considered as 'State resources' in the early *Steinike and Weinlig* case.[83] Consequently, the relevant factor was that the granting of a financial advantage to some undertakings could be seen as the result of State action. In this context, the *Van Tiggele* judgment, where the Court rejected that an aid could be financed only at the expense of consumers, thus implying that there must be a financial charge either for the State or for the State intermediaries granting the aid, does not come as surprising. Indeed, the judgment was not exceptional and it also fits well with the *instrumental* character of the Court's case law during this period, as the Commission had requested this finding.

In this regard, it has been argued in this chapter that the Commission was interested in defending a notion of aid of a *financial* character in order to isolate this notion from the internal market rules, so that its exclusive competence on the compatibility analysis would not be substituted by the judgment of national or Community courts, which could apply the fundamental freedoms directly due to their direct effect. In particular, a broad notion of 'aid granted by the State' could be confused with the rules concerning the free movement of goods, especially with Article 30 EEC, which prohibited quantitative restrictions on imports and measures having an equivalent effect.[84] Finally, the judgment was also instrumental in

are financed through compulsory contributions imposed by State legislation and as, as this case shows, they are managed and apportioned in accordance with the provisions of that legislation, they must be regarded as State resources within the meaning of Article 92, even if they are administered by institutions distinct from the public authorities'.

[82] See in this regard the para-fiscal levies case mentioned supra Case 47/69 *Government of the French Republic v Commission* [1970] ECR 487. See also some of the Commission's submissions in that case: 'aid granted to an industry must be financed by the national economy of the State concerned either by a charge on the general budget or by a quasi-fiscal charge levied on the branch in question if it is not to increase unilaterally effects which are already discriminatory in themselves, and it cannot directly or indirectly make competing foreign industry contribute even a reduced amount.' Ibid. at 492.

[83] Case C-78/76 *Steinike & Weinlig v Federal Republic of Germany* [1977] ECR 595.

[84] As referred by the Court's judgment of 22 March 1977 in Case 74/76 *Ianelli and Volpi v Meroni* [1977] ECR 557 at p. 562: 'The Commission takes the view that subsidies fall within Article 92 and not Article 30. Although almost all systems of aid have an effect on trade and are for this reason capable of influencing it, their compatibility with the provisions of the Treaty should nevertheless be considered as a whole in relation to Article 92 and with due regard to the absolute

another aspect, as it expanded the interpretation of Article 30 EEC, the crucial provision for the creation of the Common Market and the dismantling of national barriers, as the Court concluded that the loss of a competitive advantage was a sort of discrimination covered by that Article.[85] It is in this light, it is submitted, that the judgment has to be interpreted as one where both the Commission and the Court, in line with their shared goal of establishing the Common market, prioritized the use of the free movement rules over the State aid ones, far less operational in the absence of direct effect, procedural regulations, and compatibility guidelines.

Subsequently, the *Poor Farmers* case confirmed that the financial burden included in the concept of aid could fall, not only directly on the State but also (indirectly) on the public or private intermediaries instituted by the State to administer the aid. In our view, the notion of imputability that was coined by the *Van der Kooy* judgment is a reaffirmation of the same idea, that is that aid must be given directly by the State or indirectly through public or private distributors of aid that, as in *Van der Kooy*, may financed the aid by granting too favourable commercial terms at the request or, in any event, with the necessary acquiescence of the State.

In addition, the appearance of the notion of imputability reveals a transformation of the State aid rules that has been already noticed in the two previous chapters. State aid was no longer exclusively controlled in a context of the creation of the Common Market, inter-jurisdictional trade and discrimination against foreign traders, but increasingly, as in *Poor Farmers* and *Van der Kooy*, in a context of distortions of competition created and felt primarily at the national level and, particularly, created by public undertakings—or undertakings over which public authorities exercised decisive influence. As discussed in the previous chapters, these undertakings became the focus of the Commission's action in the early 1980s and evidence of that is the emergence and systematic application of the MEIP test.

During the third period, the landmark decision is the *Sloman Neptun* judgment, delivered in 1993. This case represents the first important disagreement between the outcome sought by the Commission and the decision of the Court, not only in relation to the State resources criterion but in relation to the concept of aid more generally. In this regard, the Commission defended for the first time

discretionary power which Article 93 confers on the Commission. The effect of including aids within the area of application of Article 30 would be to modify adversely the scope of this provision, to replace the Commission's discretion by that of the Court and to grant private individuals full rights in an area in which they can take no legal action because Article 92 does not have direct effect.' In this regard, AG Mancini noted that if Art. 30 could apply to situations covered by Art. 92, this latter provision could risk being rendered inoperative. See Opinion of AG Mancini in Case C-177/78 *Pigs and Bacon Commission* [1979] ECR 02161, 2207: 'Article 30 of the Treaty forbidding, as between Member States, quantitative restrictions on imports and all measures having equivalent effect could not be interpreted so widely as to extend to obstacles to trade which, as such, were covered by Articles 92 and 93. In reaching that conclusion the Court had regard to the circumstance that otherwise the provisions of Articles 92 to 94 would be rendered largely inoperative.'

[85] See Poiares Maduro, M., *We the Court: The European Court of Justice and the European Economic Constitution*, op. cit. at 64–65.

before the Court in this case that there could be State aid also in the absence of a financial burden for the State. This submission was the exact opposite to what the Commission had submitted during the 1960s, 1970s, and 1980s before the Court. It has been argued that this change of attitude can be explained by the change of circumstances present in 1993: the Commission had emphasized in the past the distinction between Article 107 TFEU and then Article 30 EEC in order to safeguard its powers on the compatibility assessment (that could be thwarted if national courts could also analyse financial measures affecting trade under Article 30 EEC) and because it prioritized the internal market rules over the State aid ones during the first phases of European integration. By 1993 the contrary was true, as there was no longer need for a broad application of Article 30 EEC given that most barriers to trade had been abolished by the 1992 deadline and, conversely, there was much more scope for action under the State aid rules, because Member States had finally recognized, in the spirit of the 1992 project, the relevance of these rules and the role of the Commission for their enforcement, a role also long recognized by private applicants.

The post-1992 context was in fact ripe for positive integration measures such as those included in the compatibility guidelines that the Commission had been publishing since the 1970s. In this regard, for example, the Commission had developed guidelines on State aid to the shipping industry, the industry involved in the *Sloman Neptun* case, that would be redundant if the measure at stake was not considered as State aid. However, as we now know, the Court did not follow the Commission's submission. The fact that the year of the judgment coincided with that of the *Keck* and *Meng* decisions has led some authors to include this judgment under the influence of the November revolution.[86] Other authors, including some judges of the Court,[87] have also emphasized the 'lighter touch' of the Court in relation to the regulation of the market that surrounded the *Sloman Neptun* judgment,[88] also in the context of the introduction of the subsidiarity principle in the Maastricht Treaty and the German Constitutional Court judgment on that Treaty.[89] Others still, also with reference to Judge Everling, have noted the overall less activist approach of the Court during this third period, starting from the mid-1980s.[90] Finally, it has been suggested, with reference to an article by Judge Mancini, that the subject matter of the case (social legislation favouring the employment of non-Community migrant workers) may have also influenced the

[86] Joined Cases C-267 and 268/91 *Keck and Mithouard* [1993], ECR I-6097, and C-2/91 *Meng* [1993] ECR I-5751.

[87] See Everling, U., 'On the Judge-made law of the European Community's Courts', in O'Keeffe, D. (ed.) *Judicial Review in European Union Law: Liber Amicorum in Honor of Lord Slynn of Hadley* (Kluwer, 2000) at 39, where the judge cites as examples of the approach followed by the Court in 1993–94 the Keck but also the *Dori* case, C-91/92 *Dori v Recreb* [1994] ECR-3325.

[88] See Ross, M., 'State Aids: Maturing into a Constitutional Problem' (1995) *Yearbook of European Law* at 82. See also the references mentioned by Ross in footnote 14 of that page.

[89] In fact the Court, in a number of cases concerning social regulation, decided in the same way. See C-189/91, *Kirsammer-Hack v Sidal*, [1993] ECR p. I-6185; C-52/97, C-53/97, and C-54/97 *Viscido* [1998] ECR p. I-2629.

[90] Gerber, *Law and Competition in Twentieth Century Europe*, op. cit. at 374.

Court's decision, as the Court was under heavy criticism from Germany for some judgments dealing with that same matter.[91]

In our view the Court may have certainly been influenced by the factors mentioned above in the *Sloman Neptun* case. However, this case has been confirmed several times and in different contexts and it has been argued in this chapter that the Court's judgment was coherent not only with its previous case-law but also with the Treaty architecture. In this regard, the Treaty foresees that legislative and regulatory measures be reviewed under the free movement rules, which also allows national courts to analyse them and Member States to plead national objectives as a defence, something that they are not entitled to do in the State aid field due to the lack of direct effect of Article 107 and the *Philip Morris* judgment, in which the Court found that only Community objectives, as interpreted by the Commission may be taken into consideration for the compatibility analysis. Finally, the case is also coherent with the *definitional* approach adopted by the Court with regard to State aids during this period, as seen with the *SFEI* case in the context of the advantage criterion and the *FNE* case in relation to the selectivity criterion, as it also clarifies its previous case law and concludes that the concept of aid does not refer to measures not entailing a burden for the State.

During the fourth period the notion of State resources has not (so far) changed significantly as the Court refused again in the *Preussen Elektra* case to open the scope of application of the concept of aid to regulatory measures. As discussed earlier, in line with its policy priorities since the achievement of the internal market in 1992, the Commission has tried to broaden the scope of the State aid rules as these remain, the Commission submits, the last resort of Member States to distort competition and trade after the achievement of the Economic and Monetary Union. The Court has however insisted on maintaining its previous position on the matter, a position that is now also consistent with the trend towards the clarification of the State aid rules for the benefit of private applicants and national jurisdictions (eg *Altmark*). In fact, legal certainty and the relevance that clearer rules might have for the role of national judges under the State aid rules have been underlined as justifications of the *Preussen Elektra* decision by an ex-President of the General Court.[92]

Having said that, it has been submitted that if Member States systematically use the *Preussen Elektra* formula (that is, if they constrain some undertakings to transfer funds to other undertakings instead of transferring the same funds the State directly or its intermediaries), then that form of regulation could be considered by the Court as entailing state resources in the same logic that it has followed in the *Gibraltar* and *EDF* cases, namely, looking at the effect beyond the form or

[91] See Mancini and Keeling., 'Language, Culture and Politics in the Life of the European Court of Justice', op. cit. at 408.

[92] Vesterndorf, B., 'A Further Comment on the New State Aid Concept as this Concept Continues to be Reshaped—Pearle—A Further Piece of the State Aid Puzzle?', op. cit. at 399. See also Biondi, A., and Farley, 'The Relationship between State Aid and the Single Market', op. cit. at 1140.

the *regulatory technique* used and preventing that aid is given to a particular group of undertakings clearly identifiable in advance. It is therefore submitted that if the 'end of formalism' approach initiated by the Court in Gibraltar and followed by *EDF* is continued, the *Preussen Elektra* case law may soon be nuanced by the Court, as indeed the most recent case-law of the EU Courts regarding this criterion appears to indicate.[93]

Finally, the clarification made by the Court in the *France Télécom* case, namely that it is not necessary for a public measure to place an inmediate burden on the budget of the State in order to be qualified as State resources, is also in line with the anti-formalist trend of the Court, the preference for a global analysis of all elements surrounding the alleged granting of aid (as in *EDF*) and, it is submitted, with the isolation of the *Preussen Elektra* judgment to its particular fact-pattern which can be also observed from other judgments of the Court during the fourth period.[94]

[93] See in this regard as mentioned before in particular C-262/12 *Vent De Colère and Others* [2013] nyr.; Regarding the General Court see the judgment in case T-251/11 *Austria v Commission* [2014] ECR nyr.

[94] See in this regard C-206/06—Essent Netwerk Noord and Others, ECR [2008] I-05497

7

The Notions of Distortion of Competition and Effect on Trade

In this section, jointly devoted to two requirements of the notion of aid—distortion of competition and effect on trade—we will apply the analytical framework of the previous chapters to the notions of distortion of competition and effect on trade that have gradually emerged from the case law of the Court of Justice and are commonly cited by the Commission and the EU Courts.

The requirements of distortion of competition and effect on trade are two distinct criteria of Article 107(1) TFEU. However, the leading cases of the Court of Justice concerning these two requirements overlap to a large extent. In this regard, the European Courts have noted that both criteria are *inextricably linked*,[1] and the European Commission has, since the early decisions, analysed them together.[2] In light of the foregoing, we will study the main formulas that have appeared in the case law of the Court concerning each of the two criteria in this chapter.

1. The *France v Commission* (*para-fiscal levies*) Case (C-47/69)

A. Introduction and background of the case

This case concerns aids financed by para-fiscal levies. The case was probably the first in which the Court was confronted with the question of whether an aid of a relatively small amount could distort competition and affect trade under Article 107 TFEU. The case is interesting as it offers the Court's early understanding of the criteria of distortion of competition and effect on trade.

The case was brought by France as an appeal to a decision of the European Commission declaring some aids to the textile industry incompatible with the

[1] See eg Joined Cases T-298/97, T-312/97, T-313/97, T-315/97, T-600/97 to 607/97, T-1/98, T-3/98 to T-6/98, and T-23/98 *Alzetta Mauro and others v Commission* ECR 2000 II-2319, or Case 173/73 *Italy v Commission* [1974] ECR 709, paras 25, 44, and 45.

[2] See, in this regard, eg the seminal Commission Decision of 25 July 1973 on Article 20 of Italian Law No. 1101 of 1 December 1971 on the restructuring, reorganization and conversion of the textile industry, OJ L 254, 1973 p. 0014–0015: 'Whereas the aid is such as to affect competition and trade directly, because it has a direct effect on manufacturing costs and, consequently, on the competitiveness of the undertakings'.

Common Market 'because of the way in which they are financed'.[3] In particular, the decision considered that the measure at stake, which dated back in its original form to 1965, distorted competition and had an effect on trade because only French textile undertakings could benefit from it, whereas foreign undertakings, which also contributed to finance the aid, did not.[4]

However, the Commission concluded, in view of the difficulties that the textile industry was experiencing in France and in other Member States, that the measure could be deemed compatible under Article 92 (3)(c) of the Treaty provided that the discriminatory effect of the para-fiscal levy was removed. France refused to do so and instead challenged the decision before the Court.

B. The policy context

The case was dealt with during the first period of evolution of the State aid policy discussed in Chapter 3. This period was generally characterized by the goal of eliminating the most prominent obstacles to trade between the EEC Treaty Members, particularly in goods. State aid rules were not an exception to this main objective. The initial focus of the Commission's enforcement was indeed to tackle those measures that were clearly discriminatory.[5] By the same token, some restrictions to competition and trade were tolerated, provided that they did not entail discrimination.[6] Indeed, discriminatory measures against out-of-State traders such as export aid—or para-fiscal levies—were the main target of the State aid rules during the first years of application of the Rome Treaties.

C. Judgment of the Court of Justice

The Court held that for the definition of a measure as aid and for the assessment of its compatibility with the Treaty it is important to assess all the relevant circumstances, including the existence of an imbalance (for out-of-State traders) between the charges imposed by the para-fiscal measure and the benefits that it

[3] See Commission Decision of 18 July 1969 on the French systems of aid for research and the reorganization of production and distribution in the textile industry, OJ L 2201969 P. 0001-0003 and Case 47/69 *Government of the French Republic v Commission* [1970] ECR 487 at p. 489.

[4] Commission Decision of 18 July 1969 on the French systems of aid for research and the reorganization of production and distribution in the textile industry, OJ L 2201969 P. 0001–0003: In the decision's terms, 'Whereas by thus strengthening the competitive position of French undertakings receiving aid, to the detriment of those established in other Member States, the aid is liable to disturb trade in textile products between the Member States.'

[5] As mentioned before, the Commission has many voices although it is depicted here as if it only had one. See in this regard, eg, Blauberger, M., 'Of "Good" and "Bad" Subsidies: European State Aid Control through Soft and Hard Law' (2009) *West European Politics* 719.

[6] P. Mathijsen, *A Guide to European Community Law* (Sweet & Maxwell, 1972) at 180. This thesis was also supported by the Judgment of the Court of Justice of 13 July 1966 in Joined Cases 56 and 58/64, *Consten Grundig v Commission*, ECR 1966, p. 429.

confers.[7] Furthermore, the Court held that '[i]t may be that aid properly so-called, although not in conformity with Community law, does not substantially affect trade between States and may thus be acknowledged as permissible but that the disturbance which it creates is increased by a method of financing it which would render the scheme as a whole incompatible with a single market and the common interest.'[8]

From this paragraph it can be interpreted that the Court admits that all aids have an effect on competition and trade yet if such effect is not 'substantial', then the aids in question may be considered permissible. It was therefore the cumulative effect of the aid and its method of financing that made the aid incompatible.[9] The Court confirmed this interpretation by holding that '[b]y automatically increasing the amount of national aid in proportion to the increase in the revenue from the charge and more especially the revenue from the charge levied on competing foreign products, the method of financing in question has a protective effect which goes beyond aid properly so-called.'[10]

Finally, the Court made a teleological statement, similar to others made during this period, by which it recalled that Member States could not make use of their competences, such as the fiscal power, in a way that could frustrate the *effet utile* of today's 107(1) TFEU: 'If such a system whereby an aid is serviced by a charge designed for that purpose, were to become general, it would have the effect of opening a loophole in Article 92 of the Treaty and of reducing the Commission's opportunities of keeping the position under constant review. In fact it leads to a system of permanent aids, the amount of which is unforeseeable and which would be difficult to review.'[11]

D. Assessment

The decision of the Court in this case reveals its understanding not only of the effect on competition and trade criteria, but also of the State aid rules more generally in the early days.

The background of the case shows how the Commission started to act against the will of the States in this field as the deadline for the custom unions (1968)

[7] Case 47/69 *Government of the French Republic v Commission* [1970] ECR 487 at para. 7: 'In order to determine whether an aid "affects trade between Member States", "distorts or threatens to distort competition by favouring certain undertakings or the production of certain goods" and "adversely affects trading conditions to an extent contrary to the common interest", it is necessary to consider all the legal and factual circumstances surrounding that aid, in particular whether there is an imbalance between the charges imposed on the undertakings or producers concerned on the one hand and the benefits derived from the aid in question on the other.'

[8] Ibid. at para. 16.

[9] Ibid. at para. 17: 'the Commission must therefore take into account all those factors which directly or indirectly characterize the measure in question, that is, not only aid, properly so-called, for selected national activities, but also the indirect aid which may be constituted both by the method of financing and by the close connexion which makes the amount of aid dependent upon the revenue from the charge.'

[10] Ibid. at para. 20.

[11] Ibid. at paras 18–19.

approached.[12] It also shows that the Commission was ready to accept the granting of national aid with only one limit: no discrimination against foreign producers. The case also left open the possibility of a *de minimis* rule for State aid as the Court notes that although all aids affect trade and distort competition, only those that do so substantially are not permissible. This would be consistent with the wording of Article 107(1) TFEU, which merely requires a threat of distortion of competition yet it did (and does) require an effect on trade, and with the Court's judgment of the same year upholding the existence of a *de minimis* rule in the field of antitrust.[13]

Indeed, already in the *Costa/Enel* judgment the Court had noted that the State aid provisions were aimed at preventing Member States from favouring certain undertakings or products in an *appreciable* way.[14] In the same vein, aid measures benefitting only or mostly domestic consumption would not be regarded as aids as they could allegedly not affect competition and/or trade at Community level.[15] Similarly, some judges of the Court, including the Judge-Rapporteur of this case would write during the first years of application of the EEC Treaty that contrary to the requirement of distortion on competition, for which the Treaty only required competition to be threatened, the Treaty required that the effect on trade be shown, and therefore this was the most important limit to the principle of incompatibility of State aids enshrined in Article 107(1).[16]

[12] See Scheuing, D.H., *Les aides financiers publiques aux enterprises en droit francaise et europeen* cit. at 321, in relation to the approach to the 'final phase' in 1968 with the achievement of the customs union. See also for another example of a decision adopted by the Commission against the same Member State around the date of entry into force of the customs union, the Joined Cases 6/69 and 11/69 *Commission v France*, Rec. 1969, p. 523 discussed earlier in the chapter devoted to the selectivity requirement.

[13] Case 5/69 *Franz Võik w SPRL Etablissements J—Vervaecke* [1969] ECR 295. See for the reference to the 'test of perceptibility', the opinion of Advocate General Lenz in the Meura case (C-234/84, *Kingdom of Belgium v Commission of the European Communities* [1986] ECR, p. 02263).

[14] C-6/64, *Flaminio Costa v E.N.E.L*, [1964] ECR 114: 'These provisions... headed "Aids granted by States", are designed, on the one hand, to eliminate progressively existing aids and, on the other hand, to prevent the individual States in the conduct of their internal affairs from introducing new aids "in any form whatsoever" which are likely directly or indirectly to favour certain undertakings or products in an appreciable way, and which threaten, even potentially, to distort competition. By virtue of Article 92, the Member States have acknowledged that such aids are incompatible with the Common Market and have thus implicitly undertaken not to create any more, save as otherwise provided in the Treaty'.

[15] C-40/75, *Produits Bertrand v Commission* [1976] ECR 1; and C-52/76, *Benedetti v Munari* [1977] ECR 163. See also the Fifth Report on Competition Policy (Office for Official Publications of the European Communities, 1976) points 126–29. See for other cases where the Commission held that there was no effect on competition and/or trade: Fourth General Report on the Activities of the Communities (European Commission, 1970) at 172, or Seventh Report on Competition Policy (Office for Official Publications of the European Communities, 1978) at 205. See also the First Report on Competition Policy (Office for Official Publications of the European Communities, 1972) at points 135–38: the Commission can only act under Article 92(1) EC, 'in cases where national aid is harmful to the economic activities of other Member States'.

[16] See Quadri, R., Monaco, R., and Trabucchi, A. (eds), *Trattato istitutivo della C.E.E. Comentario* Vol II (Giuffrè, 1965) at 722. See also Catalano, N., *Manuel de Droit des Communautés Européennes* (Dalloz, 1965) at 495.

The case also shows a feature that may be surprising for today's readers of State aid matters, namely, that the Commission concluded that the aid at stake could be declared compatible if more aid was granted; that is, if the aid in question was open to all undertakings, domestic and foreign. This point is clearly made in another early decision of the Commission. The case concerned aid granted by France for the purchase of aircraft, in particular, gliders. The aid was granted for the purchase of gliders built in France in preference to those manufactured in other Member States. The Commission decision concluded that 'whatever appropriations the French budget provides for those purposes tend to distort competition by favouring the French production of gliders.' However, the solution proposed by the Commission was not limited to the abolition of the aid and its eventual repayment (as would most likely be the case today). Rather, the operative part of the Decision established that '[t]he French Republic shall, before 23 December 1966, take the necessary measures either to abolish the aid for the purchase of gliders…or so to amend it that the aid is granted to purchasers on the same terms for gliders built in other Member States as for gliders built in France.'[17] Similarly, as discussed earlier, the Commission in the case under review gave the French government the opportunity of either abolishing the aid in question or to remove the discriminatory elements of the para-fiscal levy. The focus was not, to paraphrase a recent Commission's motto, on *less* (and better targeted) *aid* but on discrimination. Indeed, the Commission submitted in this case that the decision was justified by the close interdependence between the aid at stake and the way in which it was financed, and it advanced a notion of distortion of competition and effect on trade based on the nature of the measure, that is, on its intrinsic discriminatory character of a para-fiscal levy more than on the quantitative effects that it had on trade.[18] Similarly the Court underlined that the measure under review was aid, and an incompatible one, because of its discriminatory character, that is, because of the imbalance for out-of-State traders between the charges imposed by the para-fiscal measure and the benefits that it confers. The Court coupled this finding, as in the *French exports* case discussed in the context of the selectivity criterion, with the teleological statement by which it recalled that Member States could not make use of their competences, such as the fiscal power, in a way that could frustrate the *effet utile* of today's 107(1) TFEU.

Finally, after this judgment, the Commission called upon the Member States, with reference to this case, to modify their para-fiscal levies so as to make them

[17] Commission Decision of 23 September 1966 on the aid instituted by the Government of the French Republic for the purchase of aircraft, OJ 182, 12 October 1966, 3141–42.

[18] Case 47/69 *Government of the French Republic v Commission* [1970] ECR 487 at p. 492: 'the low rate of the charge is of no significance for the determination of this dispute which basically raises a problem of principle as to the nature of the charge, and not a quantitative problem because the question is not to determine whether the effect of the charge, the result of which is indirectly a support measure which in itself infringes Article 92 of the Treaty, is greater or less "substantial", but to examine whether it could produce a distortion of competition, independently of the extent of this effect'.

compatible with the EEC Treaty.[19] According to the Commission, there were twenty-six *like-machinery* systems in place in 1968.[20]

2. The *Philip Morris* Case (C-730/79)

A. Introduction and background of the case

In 1978 the Dutch government informed the Commission about a new law for the promotion of investment that included the possibility of granting a public 'premium' for investments projects exceeding a certain ceiling. The amount of public support would depend on the number of jobs created by the investment. The Commission considered that the law in question could be seen as a general system of aid, and asked the Netherlands government to notify any individual application of the scheme so that the Commission could assess its compatibility with the State aid rules.

One of the first projects notified under this scheme, for which public support would thus be granted, was an investment by the Dutch subsidiary of the tobacco manufacturer Philip Morris. The investment proposed by Philip Morris aimed at increasing production capacity and would make possible the employment of a significant number of workers, an important element of the project given that the tobacco manufacturer had recently closed one of the two factories it had in the country. The Commission concluded that the planned public support to this project was an aid under article 107(1) TFEU. The decision also concluded that the aid at stake could not be declared compatible under Article 107, paragraphs 2 or 3. Philip Morris challenged this decision before the Court of Justice.

B. The policy context

This judgment falls in the second period of evolution of the State aid policy described in Chapter 3. This period is characterized by a significant increase in State aids after the 1973 oil crisis and a clear evasion of the State aid rules that the Commission proved unable to enforce.[21]

[19] Fourth General Report on the Activities of the Communities (European Commission, Brussels-Luxembourg, 1970) at 34.

[20] See Scheuing, *Les aides financiers publiques aux enterprises en droit francaise et europeen*, cit. at 317, based on the Commission's reply to written question 227/67 (OJ 1968, C 20 13 March, p.4).

[21] For the increase of State aids as a reaction to the 1973 crisis, see Caspari, M. 'The Aid Rules of the EEC Treaty and Their Application', in J. Schwarze (ed.), *Discretionary Powers of the Member States in the Field of Economic Policies and Their Limits under the EEC Treaty* (Nomos Verlagsgesellschatft, 1988) at 48. For the evasion of Community rules on State aids by the Member States see, eg, Cownie, F., 'State Aids in the Eighties' (1986) *European Law Review*, 247 at 248–49, Wulff, O., 'National Economic Policy: An Obstacle to the European Community?' in J. Schwarze (ed), *Discretionary Powers of the Member States in the Field of Economic Policies and Their Limits under the EEC Treaty* (Nomos Verlagsgesellschatft, 1988) 9 at 16, and Steenbergen, J., 'Trade Regulation since the Tokyo Round' in Volker, E.L.M. (ed.), *Protectionism and the European Community* (Kluwer, 1987) 194-95.

Under these conditions, the Commission's policy during this period consisted in adopting a flexible approach with the expectation that Member States would over time refrain from giving aids as the economic situation returned to normal after the oil crisis. However, realizing that the trend towards the granting of aid was more structural than temporary, the Commission announced in the late 1970s that it was going to be stricter in the application of the State aid rules. The *Philip Morris* decision was in fact one of the first examples of this new approach.

C. Judgment of the Court of Justice

The applicant in this case, Philip Morris, had claimed that the effect on trade of the measure under review should be analysed on the basis of a competition-like test, namely, by defining the relevant market, considering the pattern of the market, and analysing the effect of the aid on the relations between competitors. The Court rejected this proposal and, in view of the circumstances of the case, established a presumption of effect on trade in the following terms: 'when state financial aid strengthens the position of an undertaking compared with other undertakings competing in intra-community trade the latter must be regarded as affected by that aid.'[22]

The Court then noted that the beneficiary was organized for international trade, as it exported much of its production to other Member States, and that the aid was granted to increase production capacity and to reduce the costs of the new factory. In light of the foregoing the Court held that those circumstances 'justify the Commission's deciding that the proposed aid would be likely to affect trade between member states and would threaten to distort competition between undertakings established in different Member States.'[23]

D. Assessment

The Court was in this case invited to rule on the 'DNA' of the State aid rules: on whether the analysis of Article 107(1) should be carried out under competition law standards, thus defining the relevant product and geographic markets, assessing whether the measure only concerned national trade (jurisdictional criterion), and whether it affected competition and trade in an appreciable fashion (beyond the *de minimis* rule), or under internal market standards, that is, without analysing the actual effects of the measure on competition and trade, and leaving no room to manoeuvre for the *de minimis* rule.

The outcome of the Court's judgment is clearly closer to the second type of analysis, that is, that of the internal market. The Court even seemed to lower the requirements included in the wording of Article 107(1). Indeed, while this Article requires that aid must *affect trade* between Member States, the Court held that '[the circumstances of the case] justify the Commission's deciding that the

[22] Case 730/79 *Philip Morris* [1980] ECR I-2671, para. 11.

[23] Ibid. at para. 12.

proposed aid would be *likely to affect* trade between Member States' (emphasis added).[24] This wording, which seems to be a Treaty revision being carried out by the Court of Justice, may has just been a realization by the Court that the *ex-ante* nature of the State aid control mechanism provided for in the Treaty makes it impossible to assess whether trade had really been affected, at least in cases such as this where the contested measure had not been put into effect.

Having said that, if there is no doubt that the Court favoured an internal market-like analysis of potential State aid measures, it failed to distance the State aid rules from the 'other' competition rules explicitly. In this regard, the Court refused to give guidance on the alleged non-applicability of the *de minimis* rule or to make a clear distinction between the competition rules addressed to undertakings and those addressed to Member States, as Advocate General Capotorti had defended. The hybrid nature of the State aid rules, between internal market and competition, was becoming clear through the silence of the Court as to the substance or 'DNA', of these rules.

Indeed, this judgment could be read as the *substantive judgment* needed to complement the *procedural judgments* adopted by the Court during the 1970s in favour of the Commission's efforts to apply the State aid rules, against the Member States' reluctance to comply with those norms and to issue procedural regulations on the matter.[25] This is so because, by refusing to admit the existence of a *de minimis* aid and by allowing, under some circumstances, the Commission to presume that trade is affected, the Court was making the Commission's task under the State aid rules far easier. It should be noted in this regard that in the previous judgment mentioned, as in others of the first period, the Court had seemingly admitted the possibility of a *de minimis* rule also in this field, a possibility that the Court now refused, it is submitted, in view of the poor enforcement of these rules. This enforcement could only become worse if Member States could claim that the effect of their aids on trade was not 'appreciable' so that there was

[24] Case 730/79 *Philip Morris* [1980] ECR I-2671, paras 10–12.

[25] In this regard, the Court had clarified during the 1970s that Member States were obliged to refrain from implementing any aid until the Commission had had sufficient time to review its compatibility with the Common Market pursuant to notification (Case 120/73 *Lorenz* [1973] ECR 1471), and that the Commission could ask for repayment of aid illegally granted (see Case 70/72 *Commission v Germany* [1973] ECR 813 at para. 13). The Commission would, however, not be able or willing to recover illegal aid until the mid-1980s. The first recovery decision was Commission Decision [1982/312/EEC] of 19 May 1982, Aid granted by the Belgian Government to an industrial and commercial group manufacturing wall coverings, OJ 1982 L 138/18. Commissioner Andriessen made explicit the Commission's determination to start demanding recovery in 1983: '*the Commission recently decided gradually to start demanding repayment of aid that has been granted without prior Commission approval.*' See Andriessen, F., 'The role of Anti-Trust in the face of economic recession' (1983) *European Competition Law Review*, 340 at 349. Furthermore, the Court had also confirmed that national courts could interpret the notion of aid in order to give full value to the direct effect of Art. 93(3) EEC (Case C-77/72 *Capolongo v Maya* [1973] ECR 611 at para. 6) and that the Commission could use the Art. 93(2) procedure to deal with cases concerning State aid and other State measures regulated by other Treaty provisions. See in this regard Gilmour, D.R., 'The Enforcement of Community Law by the Commission in the Context of State Aids: The Relationship between Articles 93 and 169 and the Choice of Remedies' (1981) *Common Market Law Review* 63.

no need to notify to the European Commission. In this vein, a contemporary commentator of this case wrote in relation to this judgment that with this decision the Court had at last supported the Commission's view that the criteria of Article 92(1) should be fairly simple because 'it is desirable that national measures should be subject to Community co-ordination.'[26]

In fact, the tendency towards non-notification in 1980, the year of the judgment, was so general that the Commission even pointed to some sort of national wilful choice to circumvent the obligation to notify State aids under Article 108(3).[27] To combat this trend, the Commission had offered in the same year the possibility of State aid playing a key role for industrial policy, yet in a Community rather than a national fashion.[28] This was strongly supported by the judgment under review as the Court held, in the part of the judgment devoted to compatibility assessment, that the compatibility of an aid ought to be determined in the context and on the basis of Community objectives, not on those of Member States.[29] In this regard, the Commission also announced after this judgment that it would resume several investigations that it had delayed awaiting for the Court's decision in this case.[30]

3. The *Leeuwarder* Case (Joined Cases 296 and 318/82)

A. Introduction and background of the case

This case is known for being the first in which the Court declared that the Commission should refer in its decisions to the situation of the relevant market, the place of the aid beneficiary in that market, and to the pattern of trade between Member States in the products in question or the beneficiary's exports for otherwise the Commission would be in violation of the duty to state reasons concerning the criteria of effect on competition and trade.[31] In this regard, the judgment could be read as qualifying the *Philip Morris* decision just discussed.

[26] Flynn, J., 'The Philip Morris Decision Upheld by the European Court, European Law Review' (1981) *European Law Review*, 208 at 212. Similarly, Judge Pescatore reminded some years after this judgment that in the field of State aids one of the main concerns of the Court had been to compensate the shortcomings arising from the lack of implementing regulations in this field. Pescatore, P., 'Public and Private Aspects of European Community Competition Law' (1987) *Fordham International Law Journal*, 373 at 393.

[27] See Tenth Report on Competition Policy (Office for Official Publications of the European Communities, 1981) at point 162. Commission communication on the notification of State aid to the Commission pursuant to Article 93(3) of the EEC Treaty: the failure of Member States to respect their obligations, OJ C 252, 30 September 1980, p. 2, quoted by Smith, M.P., 'Autonomy by the Rules: The European Commission and the Development of State Aid Policy' (1998) *Journal of Common Market Studies* at 64, footnote 6.

[28] Tenth Report on Competition Policy, op. cit. at 9.

[29] Case 730/79 *Philip Morris* [1980] ECR I-2671, para. 26.

[30] Ibid. at point 217. See also point 161.

[31] Joined Cases 296 and 318/82 *Netherlands and Leeuwarder Papierwarenfabriek v Commission* [1985] ECR 809.

The origins of the case go back to 1980 when the Commission requested from the Netherlands government information concerning alleged assistance to a paperboard-processing undertaking in the form of an acquisition of the company's capital by a public regional body. The Commission opened the formal investigation procedure during which two Member States and two trade associations supported the Commission's view as to the aid character of the measures in question. The Commission finally adopted a decision concluding that the intervention of the public body constituted State aid. Both the Dutch government and the beneficiary of the alleged aid (Leeuwarder Papierwarenfabriek BV) appealed the Commission's decision.

B. The policy context

The investigation that led to the Commission's decision and the Court's judgment in this case belong to the second period of evolution of the State aid policy discussed in Chapter 3. Reference is thus made to the policy context described earlier in relation to the *Philip Morris* judgment, decided during the same period. In essence, the Commission had adopted a flexible approach during this period in view of the difficulties that Member States were experiencing in the aftermath of the oil crisis. However, realizing that Member States were, towards the end of the decade, granting aids that were not directly related to the consequences of the oil crisis, the Commission decided to adopt a stricter approach which also coincided with an increasing focus on the activities of public undertakings and their financial relations with Member States (Transparency Directive, MEIP test, etc).

C. Judgment of the Court of Justice

The Court annulled the Commission decision for its failure to state the reasons justifying that the aid in question had an effect on trade and distorted or threatened to distort competition.

The Court was indeed quite bold as to the Commission's lack of reasoning. After noting that the decision did not include any motivation concerning the effect on trade criteria and that it merely contained instead a reference to the opinion of two Member States and two trade associations, the Court concluded that:

> [e]ven if in certain cases the very circumstances in which the aid is granted are sufficient to show that the aid is capable of affecting trade between Member States and of distorting or threatening to distort competition, the Commission must at least set out those circumstances in the statement of reasons for its decision. In this case it has failed to do so since the contested decision does not contain the slightest information concerning the situation of the relevant market, the place of Leeuwarder in that market, the pattern of trade between Member States in the products in question or the undertaking's exports.[32]

[32] Ibid. at para. 24.

In sum, the Court required the Commission to state a number of elements in its State aid decisions that could back the finding that a certain aid met the effect on trade and distortion of competition criteria.

D. Assessment

In the *Philip Morris* case the applicant maintained that '[t]he Commission must... first determine the "relevant market" and in order to do so must take account of the product, the territory and the period of time in question. It must then consider the pattern of the market in question in order to be able to assess how far the aid in question in a given case affects relations between competitors.'[33] This line of argument was only explicitly accepted in the *Leeuwarder* judgment, where the Court required the Commission to provide information 'concerning the situation of the relevant market, the place of Leeuwarder in that market, the pattern of trade between Member States in the products in question or the undertaking's exports.'[34]

In light of all this, it appears that the Court required from the Commission in *Leeuwarder* what it failed to require in the *Philip Morris* case. A closer reading of both judgments, however, reveals that the elements that the Court required the Commission to state in the *Leeuwarder* judgment were included in the *Philip Morris* decision and just restated by the Court in this judgment. By contrast, the Commission's decision in the *Leeuwarder* case only contained what Advocate General Slynn referred to as a 'bald assertion' of the effect of the measure on competition and trade.[35]

Having said that, analysing this case from a broader perspective allows us to identify another element that further explains the Court's judgment, namely, the Court's tendency during the first half of the 1980s to require more solid evidence from the Commission than in the past and, consequently, the increasing number of Commission's decisions annulled during this period. This general tendency has been recognized by a judge of the Court that took part in the Leeuwarder decision and by several other commentators in relation to the State aid field.[36] The tendency was also perceptible in the antitrust field.[37]

[33] As referred by the Court in Case 730/79 *Philip Morris* [1980] ECR I-2671, para. 9.

[34] Joined Cases 296 and 318/82 *Netherlands and Leeuwarder Papierwarenfabriek v Commission* [1985] ECR 809 at 24.

[35] Opinion of AG Slynn in Joined Cases 296 and 318/82 *Netherlands and Leeuwarder Papierwarenfabriek v Commission* [1985] ECR 809 at p. 814.

[36] See the article by Koopmans, T., 'The Role of Law in the Next Stage of European Integration' (1986) *International and Comparative Law Quarterly* 925 at 931. See also Goyder, D.G., *EEC Competition Law* (OUP, 1988) at 383–84, or Ross, M., 'A Review of Developments in State Aids 1987–88' (1989) *Common Market Law Review* at 178.

[37] Gerber, D.J., *Law and Competition in Twentieth Century Europe: Protecting Prometheus* (OUP, 1998) at 361–62. Gerber marks the beginning of this trend in the mid-1970s and places it in the broader economic context of this period (mid-1970s to mid-1980s) characterized by its difficulty for European undertakings.

In this context, the defective reasoning of the Commission's decision in this case was coupled with the fact that for the second time, the Court was analysing a (then) new test for the notion of aid: the Market Economy Investor Principle (MEIP). The Court, just as in the first application of this test,[38] supported the new test while it quashed the Commission's decision on another ground. This approach—allowing the Commission to win on the new test but quashing the decision on another ground—was not limited to the State field; Gerber also observed it in the antitrust realm during the same period.[39]

In sum, it is submitted that the explanation of the evolution in the Court's approach between *Philip Morris* and the *Leeuwarder* decisions—requiring the Commission to state explicitly a number of elements to justify the concurrence of the competition and trade criteria—is a combination of two factors: a very limited reasoning on the part of the Commission in the *Leeuwarder* decision, which was coherent with the classic assumption in the State aid field that State intervention is necessarily distortive,[40] and the Court's more exigent approach *vis-à-vis* the European Commission.

In addition, as discussed in the previous chapters, the adoption of new formulas concerning most of the criteria of the concept of aid during the early 1980s signals that something was changing in this field. In particular, it has been suggested that the State aid rules were starting to shift their main focus: from the prevention of discrimination between national and out-of-State producers (inter-jurisdiction competition) to the prevention of discrimination between public and private and even between private-only undertakings in the same Member State (intra-jurisdiction competition). In this regard, the *Philip Morris* judgment discussed above had been crucial as it had allowed the Commission to find, and even to presume, that trade was affected and competition distorted in cases of aid to a single company and not, as before, to entire industries (as in the *Italian textiles* or the *parafiscal levies* cases) or even to all domestic producers (*French export rediscount rate*).

Finally, the Commission's reaction to the *Intermills* and *Leeuwarder* judgments was included in its 1984 competition report. The Commission announced that it would examine trade statistics yet it also warned that such an examination was not conclusive as aids could also be protectionist in the sense of aiding companies to compete in their own national market and thus preventing entry from other Member States.[41]

[38] See C-323/82, *SA Intermills v Commission* [1984] ECR, p. 03809.

[39] Gerber, *Law and Competition in Twentieth Century Europe*, op. cit. at 361–62. According to him '[t]he Court's response [to the difficulties of the period in which this judgment was rendered] was to supply political progress on a conceptual and symbolic level by strengthening competition law doctrine, but to minimize the economic consequences of these substantive law moves by imposing more stringent evidentiary and procedural requirements on the Commission.'

[40] An assumption that could be traced back to the *Italian textiles* case discussed in Chapter 5.

[41] Fourteenth Report on Competition Policy (Office for Official Publications of the European Communities, 1985) at point 201, and Fifteenth Report on Competition Policy (Office for Official Publications of the European Communities, 1986) at point 176.

4. The *Boussac* Case (C-301/87)

A. Introduction and background of the case

This case is known for being the first in which the Court added two important formulas concerning the notions of distortion of competition and effect on trade to the previous case law, namely that (i) the Commission does not need to show the real effect of the aid already granted on competition and on trade between Member States,[42] and that (ii) operating aid, that is to say aid which 'is intended to release an undertaking from costs which it would normally have had to bear in its day-to-day management or normal activities, distorts the conditions of competition'.[43]

The origin of this case may be traced back to 1983 when the Commission requested France, after several complaints,[44] to submit information concerning alleged aids to the third largest French textile, clothing, and paper producer granted between 1982 and 1984. The aids in questions consisted in participation by a public body (Institut de Développement Industriel) in Boussac's capital, loans at reduced rates of interest, capital advances, and reductions in social security charges made by another public body (Sopari). In total, Boussac would have received from the French State about 99 million ECU aid according to the Commission.

The Commission decision also noted that the aid granted to Boussac was not notified and that it was also incompatible. However, the Commission accepted in 1986 to discuss with the French government at the highest level (Commission President Jacques Delors and French Prime Minister Jacques Chirac) the amount of aid provided, the amount that should be recovered, and the methods of recovery.[45] The discussions did not lead to any agreement and finally the Commission adopted a decision in July 1987 stating that illegal and incompatible aid granted to Boussac had to be recovered. The French government lodged an appeal against this decision before the Court.

B. The policy context

The judgment in this case was delivered during the third period of evolution of the State aid policy discussed in Chapter 3. In this regard, by 1984, the year of the beginning of the formal investigation, the Commission was resolved to tighten State aid enforcement. The timing was becoming more propitious for the

[42] C-301/87 *France v Commission ('Boussac)* [1990] ECR I-307 at para. 33

[43] Ibid. at paras 44 and 50.

[44] See OJ C 267, 19 January 1985 and Fourteenth Report on Competition Policy, op. cit. at points 197 and 251.

[45] See opinion of AG Jacobs in case C-301/87 *France v Commission ('Boussac)* [1990] ECR I-307 at para. 10. See also as to the personal involvement of the French Prime Minister, Goodliffe, J., 'State Aids and Recalcitrant Members' (1990) *New Law Journal* 1238.

Commission; there was 'some indication of the build-up of momentum in the Commission's exercise of its functions in controlling State aids granted by Member States.'[46] Particular emphasis was given to the presence of State aid in the provisions of capital by Member States to public undertakings.[47] The Commission's stricter line was explicitly supported by the European parliament.[48]

This momentum, supported by the arrival of the new Commissioner Peter Sutherland (1985–89), was capitalized on by the Delors Commission to try and enhance its enforcement machinery.[49] The increase in the number of cases, both notifications and complaints, brought before the Commission, which in itself shows the higher confidence in the system of this time, led the latter to adopt a decision, for the first time, to expedite cases of minor importance.[50] This decision however insisted on the Member State's duty to notify.[51] This was justified as, despite the increase in notifications, there was still a clear tendency among Member States to avoid notification which made the enforcement of these rules quite difficult for the Commission.[52] The enforcement problems of the Commission were exacerbated by the lack of procedural rules in this field for which Member States were also responsible.

Finally, regard should be given to the fact that the case concerned a sensitive sector, textiles and clothing, that employed a very large number of people in the Community, which faced strong competition from outside the Community and that was undergoing for more than a decade a serious restructuring. The Commission had in fact adopted two Community guidelines for aid to this sector in 1971 and 1977, both of which had been disregarded by France.[53]

[46] Fourteenth Report on Competition Policy, op. cit. at point 197.

[47] Ibid. at points 196–98. The Commission sent a letter on this subject to Member States in September 1984.

[48] For the support of the European Parliament see, eg, the resolution of the European Parliament on the Thirteenth Report on Competition Policy (OJ C 12, 14 January 1985).

[49] Fifteenth Report on Competition Policy, op. cit. at point 170: through 'the improvement in the effectiveness and transparency of procedures, increasing information on the current situation regarding State aid and the aid rules, and priority handling of cases that are important for competition policy.'

[50] This decision establishing some thresholds for the fast-track procedure insisted on the obligation of Member States to notify new measures. In fact, it was an incentive to notify measures fulfilling the criteria laid down by the Commission as they would be approved almost automatically. See Fourteenth Report on Competition Policy, op. cit. at point 203. The Commission would modify the thresholds in 1990, see: Information from the Commission—Notification of an aid scheme of minor importance, Official Journal C 040, 20 February 1990 P. 0002.

[51] Ibid. '[T]he Commission would underline that the introduction of the simplified operating procedure reinforces the need for Member States to observe punctiliously their obligation under Article 93(3) EEC to notify all plans to grant or alter aid in sufficient time to enable the Commission to submit its comments.'

[52] See for the resistance of Member States to notify new aid measures Advocate General Tesauro in his opinion in Case C-142/87 *Belgium v Commission (Tubemeuse)* [1990] ECR I-00959 at para. 4.

[53] See in the Commission decision in this case references to the grave difficulties existing in the textile sector, also by the time of adopting the decision: Commission Decision of 15 July 1987 on aid granted by the French Government to a producer of textiles, clothing and paper products—Boussac Saint Frères OJ L 352, 15/12/1987 P. 0042–0051.

C. The judgment of the Court of Justice

In the relevant part of the judgment, the Court of Justice held that there was no need for the Commission to show the real effect of the measure in question on competition and trade, given that '[i]f the Commission were required in its decision to demonstrate the real effect of aid which had already been granted, that would ultimately favour those Member States which grant aid in breach of the duty to notify laid down in Article 93(3) of the Treaty, to the detriment of those which do notify aid at the planning stage. It was therefore not necessary that the reasoning on which the contested decision was based should contain an up-to-date assessment of the effect of aid granted without being notified at the planning stage.'[54]

The Court also held that the operating aid granted to the beneficiary necessarily had an effect on competition and trade '[a]s it reduced the price which [Boussac] would normally have had to pay for its rationalization and modernization, the aid at issue did affect trade between Member States and distorted or threatened to distort competition.'[55] This formula thus removes for a particular type of aid, operating aid which is considered especially distortive, the need to establish in the statement of reasons the list of elements laid down by the Court in the *Leeuwarder* case.

D. Assessment

The formulas laid down by the Court in this judgment—namely that there is no need for the Commission to show the effects of an aid on competition and trade under Article 107(1) and that both criteria are met when operating aid is granted—were proposed by the Commission and endorsed by the Court almost literally.

It is submitted that both the case and the context in which this decision was rendered helps explain the appearance and boldness of both formulas. As to the case, it was characterized by a clear circumvention of the Treaty rules concerning State aids, both at the level of notification of new aid and at that of compatibility of the aid granted with the principles set by the European Commission regarding the textiles and clothing sector in France. The type of aid (large amount of operating aid) and the beneficiary (a large and failing undertaking) exacerbated the

[54] C-301/87 *France v Commission (Boussac)* [1990] ECR I-307 at para. 33.

[55] Ibid. at para. 44. See also para. 50 of the same judgment for a similar finding concerning the conditions for compatibility of the aid: 'In that context, the Commission was entitled, without exceeding the limits of its discretionary power, to form the view that the aid granted to CBSF could not come within the exemption provided for in Article 92(3)(c) of the Treaty in favour of aid designed to facilitate the development of certain economic activities or of certain economic areas, where such aid did not adversely affect trading conditions to an extent contrary to the common interest. The aid lowered CBSF's costs and thereby reduced the competitiveness of other manufacturers within the Community, at the risk of forcing them to withdraw from the market even though they had hitherto been able to continue their activities by virtue of restructuring and improvements in productivity and quality, financed by their own resources.'

distortive effect of the aid in question as several Member States and private applicants corroborated by participating in the procedures before the Commission. In the same vein, a Member State, the UK, had also supported the Commission before the Court, therefore the Commission was in a good position to require from the Court a bold judgment that could rend the enforcement of the State aid rules easier in cases such as this one, that is, cases of illegal and operating aid. The fact that the Commission considered this as a test case was indeed noted by a contemporary author.[56]

Regarding the context, not only the Commission—as discussed in the section on policy context—but also the Court seemed by this time, according to one of its judges, inspired by the *euphoria* of the foreseeable achievement of the 1992 goal. Accordingly, the Court rendered, at the time of adopting the Boussac decision, a number of strong judgments against Member States such as *Francovich*.[57]

Therefore, both the case and the context were propitious for the two formulas laid down by this judgment. In relation to the first, related to the provison regarding there to be no need to show the real effect of aid already granted, it could already be inferred from the formula used in *Philip Morris* in the sense that it sufficed that a measure was 'likely' to affect trade. In any event, this formula ensured that Member States would not profit from their own failure to notify aid measures, and that the same substantial analysis should be carried out for notified and for unnotified aid. In relation to the second formula, related to the presumption of distortion of competition and effect on trade in cases of operating aid, early commentators of the Treaty had contended that the distortion of competition element was almost automatically met because this criterion was interpreted as meaning 'any impact on costs or prices'.[58] Also the Court of Justice had held in the *Italian textiles* case that '[t]he modification of production costs in [a Member State] textile industry by the reduction of the social charges in question necessarily affects trade between the Member States.'[59]

The contribution of this judgment, following the trend initiated by the *Philip Morris* decision, was to allow for a presumption of effect on trade to be established even when the change in production costs affected a single undertaking such as Boussac, and not an entire industry as in *Italian textiles*. This contribution was very significant for the Commission as it could concentrate on cases of individual aid at a time when the application of the State aid rules was becoming, as mentioned in the previous case, increasingly focused on intra-jurisdiction competition, that is, on the situation of individual undertakings in competition

[56] Slot, P.J., 'Procedural and Substantive Compliance Required' (1991) *European Law Review* (1991) 38 at 44.

[57] See Everling, U., 'On the Judge-made law of the European Community's Courts', in O'Keeffe, D. (ed.), *Judicial Review in European Union Law: Liber Amicorum in Honor of Lord Slynn of Hadley* (Kluwer, 2000) at 39.

[58] Kapteyn, P.J.G., and Verloren van Themaat, P., *Introduction to the Law of the European Communities after the Accession of New Member States* (Sweet & Maxwell, 1973) at 245–47. See also Quadri, Monaco, and Trabucchi (eds), op. cit. at 720.

[59] Case 173/73 *Italy v Commission* [1974] ECR 709 at para. 19.

with others in the same Member State and not, as in the past, in competition with other undertakings in other Member States. In the same vein, the Court's judgment in this case favoured the trend that some senior officials of DG COMP had noted by this time, according to which the State aid rules were becoming closer to the antitrust rules (competition between undertakings) and more distanced from the internal market rules (competition between industries).[60]

Finally, the supportive approach of the Court was not unlimited as the Court refused to allow the Commission to find that aid was incompatible simply because it had not been notified under Article 108(3) TFEU. The Commission's proposal shows the test-case character of this judgment and, in this regard, as Winter has said, 'there was something in Boussac for everybody.'[61]

5. The *Tubemeuse* Case (C-142/87)

A. Introduction and background of the case

This case is known for being the first in which the Court laid down that 'the relatively small amount of aid or the relatively small size of the undertaking which receives it does not as such exclude the possibility that intra-Community trade might be affected.'[62] This passage was later interpreted by the Grand Chamber of the Court as meaning that 'there is no threshold or percentage below which it may be considered that trade between Member States is not affected.'[63] In other words, this judgment ruled out the existence of a *de minimis* rule under Article 107(1).

The origins of this case can be traced back to 1984 when the Belgian government notified to the Commission a number of funding plans to a state-owned steel pipe and tube manufacturer (Tubemeuse). The Commission launched the formal investigation procedure to analyse the notified measures. Nevertheless, in violation of the standstill provision provided for in Article 108(3), the Belgian government granted the planned aid to Tubemeuse without waiting for the Commission's clearance. In addition, the Commission learnt in the meantime that Tubemeuse had also received aid which had not been notified to it by the Belgian government.

60 Gyselen, L., 'The Emerging Interface between Competition Policy and Environmental Policy in the EC' in Cameron, J., Demaret, P., and Geradin, D. (eds), *Trade and the Environment: The Search for Balance* at 245: According to him, the legality standard that the Commission had to observe in both the internal market and the competition fields had to start with the following question: 'Is there a distortion of competition between national economies (Article 30 [then applies]) or between individual competitors (Article 85 and 92 [then apply])?' See also Ehlermann, C.D., 'State Aid Control in the European Union: Success or Failure?' (1994) *Fordham International Law Journal* at 1219.

61 Winter, J.A., 'Supervision of State Aid: Article 93 in the Court of Justice' (1993) *Common Market Law Review*, 311 at 327.

62 Case C-142/87 *Belgium v Commission* (Tubemeuse) [1990] ECR I-00959 at para. 43.

63 Case C-280/00 *Altmark* [2003] ECR I-7747 at para. 81. The Court in fact followed in this regard the opinion of AG Léger of 19 March 2002 at para. 109.

In its decision in this case, the Commission noted that the assistance granted to Tubemeuse was an aid under Article 107(1) because a normal market operator would not have invested in an industry suffering from substantial structural overcapacity, and particularly in a firm that was making heavy losses within that industry. The decision also noted that Tubemeuse produced 17 per cent of the total Community production of some seamless pipes and tubes, although it exported about 90 per cent of its output outside the Community. The decision concluded that the aids given to Tubemeuse were 'highly likely to affect trade between Member States within the meaning of Article 92 (1) of the Treaty.'[64] The aid granted to Tubemeuse could not be declared compatible under any of the provisions of Article 107(2) or (3). Lastly, the decision required Belgium to recover the aid from Tubemeuse. Belgium challenged the decision before the Court.

B. The policy context

This judgment was delivered during the third period of evolution of the State aid policy discussed in Chapter 3. The policy context of this case is essentially the same as the *Boussac* decision discussed earlier to which reference is made. In fact, both State aid investigations were initiated by the Commission in the same year (1984), both decisions were adopted in 1987, and both cases were decided by the Court in 1990. The context is therefore characterized by a clash between the Commission's determination to tighten State aid enforcement in the background of the internal market programme under the new momentum of European integration, and the resistance of Member States to notify cases of significant new aid to the European Commission in violation of Article 108(3) TFEU. The cases are also similar in that they refer to the application of the State aid rules to sectors in crisis in which the States were resorting to significant aids to large failing undertakings.

C. Judgment of the Court of Justice

The Court addressed first the argument of the Belgian government according to which there could not be an effect on trade and competition in the Community given that Tubemeuse exported 90 per cent of its production outside the Community. The Court dismissed the argument, holding that due to the interdependence on which Community undertakings operate, it was possible that aid to an undertaking could affect competition and trade. In this regard, the Court concluded that given the difficulties that the relevant sector was undergoing, any advantage to an undertaking was liable to affect competition and trade by benefitting the competitive position of the beneficiary to the detriment of that of its competitors. Furthermore, the Court noted that the Commission had shown that

[64] Commission Decision of 4 February 1987 concerning aid to a Belgian steel pipe and tube manufacturer, OJ L 227, 14 August 1987 p. 0045–0049.

it was reasonably foreseeable that Tubemeuse would redirect its exports to the Community.

Secondly, the Court refused the argument put forward by Belgium concerning the applicability of the *de minimis* rule in the field of State aid, holding that 'the relatively small amount of aid or the relatively small size of the undertaking which receives it does not as such exclude the possibility that intra-Community trade might be affected.'[65] The Court's rejection of this rule was in line with the Commission's submissions in this and other cases since the *Philip Morris* judgment.[66] The Court cited *Philip Morris* as authority for this conclusion although, as discussed earlier, that judgment was silent as to the existence (or not) of a *de minimis* rule yet it could be understood, as confirmed by this judgment, that the Court was implicitly rejecting it.

D. Assessment

From this judgment it is clear that any aid granted to an undertaking of a certain entity in a market with overcapacity affects trade and competition, the reason being that any advantage in those circumstances would affect the competitive position of the competitors of the beneficiary. This finding is thus coherent with that of *Boussac* in the sense of identifying a category of aids were it is easier to show that trade is going to be affected and competition distorted. In *Boussac*, that category was operating aid. In this case it was aid to undertakings of a certain entity in markets with overcapacity. In this regard, as discussed earlier, the Court may have been resolved to support the Commission's enforcement by lowering the standard of proof that this institution has to show in some instances of aid that could be presumed particularly distortive.

Secondly, the judgment also makes clear that there is no room for a *de minimis* exception in State aid law. In this regard, the argument of the Belgian government concerning the applicability of *de minimis* was not deprived of all force. At the end, the wording concerning effect on trade in articles 101, 102, and 107 was quite similar and, as AG Tesauro stated in his opinion to this case, it had to be interpreted in the same way for the three provisions, at least in relation to its character of jurisdictional criterion. In addition, as discussed above in relation to the *para-fiscal levies* case, the Court had originally given some indications in the sense of recognizing the applicability of that rule in the State aid field, and even the Commission had admitted its possible application in its submissions to the *Philip Morris* and *Leeuwarder* cases.[67]

[65] C-142/87 *Belgium v Commission* (Tubemeuse) [1990] ECR I-00959 at para. 43.

[66] See, eg, the Opinion of Advocate General Lenz in the *Meura* case (C-234/84 *Kingdom of Belgium v Commission of the European Communities* [1986] ECR, p. 02263). See also the Commission's position in the case Glaverbel. See Report for the Hearing in Joined Cases 62 and 72/87 *Graverbel* [1988] ECR I-1579.

[67] See for the reference to this argument in the *Philip Morris* case: Flynn, J., 'The Philip Morris Decision Upheld by the European Court, European Law Review' (1981) *European Law Review* at 211, and the reference in the Opinion of AG Slynn in Joined Cases 296 and 318/82 *Netherlands*

The Court did not give any explanation as to why the criterion on effect on trade was different between the different competition rules of the Treaty. While we can only speculate about the reasons underlying the Court's decision to reject this rule in the aid field—even though it had observed it in the antitrust field—one reason might be that the European Commission rejected this rule in the State aid field while it supported it in the antitrust one in light of the differences in the enforcement level between the two areas. Indeed, in the antitrust field the Commission required from the Court the admissibility of a *de minimis* rule in order to be able to cope with the already very high and increasing number of notifications of agreements that it was receiving.[68] By contrast, in the State aid field, the opposite was true: the Commission demanded the Court several times to reject such a rule because the enforcement situation of these rules was totally different: Member States were not notifying their aid measures.[69]

In fact, the situation that the Commission depicted before the Court in the *Tubemeuse* case was quite bleak.[70] The Commission informed the Court of more than 100 cases of aid granted in breach of then Article 93(3) only between 1984 and 1988.[71] In this context, the Court may have been persuaded about the risk of allowing Member States to claim the applicability of a *de minimis* effect and therefore to avoid further any notification of new aid measures. Indeed, the Court was well aware of the problems related to the enforcement of these rules and some

and Leeuwarder Papierwarenfabriek v Commission [1985] ECR 809 at p. 814 for the Commission's position as regards this rule in that case in which the Commission claimed that competition and trade were necessarily affected any time aid was given to keep a company holding 10 per cent of the market in its own member State afloat.

[68] See Opinion of AG C-5/69 *Franz Volk* [1969] ECR 295 at p. 349.

[69] See as to the Commission's position contrary to the existence of a *de minimis* rule in the field of State aid after the *Philip Morris* case for example the Opinion of Advocate General Lenz in the *Meura* case (C-234/84, *Kingdom of Belgium v Commission of the European Communities* [1986] ECR, p. 02263): 'The Commission contends that the assessment of the effects of aid on intra-Community trade does not depend on the degree to which those effects are perceptible. There is no *de minimis* principle in relation to the law relating to aid. Accordingly, account did not have to be taken of the undertaking's turnover or of the number of its employees'. See also the Commission's position in the case Glaverbel, litigated at the same time as the *Tubemeuse* case: 'The Commission further argues that the effect of the aid on trade and competition does not necessarily have to be "appreciable". In its judgments the Court has not held that such effects must be appreciable for the purpose of interpreting Article 92(1). According to the Commission, any parallels drawn between Article 92 (1) and Article 85 (1) are quite irrelevant.' See Report for the Hearing in Joined Cases 62 and 72/87 *Graverbel* [1988] ECR I-1579. See for some of these references also Arpio Santacruz, J.L., *State Aids in the European Community: Framework Exceptions and Implications for National Economic Policies*, defended at the European University Institute in 1996.

[70] As referred by AG Tesauro in his opinion in Case C-142/87 *Belgium v Commission* (Tubemeuse) [1990] ECR I-00959 at para. 4: 'recently, there has been an increasing tendency to grant aid without giving prior notice thereof. With increasing frequency, therefore, the Member States, rather than giving notice of the aid when it is still at the planning stage—as is required by Article 93(3)—put it into effect directly. They simply wait until the Commission, of its own motion or as a result of a complaint lodged by a third party, asks for an explanation of the measures adopted. Then and only then does the Member State transmit the information requested, thereby permitting the initiation, if necessary, of the procedure under Article 93(2).'

[71] Ibid. at footnote 2.

of its judges had criticized the lack of procedural regulations in this field caused by Member States' reluctance to adopt them.[72]

In sum, the Court eased the Commission's task in relation to some categories of aid and rejected a *de minimis* rule in the context of *Euphoria* in which both the Commission and the Court joined forces towards the achievement of the 1992 goal. The Court also confirmed the trend initiated since the early 1980s of concentrating on cases of aid to individual undertakings, usually large undertakings, and not aid to industries or sectors as has been the case in the past.

6. The *Plan Renove I* Case (C-351/98)

A. Introduction and background of the case

This case contrasts with the previous one as it is known for being the first in which the Court justified the introduction of a *de minimis* exception to the notion of aid in several State aid guidelines and communications since the early 1990s, on the basis of the Commission's discretion to assess the possible economic effects of aid.[73]

The origins of the case date back to 1995, when the Commission started an *ex officio* investigation of the 'Plan Renove Industrial', a Spanish programme for the granting of loans to 'natural persons, small and medium-sized enterprises (SMEs), regional public bodies and bodies providing local public services', with a view to renew the commercial vehicle fleet in Spain.[74]

At the end of the investigation, the Commission concluded that the assistance granted under the *Plan Renove Industrial* to regional public bodies and bodies providing local public services did not affect trade due to the lack of liberalization of these services and, therefore, that the assistance in question could not be qualified as aid under Article 107(1) TFEU. The Commission reached a similar conclusion in relation to assistance granted to natural persons or SMEs pursuing a business other than transport at an exclusive local or regional level for the purchase of a certain category of commercial vehicles, small commercial vehicles used for short journeys. Trade was not affected by this kind of assistance, the

[72] See, eg, only few months before this judgment the article by Mancini, G.F. 'The Making of a Constitution for Europe' (1989) *Common Market Law Review*, 595.

[73] The Court had reviewed several cases in which the *de minimis* rule had been discussed yet it had not decided until this case on the justification of the introduction of this rule See, eg, Case C-156/98 *Germany v Commission* [2000] ECR I-6857; C-310/99 *Italy v Commission* [2002] ECR I-2289 or Case C-382/99 *Kingdom of the Netherlands v Commission* [2002] I-05163. See for the soft-law instruments in which this rule had been introduced: Community guidelines on State aid for small and medium-sized enterprises (SMEs), OJ 1992 C 213, p. 2, Community guidelines on State aid for small and medium-sized enterprises, OJ 1996 C 213, p. 4; and Commission notice on the *de minimis* rule for State aid, OJ 1996 C 68, p. 9.

[74] Commission Decision of 1 July 1998 concerning the Spanish Plan Renove Industrial system of aid for the purchase of commercial vehicles (August 1994–December 1996), OJ L 329, 5 December 1998, p. 23–31.

Commission concluded, because the markets affected were local and their effect on trade was negligible.

However, the Commission found that all other aid granted to natural persons and SMEs constituted illegal and incompatible State aid within the meaning of Article 107(1) of the Treaty. This aid had to be recovered by the Spanish authorities. The reasons underlying this position were, in essence, that road transport (the international market for the carriage of persons by road, the international road haulage market, and the market of road passenger transport cabotage) had been completely liberalized in the Community by 1993. Consequently, the Plan Renove was likely to favour some competitors over others that could not benefit from the assistance in equal terms, and thus were discriminated and jeopardized, in intra-Community trade. The Spanish government challenged the decision before the Court. The decision was also challenged by a private applicant before the then Court of First Instance (Case CETM T-55/99).

B. The policy context

This case was decided during the fourth period of evolution of State aid policy discussed in Chapter 3. This period is characterized by a number of initiatives purporting to make State aid control more efficient and transparent through the adoption of legal procedural rules and more focus on a number of goals, so-called horizontal goals (Lisbon Agenda goals), such as research and development or environmental protection towards which State aid should be channelled. The period is also characterized by the increase in the number of State aid notifications and complaints received by the European Commission, which made the modernization of the State aid rules a necessity to cope with this unprecedented workload. In this regard, between 1990 and 1992 State aid notifications had doubled, and they had tripled during the period 1986–92.[75]

C. Judgment of the Court of Justice

The Court supported the *de minimis* rule in State aids even though it was seemingly at odds with its previous case law. In the terms used by the Court, 'whilst the Court has held that the relatively small amount of aid or the relatively small size of the undertaking which receives it does not as such exclude the possibility that intra-Community trade might be affected (see, in particular, Case C-142/87 Belgium v Commission (the "Tubemeuse" case) [1990] ECR 1-959, paragraph 43) a small amount of aid to an undertaking over a given period does not affect trade between Member States in particular economic sectors.'[76] The Court also found that the Commission could conclude that aid in amounts below that set by the

[75] Twenty-second Report on Competition Policy (Office for Official Publications of the European Communities, 1993) at para. 129, table one.

[76] C-351/98 *Spain v Commission (Plan Renove I)* [2002] ECR I-8031 at para. 51

de minimis communication did not affect trade and competition 'in the exercise of its discretion to assess the possible economic effects of aid'.[77]

Furthermore, the Court found that the Commission was bound by the guidelines and notices that it issued where they did not depart from the rules in the Treaty and were accepted by the Member States. Consequently, '[t]he Commission may not therefore refuse to apply the de minimis rule to aid granted to undertakings in sectors which the various applicable provisions do not exclude from application of the rule.'[78] Hence, the decision was partially annulled as the Commission had failed to apply the *de minimis* exception to own account transport undertakings.

D. Assessment

This case is a good example of the Court's largely deferential approach to the Commission's enforcement priorities in this field. The Court justified the *de minimis* rule, in principle *in particular economic sectors*, on the Commission's discretion to assess the possible economic effects of aid.[79] However, more than the outcome of a complex economic analysis carried out by the European Commission, the *de minimis* rule seems to have been the result of administrative and even political considerations heavily determined by the increase in workload that took place in this field since the early 1990s.

Indeed, as to the administrative considerations, the *de minimis* rule responded to the Commission's attempt to reduce its workload and to concentrate in the most important State aid cases as the number of notifications had increased substantially in the years leading to the adoption of the Commission's decision.

Regarding the political considerations, the Commission linked the introduction of the *de minimis* rule to the principle of subsidiarity in its 1992 competition report, the year of signature of the Maastricht Treaty,[80] although, as is well known, this principle does not apply to exclusive competences of the Community. In addition, the *de minimis* rule was also originally part of a comprehensive

[77] Ibid. at para. 52.

[78] Ibid. at para. 53. The Court referred in this regard to the previous its previous case law, Case 310/85 *Deufil v Commission* [1987] ECR 901, para. 22; Case C-313/90 *CIRFS and Others v Commission* [1993] ECR I-1125, para. 36; and Case C-311/94 *Ijssel- Vliet*[1996] ECR 1-5023, para. 43.

[79] Ibid. at para. 52.

[80] Twenty-second Report on Competition Policy, op. cit. at para. 120. The Report states that '[t]he Commission argues that, below a certain level, aid cannot affect trade between Member States and does not therefore distort competition at Community level. It follows that such aid measures are not caught by Article 92(1) of the Treaty and, consequently, it is for the Member States alone to decide whether to monitor the aid in accordance with competition criteria. The threshold was set at ECU 50 000 per firm over a three-year period. It is unlikely that the Commission will be able to develop this line of reasoning any further, although the scope of its notice should not be underestimated since the Commission acknowledged for the first time in a general instrument that certain aid measures were not covered by Article 92.'

program to grant favourable treatment to SMEs of the Community, an important goal that was equally favoured by the European Parliament.[81]

Furthermore, the fact that the *de minimis* rule was mostly based on enforcement considerations was admitted by the Commission before this judgment.[82] Similarly, the Court had also observed that the *rationale* of the *de minimis* rule was 'to reduce the administrative burden on both the Member States and the Commission, which must be able to concentrate its resources on cases that are genuinely important at Community level.'[83]

In sum, the so-called modernization of the competition rules, and in particular the new situation concerning the enforcement of the State aid rules, with the final acceptance of the systematic obligation to notify on the part of Member States, appear to be the real basis for the introduction of the *de minimis* rule. In this regard, the Court, which had supported the Commission when the latter argued that there was no *de minimis* rule in the field of State aids,[84] has also followed the Commission when the latter needed a *de minimis* rule to cope with the increasing workload in the new-era post internal market. Similarly, the Court, as in other cases decided during the fourth period—that we have coined as one of *balanced instrumentalism*—may have been willing to accept the political considerations underpinning the introduction of this rule, such as the support to SMEs or the principle of subsidiarity, and to balance them against the most orthodox application of the State aid rules that would have called, in light of the previous case law, for the rejection of the *de minimis* rule.

7. The *WAM* Case (C-494/06)

A. Introduction

This case is the first in which the Court of Justice established that 'the grant of aid by a Member State, in the form of a tax relief, to some of its taxable persons must be regarded as likely to have an effect on trade and, consequently, as meeting

[81] Ibid. at Annex I 327: 'Parliament insists that small and medium sized enterprises be given favourable treatment, and reiterates the recommendations it made in its Resolution of 13 December 1991 . . .'. See also para. 337.

[82] Written Question No. 2534/96 by Amedeo Amadeo to the Commission. Competition rules, OJ C 060, 26/02/1997 P. 0098.

[83] See, eg, Case C-310/99 *Italy v Commission* [2002] ECR I-2289, para. 94. The support to the administrative efforts of the Commission in the State aid field also arrived from the CFI around the same time, in 1993, with the possibility of rejecting a State aid complaint on the basis of its lack of Community interest. See Case T-49/93*SIDE* [1995] ECR II-02501 at para. 71. The CFI clarified in the same year the conditions that the Commission had to show in order to reject an antitrust complaint for its lack of Community interest (See Case T-114/92 *BENIM v Commission* [1995] ECR II-147 and Case T-5/93 *Tremblay v Commission* [1995] ECR II-00185). The CFI had allowed this possibility for the first time in its famous Automec decision, also in the field of antitrust, Case T-24/90 *Automec v Commission* [1992] ECR II-2223, paras 91–94.

[84] See for the position of the Commission the Opinion of AG Lenz in case C-234/84 *Belgium v Commission* (Meura) [1986] ECR II-02263.

that condition, where those taxable persons perform an economic activity in the field of such trade or it is conceivable that they are in competition with operators established in other Member States.'[85] In other words, as rephrased by Advocate General Kokott, that '[w]ith regard to tax legislation, it is always to be presumed that trade between Member State is affected where those favoured by such legislation perform an economic activity in the field of cross-border trade or where it is conceivable that they are in competition with operators established in other Member States.'[86]

The case thus added to the existing case law a category of aids—aids granted through tax legislation—that will almost automatically be presumed to affect trade. As discussed earlier, the Court had reached in the past a similar finding in relation to operating aid (*Boussac* presumption), and to aid given to undertakings of certain entity in markets with overcapacity (*Tubemeuse*). These categories could thus be seen as instances where the general presumption established in the *Philip Morris* case will be established more easily, thus reducing even further the evidentiary requirements that the Commission needs to put forward concerning the criteria of distortion of competition and effect on trade.

The origin of this case goes back to 1999 when the Commission received a complaint against WAM Engineering Ltd (WAM), the alleged beneficiary of an aid in the form of subsidized loans awarded by Italy with the purpose of facilitating exports to China.[87] The complaint was lodged by a competitor of WAM. The complainant claimed that WAM was able to offer competing products at one-third of its prices thanks to the Italian government funding. After receiving the complaint, the Commission initiated an investigation that lasted until 2004 when a final decision was adopted.[88] During the years of the investigation the complainant repeatedly requested information as to the status of the investigation and the date of publication of the final decision against WAM.[89]

The Commission's decision was challenged before the then Court of First Instance (CFI) by both Italy and WAM. The CFI annulled the decision for lack of sufficient reasoning to show that the loans granted by Italy were likely to affect trade, or that they distorted or threatened to distort competition.[90] The

[85] See case C-494/06 P—*Wam* [2009] ECR I-03639 at para. 51.

[86] See Opinion of Advocate General Kokott in case C-169/08 *Presidente del Consiglio dei Ministri v Regione Sardegna* [2009] ECR, p. I-10821. This formula is in fact the result of combining two previous findings made in recent cases by the Court of Justice, namely, Case C-88/03 *Portugal v Commission* [2006] ECR I-7115, para. 91 and Case C-172/03 *Heiser* [2005] ECR I-1627, para. 35.

[87] See for the background and the uncertainties concerning the amount awarded by Italy the Opinion of Advocate General Sharpston in case C-494/06 P—*WAM* [2009] I-03639 at paras 6–9.

[88] See Commission Decision of 19 May 2004 on State aid No C 4/2003 (ex NN 102/2002) implemented by Italy for WAM SpA, OJ L 63/11, 4 March 2006.

[89] See for the different exchanges between Italy and the Commission and between the latter and the complainant paras 1–30 of the Commission Decision of 19 May 2004 on State aid No. C 4/2003 (ex NN 102/2002) implemented by Italy for WAM SpA, OJ L 63/11, 4 March 2006.

[90] See Joined Cases T-304/04 and T-316/04 *Italian Republic and Wam SpA v Commission of the European Communities* [2006] ECR II-00064.

Commission appealed the judgment of the CFI to the Court of Justice and the latter rendered the judgment that is discussed below.

B. The policy context

This case was decided during the fourth period of evolution of the State aid policy discussed in Chapter 3. The main features of this period have been explained in the two previous cases reviewed in this chapter, which also belong to this period. Reference is thus made to the policy context described in those two judgments.

In addition, it should be reminded that this period is also characterized by the Commission's and Council's determination to address harmful taxation measures through the State aid rules, a goal that was supported by the issuing of a communication on State aids and direct business taxation in 1998. Furthermore, in 2000 the European Council held in Lisbon asked Member States to 'further their efforts to promote competition and reduce the general level of State aids, shifting the emphasis from supporting individual companies or sectors towards tackling horizontal objectives of Community interest, such as employment, regional development, environment and training or research.'[91] The Lisbon Agenda on State aids was taken up by Competition Commissioner Kroes in 2005 with the widely publicized 'State Aid Action Plan' (SAAP) an ambitious consultation document published in 2005 that seemed to introduce a revolution in this field.

Indeed, the SAAP, which was meant to be the first comprehensive reform of State aid policy ever,[92] marked, according to some authors, a new phase in State aid policy.[93] The SAAP called for 'less and better targeted aid',[94] and for a more refined economic approach in the field of compatibility of State aid, for more 'effective procedures', better enforcement, higher predictability, and enhanced transparency and partnership between the Commission and Member States in order to maintain State aid policy in a enlarged EU of then twenty-seven Member States.[95] The SAAP affirms that State aid is mainly forbidden because it distorts competition. Moreover, according to the SAAP, the political rational of State aid

[91] Presidency conclusions of the European Council in Lisbon on 24 March 2000.

[92] See Kleiner, T., 'The State Aid Action Plan' in Mederer, W., Pesaresi, N., and Van Hoof, M. (eds), *EU Competition Law*, Volume IV, State Aid, Book One (Claeys & Casteels, 2008).

[93] Mederer, W., Evolution of State Aid Control, in Mederer, W., Pesaresi, N., Kanninen, H., Korjus, N., and Rosas, A. (eds) *EU Competition Law in Context, Essays in Honour of Virpi Tiili* (Hart Publishing, 2009) and Van Hoof, M. (eds), *EU Competition Law* (Claeys & Casteels, 2008), Part 1, Chapter 2 at 23.

[94] COM (2005) 107 final of 7 May 2005; State Aid Action Plan. Less and better targeted State aid: a roadmap for State aid reform 2005–2009 (Consultation document); SEC(2005) 795.

[95] For a comprehensive review of the SAAP see Kleiner, 'The State Aid Action Plan', op. cit. For a less enthusiastic view on the SAAP see, eg, Buendia Sierra, J.L., and Smulders, B., 'The Limited Role of the "Refined Economic Approach" in Achieving the Objectives of State Aid Control: Time for Some Realism' in *EC State Aid Law—Le Droit des Aides d'État dans la CE, Liber Amicorum Francisco Santaolalla Gadea* (Kluwer Law International, 2008), or Buendia Sierra, J.L., 'Not like this: Some Sceptical Remarks on the "Refined Economic Approach" in State Aid', in Proceedings of 4th Experts' Forum on New Developments in European State Aid Law, 18 and 19 May 2006, European State Aid Law Institute (Berlin: Lexxion, 2006).

control has to do with efficiency, that is, State aid spending 'has to be efficient to represent value-for-money'.[96]

Finally, as the case under review was concerned with aid granted with the purpose of supporting a Community undertaking to penetrate non-EU markets, it should also be noted that at the time of receiving the complaint in this case, the Commission was developing a policy towards outward Foreign Direct Investment (FDI). In this regard, in the 1998 competition report the Commission held that it had a positive attitude towards aid for outward FDI to SMEs and a negative one for the same type of aid to large undertakings.[97]

C. Judgment of the Court of Justice

The Court restated the main formulas of the case law concerning the notions of distortion of competition and effect on trade. These formulas have been mainly laid down by the Court, as discussed earlier, in the *Philip Morris* and *Boussac* judgments. The Court included in this list the new formula mentioned in the introduction to this case, namely that '[w]ith regard more specifically to the condition that trade between Member States be affected, it follows from the case-law that the grant of aid by a Member State, in the form of a tax relief, to some of its taxable persons must be regarded as likely to have an effect on trade and, consequently, as meeting that condition, where those taxable persons perform an economic activity in the field of such trade or it is conceivable that they are in competition with operators established in other Member States'.[98] After restating the different formulas, the Court held that the CFI did not err in law by holding that the Commission was 'obliged to examine whether the aid at issue is liable to affect trade between Member States and to distort competition, giving information relevant to their likely effects in the contested decision.'[99]

In this regard, the Commission had argued that the mere fact that the beneficiary had taken part in intra-Community trade by exporting an important part of its production within the EU should serve to fulfil the criteria on distortion of competition and effect on trade. The Court, however, held that:

> the fact remains that in the circumstances of this case and contrary to the circumstances giving rise to those cases [the cases were the main formulas concerning the

[96] COM (2005) 107 final of 7 May 2005; State Aid Action Plan. Less and better targeted State aid: a roadmap for State aid reform 2005–2009 (Consultation document); SEC(2005) 795 at 70. Furthermore, 'to be compatible with the Treaty, State aid has to address objectives of common interest, which can be classified along two areas: either correcting market failures or promoting other objectives linked more to equity and re-distribution of wealth, like social and regional cohesion.'

[97] Although there was only one precedent of outward FDI to a large undertaking: Decision of 14 October 1998 concerning LiftgmbH (OJ L 142, 5 June 1999, p. 32). In this regard the Commission held that '[w]ith this decision the Commission has no intention of prejudging its future policy on state aid in support of foreign direct investment. It does not rule out the possibility that foreign direct investment by large undertakings may be eligible for state aid where it can be established that the project in question does not create an incompatible distortion of competition within the EEA. Twenty-eighth Report on Competition Policy (Office for Official Publications of the European Communities, 1999) at point 229.

[98] See Case C-494/06 P *Wam* [2009] I-03639 at para. 51.

[99] Ibid. at para. 57.

notions of distortion of competition and effect on trade were laid down] the aid at issue is not directly connected to the activity of the beneficiary on that market [a liberalised European market], but is intended to finance expenditure for a non-member State market penetration programme. In those circumstances, and all the more when it involves aid, the grant equivalent of which was of relatively low value, the effect of the aid on trade and on intra-Community competition is less immediate and even less discernible and this requires a greater effort to state reasons on the part of the Commission.[100]

However, the Court clarified that the greater effort requested from the Commission in cases such as this did not entail the carrying out of an economic analysis.[101] Finally the Court held that the aid at stake was not intended to relieve WAM from operating costs (day-to-day management or normal activities), and therefore that the Boussac presumption, the case law stating that operating aid necessarily affects competition and trade, was not relevant.

D. Assessment

In light of all this, the Court rejected in this case the automatic application of the Philip Morris presumption to undertakings operating in non-European markets. The Commission will need to explain in greater detail how competition is distorted and trade affected in these cases. The Boussac presumption concerning operating aid was however left unaffected as the aid granted to WAM was not, according to the Court, operating aid. Two other aspects of this case appear also relevant for the purposes of this work: (i) the emergence of a new formula concerning the notion of effect on trade in fiscal aid cases, and (ii) the rejection of an economic analysis for the definition of State aid in the post-SAAP scenario. Indeed, in light of the last two aspects, this case can be considered more as a victory than as a defeat for the Commission as it eases the normal application of the State aid rules for the Commission while it raises the standard of proof in some cases that remain however exceptional (cases of aid to penetrate non-EU markets).

As to the new formula adopted by the Court concerning fiscal aid, it was established in an *obiter dictum*, a restatement of two previous findings of the Court also developed during the fourth period of evolution of the State aid policy.[102] There was in fact no particular need to restate this formula as the measure at stake in this case was not one of taxation. Nevertheless, the Court included this formula among the most important concerning the notions of distortion of competition and effect on trade. This inclusion may be revealing of the influence in

[100] Ibid. at para. 62.

[101] Ibid. at para. 58: 'the Commission was not obliged to carry out an economic analysis of the actual situation of the relevant market or the patterns of the trade in question between Member States or to show the real effect of the aid at issue.'

[102] Case C-88/03 *Portugal v Commission* [2006] ECR I-7115, para. 91 and Case C-172/03 *Heiser* [2005] ECR I-1627, para. 35.

the Court's case law of one of the main policy objectives of the State aid rules during the fourth period, that is the fight against aid measures granted through tax legislation. The attention given to this type of aid may in fact be well justified as, according to the Commission's State aid scoreboard, tax aid amounted, in the period between 2009–11, to 40 per cent of all the aid granted by the Member States not related to the crisis.[103]

It remains in any event to be seen whether the presumption concerning tax measures developed by the Court during the fourth period of evolution of the State aid policy, and coined in the *WAM* case, will become the standard formula for the notion of effect on trade in fiscal aid. If that were the case, one might even wonder whether the new formula would be compatible with the recent case law of the Court stressing that the concept of aid has to be defined by reference to its effect, and not by the form or by the regulatory technique adopted to grant the aid in question. In this regard, aid granted by tax derogations has allegedly the same effect as aid granted by other means such as grants.[104]

As to the second aspect considered relevant for the purposes of this work, the rejection of an economic analysis for the definition of aid in the post-SAAP scenario, this finding may seem *prima facie* at odds with the trend towards a more economic analysis of the competition rules and with the references to a more refined economic analysis in the SAAP. However, as discussed above, it is not the first time that the Court recognizes the particular nature of the State aid rules, distinct from the competition rules addressed to undertakings. The Court has done it several times and one example is the *Philip Morris* decision, in which the Court refused to subject the effect on trade criteria to the same conditions in both fields. Similarly, in *Tubemeuse* the Court rejected the applicability of a *de minimis* rule in the State aid field and even subsequently, when this rule has been accepted, its functioning is different from that of the parallel rule in the antitrust field. Moreover, the SAAP's reference to the refined economic approach concerned the compatibility assessment, not the definitional one, as the Court rightly observed.

In relation to the aforementioned, after this judgment the Commission adopted a new decision concerning the aid granted by Italy to WAM,[105] in which it underlined that it was not obliged to carry out an economic analysis of the actual situation of the relevant market, the patterns of trade in question between Member States, or to show the real effect of the aid at issue. The new decision added three arguments in relation to the notions of distortion of competition and effect on trade to those stated in the first (annulled) decision that have recently

[103] See Scoreboard—Data on State aid expenditure (state of play: 31 December 2011) share of each aid instrument in total non-crisis aid to industry and services by Member State, percentage of total, annual average; 2009–2011.

[104] See for a recent Grand Chamber decision to the notion of regulatory technique just described: Joined Cases C-106/09 P and C-107/09 P *Government of Gibraltar v Commission* [2011] ECR nyr, paras 91–92.

[105] Commission Decision of 24 March 2010 on the State aid C 4/03 (ex NN 102/02) implemented by Italy for WAM SpA OJ L 57, 2 March 2011, pp. 29–42.

been considered sufficient by the General Court and the Court of Justice to satisfy the Commission's duty to state reasons.[106]

Therefore, the unfolding of the SAAP has, despite some early views suggesting a possible major role for economic analysis in the definition of aid under the influence of this plan,[107] left the case law on the notions of distortion of competition and effect on trade virtually unchanged.[108]

8. Conclusion

During the first period of evolution of the State aid policy the Court did not provide for any definition of the notions of distortion of competition or effect on trade under Article 107(1). These criteria could not find references either in previous attempts to control the granting of subsidies. The foregoing is in line with the Court's approach during this period in relation to the other criteria of the concept of aid, an approach that we have called, following Judge Koopmans, *institutional*, as the Court appeared to be more focused on institutional than on substantive issues.

Indeed, the Court's judgments during this period were mostly concerned with making the Treaty rules on State aid operational and with reinforcing the role of the Commission. This period was also characterized by the Court's issuance of broad teleological principles that could subsequently be clarified and limited and this could be seen also in relation to the criteria under review. In this regard, and in keeping with the two features mentioned in this paragraph, it is possible to infer the early understanding of these criteria by the Court from the *para-fiscal levies* and other cases decided during the first period.

In this regard, it emerges from the *para-fiscal levies* case that the aid at stake was only incompatible because of the way in which it had been financed—namely, through levies that discriminated against out of State producers—and that, save for that feature, the measure would have been considered 'permissible' by the

[106] See Commission Decision of 24 March 2010 on the State aid C 4/03 (ex NN 102/02) implemented by Italy for WAM SpA OJ L 57, 2 March 2011, pp. 29–42 at paras 88–91; and Cases T-303/10 *Wam Industriale SpA v European Commission* [2012] ECR nyr ad C-560/12 P Wam Industriale v Commission [2013] ECR nyr.

[107] See, eg, Coppi, L., 'The Role of Economics in State Aid Analysis and the Balancing Test' in Szyszczak, E. (ed.), *Research Handbook on State Aid* (Edward Elgar, 2011) 64 at 67: 'Distortions of competition and effect on trade would appear to be areas in which economic analysis would be relevant. However, historically, the existence of such distortions has been largely presumed whenever aid was present…Accordingly, economic analysis has had a fairly limited role in this regard, even though recent case law may indicate that the aid's effect on trade may need to be analysed in more depth in the future.'

[108] See for the view that the SAAP has not affected the case law concerning the substance of the notions of distortion of competition and effect on trade Biondi, A., 'The rationale of State aid control: a return to orthodoxy' (2010) *Cambridge Yearbook of EU Law*, 35 at 51, Buendia Sierra and Smulders, 'The Limited Role of the "Refined Economic Approach', op. cit. at 13, or Farley, M., 'The Role of Economics-based Approaches when Analysing Effects on Trade and Distortions of Competition after Wam' (2012) *European State Aid Law Quarterly*, 369 at 374.

Court, presumably because the effect of the aid was not otherwise appreciable or tangible and because the measure would not have been discriminatory.

Indeed, the view that Article 107(1) required an appreciable effect on trade was broadly accepted among judges and other commentators in the early days,[109] it was also in keeping with a literal interpretation of Article 107(1) that requires an effect on trade, and not merely a threat like the distortion of competition requirement, and could also be deduced from the early judgments of the Court.[110] This requirement was also in line with the main goal pursued by the European Commission during this period, namely, the elimination of obstacles to trade that could affect the creation of the Common Market. Measures that could not affect such trade in a perceptible way were largely ignored. As in the *French exports* case, the Court considered that the measure affected trade and was an aid because, from its discriminatory nature and purpose, it was directly aimed at harming the interests of out of state producers while benefitting national producers. Indeed, both the Commission and the Court were not concerned with the distortion of competition that could be created by the aid in question as the Commission's decision would allow the granting of more aid in this and other cases, provided that the discriminatory character was removed.[111] The focus was not, to paraphrase the recent SAAP motto on *less* (and better targeted) *aid* but instead on discrimination against out-of-State traders and on a teleological application of the rules towards the achievement of the internal market.

During the second period, referred to in the previous chapters as *instrumental*, also following Judge Koopmans, the Court adopted the landmark *Philip Morris* judgment. This decision, considered by some authors as a *sea change* in the evolution of the State aid policy,[112] was indeed crucial both at the level of the definition and at the level of the compatibility of aid measures. For our purposes, limited to the concept of aid, the judgment was clearly *instrumental* to the Commission's enforcement of the State aid rules as the Court allowed the Commission to presume that competition is distorted and trade affected in cases of aid to a single company, and not to a whole sector as in the past.[113] This, in turn, allowed the

[109] See Quadri, Monaco, and Trabucchi (eds), op. cit. At 722. Catalano, *Manuel de droit des Communautés européennes*, op. cit. at 495.

[110] Case 6/64, *Flaminio Costa v E.N.E.L.*, ECR, P. I-01141: 'These provisions…headed "Aids granted by States", are designed, on the one hand, to eliminate progressively existing aids and, on the other hand, to prevent the individual States in the conduct of their internal affairs from introducing new aids "in any form whatsoever" which are likely directly or indirectly to favour certain undertakings or products in an appreciable way, and which threaten, even potentially, to distort competition. By virtue of Article 92, the Member States have acknowledged that such aids are incompatible with the Common Market and have thus implicitly undertaken not to create any more, save as otherwise provided in the Treaty'.

[111] See for another example the Commission Decision of 23 September 1966 on the aid instituted by the Government of the French Republic for the purchase of aircraft, OJ 182, 12 October 1966, pp. 3141–42.

[112] See Allen, D., 'Competition Policy: Policing the Single Market', in Wallace, H., and Wallace, W. (eds), *Policy-Making in the European Union* (OUP, 1996) 157 at 177.

[113] Indeed, in the *Italian textiles* case discussed in Chapter 5 the Court established a similar presumption but referred to entire productions. Moreover, a literal reading of the Treaty could cast

Commission to deal with cases of individual aid in a more straightforward way at a time when the Commission was changing the focus of its enforcement action in this field towards distortions of competition primarily felt in the jurisdiction of the Member State granting the aid and not, as in the past, in other Member States. The application of the MEIP test—discussed in Chapter 4 in the context of the advantage criterion—is an example of the new focus on cases of individual aid where, if there is discrimination, it is not as in the previous period against out-of-state traders but instead primarily against competitors resident in the same jurisdiction. This 'inwards' application of the State aid rules was thus favoured by the Court through the lowering of the burden of proof that the Commission had to show in relation to the two criteria under review.

The Court's judgment in this case was also important as it negated, implicit yet necessarily, the existence of a *de minimis* rule in the State aid field. This finding, seemingly at odds with the Court's original conception of aid during the first period, was, it is submitted, motivated by the Court's realization of the poor enforcement of the State aid rules, caused mainly by the lack of Member States' compliance and the absence of procedural rules in this field due to the Council's failure to adopt them. Indeed, a *de minimis* rule in this field would have given Member States an extra argument to avoid notification of new aid measures due to their alleged lack of effect on trade.

In this context, the Commission might have felt that the Court was willing to give a supportive judgment in this case as it did not challenge the admissibility of Philip Morris' appeal, although it was the first time that an undertaking appealed a State aid decision, which is addressed to Member States. The Commission had good reasons for guessing that the Court would be supportive as it had been so since the early 1970s, both on substantive and on procedural grounds.[114] Indeed, during the 1970s the Court supported generally the Commission, not only when the latter claimed that some measures amounted to State aid but also when it claimed that some measures benefitting only or mostly domestic consumption should not be considered as aids because they would not distort competition and/or affect trade at Community level.[115] This judgment has thus been described in

some doubts as to the applicability of Art. 107 to cases of aid to a single undertaking as that article referred to aid benefitting certain '*undertakings or productions*'.

[114] See for the substantive grounds, eg, the *Italian textiles, Steinike and Weinlig*, or *Van Tiggele* decisions and, for the procedural ones, eg, case C-120/73 *Lorenz* [1973] ECR 1471 or case C-70/72 *Commission v Germany* [1973] ECR 813. These judgments clarified that Member States were obliged to refrain from implementing any aid until the Commission had sufficient time to review its compatibility with the Common Market pursuant to notification and that the Commission could ask for repayment of aid illegally granted.

[115] Case 40/75, *Produits Bertrand v Commission* [1976] ECR 1; Case 52/76 *Benedetti v Munari*, [1977] ECR 163. See also the Fifth Report on Competition Policy (Office for Official Publications of the European Communities, 1976) at points 126–29. See for other cases where the Commission held that there was no effect on competition and/or trade: Fourth General Report on the Activities of the Communities, op. cit. at 172, or Seventh Report on Competition Policy (Office for Official Publications of the European Communities, 1978) at 205. See also the First Report on Competition Policy, op. cit. at points 135–38: the Commission can only act under Article 92(1) EC, 'in cases where national aid is harmful to the economic activities of other Member States'.

this chapter as the substantive corollary to the procedural judgments laid down by the Court during this period, as all of them had the effect of making the State aid rules operative.

However, soon after this judgment, the Commission would lose two important cases for failing to state the reasons justifying the fulfilment of the criteria under review.[116] In this regard, it has been argued that these cases can be explained not only by the defective reasoning of the Commission's decisions but also by the stricter approach of the Court towards the Commission during the early 1980s. Indeed, the reasoning in the *Leeuwarder* case was clearly insufficient as it only contained what Advocate General Slynn referred to as a 'bald assertion' of the effect of the measure on competition and trade.[117] However, there was also a trend in the Court's case law towards a more rigorous control of the Commission's decision. This general tendency has been recognized by a judge of the Court who took part in the *Leeuwarder* decision and by several other commentators in relation to the State aid field.[118] The tendency was also perceptible in the antitrust field where Gerber held that during this period the Court would allow the Commission to win on new tests but it would quash the decision on another ground.[119] Indeed, the two judgments mentioned (*Leeuwarder* and *Intermills*) were the first applications of a new test, the MEIP, that reached the Court. In line with the trend just mentioned, the Court supported the application of the MEIP test in both cases and yet it annulled both Commission decisions.

During the third period, the Court issued four formulas in two cases decided in 1990:[120] that (i) the Commission does not need to show the real effect of the aid already granted on competition and on trade between Member States,[121] (ii) that operating aid, that is to say, aid which is intended to release an undertaking from costs which it would normally have had to bear in its day-to-day management or normal activities, distorts the conditions of competition,[122] (iii) that aid to undertakings of a certain entity in markets with overcapacity necessarily distort competition and affect trade, and (iv) that there is no *de minimis* rule in State aid.[123] These judgments provided for important conceptual clarifications

[116] See C-323/82 *SA Intermills v Commission* [1984] ECR, p. 03809, and Joined Cases 296 and 318/82 *Netherlands and Leeuwarder Papierwarenfabriek v Commission* [1985] ECR 809.

[117] Opinion of AG Slynn in Joined Cases 296 and 318/82 *Netherlands and Leeuwarder Papierwarenfabriek v Commission* [1985] ECR 809 at p. 814.

[118] See the article by Koopmans, 'The Role of Law in the Next Stage of European Integration', op. cit. at 931. See also Goyder, *EEC Competition Law*, op. cit. at 383–84, or Ross, 'A review of Developments in State Aids 1987', op. cit. at 178.

[119] Gerber, *Law and Competition in Twentieth Century Europe*, op. cit. at 361–62. Gerber marks the beginning of this trend in the mid-1970s and places it in the broader economic context of this period (mid-1970s to the mid-1980s) characterized by its difficulty for European undertakings.

[120] C-301/87 *France v Commission ('Boussac')* [1990] ECR I-307 and Case C-142/87 *Belgium v Commission* (Tubemeuse) [1990] ECR I-00959.

[121] C-301/87 *France v Commission ('Boussac')* [1990] ECR I-307 at para. 33

[122] Ibid. at paras 44 and 50.

[123] In other words, that 'the relatively small amount of aid or the relatively small size of the undertaking which receives it does not as such exclude the possibility that intra-Community trade might be affected.' See Case C-142/87 *Belgium v Commission* (Tubemeuse) [1990] ECR I-00959 at para. 43.

concerning the criteria under review, in line with what we have seen in relation to the other criteria of the concept of aid during the same period. Indeed, we have referred to this period previously as *definitional*.

The four conceptual clarifications mentioned earlier allowed the Commission to enforce the State aid rules more easily in relation to four categories of aid: (i) illegal aid (that should be analysed under the same standard than notified aid so no need to show effects), (ii) operating aid (that could be presumed to affect trade), (iii) aid in markets with overcapacity (that should also be presumed as distortive of competition and trade if granted to undertakings of a certain entity), and (iv) *de minimis* aid (that would not be accepted). The clarifications confirmed the line of cases initiated by *Philip Morris* and even reduced the evidentiary requirements established in that judgment (and in *Leeuwarder*) for some categories identified as particularly pernicious by the European Commission. These categories could apply both in cases of aid to industries and, as in the two cases at stake, to individual undertakings. Finally, these supportive judgments were decided in the context of *Euphoria* created by the internal market project, a context that led the Court during the same period to deliver strong judgments as *Francovich*, as Judge Everling has observed.[124]

Finally, during the fourth period, which we have described earlier as of *balanced instrumentalism*, the Court has continued supporting the European Commission yet, as we have also seen in relation to the other criteria of the concept of aid, it has done so taking into account not only the orthodox and efficient application of the State aid rules but also other interests and values now included in the Treaties. In this regard, in the *Renove I* case the Court supported the introduction of a *de minimis* rule in the field of State aids, even though it was tellingly at odds with its previous case law, and therefore with the most orthodox application of the State aid rules. As discussed in the commentary to this case, administrative and political considerations underpinning the introduction of this rule, including the support to European SMEs and the principle of subsidiarity, may have been objectives that the Court has balanced against the strict application of its case law since *Philip Morris* and *Tubemeuse*. The Court's support to the Commission in relation to the *de minimis* rule is not, however, unlimited but rather balanced, as the Court has not formally repealed its previous case law and thus the possibility remains for the annulment of any future Commission decision if the latter raises the *de minimis* threshold beyond acceptable boundaries for the Court.

Similarly, the Court's decision in *WAM* is also supportive for the Commission as it rejects the need for an economic analysis under Article 107(1)—despite the general trend towards more economic analysis in the application of the Treaty competition rules and the controversy created by the SAAP in this regard—and establishes the presumption that trade is affected when aid is granted through tax legislation. The *WAM* judgment does, in fact, contribute to the achievement of one of the main Commission's policy objectives during this period, that is the

[124] See Everling, 'On the Judge-made Law of the European Community's Courts', op. cit. at 39.

fight against harmful taxation by establishing a presumption in cases of tax legislation. This instrumental approach is however more balanced than in the 1970s or even 1990s as the Court actually refused to extend the *Philip Morris* presumption automatically to aid for undertakings active in non-European markets and annulled the Commission decision, requiring it to reason in greater detail in the future how an aid to penetrate a non-EU market might distort competition and affect trade in the internal market.

PART III

8

Case Study

State Aid for Banks during the Financial Crisis

1. Introduction

The financial crisis, and particularly the reaction of Member States to the crisis by injecting an unprecedented amount of public resources into the banking sector, has represented a major trial for the State aid regime. This chapter will analyse the Commission's policy reaction to the crisis, as it has been explained by political scientists, and whether this reaction has produced any changes on the notion of aid, as shown in recent judgments of the Court of Justice.

2. The Commission's State Aid Policy during the Financial Crisis

Political scientists have observed that the European Commission's policy on State aid during the financial crisis has evolved from a very lax approach, motivated by the high economic and political tension of the early days of the crisis and particularly soon after the collapse of Lehmann Brothers, towards a stricter approach as the financial and economic context was becoming more stable. The Commission's method to increase the toughness of State aid control progressively has been based on the publication of soft law instruments stating how it intended to approach the compatibility of aid for banks in different periods of the crisis.[1]

As discussed in Chapter 3, this method has been used by the Commission in the past to fill the gap left by the absence of legal (and particularly procedural) instruments in this field as Member States had refused to adopt them for many years. In this case, the adoption of soft law instruments, together with a very permissive interpretation of the rules—essentially accepting all bank-related aid schemes proposed by Member States in the first months of the crisis—under a exceptional legal base (Article 107(3)(b)), was motivated by a desire to avoid direct confrontation with Member States in a difficult context in which it was even proposed to

[1] See in this regard, eg, Doleys, T.J., 'Managing State Aid in a Time of Crisis: Commission Crisis Communications and the Financial Sector Bailout', *Journal of European Integration* (2012) 549.

suspend the application of the State aid discipline altogether.[2] The Commission's method has also in this case attempted to fill a gap in the regulation at EU level concerning banks' supervision, a regulation that has only been drafted during the crisis.[3] In this regard, as the first Commissioner for Competition stated many years ago, '[i]t is true that the Treaty prohibits aids which distort competition, but it is difficult to find a satisfactory solution when an emergency has already arisen.'[4] The Commission thus responded with a 'crisis regime' specially devised to combine the needs for rapid and flexible State intervention with the safeguard of competition and the avoidance of subsidy races.[5] Over time, the European Commission also pursued a number of regulatory objectives, in addition to the traditional protection of competition and of the integrity of the internal market. Indeed, through its enforcement of the EU State aid rules in the context of the financial crisis, the Commission has addressed issues such as financial stability, moral hazard, or the return to long-term viability of financial institutions.[6]

Today it is widely recognized that the European Commission has managed to help Member States prevent a banking meltdown, and to avoid significant distortions of competition in the internal market throughout the crisis while maintaining the

[2] See in this regard, eg, the speech by H. Ungerer, Deputy Director General of DG Competition with special responsibility for State Aids, at the EU State Aid Summit State Aid Policy, Procedure and Enforcement through the Economic Crisis and Beyond C5 Business Information in a Global Context, Brussels, at 13. It is available at: <http://ec.europa.eu/competition/speeches/text/sp2009_11_en.pdf>. He referred to Art. 107(3)(b) as a 'nuclear option' of State aid law. See also in this regard the Business and Advisory Committee (BIAC) to the OECD: 'An aggressive enforcement of subsidies bans would also have put into danger the very existence of State aid rules, given the strong political and economic reasons for granting aid.' Global Forum on Competition, Roundtable on competition, state aids and subsidies (DAF/COMP/GF(2010)5) at 228.

[3] See in this regard, *inter alia*, Council Regulation (EU) No. 1024/2013 of 15 October 2013 conferring specific tasks on the European Central Bank concerning policies relating to the prudential supervision of credit institutions, and Regulation (EU) No. 1022/2013 of the European Parliament and of the Council of 22 October 2013 amending Regulation (EU) No. 1093/2010 establishing a European Supervisory Authority (European Banking Authority) as regards the conferral of specific tasks on the European Central Bank pursuant to Council Regulation (EU) No. 1024/2013.

[4] Von der Groeben, H., *The European Community—The Formative Years: The Struggle to Establish the Common Market and the Political Union (1958–66)* (Office for Official Publications of the European Communities, 1987) at 215.

[5] The crisis regime was based on four communications, namely, the Banking Communication (Communication from the Commission—The application of State aid rules to measures taken in relation to financial institutions in the context of the current global financial crisis [2008] OJ C 270/8), the Recapitalization Communication (Communication on the recapitalization of financial institutions in the current financial crisis: limitation of aid to the minimum necessary and safeguards against undue distortions of competition [2009] OJ C 10/2), the Impaired Assets Communication (Communication on the treatment of impaired assets in the Community banking sector [2009] OJ C 72/1), and the Restructuring Communication (Commission Communication on the return to viability and the assessment of restructuring measures in the financial sector in the current crisis under the State aid rules [2009] OJ C 195/9).

[6] See, eg, Gerard, D.M.B., 'Managing the Financial Crisis in Europe: The Role of EU State Aid Law Enforcement', in Merola, M., Derenne J., and Rivas J. (eds), *Competition Law at Times of Economic Crisis—In Need for Adjustment?* (Bruylant, 2013) 248–49, or Andreangeli, A., 'EU Competition Law in Times of Crisis: Between Present Challenges and a largely Unwritten Future' (2013) *Competition Law Review* 91 at 103.

State aid rules in place.[7] As Commissioner Almunia has underlined, 'on the basis of these rules, the Commission has acted as a de facto crisis-management and resolution authority at EU level.'[8] The central position of the European Commission was substantially reinforced by the Member States' realization that traditional national protectionist policies could be extremely dangerous in the current level of economic integration. In this regard, the enormous tension generated by the Irish bank guarantee scheme in favour only of Irish majority-owned banks, introduced two weeks after the collapse of Lehman Brothers, made Member States appreciate the importance of avoiding 'beggar-thy-neighbour policies' in the context of the crisis. The Irish scheme had provoked a remarkable migration of funds to Irish banks benefitting from the scheme to the detriment of other Irish and European banks, and this was rightly perceived by European leaders as a very risky way to proceed. Soon after these events, on 7 October 2008 Member States welcomed 'the Commission's continued commitment to act quickly and apply flexibility in State aid decisions, within the framework of the single market and state aid regime [and] the Commission's commitment to shortly issue guidance setting out the broad framework within which the State aid compatibility of recapitalisation and guarantee schemes, and cases of application of such schemes, could be rapidly assessed'. They also recognized that 'legitimate interest of competitors must be protected, in particular through the State aids rules.'[9]

The reaction of Member States to this crisis, and their favourable position towards the flexible observance of the State aid rules, due in great part to the level of economic integration achieved by the Union—as exemplified by the Irish guarantee scheme—contrasts with that followed by Member States in previous crises discussed in the book, particularly during the 1973 oil crisis, where a *de facto* abandonment of the discipline took place.

The Council's demand for Commission's action and flexibility was met by the latter by its virtually accepting all aid schemes notified by Member States in relation to the crisis, provided that they accepted a rescue and restructuring logic for a future phase as they emerged from the crisis. This first period has been named by Doleys as the 'crisis response' period, which was followed, according to this author, by another two phases in the Commission's State aid policy during the crisis, namely, a 'crisis management' phase which covers late 2008 until early 2009, 'and

[7] See in this regard, eg, Gebski, S., 'Competition First? Application of State Aid Rules in the Banking Sector', *The Competition Law Review*, 89 at 95; Spector, D., 'Competition Policy in Times of Crisis', *Concurrences*, 2-2009 at 1; Quigley, C., 'Review of the Temporary State Aid Rules Adopted in the Context of the Financial and Economic Crisis' (2012) *Journal of European Competition Law and Practice* at 237 or Gerard, D.M.B., 'Managing the Financial Crisis in Europe: The Role of EU State Aid Law Enforcement' in Merola, M., Derenne J., and Rivas J. (eds), *Competition Law at Times of Economic Crisis—In Need for Adjustment?* (Bruylant, 2013) at 231, or Doleys, 'Managing State Aid in a Time of Crisis', op. cit. at 551.

[8] Speech by Commissioner Almunia entitled 'Banking crisis, financial stability and State aid: The experience so far', delivered in Brussels, 8 March 2013.

[9] Immediate responses to financial turmoil, Council Conclusions—Ecofin Council of 7 October 2008, Luxembourg, 7 October 2008 13930/08 (Presse 284), 2–3. It is available at: <http://www.consilium.europa.eu/ueDocs/cms_Data/docs/pressData/en/misc/103202.pdf>.

addresses events surrounding the publication of the Commission's Restructuring and Impaired Assets Communications', and the 'crisis resolution' phase which covers the period from early 2009 onward 'and encompasses the Commissions Restructuring Communication and ongoing efforts by the industry to exit the crisis.'[10] This periodization broadly coincides with the evolution described in other accounts of the Commission's State aid policy during the crisis.[11]

During the first phase of the crisis, the most acute period, the European Commission adopted a very lax approach with the publication of the early Banking Communication (October 2008) that introduced two main novelties: the new legal basis for compatibility of measures related to the financial sector mentioned earlier (Article 107(3)(b)), which allowed the Commission to treat the financial sector as special, and therefore to be more flexible and lenient with this sector than with others under the rescue and restructuring compatibility rules, and the commitment to approve State aid measures within 24 working hours or even during weekends, and, in case of doubt, to offer preliminary authorization of them while continuing to investigate. This led to a significant number of notifications and of authorization decisions in the first weeks and months of the financial crisis.[12]

During the second phase of the crisis, the Commission published the Recapitalization Communication in which it adopted a pragmatic and lenient approach towards 'fundamentally sound' banks at the request of some Member States, while it became stricter *vis-à-vis* distressed banks, imposing conditions for them to obtain compatible State aid that had not been previously demanded of banks in the Banking Communication. Among the new conditions, some reflected a number of regulatory goals such as addressing moral hazard (eg limit executive compensation), beyond the traditional competition-related objectives pursued under the compatibility analysis. During this *crisis management* period the Commission would also adopt the Impaired Assets Communication in which it struck again a balance between accommodating the demands of Member States such as Germany, which wanted to remove toxic assets from the banks' balance sheets, with those of competitors and the industry that feared that governments could overvalue the toxic assets and thus confer an unfair advantage to the aided firms.

After the publication of the Impaired Assets Communication, because the macroeconomic and financial situation was at that stage becoming more stable, the Commission turned its focus to restructuring. During this period the Commission was able to impose strict conditions on aided banks and to pursue more clearly its regulatory goals. As referred by some commentators, it was

[10] See Doleys, 'Managing State Aid in a Time of Crisis', op. cit. at 7.

[11] See in this regard, eg, Sutton, A., Lannoo, K., and Napoli,C., on the evolutionary character of the policy and its increasing strictness and derivation towards industrial policy-like measures: 'Bank State Aid in the Financial Crisis Fragmentation or Level Playing Field? A CEPS Task Force Report' (CEPS, 2010), or the second period (crisis-related regimes) identified by Lo Schiavo, G., 'The Impact of the EU Crisis-Related Framework on State Aids to Financial Institutions: From Past Practice to Future Prospects' (2013) *The Competition Law Review* 135 at 139.

[12] See Doleys, 'Managing State Aid in a Time of Crisis', op. cit. at 555–58.

'payback time'.[13] The Commission adopted the Restructuring Communication which was met with criticism in some quarters precisely for including criteria that seemed to go beyond the protection of competition in the internal market and closer to industrial policy, specifically the requirement that aided firms should consider divesting themselves of non-core activities. This approach, started under the mandate of Commissioner Krooes, was continued by Commissioner Almunia who held, after summarizing the main steps taken by the Commission under the State aid rules during the crisis,[14] that 'we want a leaner, cleaner and healthier banking system centred on the financing of the real economy.'[15]

Finally, during this last phase the Commission has adopted a new Banking Communication that codifies the practice of the Commission in the Spanish and Cyprus cases.[16] The new Communication replaces the 2008 Banking Communication and supplements the remaining crisis rules. The Commission further tightens the rules applicable to State aid for the financial sector by, for example, making the temporary authorizations of recapitalizations exceptional (the former general rule and one of the two main novelties of the 2008 Communication discussed previously). Under the new Communication, banks will need in principle to work out a restructuring plan, including a capital-raising plan, before they can receive recapitalization measures. In addition, in case of capital shortfalls, bank owners and junior creditors will be required to contribute as a first resort before banks can resort to public funding. The new rules are also intended to prepare the transition to a banking Union.

In sum, the European Commission has emerged through the application of the EU State aid rules as a pragmatic crisis-management and resolution authority which adopted a strategically permissive stance at the beginning of the crisis when the latter was most acute, and became stricter over time, as the macroeconomic situation was more stable and the political pressure to authorize aid schemes diminished. Finally, in the last phase of the crisis, the European Commission has been able to pursue regulatory goals beyond the mere preservation of competition in the market and the integrity of the internal market. Overall, the Commission has been praised for finding the right balance between preventing significant

[13] See the reference in Doleys, 'Managing State Aid in a Time of Crisis', op. cit. at 560.

[14] Speech of Commissioner Almunia at the 23rd World Savings Banks Institute Congress, Marrakech, 10 May 2012 'we responded to the call swiftly introducing special rules for State aid to banks in 2008 and 2009. Under these rules, we have decided on the viability, restructuring or liquidation of 43 banks, and are still working on more than 20 other cases. The emergency regime has given guidance on the pricing, duration and type of liabilities that national authorities across the EU can guarantee for a bank. It has also provided common criteria on how banks must remunerate the government for recapitalisation and impaired-asset measures. Finally, it set out the terms for the restructuring or orderly liquidation of aided banks, depending on the size of the support received and on the soundness of a bank's business model.'

[15] Ibid.

[16] Communication from the Commission on the application, from 1 August 2013, of State aid rules to support measures in favour of banks in the context of the financial crisis, OJ C 216, 30 July 2013, pp. 1–15.

distortions of competition and allowing national interventions in the absence of a European Union framework to deal with such a severe crisis.

3. The Evolution of the Legal Notion of Aid during the Crisis

The notion of State aid has not remained unaffected by these extraordinary policy developments outlined.[17] Indeed, the avalanche of State aid decisions pertaining to the banking sector has brought about a number of clarifications concerning most of the criteria of Article 107(1) TFEU.

In this regard, the European Commission has considered that an aid to a bank was effectively granted not when the funds were made available to the bank at stake, but when the authorities made declarations announcing the concrete support to be granted.[18] This innovative interpretation of the notion of State resources had a clear precedent in the Commission's practice (the *France Télécom* decision), where the Commission noted that 'an announcement which induced the rating agencies from further downgrading France Telecom was capable of constituting state aid, because such public declarations are equivalent from a legal standpoint to a guarantee and were placing the State's reputation on the line, with economic costs in the event of non-compliance'.[19] This interpretation has recently been upheld by the Court of Justice in Grand Chamber formation in the *France Télécom* case, covered in detail in Chapter 6.[20]

The European Commission has also concluded that measures of national central banks benefitting financial institutions, therefore in principle benefitting a particular sector of the economy (a sectorial measure), can be qualified as general measures, and hence not selective under Article 107(1) TFEU, if certain conditions are met. Essentially, these measures will not be selective if the beneficiaries are solvent, the liquidity is fully secured by collateral, and the measures are provided at a market rate.[21] As the Commission has recently stated: 'where a central bank reacts to a banking crisis not with selective measures in favour of individual banks, but with general measures open to all comparable market players in the market (eg lending to the whole market on equal terms), such general measures often fall outside the scope of State aid control.'[22]

[17] Given the recent character of most of the State aid decisions in this field, this section reviews significant novelties related to the notion of aid included in Commission documents and in cases decided by the General Court and not only Court of Justice judgments as in the rest of the book.

[18] Commission Decision NN 25/2008 of 30 April 2008 WestLB riskshield, paras 37–38.

[19] Gebski, S., 'Competition First?', op. cit. at footnote 11, and Commission Decision C 13a/2003 of 2 August 2004 France Telecom, OJ 2006, L 257/55, para. 194.

[20] Joined Cases C-399/10 P and C-401/10 P *Bouygues SA, Bouygues Télécom SA v Commission*, nyp.

[21] See in this regard Gebski, S., 'Competition First?', op. cit. at 92, and references cited therein. See also Communication from the Commission on the application, from 1 August 2013, of State aid rules to support measures in favour of banks in the context of the financial crisis ('Banking Communication') 2013/C 216/01 at 62.

[22] Draft Commission Notice on the notion of State aid pursuant to Article 107(1) TFEU at point 50 and footnote 72.

This conjunctural interpretation—'reacts to a banking crisis'—of the selectivity criterion appears at odds with the established case law of the Court of Justice concerning the objective character of the notion of aid.[23] In addition, this interpretation seems to contradict the traditional case law of the Court according to which measures affecting an entire sector are selective,[24] also in cases related exclusively to the banking sector.[25] In this regard, the exceptional circumstances under which the Commission adopted the first Banking Communication, together with the need to reassure financial institutions and Member States, and to reduce the number of notifications to the Commission in the first months of the crisis might perhaps explain this sort of 'interpretative exemption' in cases of measures adopted by central banks and applicable to all financial institutions in their Member State. However, these are not valid justifications for deviating from the case law of the Union courts concerning the notion of aid. To this extent, as the Union courts have recently observed, 'although the Commission is bound by the guidelines and notices that it issues in the field of State aid, that is so only to the extent that those texts do not depart from the proper application of the rules in the Treaty, since the texts cannot be interpreted in a way which reduces the scope of Articles 87 EC and 88 EC or which contravenes the aims of those articles.'[26]

Nevertheless, the clearest impact of the financial crisis on the notion of aid has been on the advantage criterion, and more particularly on the Market Economy Investor Principle (MEIP) test. This test had been applied to the banking sector in the past.[27] However, during the crisis, the Commission has followed a qualitative assessment based on the assumption that, after the second half of 2008, when the crisis became more acute, no reasonable private investor would have granted the same or similar facilities to banks under circumstances similar to those prevailing at the time.[28] The Commission has indeed refused to conceive the applicability of the MEIP to national rescue packages which were aimed, the Commission found, at avoiding large negative spill-over effects into the national banking system and economy. In addition, the Commission has underlined in several decisions that even if it were to apply the MEIP, no private investor would have been able to provide the amount of capital and funding provided by the State, and no private investor would have been willing to assume the same risks as the State,[29] and with

[23] See, eg, Case C-83/98 P *France v Ladbroke Racing and Commission* [2000] ECR I-3271, para. 25 or C-487/06 P *British Aggregates v Commission* [2008] ECR I-10515, paras 111–14 and 185–86.

[24] See, eg, the landmark judgments of the Court in case C-173/73 *Italy v Commission* [1974] ECR 00709 and Case C-75/97 *Belgium v Commission* [1999] ECR I-3671, para. 33.

[25] See, among others, the case C-148/04 Unicredito Italiano [2005] I-11137 at 45–46.

[26] See T-443/08 and T-455/08—*Freistaat Sachsen and Others v Commission* [2011] II-01311 at p. 104 and, on appeal, C-288/11 P—*Mitteldeutsche Flughafen and Flughafen Leipzig-Halle v Commission*, nyr at pp. 38–39.

[27] See Joined Cases T-228/99 and T-233/99, T-228/99, *Westdeutsche Landesbank Girozentrale v Commission* ECR [2003] II-00435.

[28] See Gerard, 'Managing the Financial Crisis in Europe: The Role of EU State Aid Law Enforcement', op. cit. at 234; see also Gilliams, H., 'The Notion of Aid in the Financial Crisis' in Merola, Derenne, and Rivas (eds), op. cit. at 262.

[29] See Gilliams, 'The Notion of Aid in the Financial Crisis', op. cit. at 263, and, *inter alia*, Commission decision of 29 June 2011 on the state aids Nos SA.32504 (2011/N) and C 11/2010 (ex

the same rapidity, the State being interested in avoiding a serious disruption of the banking system, a concern which a private investor would not have shared.[30]

Similarly, during the crisis the Commission has interpreted the notion of *pari passu* transaction and the related concomitance test, both related to the MEIP, very strictly. According to the case law of the General Court, 'a capital contribution from public funds must therefore be regarded as satisfying the private investor test and not constituting State aid if, inter alia, it was made at the same time as a *significant capital contribution* on the part of a private investor made in comparable circumstances'[31] (emphasis added). The notion of significant capital contribution has been interpreted in the past by the Commission as requiring that the private partner provides 30 per cent of the total investment needed.[32] However, during the crisis the Commission required a much higher contribution in order to exclude the existence of aid, namely, a 75 per cent contribution, rejecting contributions of up to 50 per cent of the total investment as insufficient.[33]

Consequently, as already mentioned, the European Commission has found that virtually any public support to financial institutions amounted to State aid as the MEIP was not applicable. Indeed, to this author's knowledge, only in one case of the more than 300 decisions adopted during the crisis, did the Commission accept the application of the MEIP, and this after noting that the private owner of the Bank participated in the recapitalization with 75 per cent of the funds needed, as mentioned above.[34] This approach towards the MEIP, and more generally towards the notion of aid, allowed the Commission to consider as State aid most of the national measures adopted during the crisis, and therefore to advance the regulatory objectives discussed in the previous section during the compatibility analysis of those measures under Article 107(3)(b).

Interestingly, despite the broad notion of aid defended by the Commission during the crisis, Member States and/or banks (beneficiaries or competitors) very seldom challenged its decisions before the Union courts. Indeed, the number of appeals against Commission decisions related to aids for banks, no more than five until 2013,[35] is extremely limited if one takes into account that the Commission

N 667/2009) implemented by Ireland for Anglo Irish Bank and Irish Nationwide Building Society at point 103.

[30] Ibid. at 263–64, and Commission decision of 5 April 2011 on the measures No. C 11/2009 (ex NN 53b/2008, NN 2/2010 and N 19/2010) implemented by the Dutch State for ABN AMRO Group NV (created following the merger between Fortis Bank Nederland and ABN AMRO N) at point 224.

[31] See, among others, Case T-296/97 *Alitalia v Commission* [2000] ECR II-3871, para. 81.

[32] See Commission Decision 2008/729/EC of 11 December 2007 on State aid C53/2006 Citynet Amsterdam, the Netherlands. OJ L 247, 16 September 2008, p. 27 recitals 96–100, and the Draft Commission Notice on the notion of State aid pursuant to Article 107(1) TFEU at point 89.

[33] See Buendía Sierra, J.L., Muñoz de Juan, M., and Visser M., 'Public Intervention in the Economy in Times of Crisis', in Merola, Derenne, and Rivas (eds), op. cit. at 422–23.

[34] See State aid NN 40/2009—Austria Recapitalisation of Landes-Hypotheke nbank Steiermark Aktiengesellschaft. See Buendía Sierra, Muñoz de Juan, and Visser, 'Public Intervention in the Economy in Times of Crisis', op. cit. at 415–28.

[35] See in this Laprevote F.C., 'Judicial Review (States, Beneficiary & Third Parties)' in Merola, Derenne, and Rivas (eds), op. cit. at 309. See also Gerard, 'Managing the Financial Crisis in Europe', op. cit. 239.

adopted no less than 325 State aid decisions in relation to the financial sector between September 2008 and September 2012.[36] The absence of Court challenges is revealing of the general satisfaction of Member States and banks towards the permissive approach adopted by the Commission under the compatibility analysis of rescue and restructuring plans.

The absence of Court challenges has ensured that the scant application of the MEIP test in practice and the broad definition of aid defended by the Commission during the crisis have largely escaped the review of the Union courts. There is, however, a remarkable exception. The judicial case in point for the application of the notion of aid, and particularly the MEIP test, during the financial crisis is *ING Groep*.[37] The main facts of the case can be summarized as follows. In November 2008, at the beginning of the first phase of the Commission's State aid policy during the financial crisis described above, ING Groep (ING) received a capital injection of €10 billion from the Dutch State through the purchase of securities. ING and the State agreed that the bank would decide either to repurchase the securities bought by the State with a 50 per cent premium (at €15 per security instead of the €10 paid by the State), or, after three years, to convert those securities into ordinary shares. The Commission considered the referred purchase of securities as State aid, compatible under Article 107(3)(b) TFEU in November 2008.[38]

Almost a year later, in October 2009, and as part of the restructuring plan to be submitted to the Commission under the original decision, ING and the State agreed to amend their original deal given that ING was then in a position to repurchase up to half of the securities. ING would, however, pay a lower price than that originally agreed: €10 per security (the issue price) instead of the €15 agreed. In exchange, ING would pay accrued interest plus a penalty of no less than €340 million and a maximum of €705 million.

Within a month of this amendment, the Commission adopted a decision stating that the amendment constituted new State aid that had to be added to the original capital injection. The Commission calculated the new aid in approximately €2 billion. The Commission based its decision on the inapplicability of the MEIP test, as no private investor could grant State aid to another undertaking. In other words, the Commission applied the so-called 'pollution theory' according to which once an undertaking has received State aid, any future public investment will also constitute State aid, a theory that the Commission has adopted during

[36] See for this figure Gerard, 'Managing the Financial Crisis in Europe', op. cit. 233.

[37] C-224/12 P, *Commission v Netherlands and ING Groep*. The judgment of the Court of Justice in this case is also perceived as the leading case for future challenges in the financial sector, such as cases of assistance provided to banks in response to losses on sovereign debt. See in this regard, the briefing published by 'OXERA: Agenda, Advancing economics in businesses, Passing judgment on crisis state aid control: the ING MEIP case' at 4. It is available at: <http://www.oxera.com/Oxera/media/Oxera/downloads/Agenda/The-ING-MEIP-state-aid-case.pdf?ext=.pdf>.

[38] Commission Decision C(2008) 6936, in Case N 528/08, on State aid granted by the Kingdom of the Netherlands to ING.

the crisis.[39] The Commission added, in keeping with its approach towards the application of the MEIP during the crisis that, in any event, no private investor would have ever accepted such a price reduction.[40] Nevertheless, the Commission considered the aid compatible under Article 107(3)(b) TFEU subject to a number of commitments, also in line with the decisions adopted by the Commission during the crisis. ING and the Dutch State disagreed with the Commission's assessment and decided to proceed with the deal as amended and to challenge the Commission's decision in January 2010. The appeal shows that Member States and banks started to consider that the time for the exceptional application (virtual inapplicability) of the MEIP had ended, even if the measure at stake had been considered compatible aid.

In 2012 the General Court ruled in favour of the applicants, criticizing the Commission for having refused to apply the MEIP test in light of the evolution of the market conditions between the adoption of the original deal, when the crisis was very acute, and the adoption of the amendment, when the economic situation had improved. The Court rejected the 'pollution theory' in bold terms:

> ... the Commission cannot evade—as it proposes—its obligation to assess the economic rationality of the amendment to the repayment terms in the light of the private investor principle solely on the ground that the capital injection subject to repayment already itself constitutes State aid. It is only after such an assessment that the Commission is in a position to conclude whether an additional advantage within the meaning of Article 87(1) EC has been granted.[41]

The General Court further noted that the Commission was required, under the principle of good administration applicable to the State aid rules, to conduct a diligent and impartial examination of the evidence at its disposal.[42] In particular, the judgment underlined that the Commission should have analysed whether a private investor would have been encouraged to substitute a certain outcome (the new deal) for an uncertain one (the original one), 'and obtain in that regard a fixed and satisfactory return in the place of one that could not be predicted at the time of the amendment of the initial terms'.[43] Pursuant to this judgment, the

[39] See for an application of this theory State aid N 428/2009—United Kingdom Restructuring of Lloyds Banking Group [2009], p. 128: 'a private investor would not find itself in the situation of the State since it would not have granted the £14.7 billion recapitalisation.' See for this Buendía Sierra, Muñoz de Juan, and Visser 'Public Intervention in the Economy in Times of Crisis', op. cit. at 424.

[40] Commission Decision 2010/608/EC of 18 November 2009 on State aid C 10/09 (ex N 138/09) implemented by the Netherlands for ING's Illiquid Assets Back Facility and Restructuring Plan OJ 2010 L 274, p. 139.

[41] Joined Cases T-29/10 and T-33/10, *Netherlands and ING Groep v Commission*, ECLI [2012] 98 at 99.

[42] Ibid. at 108. See also Case C-367/95 P *Commission v Sytraval and Brink's France* [1998] ECR I-1719, para. 62. See on this principle Pastor Merchante, F., *The Role of Competitors in the Enforcement of State Aid Law*, Ph.D. thesis defended at the European University Institute, 6 October 2014 at 116 *et seq.*

[43] Joined Cases T-29/10 and T-33/10, *Netherlands and ING Groep v Commission*, ECLI [2012] 98 at 123.

Commission adopted a new decision in which it applied the private investor test. The new decision concluded that a market economy private investor would not have agreed to the new terms. Consequently, it considered the amendment to the original terms as State aid but it declared, again, the aid compatible subject to a number of commitments. ING and the Netherlands also appealed this decision yet later withdrew their actions. This new decision is therefore final.[44]

In spite of the confirmation of the new decision, the Commission continued with its appeal to the General Court judgment. The Commission thus aimed at setting a clear principle in the case law, namely, that a private investor could never find itself in a situation in which it had provided State aid to an undertaking and, therefore, that the MEIP is not applicable. In other words, at stake was the so-called pollution theory that the Commission had applied to the financial sector during the crisis.

Policy reasons may explain the Commission's position in this case. The pollution theory allowed the Commission to treat as aid any measure adopted in relation to the financial institutions that received aid at the beginning of the crisis (crisis response phase) facilitating in this way the imposition of conditions for compatibility during the crisis management and crisis resolution phases. Indeed, as discussed previously, it is precisely in the third phase of the crisis when the Commssion has been able to impose its conditions and to advance regulatory goals through the compatibility criteria, something the Commission could not have done if the new State aid measures fell short of the notion of aid due to the fulfillment of the MEIP test. The Advocate General in the ING case also observed that behind the Commission's position might have been a pragmatic consideration, that is, that the systematic application of the MEIP would impose too great a strain on the Commission's resources.[45]

The Court of Justice clearly rejected the principle defended by the Commission and confirmed the judgment of the General Court, in agreement on this point with its Advocate General.[46] The Court did so by deducing from the Grand Chamber EDF judgment[47] that the applicability of the MEIP test to a public intervention does not depend on the form in which the advantage is conferred, but on the classification of the intervention as a decision adopted by a shareholder of the undertaking in question. In other words, what matters is that the State was a shareholder of the alleged beneficiary and, therefore, that the Commission could not lawfully refuse to apply the MEIP test in this context. Indeed, the Court concluded, the Commission should have analysed whether a private shareholder of ING would have accepted the terms as renegotiated by the Dutch State.

In addition, the Court also reminded, in line with the EDF judgment, that the MEIP test must be applied by default and not as an exception that applies

[44] Decision C(2012) 3150 final—State aid SA.28855 (N 373/2009) (ex C 10/2009 and ex N 528/2009)—The Netherlands—ING—restructuring aid.

[45] C-224/12 P, *Commission v Netherlands and ING Groep*. See Opinion of AG Sharpston in this case at point 36.

[46] Ibid. at point 43.

[47] C-124/10 P, *Commission v EDF* [2012] ECR, nyr.

only if a Member State so requests. Consequently, 'where it appears that the private investor test may be applicable, the Commission is under a duty to ask the Member State concerned to provide it with all relevant information enabling it to determine whether the conditions governing the applicability and the application of that test are met.'[48] The Court further found that the private investor test appeared applicable given that any holder of securities may wish to renegotiate the conditions of their redemption and the Commission could not evade the application of this test merely because the securities had been acquired in return for State aid.

The Court's judgment has been seen as an application of the EDF Grand Chamber decision, and as a further antiformalist step in the application of the State aid rules.[49] There are indeed similarities between the two cases. In EDF the Commission had refused to apply the MEIP test to fiscal measures. In ING the Commission also refused to apply the MEIP test to previously declared aid measures. In both cases the Court criticized the Commission for not carrying out the test and justified its decision on the effects-based formula. The Court indeed linked the two decisions by holding that what matters for the purposes of the MEIP is that the public authorities are shareholders of the undertakings at issue and, consequently, that their actions must be judged under an economic rationality test, by their effects.

However, despite the many references to the EDF judgment, in our view the decision of the Court in the ING case is more justified than in the EDF one for three main reasons: (i) the form of the measure under review in ING was not an act of public authority, (ii) there are less risks for circumvention of the State aid rules as a result of this judgment, and (iii) the measure was not more likely to favour public undertakings in detriment of private ones.

In this regard, the measure under review in the ING case was the renegotiation of the conditions for the redemption of securities, a measure open to any holder of securities. Therefore, the Commission's refusal to analyse this measure under the MEIP was less justified as it was a conceivable commercial transaction. In addition, the contested measure was notified to the European Commission as part of the restructuring package, as it was the case with other measures in which the Commission applied the pollution theory during the crisis. Indeed, the pollution theory applies, by definition, to measures that have been considered aid by the European Commission. Consequently, there is almost no risk of a ING-type measure being adopted without the European Commission being notified, something that, regrettably, cannot be said of the EDF-type measures as they refer to dealings between public companies and the State without any link to an ongoing Commission procedure. Related to the foregoing is the point that the EDF's

[48] C-224/12 P, *Commission v Netherlands and ING Groep*. See Opinion of AG Sharpston in this case at point 33.

[49] See, eg, Sánchez Graels, A., 'CJEU further pushes for a universal application of the 'market economy private investor test' (C-224/12)' blog entry posted on 18 April 2014, available at: <http://howtocrackanut.blogspot.com.es/2014/04/cjeu-further-pushes-for-universal.html>.

decision is more likely to favour public undertakings, as they have more dealings with public authorities that could be settled by the cancellation of a fiscal debt without notification to the Commission or any publicity.

The Court seems in the last years to be sanctioning the Commission for refusing to apply an economic test precisely at a time, after the SAAP–SAM initiatives, where the Commission has placed more emphasis than ever on the importance of economic analysis in the State aid field. In this regard, while the Commission has limited the *refined economic approach* to the compatibility analysis, this approach may be permeating the EU Courts' case law on the notion of aid. In this regard, the General Court has recently held that the concept of market failure, included in compatibility guidelines, may be also relevant for the definition of State aid, particularly in the context of a service of general economic interest (SGEI).[50] The refined economic approach may also be having the collateral effect of making more difficult for the Commission to refer to the form of a measure, as in EDF, or to its previous categorization as aid in this case, to reject the application of the MEIP, and consequently, to define them as State aid. The more economic approach may have also resulted in a higher standard for the Commission to win cases based on the MEIP before the EU Courts. To this extent, according to a recent study, since 2004 the 'private investor test' has been one of the most litigated areas of EU State Aid law and the annulment of State aid decisions have been more likely where the 'private investor test' was raised as a ground.[51]

This situation is problematic as both the form and the previous categorization of a measure as aid may be important for the definition of aid. In other words, if through the extension of the effects-based formula to fiscal measures, the Court wanted in EDF to simplify the case law on the notion of aid by proposing an overall economic (effects-based) analysis that disregards the form of a measure, more recent case law shows that it is not simple or even always possible. Indeed, in a recent case also related to financial institutions, the Commission refused to consider a public guarantee granted by an Austrian Land to a bank as one of the elements that such Land should take into consideration when evaluating offers to privatize that bank as a shareholder under the MEIP. The Commission held that such guarantee—which had been considered State aid by the Commission in 2003—would not have been granted by a market operator under normal market conditions. The Court of Justice, with the same rapporteur than in the EDF case, agreed with the Commission.[52] The guarantee was thus granted by the public shareholder but in its condition of public authority.[53] In other words, the

[50] See T-79/10—*Colt Télécommunications France v Commission* [2013] nyp at p. 150.

[51] Ibañez Colomo, P., 'State Aid Litigation before EU Courts (2004-2012): A Statistical Overview', *Journal of European Competition Law and Practice* (2013) 4(6) 469–84.

[52] See C-214/12 P—*Land Burgenland and Others v Commission* [2013] nyp.

[53] Ibid. at 56: 'In those circumstances, and since, by granting aid, a Member State pursues, by definition, objectives other than that of making a profit from the resources granted to an undertaking belonging to it, it must be held that those resources are, in principle, granted by the State exercising its prerogatives as a public authority.'

economic analysis alone will not suffice to qualify a measure as MEIP conforming in all cases in which a public authority is a shareholder in an undertaking.

In light of the foregoing, the Court could have based its decision on the Commission's duty to review all information available to it under the principle of good administration rather than on the EDF case, as the General Court had hinted at, and more so after this principle has been incorporated as EU primary law under Article 41 of the Charter of Fundamental Rights. This would be in line with a trend of the case law of the EU Courts identified in previous chapters, namely, the Courts' criticism for the Commission's refusal to analyse the applicability of the MEIP as a matter of principle.[54] Indeed, the Commission should not have refused to apply the MEIP test to a commercial transaction that was defended by a Member State as market conforming. This approach would have allowed the Court to reach the same outcome without insisting on giving the (flawed) impression that after the EDF judgment only the effects of the contested measure matters under the MEIP test if the Member State under investigation is a shareholder of the alleged beneficiary.

The Court of Justice seems to insist on the invocation of recent Grand Chamber judgments in an attempt to bring clarity and to simplify the application of the State aid rules through the effects-based formula and a more economic approach towards these rules. It is however doubtful whether the 'economic rationality' test will achieve that aim alone, as shown by subsequent judgments. It therefore seems to us that the Court should circumscribe the EDF judgment to a good administration obligation by the Commission to carry out the MEIP test once a public authority adopts a measure in relation to an undertaking in which it has a shareholding that could, at least potentially, be adopted by any holder of securities. This 'good administration' logic seems plausible in cases such as *ING*, where the Commission knew about the measure because it was notified to it. However, the Court's approach does not seem justified in the case of fiscal or social measures that a private undertaking could not possible adopt and which, through the application of the MEIP, may escape the notification obligation under Article 108(3) TFEU even in cases such as *EDF*, where the aid amount was about €1 billion.

4. Conclusion

During the crisis the European Commission has been strict about the definition of aid and flexible on the compatibility analysis of aid measures for banks, especially during the first and second phases described in the policy section. The Commission has applied a broad notion of aid based on the virtual inapplicability of the MEIP, the pollution theory, and the fulfiment of the State resources

[54] See also in this regard, eg, the case T-196/04 *Commission v Ryanair* [2008] ECR II-3643, and Köhler, M, 'New Trends Concerning the Application of the Private Investor Test' (2011) *European State Aid Law Quarterly* 21.

criterion when public authorities made declarations announcing the support to be granted to banks. By contrast, the Commission has accepted as general some measures adopted by central banks that appear to favour only the financial sector. This innovative interpretation of the concept of selectivity, which might be explained against the contrast of hundreds of cases being notified in a matter of weeks, has not been reviewed by the EU Courts yet. Indeed, most of the decisions adopted by the Commission during the crisis in this field have escaped judicial review due to the lack of Court challenges, surely influenced by the very flexible stance of the Commission regarding compatibility.

The exception is the *ING* case where the Court of Justice rejected the pollution theory defended by the Commission as a matter of principle. In this regard, it is submitted that the analysis of the impact of the aids for banks on the notion of aid during the crisis from a policy and dynamic perspective allows the reader to better understand the relevant decisions of the Court, the Commission submissions, and to analyse critically the applicability of certain formulas, such as the effects-based formula, mentioned in the Court's judgment. In addition, the analysis also shows that the main trends identified in the previous chapters in the recent case law of the Court are also present in *ING* and other cases related to the financial sector. In other words, the Court has not accepted in the *ING* case the extraordinary application (or rather inapplication) of the MEIP that has allowed the Commission to treat many State measures related to banks as aid in a very expedient way, and that has been largely accepted by Member States and banks, as exemplified by the remarkable lack of Court challenges. The Court has thus shown again to have '*une certain idée des aides*' which can be only fully understood by looking at formulas identified in the previous chapters in the context in which they first appeared.

9

The Concept of State Aid under EU Law

From Internal Market to Competition and Beyond

In 1513 Machiavelli identified one of the problems usually associated with the granting of aids: their unfair and discriminatory character related to their selectivity. Machiavelli claimed that a too-generous prince would be compelled in the end 'to lay excessive burdens on the people, to impose extortionate taxes, and to do everything else he can to get money. This will start to make his subjects hate him, and, since he will have impoverished himself, he will be generally despised. As a result, because of this generosity of his, having injured many and rewarded few, he will be vulnerable to the first minor setback'.[1] Other problems related to the granting of aids, such as their inefficiency or their potential for conflict between subsidizing and non-subsidizing nations, have also been known for centuries, yet it was not until the twentieth century that some form of multinational control of subsidies was established, and this for a single commodity: sugar.

Indeed, as discussed in Chapter 1 of the book, after some unsuccessful attempts,[2] a number of States decided in 1902 to establish a multilateral system of control of subsidies in the Brussels Sugar Convention.[3] Three features should be recalled from this pioneer system, namely: (i) the prohibition of all subsidies for the production and export of sugar, (ii) the introduction of a broad notion of subsidy (bounty) that was not defined yet it covered 'all advantages derived directly or indirectly...from State fiscal legislation,[4] and (iii) the creation of a

[1] Machiavelli, N., *The Prince*, Ch. 16, translated by Bull, G. (Penguin Books, 1999) at 51. Similarly, as discussed in Ch. 2, Turgot criticized French King Louis XVI in 1774 in the sense that his 'gracious' policy entailed unfair discrimination between the beneficiaries of the subsidies (the minority with access to the Crown) and the payers of those subsidies (the majority without that access).

[2] See, eg, the Sugar Convention entered into between Great Britain, France, Holland, and Belgium of 1864.

[3] See Convention between Great Britain, Germany, Austria, Hungary, Belgium, Spain, France, Italy, Netherlands, and Sweden, relative to Bounties on Sugar, signed at Brussels, 5 March 1902, Cd. 1535, 191 Parry 56.

[4] And in particular: (a) direct bonuses granted on exportation; (b) direct bonuses granted to production; (c) total or partial exemptions from taxation which profit a part of the products of manufacture; (d) profits derived from excess of yield; and (e) profits derived from too high a drawback; and (f) advantages derived from any surtax in excess of the rate fixed by Art. 3. Ibid. at Art. I of the Convention.

supranational commission capable of adopting binding decisions to monitor the execution of the Convention.[5]

This convention may have been inspirational for the drafters of the European Coal and Steel Community (ECSC) Treaty, which incorporated three similar features in the new Treaty. Indeed, all subsidies and aids to the coal and steel industries were prohibited, neither of these terms was defined, and a supranational authority would monitor the prohibition. However, the ECSC regulation was more invasive as it sought to replace the granting of national aid by aid granted at Community level by the High Authority. As AG Lagrange would phrase it, Member States had 'lost jurisdiction' in relation to the granting of aids.[6] However, the ECSC system did not work as expected and it showed that a total abolition of national aid was not realistic.[7] Some form of mixed or compromised solution would need to be found.

Certainly, the analysis of the legislative history of today's article 107 TFEU carried out in Chapter 2 shows that this provision is a product of the new approach to European integration adopted after the fall of Monnetism, an approach characterized by the transfer to the European institutions of the minimum powers considered necessary to achieve economic and subsequently political union. The approach was thus significantly different from that followed for the ECSC Treaty, based on the full transfer of sovereignty to the supranational institution (the High Authority), the only competent body to grant aid originally, on a sector-by-sector basis.[8] In this regard, the solution found in the Rome Treaties included a broad notion of (national) aid that excluded general legislative measures and State measures not affecting trade. This notion of aid was in principle incompatible with the Treaty and was coupled, realistically, with a long list of exceptions (or compatibility provisions) to be assessed by a supranational monitoring authority capable of adopting binding decisions: the European Commission. Therefore, three features characterize the EEC Treaty system: (1) a broad notion of aid, (2) a supranational monitoring system, and (3) the introduction of flexibility through a number of exemptions.[9]

[5] See Art. VII of the Convention.

[6] See Opinion of Advocate General Lagrange, C 30-59 *Gezamenlijke Steenkolenmijnen*, delivered on 5 November [1961] ECR 42.

[7] See in this regard, eg, Ehlermann, 'State Aid Control in the European Union: Success or Failure?' (1994) *Fordham International Law Journal* at 1216.

[8] See address given by Gaetano Martino, Italian Foreign Minister on 18 January 1957, 'From the ECSC to the Common Market.' Ministerio degli affari esteri (ed.). It is available at: <http://www.ena.lu/>. 'Experience of the ECSC has taught us that it is impossible to establish a federal power or achieve the political unification of Europe through the juxtaposition of a number of partial cessions of sovereignty, and we are therefore sceptical about the idea of constructing Europe by increasing the number of 'supranational authorities' with powers confined to a single sector... what [the draftsmen] did not want, either in Messina or at subsequent conferences, was to put the cart before the horse, political unification before economic union.'

[9] It should also be mentioned in this context that the 1947 General Agreement on Tariffs and Trade also introduced in its Art. 16 some provisions concerning subsidies, yet they merely established some reporting obligations and a possibility of countervailing duties and therefore they may have been less relevant for the type of monitoring system laid down in the Rome Treaties. However, one feature was similar, namely, the lack of a definition of subsidy, this feature being welcomed as it

The analysis of the legislative history of today's Article 107 TFEU also shows that the allusion to State resources in the original notion of aid seems to have referred to public distributors of aid belonging to the State, and not to State money or funds, that the notion of aid was broader than that of subsidy (the Court would ratify this five years later in the *miners' bonus* case (1961) under the ECSC Treaty), that the notion of selectivity allowed to distinguish between artificial distortions of competition created by advantages granted to some undertakings or sectors, prohibited under the State aid rules, and non-artificial distortions of competition created by general legislative or regulatory measures equally distortive and '*qui formellement sont des aides ou des subventions*'[10] that could not be addressed through *ex-ante* analysis by the European Commission and would be controlled *ex post* and would, if necessary, be subject to harmonization. Finally, this analysis also shows that the compatibility of aids '*avec le marché commun*' may have referred not only to the 'establishment' of the Common Market but also to its 'functioning', at least for some delegations like Germany, thus forecasting the evolution of this provision described in this work.

This book has shown that, once established in the Rome Treaties, the concept of aid has evolved broadly in line with (i) the policy priorities of the European Commission, and (ii) the evolution of the case law of the Court of Justice of the European Union. As to the former, this book has studied how several developments in State aid law enforcement priorities affected the way the Commission went about constructing the concept of aid, and that such advances were, generally, ratified by the Court.[11] As for the latter, while most authors have portrayed State aid control as a very technical sub-discipline, a poor relative of antitrust, or as a latecomer in legal development,[12] the analysis in this book shows that the way the case law concerning the concept of aid has evolved tracks the way the Court has handled mainstream fields of European economic law, in particular free movement and competition law. The analysis also shows that the main features of the different periods of evolution of the case law of the Court of Justice,

could help avoid circumvention. See in this regard the conclusions of an early panel in 1961: L/1442 and Add.1-2, adopted on 21 November 1961, 10S/201, 209, para. 23.

[10] Trans. 'which formally are aids or subsidies'.

[11] This may seem puzzling in view of the Court's statements on the objective character of the concept of aid and the Commission's recognition that it has no margin of discretion as regards this concept. See, eg, Case C-83/98 P *France v Ladbroke Racing and Commission* [2000] ECR I-3271, para. 25, or C-487/06 P *British Aggregates v Commission* [2008] ECR I-10515, paras 111–14 and 185–86; for the Commission's (lack of) margin of discretion, see the Report on the implementation of the Commission notice on the application of the state aid rules to measures relating to direct business taxation. Brussels 9 February 2004. C2004(434) at 6: 'The concept of aid is an objective concept that leaves the Commission no margin of discretion'.

[12] See in this regard, Ehlermann, C.D. 'Introduction' in Ehlermann, C.D., and Everson, M. (eds), *European Competition Law Annual 1999: Selected Issues in the Field of State Aids* (Hart Publishing, 2001) at xii. He also refers to State aid control as 'the Cinderella of EU competition policy'; See also Hancher, L., 'EC State Aid Law—No Longer the Cinderella of European Competition Law But Not Quite the Ugly Sister?' in Hancher, L., Ottervanger, T., and Slot, P.J. (eds), *EC State Aids* (Sweet & Maxwell, 2006) at 1. See for the 'latecomer' reference Ross, 'State Aids: Maturing into a Constitutional Problem' (1995) *Yearbook of European Law* at 79.

as they have been summarized by some of its judges, can also be observed in relation to the case law on the concept of aid during those periods. Finally, as will be noted, there is some correlation between the periods in which different authors have divided the evolution of State aid policy, on the one hand, and those in which some judges have divided the evolution of the case law of the Court, on the other. This is so, as will be discussed, because both evolutions have been influenced by the main political and economic milestones that have shaped the process of European integration.

1. The Concept of State Aid and the Policy Priorities of the European Commission

This book shows that many of the current formulas that today depict the concept of aid were proposed by the European Commission pursuant to its policy and enforcement priorities at the time when the formulas were coined by the Court of Justice. To prove this point, the following sections will review the main features of the periods in which the evolution of the State aid policy has been divided together with the main formulas that have appeared in the case law of the Court during each of those periods.

2. The First Period: 1958 to the Early 1970s

During this period, ranging broadly from 1958 to 1973,[13] the Commission's main goal was the creation of the Common Market, for which the elimination of all sort of discriminatory measures against out-of-State traders was the main concern. The State aid rules were, however, a limited instrument in the hands of the Commission due to their innovative character, the lack of a procedural regulation concerning these rules (as the Council had rejected a proposal for this in 1966 and 1972), and the Member States' reluctance to notify State aids. In light of these difficulties, coupled with the political sensitivity of the State aid rules and the fact that the Commission was busy reviewing the high number of antitrust notifications, the Commission adopted a low-profile approach. The Commission focused on cases strictly related to the creation of the Common Market, such as export aid

[13] See in this regard, eg, Doleys, T., 'Fifty Years of Moulding Article 87: The European Commission and the Development of EU State Aid Law & Policy (1958–2008)', Paper prepared for presentation at the 11th Biennial International Conference of the European Union Studies Association in Marina Del Ray, California, 23–25 April 2009, who frames the first period from 1957 to early 1970s. Weiler has referred to this period as comprising 1958–73 and so has Gerber in the antitrust field. See Weiler, J. 'The Transformation of Europe' (1990–91) *Yale Law Journal* 2403, and Gerber, D.J., *Law and Competition in Twentieth Century Europe: Protecting Prometheus* (OUP, 1998) at 354 *et seq.*

or para-fiscal levies that were clearly discriminatory against out-of-State traders,[14] particularly towards the earlier than planned achievement of the customs union in 1968, and these were among the first cases on State aid that reached the Court of Justice.

The Court supported the Commission's decisions in these cases, in which it underlined their importance for the creation of the Common Market, the main goal pursued by the Commission, and the latter's important role and prerogatives under the Treaty. The Court's judgments did not include detailed definitions of the concept of aid, instead, they laid down broad principles more designed to remind Member States of their obligations under the Treaty than to provide substantive clarifications concerning the criteria for defining the concept of aid. In this regard, in the *French exports* case the Court made clear that Member States could not adopt unilateral measures that harmed the economies of other Member States, even if those measures were adopted in reserved fields such as monetary or fiscal policy.[15] In the words of Judge Pescatore with reference to this judgment, 'the residual authority of the Member States is placed at the service of the Community'.[16] In addition, the formula adopted by the Court in this case to find the aid character of the French measure under review was subjective, based on the intent, the purpose of the measure, and not objective, based on the effects.[17] Furthermore, the Court referred to products (national products exported) and not to beneficiary undertakings to find the aid character of the measure, what also contributed to the internal market flavour of the entire judgment. In the same vein, in the *parafiscal levies* case,[18] the Court supported the Commission's decision to consider a State measure as incompatible aid due to its discriminatory effect against out of State traders produced by the way in which it was financed (subjecting out of state traders to the para-fiscal charge although they would not benefit from the yields of the charge). Also in this judgment, the Court underlined the Commission's prerogatives in this field and warned against any measure that could open loopholes in the application of the Treaty rules in this field.[19]

Finally, although the Court supported the Commission's decisions and policy priorities during this period, it adopted its own language to refer to this concept

[14] The fact that the Commission was not interested in assessing under these rules cases of discriminatory taxation between competitors of the same Member State can also be seen in the Commission submissions in the early C-9/70 *Franz Grad v Finanzamt Traunstein* [1970] ECR 825 at p. 835.

[15] See Joined Cases C-6/69 and 11/69 *Commission v France* [1969] ECR 523 at, eg, para. 15.

[16] Pescatore, P., *The Law of Integration: Emergence of a New Phenomenon* (Sijhoof, 1974) at 39–40.

[17] See Brinkhorst, L.J., and Verougstraete, I.M., 'Annotation in Joined Cases C-6/69 and C-11/69, Commission v France, [1969] ECR 523' (1970) *Common Market Law Review* at p. 487: 'It should be noted that the Court used in this respect a *subjective formula* ("granted…with a view to") thus emphasizing the intent of the measure, *rather than an objective formula*, considering its effect.' (emphasis added). A subjective formula was also consistent with the wording of the Spaak Report that prevented Member States from granting aids having as their *object* and *effect* the distortion of competition. See introduction to the Report of the Heads of Delegation to the Ministers of Foreign Affairs, 21 April 1956, Mae 120 f56 (corrigé), 16–17.

[18] Case 47/69 *Government of the French Republic v Commission* [1970] ECR 487.

[19] Ibid. at 18.

and some arguments to defend its applicability that were different from those submitted by the Commission or the Advocate Generals in the judgments under review.[20] The Court's view of this concept was even broader and more teleological (more related to the goal of the creation of the Common Market) than that of the Commission. It therefore seems, paraphrasing Judge Pescatore, that the judges of the Court had from the very beginning '*une certain idée des aides*'.[21]

3. The Second Period: Early 1970s to the Mid-1980s

The policy priorities of the Commission continued to be focused on the elimination of obstacles to the creation of the Common Market, especially during the first half of this period. However, aware of the dimension of the economic problems affecting the Member States after the 1973 oil crisis, it opted for a pragmatic approach, supportive to the Member States' efforts to recover from the shock. Indeed, the Commission considered that the national protectionist measures adopted during these early years following the crisis would be temporary and therefore decided not to intervene decisively.[22]

The Court was especially supportive to the Commission during the first half of this period. Significant among the cases decided during this time was the *Italian textiles* judgment. In this regard, the Court held in the *Italian textiles* case that the fiscal nature or social aim of a national measure could not suffice to shield it from the application of today's Article 107 TFEU and that this provision does not distinguish between the measures of State intervention concerned by reference to their causes or aims but defines them in relation to their effects.[23] The Court supported in this way an effects-based formula for the notion of aid. This formula contrasted with the subjective one adopted by the Court in the previous period (in the *French exports rediscount rate* case). It is submitted that the change in the Court's formula, from subjective to objective, responded to the requests made by

[20] Eg, as mentioned earlier, in *French exports rediscount rate*, both the Advocate General and the Commission had argued that the measures under review were selective because they favoured exports undertakings against those that produced for the domestic market, and that the contested measures were aids by reference to their effects. However, the Court did not discuss the distorting effect of the measure in the French market or whether there was competition between exporting and non-exporting undertakings. Rather, the Court adopted a subjective formula based on the distortive nature, not on the effects, of the measures under review in the internal market context. Similarly, the Commission had claimed that the measures under review could create a distortion on the intra-Community level 'when such system has no equivalent in the other Member States'. However, the Court found that the situation in other Member States could not remove the aid character of the measure in any event. See Joined Cases C-6/69 and 11/69 *Commission v France* [1969] ECR 523 at para. 21.

[21] See the famous article by Pescatore, P., 'The Doctrine of 'Direct Effect': An Infant Disease of Community Law' (Sijhoof, 1974) at 157, where Judge Pescatore affirms that the reasoning of the Court in the *Van Gend and Loos* case shows that the judges had '*une certaine idée de l'Europe*'.

[22] Lavdas, K.A., and Mendrinou, M.M., *Politics, Subsidies, and Competition: The New Politics of State Intervention in the European Union* (Edward Elgar, 1999) at 31.

[23] Case 173/73 *Italy v Commission* [1974] ECR 709 at para. 13.

the Commission in order to avoid *subjective* arguments such as those raised by Italy in this case, that is, that the measure was not an aid but a social measure. This objective formula was long favoured by the Commission for the State aid field,[24] and was defended by the latter before the Court also in this case to define the contested measure as aid.[25] The formula was also coherent with that followed in the internal market context in cases such as *Dassonville*, decided within nine days of this case. Indeed, in that case the Commission had also advocated for an effects-based formula that the Court followed.[26] The Court also confirmed in this case, in line with the Commission, that not only direct benefits but also indirect ones, such as the mitigation of normally applicable charges, were covered by Article 107(1).

Furthermore, the support of the Court to the Commission's position during these years covered not only cases in which the latter considered a given measure as aid, but also those where the Commission proposed a no-aid finding,[27] or even did not reach a definitive position.[28] The most significant among the cases in which the Commission defended a no-aid finding was the *Van Tiggele* decision.[29] The Court held that price-fixing regulation was not 'granted by the State' under today's Article 107(1) TFEU, as the alleged advantage was not financed by the State but rather by consumers directly. The conclusion reached by the Court in this judgment was suggested by the European Commission, which submitted that the notion of aid necessarily entailed some sort of financial burden for the State.[30] It has been suggested in Chapter 6 that the Commission proposed this finding, that limited its competence under the State aid rules, as otherwise Article 107 could be confused with (and encapsulated by) Article 30 EEC, a result that would have limited the Commission's prerogatives under the compatibility rules because Article 30 is directly effective, and thus national courts can apply it and also accept justifications for its restriction, while Article 107 is not directly effective

[24] See the reference in Doleys, T., 'Fifty Years of Moulding Article 87', op. cit. at 9, footnote 19, to the following Commission's statement: 'Included among the modalities that the Commission understood to fall within the meaning of Article [107(1)] were: "tax exemptions, preferential interest rates, guarantees of loans on especially favorable terms, acquisition of land or buildings either gratuitously or on favorable terms, provisions of goods and services on preferential terms, indemnities against losses *and other measures having equivalent effect*."'

[25] See for the arguments of the Commission as summarized by the judgment in Case 173/73 *Italy v Commission* [1974] ECR 709 at 714 and 715.

[26] See the argument of the Commission in *Dassonville* as referred in the Court's judgment: 'According to the Commission, any measure, whatever its nature or content may, by reason of its effect on the free movement of goods, constitute a measure having equivalent effect, provided that it is not covered by another provision of the Treaty.' Case 8/74 *Dassonville* [1974] ECR 837 at 846.

[27] See, eg, the Case 40/75, *Produits Bertrand v Commission* [1976] ECR 1.

[28] As in C-52/76 *Benedetti v Munari* [1977] ECR 00163 where the Commission held that it had no evidence to conclude whether trade was affected and the same was found by the Court.

[29] Case 82/77 *Openbaar Ministerie v Van Tiggele* [1978] ECR 25.

[30] See, as referred in the judgment: 'The Commission considers that the rules in dispute do not constitute an aid within the meaning of Articles 92 to 94 since they entail neither the provision by the public authorities, directly, indirectly or a posteriori, of a benefit in cash or in kind, nor the renunciation by the authorities of the imposition of taxation or other benefits in cash or in kind owed to them.' See Case 82/77 *Openbaar Ministerie v Van Tiggele* [1978] ECR 25 at 37.

and only the Commission can decide about the compatibility of an aid with the internal market.

During the second half of this period, particularly towards the end of the 1970s, the Commission realized that the economic problems affecting Member States were structural more than contingent and decided to become stricter, a fact also favoured by the arrival of a more liberal Commissioner for competition policy, Commissioner Andriessen. In this context, the reduction of public budgets and inefficient public undertakings were considered suitable aims to be pursued by State aid law by the Commission, but also by Member States. With this background, the Commission, supported by the Council, proposed the systematic application of the Market Economy Investor Principle (MEIP) test, a test originally devised in 1963,[31] yet little used after that.[32] The main target of this test during the first years of its application was related to the activities of public undertakings as creditors of non-efficient projects. This proposal was parallel to the approval of the Transparency Directive, also aimed at clarifying the financial relationships between public undertakings and States. The Court upheld the validity of that Directive and underlined the differences between private and prublic undertakings and the special relationship between the latter and the State that justified its adoption.[33] The Court also supported this Commission's initiative

[31] See the Reply to Parliamentary Question No. 48 of Mr Burgbecher, 30 July 1963, OJ 2235/63: '*Au cas où la puissance publique renonce, en tout ou en partie, a la rémunération du capital propre d'une entreprise d'État ou de toute autre entreprise publique, un telle renociation pourrait, le cas échéant, être considérée comme une aide d'État. De l'avis de la Commission, ceci pourrait se concevoir dans la mesure ou un propriétaire ou actionnaire privé se trouvant dans une situation comparable et agissant en vertu de considérations d'ordre économique, ne renoncerait pas—ou ne renoncerait que dans un mesure limitée—á la rémunération de son capital propre; autrement dit, la renonciation a laquelle consentirait la puissance publique résulterait en l'occurrence non pas considérations d'ordre économique, mais de motifs d'ordre politique.*'

[32] Second Report on Competition Policy (Office for Official Publications of the European Communities, 1973) at point 124: 'In certain cases (establishment by a central government of new undertakings, acquisition of non-precarious holdings in firms already existing or to be set up in association with private interests), the central government normally assumes the role of entrepreneur or venture capital investor. Although the official measure is normally dictated by exigencies going beyond the profit motive, this factor is inherent in the public ownership, the existence and the special nature of which is confirmed by Article 222, and it could not be used alone to justify the bringing into play of the Treaty rules on aids. This is not the case, however, where the central authority, through financial agencies it sets up at its initiative and with its financial support, confines itself to the acquisition in certain firms of holdings which by their special nature (eg duration, purpose, terms) show clearly what the aim of the acquisition is to help the firms until such time as they will have overcome temporary difficulties.'

[33] Joined Cases 188 to 190/80, *French Republic, Italian Republic, and United Kingdom of Great Britain and Northern Ireland v Commission of the European Communities*, ECR [1982] I-02545 at 21: 'within the limits laid down by the applicable legislation, private undertakings determine their industrial and commercial strategy by taking into account in particular requirements of profitability. Decisions of public undertakings, on the other hand, may be affected by factors of a different kind within the framework of the pursuit of objectives of public interest by public authorities which may exercise an influence over those decisions. The economic and financial consequences of the impact of such factors lead to the establishment between those undertakings and public authorities of financial relations of a special kind which differ from those existing between public authorities and private undertakings.'

and the MEIP test became the standard test for judging the investments of public undertakings under the advantage criterion of Article 107 TFEU in the *Meura* judgment.[34]

The adoption of the MEIP reveals an evolution in the role assigned to the concept of aid within the Treaty. If during the first period this concept was mostly used for the elimination of obstacles to trade between Member States (inter-jurisdictional competition), during the second period this concept would start to be used to eliminate distortions of competition felt within individual Member States (intra-jurisdictional competition). Indeed, a similar evolution was experienced in the internal market context where, also increasingly since the 1980s, many measures and regulations were 'challenged in the Court by nationals of the State in question, not other EU nationals or importers'.[35] A comparable development is also observable in the antitrust field, in relation to which it has been noted that from the 1980s onwards the Commission shifted focus from establishing the internal market to regulating processes within that market.[36]

However, the changing priorities of the European Commission were not only reflected in the new notion of advantage. Other criteria of the concept of aid also changed and tellingly in the same direction. This was the case of the distortion of competition and effect on trade criteria in relation to which the Court established a presumption of fulfilment of these criteria in cases of aid to a single company in the *Philip Morris* case.[37] Through this judgment the Court was in fact extending to cases of individual aid a presumption that it had established to entire sectors in the *Italian textiles* case.[38] The establishment of the presumption, which confirmed the Commission's position in this case,[39] allowed the latter to deal with cases of individual aid, those typically covered by the MEIP test, in a more straightforward fashion. Therefore, the establishment of this presumption also contributed to the change in focus of the State aid rules from inter-jurisdictional to intra-jurisdictional competition. The case was also very important for the Commission as the Court held that only the Community and not national objectives could justify the granting of aid under the Treaty compatibility rules,[40] a crucial development at a time when the Commission was starting to depart from

[34] C-234/84 *Belgium v Commission* ('Meura') [1986] ECR p. 02271.

[35] See in this regard Poiares Maduro, M., *We the Court: The European Court of Justice and the European Economic Constitution* (Hart Publishing, 1998) at 63 where he cites the following cases as examples of this trend: Case 286/81 *Oosthoek's* [1982] ECR 4575; Case 126/82 *Smit* [1983] ECR 73; Case 237/82 *Jongeneel Kaas* [1984] ECR 483; Joined Cases 80 and 159/85 *Edah* [1986] ECR 3359; and Case C–241/89 *SARPP* [1990] ECR I–4695.

[36] Wesseling, R., *The Modernisation of EC Antitrust Law* (Hart, 2000) at 33.

[37] Case 730/79 *Philip Morris Holland BV v Commission* [1980] ECR 2671.

[38] Case 173/73 *Italy v Commission* [1974] ECR 709 at 19.

[39] See in this regard Flynn, J., 'The Philip Morris Decision Upheld by the European Court' (1981) *European Law Review*, 208.

[40] As the Commission summarized in the Eleventh Report on Competition Policy 'the [Philip Morris] judgment underlined that the Commission in its evaluation of aid proposals cannot accept national objectives are sufficient to justify the use of aids. They can only be considered compatible with the common market if they further Community objectives.' Eleventh Report on Competition Policy (Office for Official Publications of the European Communities, 1982) at 178.

the 'mere enforcement of legal rules' with the aim of market integration towards the development of a competition *policy* influenced by economic and industrial policy goals.[41] In the same vein, the increased interest in the commercial activities of the State and no longer exclusively in its acts of public authority (such as monetary, social, or fiscal and para-fiscal measures) as in the previous period, led to cases in which it was not clear whether a certain conduct could be attributed to the State, in turn leading to the concept of imputability in the context of the State resources criterion.[42]

To conclude, the Court supported the policy priorities set by the European Commission and, this time, the language and arguments included in the judgments were very similar to those used by the European Commission. This is the case, for example, of the effects-based formula for the concept of aid defended by the Commission (and adopted by the Court) in the *Italian textiles* case, of the presumption of distortion of competition and effect on trade also defended by the Commission and supported by the Court in the *Philip Morris* judgment, or of the MEIP test proposed by the Commission and adopted by the Court in the *Meura* judgment. Indeed, the Court even went beyond the Commission's submissions during this period in order to make the State aid rules more operational. The Court did so in the *Philip Morris* judgment by rejecting the possibility of a *de minimis* rule in this field (that the Commission had admitted in its pleadings), in the *Steinike and Weinlig* judgment, reinterpreting its case law to hold that aid could be granted not only by public authorities but also by private bodies,[43] or in the *Poor Farmers* case by extending the concept of aid (beyond the Commission's submissions) to hold that the financial burden included in the concept of aid could also fall on the private or public bodies instituted by the State to grant the aid (and therefore not necessarily on the State directly).[44]

4. The Third Period: Mid-1980s to Mid- to Late 1990s

During this period,[45] initiated in parallel with the Single European Act and the 1992 programme, the Commission profited from the increasing support to the

[41] See in this regard Verstrynge, J.F., 'Current Antitrust Policy Issues in the EEC: Some Reflections on the Second Generation of Competition Policy' (1984) *Fordham Corporate Law Institute* 673 at 676.

[42] See Joined Cases 67, 68, and 70/85 *Van der Kooy and others* [1988] ECR 219.

[43] Case C-78/76 *Steinike & Weinlig v Federal Republic of Germany* [1977] ECR p. 00595 at para. 21. The Court reinterpreted in this case the formula laid down in the Italian textiles case. See in this regard C-173/73 *Italy v Commission* [1974] ECR 709 at 13: 'The aim of Article 92 is to prevent trade between Member States from being affected by benefits *granted by the public authorities* which, in various forms, distort or threaten to distort competition by favouring certain undertakings or the production of certain goods' (underline added).

[44] C-290/83 *Commission v France* [1985] ECR 439 at para. 14. The Court would confirm this opinion in the *Van der Kooy* judgment, also decided during this period. Joined Cases 67, 68, and 70/85, *Van der Kooy and others*, [1988] ECR p. 219.

[45] This period lasted until the mid- to late 1990s. See also for this periodization Lavdas and Mendrinou, *Politics, Subsidies, and Competition*, op. cit.; Doleys, 'Fifty Years of Moulding Article 87',

integration process to make State aid control stricter.[46] In addition, as the internal market was being achieved, the Commission started to regard the State aid rules increasingly as competition tools (competition between undertakings) and no longer as internal market ones (competition between economies).[47] During this phase, the Court also observed that the State aid and competition rules pursued the same objective in the *Matra I* case.[48]

In this more competition-oriented context the Commission suggested a notion of general measures (thus non-selective measures) based on the absence of discrimination or discretion on the part of national authorities among undertakings placed in a single Member State.[49] The Court endorsed this view in the *FNE* case, in which it upheld the discretion test and concluded that the national measure under review had the effect of placing 'some undertakings in a more favourable position than others'.[50]

op. cit.; Weiler, 'The Transformation of Europe', op. cit.; and Gerber, *Law and Competition in Twentieth Century Europe*, op. cit.

[46] See, *inter alia*, Brittan, L., '1992: A Bonfire of Subsidies? A Review of State Aids in the European Community', *European Access* 3:1989 at 14: '[the Commission has changed strategy] *from merely reacting to new schemes, to a more positive one of the Commission actively selecting the important areas it should critically examine.*' See for a concrete example, related to the automobile industry, of the trend 'towards a more courageous approach' since 1986, the article by Dancet, G., and Rosenstock, M., 'State Aid Control by the European Commission: The Case of the Automobile Sector' (1995), available at: <http://ec.europa.eu/competition/speeches/text/sp1995_043_en.html>.

[47] See in this regard the words of the then Director General for Competition: 'Aid granted by a Member State is no longer controlled exclusively or principally in the interest of other Member States, but also, and perhaps even more so, in the interest of the competitors of the intended beneficiaries of the aid. The original macroeconomic approach of the authors of the EEC Treaty is being supplanted progressively by a microeconomic perspective, similar to that which has always dominated substantive and procedural antitrust law.' Ehlermann, C.D., 'State Aid Control in the European Union', op. cit. at 1219. See for other officials Gyselen, L., 'The Emerging Interface between Competition Policy and Environmental Policy in the EC', in Cameron, J., Demaret, P., and Geradin, D. (eds), *Trade and the Environment: The Search tor Balance* at 245, or Kobia, R.A.J., 'Introduction to the Law, Practice and Policy of State Aids in the European Community', speech delivered at the Institute for European Business Administration, Gand, 1996, available at: <http://ec.europa.eu/competition/speeches/text/sp1996_007_en.html>, or Jonathan Faull, according to whom the State aid enforcement system was widely acknowledged and mature by this time: Faull, J., 'The Enforcement of Competition Policy in the European Community: A Mature System' (1991–92) *Fordham International Law Journal*, 219 at 222.

[48] See Case C-225/91 *Matra v Commission* [1993] ECR I-3203, para. 41. See also para. 42: 'That obligation on the part of the Commission to ensure that Articles 92 and 93 are applied consistently with other provisions of the Treaty is all the more necessary where those other provisions also pursue, as in the present case, *the objective of undistorted competition in the common market.*' The Court had reached the same conclusion before with respect to discriminatory taxation or internal market measures in, eg, Case 73/79 *Commission v Italy* [1980] ECR 1533, para. 11; or C-21/88 *Du Pont de Nemours Italiana* [1990] ECR I-889, para. 20. See Giolito, C., 'La procédure de contrôle des aides d'État peut-elle être utilisée pour contrôler la bonne application d'autres dispositions de droit communautaire?' in *EC State Aid law—Le Droit des Aides d'Etat dans la CE, Liber Amicorum Francisco Santaolalla Gadea* (The Hague, 2008) 145.

[49] See Twenty-fourth Report on Competition Policy (Office for Official Publications of the European Communities, 1994) at p. 167, point 347.

[50] The closer interdependence of the competition rules addressed to undertakings and the State aid ones, together with the increasing role of private applicants in the State aid field, were present in

Similarly, in this context the Court also laid down a notion of aid based on the MEIP test for advantage. This notion made all State measures, and not only capital injections, subject to review under market conditions.[51]

In the same vein, the Court diminished the evidence that the Commission had to put forward to show that competition was distorted and trade affected and declared the inapplicability of a *de minimis* rule in the State aid field in cases of aid to a single undertaking.[52] The Court thus further favoured with these judgments the trend initiated in the previous period towards the application of the State aid rules in an intra-jurisdictional context and the Commission's conception of these rules as competition tools. Finally, the closer relationship between the concept of aid, that of discrimination, and the competition rules was also fostered by the increasingly important role of private applicants, that during this period started to claim before the Commission (and the Court) that their competitors were receiving benefits that they were not receiving, and therefore that they were discriminated against as they had been placed in a competitively disadvantaged position.

To conclude, although the Court was largely supportive of the Commission's priorities, it would reject the expansion of the concept of State resources submitted by the Commission in the *Sloman Neptun* case.[53] As discussed in Chapter 6, the Commission changed its initial position regarding the financial nature of the concept of aid in this case and asked for a broader notion of aid that was not necessarily limited to the financial. In this regard, it has been suggested that the change in the Commission's position obeyed to the decision to use the State aid rules instead of the internal market rules in order to deal with measures such as those at stake in the *Sloman Neptun* case, and this for two main reasons: (i) the internal market was formally achieved and therefore there was less need for the application of the internal market provisions, and (ii) the Commission had developed a number of soft-law instruments to deal with the compatibility of aid measures with the internal market that it was now ready to use in the more propitious context described above in relation to this period. However, the Court confirmed its traditional case law on this requirement and rejected the Commission's submission. The reasons that may have led the Court to this decision are discussed below at the end of the fourth period.

the *Matra* I case, decided in 1993, in which the Court, while upholding the Commission's decision, concluded that the State aid procedures could not lead to a result contrary to the Treaty competition rules addressed to undertakings. C-241/94 *France v Commission* [1996] ECR I-4551 at 24.

[51] Case C-39/94 *SFEI v La Poste* [1996] ECR p. I-03547 at para. 60: 'in order to determine whether a State measure constitutes aid, it is necessary to establish whether the recipient undertaking receives an economic advantage which it would not have obtained under normal market conditions'.

[52] Case C-142/87, *Belgium v Commission* (Tubemeuse) [1990] ECR I-00959 at para. 43; C-301/87 *France v Commission* (Boussac) [1990] ECR I-307.

[53] Joined Cases C-72/91 and C-73/91 *Sloman Neptun* et al. [1993] ECR I-887.

5. The Fourth Period: Mid- to Late 1990s to the Present

During this period, initiated by the mid- to late 1990s,[54] the Commission has increased transparency and legal certainty and has clarified the procedural rules concerning State aid. This was only possible after the Council agreed to adopt a procedural regulation in this field, almost forty years after adopting the corresponding rules in the antitrust field.[55] One of the most significant policy initiatives pursued by the European Commission during this period, also supported by the Council, has been the use of the State aid rules to combat harmful business taxation.[56] In the *Maribel* and *Adria–Wien* judgments, the Court has backed this initiative by endorsing the (derogation justification) test for selectivity included in the Commission Notice on the application of the State aid rules to measures relating to direct business taxation.[57] The Court has also accepted, after some hesitation,[58] that the only available justification of a *prima facie* selective measure by the nature or general scheme of the system has to be based on the intrinsic technical features of the system, as suggested by the Commission, and not on the extrinsic goals assigned to a particular tax scheme.[59] In this same sense, the Court has also established a presumption of distortion of competition and effect on trade for aid granted through fiscal measures in the *WAM* case.[60] Finally, the Court has also justified the introduction of a *de minimis* rule in this field; that is, a ceiling below which aid is deemed not to fall within the scope of Article 107(1) TFEU.[61] All these judgments backed the Commission's enforcement policy.

However, the Court's support for the Commission's policy priorities in this last period is limited in circumstances where the Court pursues another concern

[54] See for this periodization, eg, Mederer, W., 'The Future of State Aid Control' (1996) Competition Policy Newsletter; Lavdas and Mendrinou, *Politics, Subsidies, and Competition*, op. cit. at 44. See also Doleys, 'Fifty Years of Moulding Article 87', op. cit. at 22. He marks the beginning of this period in the late 1990s.

[55] Procedural rules were adopted in the antitrust field with the regulation 17/62. The main procedural regulation in the State aid field was adopted in 1999 (Council Regulation No 659/1999 of 22 March 1999 laying down detailed rules for the application of Article 93 of the EC Treaty Official Journal L 83/1, 27 March 1999, pp. 1–9).

[56] See Conclusions of the ECOFIN Council Meeting on 1 December 1997 concerning taxation policy—Resolution of the Council and the Representatives of the Governments of the Member States, meeting within the Council of 1 December 1997 on a code of conduct for business taxation—Taxation of saving Official Journal C 002, 6 January 1998 p. 0001–0006. 'The Council held a wide-ranging debate in the light of the Commission communication entitled "A package to tackle harmful tax competition in the European Union", which takes stock of a discussion initiated by the Commission at the informal meeting of Ministers for Economic Affairs and Finance in Verona in April 1996 and given more substantial shape at the informal meeting in Mondorf-les-Bains in September 1997 ...'.

[57] OJ C 384, 10/12/1998 p. 0003–0009.

[58] It has been submitted that in the *Maribel* and *Adria–Wien* judgments the Court seemed to give weight to the social and environmental goals pursued by the general system in question and not only to its intrinsic technical features as required by the notice.

[59] C-88/03 *Portugal v Commission* (Azores) [2006] ECR I-7115 at 81.

[60] See Case C-494/06 P *Wam* [2009] I-03639 at para. 51.

[61] C-351/98 *Spain v Commission* (Plan Renove I) [2002] ECR I-08031.

also now included in the Treaties, such as the respect for the special role of services of general economic interest in the Union, included since the Amsterdam Treaty (today in Article 14 TFEU), or the respect for the role of regions in the integration process, initiated in Maastricht and gradually reinforced until arriving at the wording of the current Article 4(2) TEU, that recognizes regional and local self-government as part of the national (constitutional) identity of Member States. These other Treaty goals may help explain judgments such as *Chronopost* or *Altmark*, concerning services of general economic interest (SGEIs), or *Azores* and *UGT–Rioja* in relation to the respect for regional government and the national constitutional identity of Member States. In both instances, judges of the Court have recognized the balancing exercise carried out by the Court among the mentioned Treaty articles.[62]

Finally, as in previous periods, the Court has maintained its own view on the notion of aid and this had led to discrepancies with the European Commission as to the substance of such notion. The most significant remains the concept of State resources under Article 107(1) TFEU, which does not cover regulatory measures, as the Court confirmed again in the *Preussen Elektra* case.[63] Similarly, the Court refused the extension of the presumption established in the *Philip Morris* case to the situation of undertakings benefitting from aid to penetrate non-EU markets, and it also clarified in the *Maribel bis/ter* and *Adria–Wien* cases that the term 'all undertakings' that the Commission uses to refer to general measures (measures open to all undertakings in a given Member State),[64] has to be limited to those undertakings that are in a comparable position in the light of the objective pursued by the measure under review.[65] Furthermore, in *British Aggregates*, the Court has considered, against the Commission's submissions, that the effects-based

[62] See von Danwitz, T., 'The Concept of State Aid in Liberalised Sectors' in Cremona (ed.) *Market Integration and Public Services in the European Union* (OUP, 2011) where he highlights the balancing between the application of the State aid rules and the liberalization of public services, eg, at 12: 'In essence, it seems to me that the jurisprudence is well established on a balanced approach which takes the necessities of a stringent state aid control seriously without neglecting the importance of maintaining the good functioning of services of general economic interest'; and Rosas, A., and Armati, L., *EU constitutional Law: An Introduction* (Hart, 2012) at 108: 'the status autonomus regions enjoy under the national constitution may affect the way in which Union Law will apply to them. The clearest example of such an effect concerns state aid law, where the ECJ has departed somewhat from the traditional Union/Member State dichotomy, looking beyond this distinction to the actual power of regional bodies to determine the applicable legal and economic framework for action'. Judge Rosas refers in this regard to Art. 4(TEU) of the Lisbon Treaty (also included in the unratified Constitutional Treaty), and the *Azores* (C-88/03 *Portugal v Commission* (Azores) [2006] ECR I-7115) and *UGT–Rioja* (C-428/06 to C-434/06 *UGT–Rioja and Others* [2008] ECR I-06747) judgments.

[63] C-379/98 *Preussen Elektra* [2001] ECR I-2099.

[64] See also the Commission Notice on the application of the State aid rules to measures relating to direct business taxation, OJ C 384, 10/12/1998 P. 0003–0009 at point 13 in this regard: 'Tax measures which are open to all economic agents operating within a Member State are in principle general measures.'

[65] As discussed in Ch. 5, the Court applied this conception in the *Maribel bis/ter* case although it coined the formula usually repeated in the *Adria–Wien* judgment, in particular in C-143/99 *Adria–Wien Pipeline* [2001] ECR I-8365 at para. 41.

approach to the notion of aid does not allow for the consideration of some measures as general systems if these measures treat differently undertakings that are in a comparable position. More recently, in the *EDF* and *ING* cases, the Court has considered that the Commission may not refrain from applying the MEIP test to fiscal measures just because they are fiscal under the effects-based approach to the concept of aid established in the case-law, and has also confirmed the applicability of the MEIP to situations where the public shareholding in the alleged beneficiary was obtained through State aid.

Nevertheless, in light of the analysis described above and throughout this book, it can be concluded that the Court has been largely supportive of the Commission's evolving policy and enforcement priorities in relation to the concept of aid. Several reasons may explain the Court's deference. First, the Court has allowed the Commission a broad discretion to interpret the 'economic criteria that govern the application of Article [107]'.[66] Secondly, some of the policy goals pursued by the European Commission, such as the early goal of eliminating discriminatory measures against out of State traders, were broadly shared by the Court, which contributed with its support to the creation of the Common Market. Thirdly, even after the more 'teleological' period of the Court's case law, represented by the first and second periods, the Court has felt that it needed to contribute to fill the gaps left by the absence of procedural rules in this field due to the refusal of the Council to adopt them. This has been recognized by some judges of the Court,[67] and even noted in some judgments.[68] In this regard, it has been submitted in this book that there has been a spill-over effect from the procedural to the substantive requirements of these rules, and that the Court has in some instances, particularly in relation to the notions of distortion of competition and effect on trade, laid down formulas that have eased the Commission's task against the unwilling and uncooperative Member States. The refusal during some time of a *de minimis* rule in this field is probably the best example of this spill-over effect as it had been allegedly admitted by the Court and some of its judges in the first period,[69] and yet the Court rejected it when the enforcement of the State aid rules was poor

[66] Pescatore, P., 'Public and Private Aspects of European Community Competition Law' (1987) *Fordham International Law Journal*, 373 at 393: 'For the time being there remains great, and so far unchallenged, discretion in the hands of the Commission.' This discretion has also been noted by the Court in some of the cases reviewed. The Court has, eg, found that the Commission can conclude that aid in amounts below that set by the De minimis communication does not affect trade and/or distort competition 'in the exercise of its discretion to assess the possible economic effects of aid'. See C-351/98 *Spain v Commission* (Plan Renove I) [2002] ECR p. I-08031 at para. 52.

[67] See, eg, Judge Pescatore, 'Public and Private Aspects of European Community Competition Law', op. cit. at 393: '[The Court] has not allowed Member States to take refuge behind the procedural shortcomings arising from the absence of implementing regulations in conjunction with Article [109].' See also Mancini, G.F. 'The Making of a Constitution for Europe' (1989) *Common Market Law Review* at 613.

[68] See, eg, C-84/82 *Germany v Commission* [1984] ECR 1451 at para. 10 and Case C-301/87 *France v Commission* ('Boussac) [1990] ECR I-307 at para. 14. See in this regard also Slot, P.J., 'Procedural Aspects of State Aids: The Guardian of Competition versus the Subsidiy Villains?' CMLR, 27 741 (1990).

[69] Case 6/64 *Flaminio Costa v E.N.E.L.* [1964] ECR, P. I-01141: 'These provisions…headed "Aids granted by States", are designed, on the one hand, to eliminate progressively existing aids and, on the other hand, to prevent the individual States in the conduct of their internal affairs

in the second and third periods,[70] only to accept it again when this enforcement had improved considerably since the early 2000s.[71]

On the other hand, the cases in which the Court has departed from the Commission's submissions are rather exceptional in this field, and most of them concern procedural reasons or defective motivation. Substantially, the main disagreement between the two institutions has been related to the notion of aid granted by the State or through State resources since the early 1990s, and, in particular, to one aspect of that notion: the consideration of regulatory and legislative measures as State resources that the Court refuses to admit. In this regard, it is submitted that the Court's position is justified by the general architecture of the Treaty that leaves the control of regulatory and legislative measures to national and European courts under the direct effect of the free movement rules. These rules also allow Member States to plead justifications and mandatory requirements based on their national objectives, such as the protection of the environment, for example, something that they could not do under the State aid rules, as only community objectives are acceptable under the compatibility analysis since the *Philip Morris* case law, and only the Commission may carry out that analysis. Finally, another factor of disagreement between the Commission and the Court in recent years has been the role of private parties in State aid proceedings. Private complainants were traditionally allies of the European Commission as they brought to the latter's attention cases of non-notified aid, and reinforced the Commission's role as a neutral arbiter between States.[72] However, recently, as many formerly reserved sectors have been open to competition, private complainants have brought to the Commission politically sensitive cases involving aids to incumbents in important sectors and have not hesitated to bring the Commission before the Court for failing to act on their complaints or for doing it incorrectly. The *SFEI* judgment discussed in Chapter 4 is an example of this new trend.

To conclude this section, although the book has focused on the interaction between the Commission and the Court, the study of this relationship has also revealed what could be referred to, in very broad terms, as an evolving role in the Council from an initial hostility towards these rules to a more collaborative

from introducing new aids "in any form whatsoever" which are likely directly or indirectly to favour certain undertakings or products *in an appreciable way*, and which threaten, even potentially, to distort competition. By virtue of Article 92, the Member States have acknowledged that such aids are incompatible with the Common Market and have thus implicitly undertaken not to create any more, save as otherwise provided in the Treaty' (emphasis added). As to the judges, see Quadri, R., Monaco, R., and Trabucchi, A. (eds), *Trattato istitutivo della C.E.E. Comentario*, Vol II (Giuffrè, 1965) at 722; and Catalano, N., *Manuel de droit des Communautes europeennes* (Dalloz, 1965) at 495.

70 See Case 730/79 *Philip Morris Holland BV v Commission* [1980] ECR 2671, and Case C-142/87, *Belgium v Commission* (Tubemeuse) [1990] ECR I-00959.

71 See, eg, C-351/98 *Spain v Commission* (Plan Renove I) [2002] ECR I-08031.

72 Smith, M.P., 'Autonomy by the Rules: The European Commission and the Development of State Aid Policy' (1998) *Journal of Common Market Studies* at 63.

attitude.[73] In this regard, until the 1980s, and particularly during the difficult years of the *empty chair* and its aftermath (the Luxembourg compromise), the Council was quite unreceptive to these rules, the best example of this probably being the double refusal to adopt a procedural regulation in 1966 and 1972, as proposed by the European Commission. However, during the early 1980s, and at least as a mechanism to address the situation of some sectors (such as shipbuilding) and undertakings, many public enterprises needed to become more efficient or be liquidated and the Council supported the Commission's adoption of the MEIP test, and even included it in the shipbuilding code adopted by the Council in 1981. Member States remained reluctant to comply with the State aid rules during the 1980s, although they supported a greater role for these rules in the context of the 1992 programme, when notifications of new aid increased. Finally, since the mid-1990s, the Council has supported and sometimes even proposed important initiatives such as the drafting of a procedural regulation, the adoption of a strategy against harmful taxation, of a strategy for the coordination of aids for financial institutions during the most recent crisis, or the discussion over how to reconcile the application of the State aid rules to SGEIs, this latter initiative also motivated by the increasing number of private complaints against former public monopolists. Therefore, although in principle the position of Member States and that of the Commission in relation to State aid should lead to friction, it has been collaborative in some important instances and this, too, has not been only specific to the State aid field.[74]

6. The Concept of State Aid and the Evolution of the Case Law of the Court of Justice of the European Union

The second argument defended in this book shows that the legal concept of aid has experienced an evolution that shares many features with the general evolution of the case law of the Court of Justice as described by some of its judges. Indeed, as will be discussed in this section, the characteristics of the periods in which Judge Koopmans divided the evolution of EU case law until the mid-1980s,[75] and those identified by Judge Everling subsequently,[76] are also generally transposable

[73] The position of the Parliament has been less discussed in this work yet, at least during the early 1980s, it has supported the Commission decisively in the latter efforts to apply the State aid rules more strictly: Lavdas and Mendrinou, *Politics, Subsidies, and Competition*, op. cit. at 33, and Debates of the European Parliament (EP) 14/15 October 1981; EP Resolution 1-608/81, OJ C 287/61-62 1981; EP Resolution 1-610/81, OJ C 287/63 1981.

[74] Thatcher, M., 'The Commission and National Governments as Partners: EC Regulatory Expansion in Telecommunications 1979–2000' (2001) *Journal of European Public Policy* 558.

[75] See Koopmans, T., 'The Role of Law in the Next Stage of European Integration' (1986) *International and Comparative Law Quarterly* 925.

[76] See Everling, U., 'On the Judge-made Law of the European Community's Courts' in O'Keeffe, D. (ed.), *Judicial Review in European Union Law: Liber Amicorum in Honor of Lord Slynn of Hadley* (Kluwer, 2000).

with the case law on the concept of aid. Similarly, many of the features identified by authors such as *Maduro*, in relation to the evolution of the case law in today's Article 34 TFEU,[77] or Gerber and Wesselling regarding the case law on Articles 85 and 86 EEC,[78] are also largely applicable to the evolution of the case law on State aids.

In this vein, Judge Koopmans considered that during the 1950s and 1960s the case law of the Court of Justice focused on institutional issues, such as the direct effect of Treaty provisions or the relation between domestic and the European legal order, more than on substantive ones. He referred to this period as *institutional*.

In the State aid field, the Court of Justice also dealt with the issue of the direct effect of today's Article 108 in the *Costa/Enel* case, or whether the Commission had competence to review national measures pertaining to retained fields such as monetary and fiscal policy under the State aid rules (in the *French exports* and *para-fiscal levies* cases). In all three cases the Court sided with the European Commission, reinforcing its prerogatives to the detriment of those of Member States, as it also did in other fields.[79] The Court, also in line with the institutional tenets of the period, refrained from defining the concept of aid or any of its substantive criteria. Instead, as mentioned in the previous section of these conclusions, the Court issued broad principles in succinct judgments that established clearly the Commission's prerogatives in this field and the obligations of Member States under these rules and, more generally under the Treaty.[80]

During the 1970s, Judge Koopmans claimed that the case law of the Court was characterized by cases that no longer concerned institutional problems but rather dealt with the way in which courts could 'contribute to realising the European treaties' general aims'. He referred to this period as *instrumental*. Judgments handed down during this period such as *ERTA*,[81] *Dassonville*,[82] or *Continental Can*,[83] could be cited as examples of this approach.

[77] See Poiares Maduro, *We the Court, The European Court of Justice and the European Economic Constitution*, op. cit.

[78] Gerber, *Law and Competition in Twentieth Century Europe*, op. cit., and Wesseling, R., *The Modernisation of EC Antitrust Law* (Hart, 2000).

[79] In this context, Gerber observed for the competition rules addressed to undertakings that in this first period of European integration (up to 1973) the Court reinforced the prerogatives of the Commission to the detriment of those of Member States, and laid down broad teleological principles, two features that also appear in the first State aid case law. See Gerber, *Law and Competition in Twentieth Century Europe*, op. cit. at 351–53. Similarly, Maduro observed an alliance between the Court and the Commission's priorities during the early years of integration in the internal market field in order to create a 'habit of obedience'. See Poiares Maduro, *We the Court*, op. cit. at 9–10.

[80] See for an example of this approach Joined Cases C-6/69 and C-11/69 *Commission v France* [1969] ECR 523. Similarly, the Court's preference for broad principles during this period was also the main feature of the early cases concerning Art. 5 EEC, the so-called principle of loyal cooperation. See Temple Lang, J., 'The Development by the Court of Justice of the Duties of Cooperation of National Authorities and Community Institutions under Article 10 EC', *Fordham International Law Journal*, 2007–08, 1483 at 1484–85.

[81] Case 22/70 *Commission v Council* (ERTA) [1971] ECR 263.

[82] Case 8/74 *Procureur du Roi v Benoît and Gustave Dassonville* [1974] ECR 00837

[83] Case C-6/72 *Continental Can v Commission* [1973] ECR 215.

In the State aid field, the 1970s were also characterized by the Court's support for the Community's ends. The Court supported the Commission's proposals and even went beyond them in order make the State aid rules operational and, in this fashion, to help them achieve the Community's ends. Three cases concerning the concept of aid could be mentioned from this period: *Italian textiles, Van Tiggele*, and *Steinike and Weinlig*. The three have been discussed in some detail thus it will only be added here that in *Italian Textiles*, together with the support to the effects-based formula proposed by the Commission discussed earlier, the Court held that the concept of advantage granted to some undertakings must be established by comparison with other undertakings established in the same Member State, and not in different Member States, as had been suggested by Italy and partially admitted by the Commission. Therefore, consistent with the instrumental approach of the period, the Court went beyond the Commission's position in order to make the Treaty rules operational, and this even though the Commission's position in this case could find support in the influential Spaak Report.[84]

To conclude, two more cases decided during this period should be mentioned, although they relate to procedure and not to substance.[85] The cases are relevant as the Court contributed through them to fill the procedural and enforcement gaps left by the Council's reluctance to adopt a procedural regulation in this field, and to give the State aid rules 'a practical effect'. Finally, the Court instrumental support to the Community objectives during this period was also observed by other authors in different areas.[86]

[84] The Commission's partial acceptance of a comparison found in fact some support in the Spaak Report. See Spaak Report, Report of the Heads of Delegation to the Ministers of Foreign Affairs, of 21 April 1956, p. 62 of the French version : '*Il apparait cependant qu'une industrie apparemment désavantagée cesse de l'être si la même surcharge relative existe dans même industrie des autres pays. Au contraire, ce désavantage se maintient si cette surcharge n existe pas ailleurs, et s'accroit si la même industrie est relativement déchargée dans l'autre pays considère*.' (Trans. 'It appears, however, that an apparently disadvantaged industry ceases to be so if the same relative overload exists in the same industry in other countries. On the contrary, this disadvantage is maintained if the overload exists elsewhere, and increases if the same industry is relatively relieved in the other countries considered.') However, the Court refused this comparison as mentioned before. The Court had in fact already refused a similar argument in the Joined Cases C-6/69 and 11/69 *Commission v France* [1969] ECR 523 at para. 21. In this regard, as underlined by AG Warner, the availability of such a defense (the existence of similar advantages in other Member States) could make the enforcement of the State aid provisions a 'dead letter'. See Opinion of Advocate General Warner in Case 173/73 *Italy v Commission* [1974] ECR 727. See also for a similar finding of the Court during the 1970s, this time concerning the notion of distortion of competition Case C-78/76, *Steinike & Weinlig v Federal Republic of Germany* [1977] ECR p. 00595 at para. 24.

[85] See Case C-120/73 *Lorenz* [1973] ECR 1471. In reality the Court delivered on the same day, 11 December 1973, four judgments, including *Lorenz*, clarifying that Member States were obliged to refrain from implementing any aid until the Commission had sufficient time to review its compatibility with the Common Market pursuant to notification: 121/73 *Markmann* [1973] ECR 1495; 122/73 *Nordsee GmbH* [1973] ECR 1511; 141/73 *Lohrey* [1973] ECR 1527. See also Case 70/72 *Commission v Germany* [1973] ECR 813 at para. 13 in which the Commission was allowed to ask for the repayment of incompatible aid.

[86] See in this regard, eg, Wesseling, R., *The Modernisation of EC Antitrust Law* (Hart, 2000) at 28–33. Similarly, the Court's case law on the antitrust rules was also far reaching and integration oriented, so much so that Gerber even noted that the weight of the integration objectives eroded

Subsequently, during the 1980s, both Judge Koopmans and Judge Everling noted a tendency in the Court's case-law towards less activism. During this period, the Court, while overall supportive to the Commission's position, would require from it stricter minimum standards and a more solid legal basis in order to uphold measures fostering integration. Koopmans referred to this period as *minimalist.*

In the State aid field, this trend was initiated by the *Philip Morris* judgment, discussed in the previous section of these conclusions. This judgment was very supportive of the Commission. However, the minimalist approach of the Court could already be perceived as the Court linked the establishment of the presumption of distortion of competition and trade to the circumstances of the case, in particular the beneficiary in this case, a large undertaking with an important share of intra-community trade, and was silent in relation to the applicability of the *de minimis* rule in this field (although this silence could be interpreted as a tacit rejection of it), even though the Advocate General had requested its explicit rejection and the Commission had requested guidance as to its applicability.

However, the minimalist approach of the Court was clearer in three cases decided during the early 1980s which represented the first annulments of State aid decisions, precisely for faulty motivation or incorrect legal basis. This was the situation with the *Leeuwarders* and *Intermills* cases, the first applications of the MEIP test that reached the Court, and with the *Poor Farmers* case, where the Court rejected the existence of 'measures having an effect equivalent to State aid' as the Commission had suggested.[87] Despite these set backs the Court remained overall supportive of the Commission in this field as it, for example, endorsed the MEIP test in *Meura* and other judgments and upheld the important, and related, Transparency Directive.[88] Indeed, the same tendency was perceptible in the antitrust field where Gerber held

to some extent the 'juridical' conception of Community competition law. See Gerber, *Law and Competition in Twentieth Century Europe*, op. cit. at 360. Likewise, Van Gerven commented in the early 1970s that faced with an inactive legislator (the Council after the Luxembourg compromise), the Court was bound to take policy decisions and that it would be 'induced to take even more important policy decisions in the future'. See Van Gerven, W., 'Twelve Years of EEC Competition Law (1962–73) Revisited' (1974) *Common Market Law Review*, 38 at 60.

[87] See Case 323/82 *Intermills v Commission* [1984] ECR 3809, Joined Cases 296 and 318/82 *Netherlands and Leeuwarder Papierwarenfabriek v Commission* [1985] ECR 809, and C-290/83 *Commission v France* [1985] ECR 439.

[88] Likewise, in the competition field, while the Court broadly supported the so-called second generation of competition law, led by a 'second generation of competition lawyers in the Commission' (Whish, R., and Sufrin, B., 'Article 85 and the Rule of Reason' (1987) *Yearbook of European Law* 12 at 38) it increased its rigor and, just like in the State aid field, started to annul Commission decisions for lack of evidence to support the Commission's claims. See in this regard Verstrynge, J.F., 'Current Antitrust Policy Issues in the EEC: Some Reflections on the Second Generation of Competition Policy' (1984) *Fordham Corporate Law Institute* at 676. Gerber notes this development since the mid-1970s also in the antitrust field and cites as an example Case C-27/76 *United Brands Co. v Commission* [1978] ECR 207), but also during the 1980s citing also as example the Case C-86/82 *Hasselblad (GB) Ltd v Commission* [1984] ECR 883. Gerber, *Law and Competition in Twentieth Century Europe*, op. cit. at 361–62.

that during this period the Court would allow the Commission to win on new tests but it would quash the decision on another ground.[89]

In addition, towards the end of the decade, the success of the internal market programme led to a time distinguished by a sense of euphoria, as underlined by Judge Everling,[90] in which the Court adopted courageous decisions such as *Francovich*.[91] In the State aid field, the Court supported the Commission's bold submissions concerning the absence of a *de minimis* rule and the presumption that operating aid always distorts competition and affects trade in the *Tubemeuse* and *Boussac* judgments.[92]

During the 1990s, particularly in the context of the difficult ratification of the Maastricht Treaty (signed in February 1992), several authors, including judges of the Court, noted a more cautious approach in the Court's case law and its overall 'lighter touch' with respect to State regulation.[93] This was the context in which the Court decided the famous *Keck* or *Meng* cases, in the internal market and competition fields, and the *Sloman Neptun* case in the State aid field. It has been suggested, with reference to an article by Judge Mancini, that the subject matter of this case (social legislation favouring the employment of non-Community migrant workers) may have also influenced the Court's decision in *Sloman Neptun*, as the Court was under heavy criticism at the time of the decision from Germany for some judgments dealing with that same matter.[94] In any event, this case has been confirmed several times in different contexts and it has been argued in this book that the Court's finding is justified under the general architecture of the Treaty.[95]

Finally, towards the end of the 1990s, after the ratification of the Amsterdam Treaty, Judge Everling observed a more balanced approach in the Court's case law.[96] Similarly, AG Jacobs has also observed that the evolution of the case law, together with the successive Treaty amendments have led the Court to strike a balance between the market and other values now enshrined in the Treaties.[97]

[89] Gerber, *Law and Competition in Twentieth Century Europe*, op. cit. at 361–62. Gerber marks the beginning of this trend in the mid-1970s and places it in the broader economic context of this period (the mid-1970s to the mid-1980s) characterized by its difficulty for European undertakings.

[90] See Everling, 'On the Judge-made Law of the European Community's Courts', op. cit. at 39.

[91] Joined Cases C-6/90 and C-9/90 *Francovich and others v Italy* [1991] ECR 1-5403.

[92] Although, as mentioned before, even in this propitious context the Court refused in the latter the Commission's submission in the sense that illegal aids should be deemed incompatible just because of their illegality (because they were granted without prior notification to the Commission).

[93] See, eg, Ross, 'State Aids: Maturing into a Constitutional Problem', op. cit. at 82. See also the references mentioned by Ross in footnote 14 of that page, and see Everling, 'On the Judge-made Law of the European Community's Courts', op. cit. at 39.

[94] See Mancini and Keeling, 'Language, Culture and Politics in the Life of the European Court of Justice', op. cit. at 408.

[95] As mentioned in previous sections, this architecture foresees that legislative and regulatory measures are reviewed under the free movement rules, which also allows national courts to analyse them and Member States to plead national objectives as a defence, something that they are not entitled to do in the State aid field after the *Philip Morris* judgment, in which the Court found that only Community objectives, as interpreted exclusively by the Commission, may be taken into consideration for the compatibility analysis.

[96] See Everling, 'On the Judge-made Law of the European Community's Courts', op. cit. at 39.

[97] Jacobs, F.G., (2004) CMLR 41 303 at 305: 'More generally, the case law, the legislation and progressive Treaty amendments seek to delimit the contours of the market: to strike a balance

This more balanced approach has also been noted in the State aid field and some of the judgments included in the previous section under the fourth period (such as *Altmark* or *Azores*) are evidence of this trend which, as mentioned previously, has also been admitted by several judges of the Court in the State aid field.[98] Indeed, from the 2000s onwards the concept of aid has changed to take into account new goals included in the Treaties, and this tendency continues. The last example might be the now binding character of the Charter of Fundamental Rights, which recognizes in its Article 36 access to SGEIs as a fundamental right. This Article has already been invoked by an Advocate General in relation to the *Altmark* criteria for the notion of advantage and the new rules on SGEIs.[99]

between deregulation and other values—with an evolving recognition, for example, of the importance of social policy and of public services.'

[98] See Von Danwitz, T., 'The Concept of State Aid in Liberalised Sectors', op. cit., where he highlights the balancing between the application of the State aid rules and the liberalization of public services, at 12, and Judge Rosas and Armati, *EU Constitutional Law*, op. cit. at 108.

[99] Jääskinen, N., 'The New Rules on SGEI' (2011) *European State Aid Law Quarterly*. See also for another invocation of the Charter of Fundamental Rights in the context of State aids the opinion of AG Mengozzi in Case 290/07 *Commission v Scott* [2010] ECR 2010 I-07763 at para. 60.

The Book in a Nutshell

This book has shown that the concept of aid is a 'living instrument' that has been applied in accordance with the main policy priorities of the European Commission, a fact that had been under-explored and the implications of this connection seldom studied. The book has also demonstrated, contrary to what has been affirmed before by other authors, that the evolution of this concept has been influenced by the broader evolution of the case law of the Court of Justice in different periods of the integration process. As advanced in the introductory chapter, it is submitted that the study of the policy and enforcement considerations that have affected the evolution of the concept of aid is not only enriching from an intellectual point of view but also useful to help decide difficult cases. In this regard, together with the *EDF* and *Gibraltar* judgments discussed in the introduction, the book has provided criteria to interpret and discuss cases such as *Sloman Neptun, Philip Morris,* and *Azores* beyond the analysis traditionally carried out in this field, too often limited to the compatibility of these cases with the effects-based formula to the notion of aid first established in the *Italian textiles* case. Indeed, the emergence of that formula, of the MEIP test, the Adria–Wien test for selectivity, the ups and downs of the *de minimis* rule in this field, or the exclusion of regulatory measures from the notion of State resources, cannot be understood solely by looking at the economic or even the legal reasoning behind the relevant judgments. Instead, policy and enforcement considerations are useful interpretative tools to understand these developments, a point that this book has hopefully contributed to making.

The book also offers new insights to the current understanding of the concept of aid by showing that it has not been a technical sub-discipline detached from the general evolution of the Community, or a latecomer in legal development. Indeed, although commentators are right to underline the scarce number of cases in this field until the 1980s, the problems associated with the lack of procedural rules during past decades, or the limited academic enthusiasm for this field when compared with the antitrust one,[1] the analysis carried out in the book shows that the

[1] See in this regard, Ehlermann, C.D., 'Introduction' in Ehlermann, C.D., and Everson, M. (eds), *European Competition Law Annual: 1999 Selected Issues in the Field of State Aid*, (Hart, 2001) at xii. See also Hancher, L., 'EC State Aid Law—No Longer the Cinderella of European Competition Law But Not Quite the Ugly Sister?' in Hancher, L., Ottervanger, T., and Slot, P.J. (eds), *EC State Aids* 3rd edn (Sweet & Maxwell 2006) 1; and Ross, M., 'State Aids: Maturing into a Constitutional Problem', (2000) *Common Market Law Review* 401, at 79.

concept of aid has followed an evolution parallel to that of the main economic law provisions of the Treaty, and has been, as have they, influenced by the political, constitutional, and economic events affecting the Community. In addition, the book has also sought to bring to the legal discipline the work of political scientists in this field, considered crucial to understand the law of State aid. In this regard, perhaps future research will build on their knowledge to study issues that have not been covered here, such as whether the picture painted of the evolution of the concept of aid might offer insights into a similar evolution concerning the compatibility provisions of Article 107 TFEU or in relation to the concept of economic activity—that is a precondition to the application of the State aid rules—whether the relation between the evolution of the Community and that of the concept of aid could justify a different concept of aid (of subsidy) in the GATT context, or whether the close relationship between the policy priorities of the Commission and the current concept of aid may also cast doubts as to the desirability of an independent agency for competition matters that would include State aid cases.

To conclude, the concept of aid has evolved from an internal market conception, which predominated during the 1960s and 1970s, to a competition-based one during the 1980s and especially the 1990s, and from there to the current comprehensive conception. What will follow is unknown, but new formulas will tell.

Bibliography

ACADEMIC SOURCES

Abate, A., 'Privatisations et Déréglementations en Droit Communautaire' in Di Bucci, V., Buendia Sierra, J.L., Smulders, B., et al. (eds), *EC State Aid Law—Le Droit des Aides d'État dans la CE, Liber Amicorum Francisco Santaolalla Gadea* (The Hague : Kluwer Law International, 2008) 239.

Ahlborn, C., and Piccinin, D., 'The Great Recession and Other Mishaps: The Commission's Policy of Restructuring in a Time of Crisis', in Szyszczak, E. (ed.), *Research Handbook on State Aid* (Cheltenham: Edward Elgar, 2011) 124.

Ahlborn, C., and Berg, C., 'Can State Aid Control Learn from Antitrust? The Need for Greater Role for Competition Analysis under the State Aid rules' in Biondi, A., Eeckhout, P., and Flynn, J. (eds), *The Law of State Aid in the European Union* (Oxford: Oxford University Press, 2004) 41.

Akyürek-Kievits, H.E., 'Case 82/77, Openbaar Ministerie (Public Prosecutor) of the Kingdom of the Netherlands v. Jacobus Philippus van Tiggele. Preliminary ruling of 24 January 1978 at the request of the Gerechtshof, Amsterdam (1978) E.C.R. 26.' (1979) *Common Market Law Review*, 16(1):139.

Allen, D., 'Competition Policy: Policing the Single Market', in Wallace H., and Wallace, W. (eds), *Policy-Making in the European Union* (Oxford: Oxford University Press 1996) 157.

Amato, G., *Antitrust and the Bounds of Power: The Dilemma of Liberal Democracy in the History of the Market* (Oxford: Hart Publishing, 1997).

Andreangeli, A., 'EU Competition Law in Times of Crisis: Between Present Challenges and a Largely Unwritten Future' (2013) *Competition Law Review*, 9(2):91.

Andriessen, F., 'The Role of Anti-Trust in the Face of Economic Recession' (1983) *European Competition Law Review*, 2:340.

Anestis, P., and Mavroghenis, S., 'The Market Investor Test', in Rydelski, M.S. (ed.) *The EC State Aid Regime: Distortive Effects of State Aid on Competition and Trade* (London: Cameron May, 2006) 109.

Arnull, A., *The European Court of Justice* 2nd edn (Oxford: Oxford University Press, 2006).

Arpio Santacruz, J.L., *State Aids in the European Community: Framework Exceptions and Implications for National Economic Policies*, Doctoral thesis defended at the European University Institute in 1996.

Atanasiu, I., 'Chronopost II: The Application of the Market Economy Investor Principle in Reserved Sectors' (2008) *European State Aid Law Quarterly* 571.

Atanasiu, I., 'EC State Aid Policy with Respect to Soft Budgetary Constraints: Tax and Social Security Contribution Payment Arrears' (2005) *European State Aid Law Quarterly*, 4:597.

Bacon, K., 'State Aids and General Measures' (1997) Master thesis defended at the European University Institute in 1997.

Bacon, K., 'State Aids and General Measures' (1997) *Yearbook of European Law*, 17(1) 269.

Bacon, K., 'Differential Taxes, State Aids and the Lunn Poly Case' (1999) *European Competition Law Review*, 7:384.

Bacon, K., 'State Aids in the English Courts: Definition and Other Problems', in Biondi, A., Eeckhout, P., and Flynn, J. (eds) *The Law of State Aid in the European Union* (Oxford: Oxford University Press, 2004) 337.

Bacon, K., *European Community Law of State Aid* (Oxford: Oxford University Press, 2009).

Bagwell, K.W., Bermann, G.A., and Mavroidis P.C. (eds), *Law and Economics of Contingent Protection in International Trade* (New York, NY: Cambridge University Press, 2009).

Baquero Cruz, J., and Castillo de la Torre, F., 'A Note on Preussen Elektra' (2001) *European Law Review*, 5:489.

Baquero Cruz, J., *Between Competition and Free Movement* (Oxford: Hart Publishing, 2002).

Barnard, C., and Deakin, S., 'Market Access and Regulatory Competition' in Barnard, C., and Scott, J. (eds), *The Law of The Single European Market: Unpacking the Premises* (Oxford: Hart Publishing, 2002) 197.

Bartosch, A., 'Is there a Need for a Rule of Reason in European State Aid Law?' (2010) *Common Market Law Review*, 47:729.

Bartosch, A., 'Clarification or Confusion? How to Reconcile the ECJ's Rulings in Altmark and Chronopost' (2003) *European State Aid Law Quarterly*, 3:375.

Bengoetxea, J., *The Legal Reasoning of the European Court of Justice* (Oxford: Clarendon Press, 1993).

Besselink, L.F.M., 'National and Constitutional Identity Before and After Lisbon' (2010) *Utrecht Law Review*, 6(3): 36.

Biondi, A., 'State Aid is Falling Down, Falling Down: An Analysis of the Case Law on the Notion of Aid' (2013) 50 *Common Market Law Review* 50(6):1719.

Biondi, A., and Farley, M., 'The Relationship between State Aid and the Single Market' in Szyszczak, E. (ed.), *Research Handbook on State Aid* (Cheltenham: Edward Elgar, 2011) 277.

Biondi, A., 'The Rationale of State Aid Control: A Return to Orthodoxy' (2010) Barnard, C. Odudu, O. (eds), *Cambridge Yearbook of European Legal Studies*, 12:35.

Biondi, A., 'BUPA v Commission' (2008) *European State Aid Law Quarterly*, 7(2):401.

Biondi, A., 'Free Trade, A Mountain Road and the Right to Protest: European Economic Freedoms and Fundamental Individual Rights' (2004) *European Human Rights Law Review* 51.

Biondi, A., 'Justifying State Aid: The Financing of Services of General Economic Interest' in Tridimas, T., and Nebbia P. (eds), *European Union Law for the Twenty-First Century*, Vol. II (Oxford: Hart Publishing, 2004).

Biondi, A., Eeckhout, P., and Flynn, J. (eds), *The Law of State Aid in the European Union* (Oxford: Oxford Univeristy Press, 2004).

Biondi, A., and Eeckhout, .P, 'State Aid and Obstacles to Trade' in Biondi, A., Eeckhout, P., and Flynn, J. (eds), *The Law of State Aid in the European Union* (Oxford: Oxford University Press, 2004) 103.

Biondi, A., and Rubini, L., 'Aims, Effects and Justifications: EC State Aid Law and Its Impact on National Social Policies' in Dougan, M., and Spaventa, E. (eds), *Social Welfare and EU Law* (Oxford: Hart Publishing, 2005) 79.

Biondi, A., 'Review of Judgment in Case C-222/04—Ministero dell'Economia e delle Finanze v. Cassa di Risparmio di Firenze SpA et al.' (2006) *European State Aid Law Quarterly*, 3:371.

Biondi, A., 'Some Reflections on the Notion of "State Resources" in European Community State Aid Law' (2007) *Fordham International Law Journal*, 30(5):1426.

Bishop, B., 'From Trade to Tutelage: State Aid and Public Choice in the European Union', Presentation to Conference to ACE, Copenhagen, 2 December 2005.

Boulois, J., 'Jurisprudence de la Cour de Justice des Communautés Européennes' (1961) *Annuaire Français de Droit International*, 7:267.

Bourgeois, J.H.J., 'State Aids, Taxation Measures and Specificity. Some Thoughts' in Dony, M., and De Walsche, A., *Mélanges en hommage à Michel Waelbroeck*, Vol 2 (Bruxelles: Bruylant, 1999) 765.

Bovis, C.H., 'Financing Services of General Interest in the EU: How do Public Procurement and State Aids Interact to Demarcate between Market Forces and Protection' (2005) *European Law Journal*, 11(1):79.

Blauberger, M., 'Of "Good" and "Bad" Subsidies: European State Aid Control through Soft and Hard Law' (2009) *West European Politics*, 32(4):719.

Blockley, R.C., 'Subsidies and Diplomacy: Rome and Persia in Late Antiquity' (1985) *Phoenix*, 30(1):62.

Brinkhorst, L.J., and Verougstraete, I.M., 'Annotation in Joined Cases C-6/69 and C-11/69, Commission v France, [1969] ECR 523' (1970) *Common Market Law Review*, 7(4):483.

Brittan, L., '1992: A Bonfire of Subsidies? A Review of State Aids in the European Community' (1989) *European Access*, 3.

Brogan, O., 'Trade between the Roman Empire and the Free Germans' (1936) *Journal of Roman Studies*, 26(2):195.

Bucirossi, P. (ed.), *Handbook of Antitrust Economics* (Cambridge, MA: MIT Press, 2008).

Buendía Sierra, J.L., and Smulders, B., 'The Limited Role of the "Refined Economic Approach" in Achieving the Objectives of State Aid Control: Time for Some Realism', in Di Bucci, V., Buendia Sierra, J.L., Smulders, B., et al. (eds), *EC State Aid Law—Le Droit des Aides d'État dans la CE, Liber Amicorum Francisco Santaolalla Gadea* (The Hague, Kluwer Law International, 2008) 18.

Buendía Sierra, J.L., 'Finding the Right Balance: State Aid and Services of General Economic Interest', in Di Bucci, V., Buendia Sierra, J.L., Smulders, B., et al. (eds), *EC State aid law—Le Droit des Aides d'État dans la CE, Liber Amicorum Francisco Santaolalla Gadea* (The Hague: Kluwer Law International, 2008) 191.

Buendía Sierra, J.L., 'Not Like This: Some Sceptical Remarks on the "Refined Economic Approach" in State Aid', in Proceedings of 4th Experts' Forum on New Developments in European State Aid Law, 18 and 19 May 2006, European State Aid Law Institute (Berlin: Lexxion, 2006) 59.

Buendía Sierra, J.L., Muñoz de Juan, M., and Visser, M., 'Public Intervention in the Economy in Times of Crisis', in Merola, M., Derenne, J., and Rivas, J. (eds), *Competition Law in Times of Economic Crisis—In Need of Adjustment? 2012 GCLC Annual Conference EU Competition Law in Times of Economic Crisis* (Brussels: Bruylant, 2013).

Burley, A.M., and Mattili, W., 'Europe Before the Court: A Political Theory of Legal Integration' (1993) *International Organization*, 47(1):41.

Cameron, J., Demaret, P., and Geradin, D. (eds), *Trade and the Environment: The Search for Balance* (London: Cameron May, 1994).

Caspari, M., 'The Aid Rules of the EEC Treaty and Their Application' in J. Schwarze (ed.), *Discretionary Powers of the Member States in the Field of Economic Policies and Their Limits under the EEC Treaty* (Baden-Baden: Nomos Verlagsgesellschatft, 1988) 40.

Catalano, N., *Manuel de Droit des Communautés Européennes* 2nd edn (Paris: Dalloz, 1965).

Catherine, R., and Gousset, P., *L'état et l'essor industriel; du dirigisme colbertien a l'économie concertée* (Paris: Berger-Levrault, 1965).

Chevallier, R.M., 'L'arrêt 30-59 de la Cour de justice des Communautés européennes' (1962) *Revue Générale de Droit International Public*, 33(3):46.

Chevallier, R.M., 'Methods and Reasoning of European Court in its Interpretation of Community Law' (1965) *Common Market Law Review*, 2(1):21.

Cini, M., 2001 'The Soft Law Approach: Commission Rule-Making in the EU's State Aid Regime' (2001) *Journal of European Public Policy*, 8(2):192.

Cini, M., and McGowan, L., *Competition Policy in the European Union* (Basingstoke: Macmillan, 1998).

Colbert, J.B., *Letters of 5 and 26 December*, 1670, and *privilege* of 17 February, 1671, Clement, P. (ed.), *Lettres, Instructions et Mémoires* (Imprimerie Imperiale, Paris, 1861–73).

Colbert, J.B., *Memorandum on Trade*, 1664, Clement, P. (ed.), *Lettres, Instructions et Mémoires* (Imprimerie Imperiale, Paris, 1861–73).

Comín, F., Hernández, M., and Llopis, E. (eds), *Historia económica mundial: siglos X–XX*, 2ª edn (Barcelona: Crítica, 2009).

Cornish, W.R., 'Legal Control over Cartels and Monopolization 1880–1914: A Comparison', in Hohn, N., and Kocka, J. (eds), *Law and the Formation of Big Enterprises in the 19th and 20th Centuries* (Gottingen: Vandenhoeck & Ruprecht 1979) 280.

Coppi, L., 'The Role of Economics in State Aid Analysis and the Balancing Test' in Szyszczak, E. (ed.), *Research Handbook on State Aid* (Cheltenham: Edward Elgar, 2011) 64.

Cownie, F., 'State Aids in the Eighties' (1986) *European Law Review*, 247.

Craig, P., and De Búrca, G., *EU Law—Text, Cases and Materials* 4th edn (Oxford: Oxford University Press, 2007).

Cremona, M. (ed.) *Market Integration and Public Services in the European Union* (Oxford: Oxford University Press, 2011).

Crocioni, P., 'Can State Aid Policy Become more Economic-Friendly?' (2006) *World Competition*, 29(1):89.

Cruz Vilaca, J., 'Material and Geographic Selectivity in State Aid—Recent Developments' (2009) *European State Aid Law Quarterly*, 4:444.

Dam, K., *The GATT: Law and International Economic Organization* (Chicago: University of Chicago Press, 1970).

Dancet, G., and Rosenstock, M., 'State Aid Control by the European Commission: The Case of the Automobile Sector' (1995), available at: <http://ec.europa.eu/competition/speeches/text/sp1995_043_en.html>.

Dashwood, A., 'Control of State Aids in the EEC: Prevention and Cure under Article 93' (1975) *Common Market Law Review*, 12(1):43.

Davies, P., 'Market Integration and Social Policy in the Court of Justice' (1995) *Industrial Law Journal*, 24(1):49.

Davignon, E., 'Subsidies and Competition in the European Union', in Stuyck, J., Abraham, F., and Goemans, Ch. (eds), *Subsidies and Competition in the European Union: Generale Bank lectures 1994–1995* (Leuven: Leuven University Press, 1996) 1.

De Búrca, G. (ed.), *EU and the Welfare State—In Search of Solidarity* (Oxford: Oxford University Press, 2006).

De Búrca, G., 'Unpacking the Concept of Discrimination in EC and International Trade Law', in Barnard, C., and Scott, J. (eds), *The Law of the Single European Market: Unpacking the Premises* (Oxford: Hart Publishing, 2002) 181.

De Búrca, G., and Scott, J., *The EU and the WTO—Legal and Constitutional Issues* (Oxford: Hart Publishing, 2001).

De Cecco, F., *State Aid and the European Economic Constitution* (Oxford: Hart, 2013).

De Cecco F., 'State Aid and Self-Government: Regional Taxation and the Shifting Spaces of Constitutional Autonomy' in Shuibhne, N., and Gormley, L. (eds), *From Single Market to Economic Union: Essays in Memory of John A. Usher* (Oxford: Oxford University Press, 2012) 221.

Derenne, J., and Merola, M. (eds), *Economic Analysis of State Aid Rules—Contributions and Limits* (Berlin: Lexxion, 2004).

De Wilmars, J.M., 'Aides CECA et aides CEE: aspects juridique d'une convergence economique' in Capotorti, F. (ed.). *Du droit international au droit de l'intégration: liber amicorum Pierre Pescatore* (Baden-Baden: Nomos Verlagsgesellschaft, 1987) 421.

Di Bucci, V., 'Quelques Aspects Institutionnels du Droit des Aides d'État' in Di Bucci, V., Buendia Sierra, J.L., Smulders, B., et al. (eds), *EC State Aid Law—Le Droit des Aides d'État dans la CE, Liber Amicorum Francisco Santaolalla Gadea* (The Hague: Kluwer Law International, 2008) 43.

Di Bucci, V., 'Direct Taxation—State Aid in the Form of Fiscal Measures', in Rydelski, M.S. (ed.), *The EC State Aid Regime: Distortive Effects of State Aid on Competition and Trade* (London: Cameron May, 2006) 73.

Di Bucci, V., 'Comments on the Paper "Selectivity, Economic Advantage, Distortion of Competition and Effect on Trade"' in Derenne, J. and Merola, M. (eds) *Economic Analysis of State Aid Rules—Contributions and Limits* (Berlin: Lexxion, 2007) 156.

Doleys, T., 'Fifty years of Moulding Article 87: The European Commission and the Development of EU State Aid Law & Policy (1958–2008)', Paper prepared for presentation at the 11th Biennial International Conference of the European Union Studies Association in Marina Del Ray, California, 23–25 April 2009.

Doleys, T.J., 'Managing State Aid in a Time of Crisis: Commission Crisis Communications and the Financial Sector Bailout' (2012) *Journal of European Integration*, 34(6):549.

Dony, M., Renard, F., and Smits, C., *Contrôle des aides d'Etat* 3rd edn (Brussels: Editions de l'université de Bruxelles, 2007).

Dougan, M., and Spaventa, E. (eds) *Social Welfare and EU Law* (Oxford: Hart Publishing: 2005).

Douglas-Scott, S., *Constitutional Law of the European Union* (Harlow: Pearson Longman, 2002).

Due, O., 'The Law-making Role of the European Court of Justice Considered in Particular from the Perspective of Individuals and Undertakings' (1994) *Nordic Journal of International Law*, 63:123.

Dumoulin, M. (ed.) *The European Commission, 1958–72: History and Memories* (Brussels: European Commission, 2007).

Ehlermann, C.D., 'State Aids under European Community Competition Law' (1994) *Fordham International Law Journal*, 18(2):408.

Elhermann, C.D., 'State Aid Control in the European Union: Success or Failure?' (1994) *Fordham International Law Journal*, 18(4):1210.

Ehlermann, C.D., 'The Contribution of EC Competition Policy to the Single Market' (1992) *Common Market Law Review*, 29(2): 257.

Ehlermann, C.D., 'Commission Lacks Power in 1992 Process' (1990) *European Affairs* 65.

Ehlermann, C.D., and Goyette, M., 'The Interface between EU State Aid Control and the WTO Disciplines on Subsidies' (2006) *European State Aid Law Quarterly*, 4:695.

Ehlermann, C.D., and Vallery, A., 'Giving Meaning to the Condition of Effect on Trade: The Court's Judgment in Xunta de Galicia, a Missed Opportunity?' (2005) *European State Aid Law Quarterly*, 4:709.

Ehlermann, C.D., and Everson, M. (eds) *European Competition Law Annual 1999: Selected Issues in the Field of State Aids* (Oxford: Hart Publishing, 2001).

Evans, A., *European Community Law of State Aid* (Oxford: Clarendon Press, 1997).

Everling, U. 'The Court of Justice as a Decision Making Authority', in Stein, E. (ed.), *The Art of Governance: Festschrift in Honor of Eric Stein* (Baden-Baden: Nomos Verlagsgesellschaft, 1987), 156.

Everling, U., 'On the Judge-made Law of the European Community's Courts', in O'Keeffe, D. (ed.), *Judicial Review in European Union Law: Liber Amicorum in Honor of Lord Slynn of Hadley* (The Hague: Kluwer, 2000), 36.

Farley, M., 'The Role of Economics-based Approaches when Analysing Effects on Trade and Distortions of Competition after WAM' (2012) *European State Aid Law Quarterly*, 9(2):369.

Faull, J., 'The Enforcement of Competition Policy in the European Community: A Mature System' (1991–92) *Fordham International Law Journal*, 15(2):219.

Flynn, J., 'The Philip Morris Decision Upheld by the European Court, European Law Review' (1981) *European Law Review*, 6(1):208.

Focsaneanu, L., 'Réglementations nationales de prix et droit communautaire—Jurisprudence de la Cour de justice des Communautés européennes—Prix de produits industriels' (1986) *Revue du Marché Commun*, 294:281.

Frazer, I., 'The New Structural Funds, State Aids and Interventions on the Single Market' (1995) *European Law Review* 3.

Friederiszick, H.W., Röller, L.H., and Verouden, V., *European State Aid Control: An Economic Framework*, in Bucirossi, P. (ed.), *Handbook of Antitrust Economics* (Cambridge, MA: MIT Press, 2008) 625.

Garcia, J., and Neven, D., 'Identification of Sensitive Sectors in which State Aid may have Significant Distorting Effects', London: HM Treasury, 2004.

Gardner, A., 'The Velvet Revolution: Article 90 and the Triumph of the Free Market in Europe's Regulated Sectors' (1995) *European Competition Law Review*, 78.

Gebski, S., 'Competition First? Application of State Aid Rules in the Banking Sector' (2009) *The Competition Law Review*, 6(1):89;

Quigley, C., 'Review of the Temporary State Aid Rules Adopted in the Context of the Financial and Economic Crisis' (2012) *Journal of European Competition Law and Practice*, 3(3):237.

Geelhoed, L.A., 'The Demarcation of State Aid and Regulatory Charges' in (2005) *European State Aid Law Quarterly*, 4:40.

George, K.D., Joll, C. (eds), *Competition Policy in the UK and the EEC* (Cambridge: Cambridge University Press, 1975).

Gerard, D.M.B., 'Managing The Financial Crisis in Europe: The Role Of EU State Aid Law Enforcement' in Merola, M., Derenne J., and Rivas J. (eds), *Competition Law at Times of Economic Crisis—In Need for Adjustment?* (Brussels: Bruylant, 2013).

Gerber, D.J., *Global Competition: Law, Markets, and Globalization* (Oxford: Oxford University Press, 2010).

Gerber, D.J., *Law and Competition in Twentieth Century Europe: Protecting Prometheus* (Oxford: Oxford University Press, 1998).

Gerber, D.J., 'The Transformation of European Community Competition Law?' (1994) *Harvard International Law Journal*, 35(97):137.

Gilliams, H., 'The Notion Of Aid In The Financial Crisis' in Merola, M., Derenne, J., and Rivas, J. (eds), *Competition Law in times of Economic crisis—In need of Adjustment?* 2012 GCLC Annual Conference EU Competition Law in Times of Economic Crisis (Brussels: Bruylant, 2013).

Gillingham, J., *European Integration 1950–2003: Superstate or New Market Economy?* (Cambridge: Cambridge University Press, 2003).

Gilmour, D.R., 'The Enforcement of Community Law by the Commission in the Context of State Aids: The Relationship between Articles 93 and 169 and the Choice of Remedies' (1981) *Common Market Law Review*, 18(1):63.

Giolito, C., 'La procédure de contrôle des aides d'État peut-elle être utilisée pour contrôler la bonne application d'autres dispositions de droit communautaire?' in Di Bucci, V., Buendia Sierra, J.L., Smulders, B., et al. (eds), *EC State Aid law—Le Droit des Aides d'État dans la CE, Liber Amicorum Francisco Santaolalla Gadea* (The Hague, Kluwer Law International, 2008) 145.

Goodliffe, J., 'State Aids and Recalcitrant Members' (1990) *New Law Journal*, 140:1238.

Gordon, C.D., 'Subsidies in Roman Imperial Defence' (1949) *Phoenix*, 3:60.

Goyder, D.G., *EEC Competition Law* (Oxford: Oxford University Press, 1988).

Grespan, D., and Santamato, S., "Favouring Certain Undertakings or the Production of Certain Goods': Advantage' in Mederer, W., Pesaresi, N., and Van Hoof, M. (eds), *EU Competition Law*, Volume IV, State Aid, Book One (Leuven: Claeys & Casteels, 2008) 273.

Gyselen, L., 'The Emerging Interface between Competition Policy and Environmental Policy in the EC', in Cameron, J., Demaret, P., and Geradin, D. (eds), *Trade and the Environment: The Search for Balance* (London: Cameron May 1994) 242.

Haas, E., *The Uniting of Europe: Political, Social, and Economic Forces, 1950–1957* (Stanford, CA: Stanford University Press, 1958).

Hancher, L., Ottervanger, T., and Slot, P.J., *EU State Aids* 4th edn (London: Sweet & Maxwell, 2012).

Hancher, L, and Larouche, P, 'EU Regulation of Network Industries and Services' in Craig, P., and de Búrca, G. (eds), *The Evolution of EU Law* 2nd edn (Oxford: Oxford University Press, 2011) 643.

Hancher, L., 'EC State Aid Law—No Longer the Cinderella of European Competition Law But Not Quite the Ugly Sister?' in Hancher, L., Ottervanger, T., and Slot, P.J. (eds), *EC State Aids* 3rd edn (London: Sweet & Maxwell 2006) 1.

Hancher, L., 'Towards an Economic Analysis of State Aid' (2005) *European State Aid Law Quarterly*, 3:425.

Hancher, L., 'A Pearle of Wisdom' (2004) *European State Aid Law Quarterly*, 3:363.

Hancher, L., 'Towards a New Definition of a State Aid under European Law' (2003) *European State Aid Law Review*, 3:365.

Hancher, L., 'State Aids and Judicial Control in the European Community' (1994) *European Competition Law Review*, 15(3):134.

Hildebrand, D., *The Role of Economic Analysis in the EC Competition Rules*, 3rd edn (Alphen aan den Rijn: Kluwer Law International 2009).

Hill, M., *The Economic and Financial Organization of the League of Nation* (Washington DC: Carnegie Endowment for International Peace, 1946).

Home, H. (Lord Karnes), *Sketches of the History of Man* 2 vols. (Edinburgh, Harris, JA, 1774).

Ibañez Colomo, P., 'State Aid Litigation before EU Courts (2004–2012): A Statistical Overview' (2013) *Journal of European Competition Law and Practice* 4(6):469.

Jacobs, F.G., *The Sovereignty of Law—The European Way*, The Hamlyn Lectures 2006 (Cambridge: Cambridge University Press, 2007).

Jacobs, F.G., 'The Evolution of the European Legal Order' (2004) *Common Market Law Review*, 41(2):303.

Jacobs, F.G., 'Is the Court of Justice of the European Communities a Constitutional Court?' in Curtin, D., and O'Keeffe, D. (eds), *Constitutional Adjudication in European Community and National Law* (Dublin: Butterworths, 1992) 25.

Jaeger, T., 'Goodbye Old Friend: Article 107's Double Control Criterion' (2012) *European State Aid Law Quarterly*, 3:535.

Jackson, J.H., *The World Trading System—Law and Policy of International Economic Relations* 2nd edn (Cambridge, MA: MIT Press, 1997).

James, E., 'L'État au Secours des Entreprisses Défaillantes' (1932) *Revue d'Economie Politique*, 45:1511.

Jääskinen, N, 'The New Rules on SGEI' (2011) *European State Aid Law Quarterly*, 4:599.

Jenny, F.Y., 'Competition and State Aid Policy in the European Community' (1994) *Fordham International Law Journal*, 18(2):525.

Joerges, C., and Petersmann, E.U., *Constitutionalism, Multilevel Trade Governance and Social Regulation* (Oxford: Hart Publishing, 2006).

Jordan, J., 'State Aids: The Compatibility of Regional Aid Systems with the Common Market' (1976) *European Law Review*, 1:236.

Kanninen, H., Korjus, N., and Rosas, A. (eds), *EU Competition Law in Context, Essays in Honour of Virpi Tiili* (Oxford: Hart Publishing, 2009).

Kapteyn, P.J.G., 'Outgrowing the Treaty of Rome: From Market Integration to Policy Integration', in *Melanges Fernand Dehousse* (Bruxelles: Labor, 1979) 45.

Kapteyn, P.J.G., and Verloren van Themaat, P., *Introduction to the Law of the European Communities after the Accession of New Member States* (London: Sweet & Maxwell, 1973).

Keppenne, J.P., *Guide des aides d'état en droit communautaire: réglementation, jurisprudence et pratique de la Commission* (Brussels: Bruylant, 1999).

Khan, N., and Borchardt, K.D., 'The Private Market Investor Principle: Reality Check or Distorting Mirror?' in Di Bucci, V., Buendia Sierra, J.L., Smulders, B., et al. (eds), *EC State Aid Law—Le Droit des Aides d'État dans la CE, Liber Amicorum Francisco Santaolalla Gadea* (The Hague: Kluwer Law International, 2008) 109.

Kleiner, T., 'Modernization of State Aid Policy' in Szyszczak, E. (ed.), *Research Handbook on State Aid* (Cheltenham: Edward Elgar, 2011) 1.

Kleiner, T., 'The State Aid Action Plan', in Mederer, W., Pesaresi, N., and Van Hoof, M. (eds), *EU Competition Law*, Volume IV, State Aid (Leuven: Claeys & Casteels, 2008) 65.

Kirch, P., d'Ormesson, O., Rodriguez Curiel, J.W., 'Transfer of State Resources' in Derenne, J., and Merola, M. (eds), *Economic Analysis of State Aid Rules—Contributions and Limits* (Berlin: Lexxion, 2007) 105.

Kobia, R.A.J., 'Introduction to the Law, Practice and Policy of State Aids in the European Community' (1996), available at: <http://ec.europa.eu/competition/speeches/text/sp1996_007_en.html>.

Koenig, C., and Haratsch, A., 'The Logic of Infrastructure Funding under EC State Aid Control' (2004) *European State Aid Law Quarterly*, 3:393.

Köhler, M., 'New Trends Concerning the Application of the Private Investor Test' (2011) *European State Aid Law Quarterly*, 1:21.

Konstadinides, T., 'Constitutional Identity as a Shield and as a Sword: The European Legal Order within the Framework of National Constitutional Settlement' (2010–11) *Cambridge Yearbook of European Legal Studies*, 13:195.

Koopmans, T., 'The Role of Law in the Next Stage of European Integration' (1986) *International and Comparative Law Quarterly*, 35:925.

Krsjak, P., 'annotation case C-173/73' (1975) *Gazette du Palais*, 91:481.

Kurcz, B., and Vallindas, D., 'Can General Measures be...Selective? Some Thoughts on the Interpretation of a State Aid Definition' (2008) *Common Market Law Review*, 45(1):159.

Kusters, H.J., *Fondements de la Communauté économique européenne*, Office des publications officielles des Communautés européennes (Brussels–Luxembourg: Labor, 1990).

Lavdas, K.A., and Mendrinou, M.M., *Politics, Subsidies, and Competition: The New Politics of State Intervention in the European Union* (Cheltenham: Edward Elgar, 1999).

Laprevote, F.C., 'Selected Issues Raised by Bank Restructuring Plans under EU State Aid Rules' (2012) *European State Aid Law Quarterly*, 1:93.

Laprevote, F.C., 'Judicial Review (States, Beneficiary & Third Parties)' in Merola, M., Derenne, J., and Rivas, J. (eds), *Competition Law in Times of Economic Crisis—In Need of Adjustment? 2012 GCLC Annual Conference EU Competition Law in Times of Economic Crisis* (Brussels: Bruylant 2013).

Lehmkuhl, D., 'On Government, Governance and Judicial Review: The Case of European Competition Policy' (2008) *Journal of Public Policy*, 28(1):139.

Lemaitre, P., 'Un conflit qui aurait pu être évité—Devant la Cour de Luxembourg la Commissione reproche à la France le maintien d'un taux de réescompte favorable à ses exportations' (1969) *Revue du Marché Commun*, 34(1):57.

Lenaerts, K., 'State Aid and Direct taxation', in Kanninen, H., Korjus, N., Rosas, A. (eds), *EU Competition Law in Context, Essays in Honour of Virpi Tiili* (Oxford: Hart Publishing, 2009) 291.

Lenaerts, K., 'Constitutionalism and the Many Faces of Federalism' (1990) *American Journal of Comparative Law*, 38:205.

Lo Schiavo, G., 'The Impact of the EU Crisis-Related Framework on State Aids to Financial Institutions: From Past Practice to Future Prospects' (2013) *Competition Law Review*, 9(2):135.

Luengo Hernández de Madrid, G., *Regulation of Subsidies and State Aids in WTO and EC Law—Conflicts in International Trade Law* (Alphen aan den Rijn: Kluwer Law International, 2007).

Macchiavelli, N., *The Prince* (New York, NY: Penguin Books, 1999).

Poiares Maduro, M., *We the Court: The European Court of Justice and the European Economic Constitution* (Oxford: Hart Publishing, 1998).

Majone, G.D., 'The Rise of the Regulatory State in Europe' (1994) *West European Politics*, 17(3):77.

Mancini G.F., and Keeling, D.T., 'Language, Culture and Politics in the Life of the European Court of Justice' (1994–95) *Columbia Journal of European Law*, 1:397.

Mancini, G.F., 'The Making of a Constitution for Europe' (1989) *Common Market Law Review*, 26(4):595.

Mathijsen, P., *A Guide to European Community Law* (London: Sweet & Maxwell, 1972).

Mathijsen, P., in George, K.D., Joll, C. (eds), *Competition Policy in the UK and the EEC* (Cambridge: Cambridge University Press, 1975).

Martineau, G., 'The Brussels Sugar Convention' (1904) *Economic Journal*, 14:34.

Martino, G. (ed.), 'From the ECSC to the Common Market.' Ministerio degli affari esteri. *Gaetano Martino e l'Europa, Dalla Conferenza di Messina al Parlamento europeo* (Rome: Istituto poligrafico e zecca dello stato, 1995. Translated by the CVCE) 66.

Mederer, W., 'Evolution of State Aid Control' in Mederer, W., Pesaresi, N., and Van Hoof, M. (eds), *EU Competition Law*, Volume IV, State Aid, Book One (Leuven: Claeys & Casteels, 2008), 19.

Mederer, W., 'The Future of State Aid Control' (1996) *Competition Policy Newsletter*, 3(2):12.

Megret, J., Waelbroeck, M., Vignes, D., *Le droit de la Communauté Economique Europeen* Vol. 4 (Brussels: Concurrence, 1972).

Mengozzi, P., 'Il Principio dell'Investitore in una Economia di Mercato e i Valori del Diritto Comunitario' (1995) *Rivista di Diritto Europeo*, 35(1):19.

Merola, M., 'Comments on the Paper "The Most Appropriate Economic Tools for a Better Targeted State Aid Policy"', in Derenne, J., and Merola, M. (eds), *Economic Analysis of State Aid Rules—Contributions and Limits* (Berlin: Lexxion, 2007) 68.

Miro, P., 'The requirement of Selectivity in the Recent Case-law of the Court of Justice' (2012) *European State Aid Law Quarterly*, 2:335.

Monti, G., 'Article 81 and Public Policy' (2002) *CML Review*, 39(5):1057.

Moravcsik, A., 'Negotiating the Single European Act: National Interests and Conventional Statecraft in the European Community' (1991) *International Organization*, 45(1):19.

Mortelmans, K., 'Towards Convergence in the Application of the Rules on Free Movement and on Competition?' (2001) *Common Market Law Review*, 39(3):613.

Mortelmans, K., 'The Compensatory Justification Criterion in the Practice of the commission in Decisions on State Aids' (1984) *Common Market Law Review*, 21(2):405.

Moura Filho, H.P., 'Pioneering Multilateralism: The Sugar Agreements 1864–1914', paper presented at the XVI International Economic History Congress, Helsinki, Session 109, 2006.

Neven, D., and Verouden, V., 'Towards a More Refined Economic Approach in State Aid Control' in Mederer, W., Pesaresi, N., and Van Hoof, M. (eds), *EU Competition Law*, Volume IV, State Aid, Book One (Leuven: Claeys & Casteels, 2008) 99.

Nicolaides, P., 'State Aid, Advantage and Competitive Selection: What is a Normal Market Transaction?' (2010) *European State Aid Law Quarterly*, 1:65.

Nicolaides, P., 'Fiscal State Aid in the EU: The Limits of Tax Autonomy' (2004) *World Competition*, 27(3):365.

Nicolaides, P., 'Fiscal Aid in the EC: A Critical Review of Current Practice' (2001) *World Competition*, 24(3):319.

Nitsche, R., and Heidhues, P., *Study on Methods to Analyse the Impact of State Aid on Competition*, Report prepared for the European Commission, Directorate General for Economics and Financial Affairs (Final Report ECFIN/R/2004/004): Bruxelles (2005).

Notz, W, 'International Private Agreements in the form of Cartels, Syndicates and other Combinations' (1920) *Journal of Political Economy*, 28:658.

Odudu, O., 'Economic Activity as a Limit to Community Law' in Barnard, C., and Odudu, O. (eds), *The Outer Limits of European Union Law* (Oxford, Hart Publishing, 2009) 225.

O'Keeffe, D. (ed.), *Judicial Review in European Union Law: Liber Amicorum in honor of Lord Slynn of Hadley* (The Hague: Kluwer, 2000).

O'Keeffe, D., and Bavasso, A., 'Four Freedoms, One Market and National Competence: In Search of a Dividing Line' in Andenas, M., and Fairgrieve, D. (eds), *Judicial Review in International Perspective: Liber Amicorum in Honour of Lord Slynn of Hadley* (London: Aspen, 2000) 541.

Pastor Merchante, F., *The Role of Competitors in the Enforcement of State Aid Law*, Ph.D. thesis defended at the European University Institute, Florence, 6 October 2014.

Pelkmans, J., *European Integration—Methods and Economic Analysis* 2nd edn (London: FT–Prentice Hall, 2001).

Petersen, A., 'State Aid and European Union: State Aid in the Light of Trade and Competition, Industrial and Cohesion Policies', in Harden, I.(ed.), *State Aid: Community Law and Policy* (Cologne: Bundesanzeiger, 1993) 20.

Pescatore, P., 'Public and Private Aspects of European Community Competition Law' (1987) *Fordham International Law Journal*, 10(3):373.

Pescatore, P., 'The Doctrine of "Direct Effect": An Infant Disease of Community Law' (1983) *European Law Review*, 8:155.

Pescatore, P., *The Law of Integration: Emergence of a New Phenomenon* (Leiden: Sijhoof, 1974).

Pigman, G.A., 'Hegemony and Trade Liberalization Policy: Britain and the Brussels Sugar Convention of 1902' (1997) *Review of International Studies*, 23:185.

Plender, R., 'Definition of Aid' in Biondi, A., Eeckhout, P., and Flynn, J. (eds), *The Law of State Aid in the European Union* (Oxford: Oxford University Press, 2004) 3.

Prechal, S., and de Vries, S., 'Seamless Web of Judicial Protection in the Internal Market?' (2009) *European Law Review*, 34:5.

Priaux, F., *La Question des Sucres et les Conventions Sucrières de Bruxelles*, Thèse de Doctorat (Faculté de Droit), Université de Rennes. Rennes. 1910.

Quadri, R., Monaco, R., and Trabucchi, A., (eds), *Trattato istitutivo della C.E.E. Comentario* (Milan: Giuffrè, 1965, vol. II).

Quigley, C., *European State Aid Law and Policy* 2nd edn (Oxford: Hart Publishing, 2009).

Quigley, C., 'The Notion of a State Aid in the EEC' (1988) *European Law Review*, 13:242.

Quigley, C., and Collins, A.M., *EC State Aid Law and Policy* (Oxford: Hart Publishing, 2003).

Quigley, C., 'General Taxation and State Aid', in Biondi, A., Eeckhout, P., and Flynn, J. (eds), *The Law of State Aid in the European Union* (Oxford: Oxford University Press, 2004) 207.

Rasmussen, H., 'Between Self-Restraint and Activism: A Judicial Policy for the European Court' (1988) *European Law Review*, 13:28.

Rasmussen, H., *On Law and Policy in the European Court of Justice* (Lancaster: Martinus Nijhoff, 1986).

Rawlinson, F., 'The Role of Policy Frameworks, Codes, and Guidelines in the Control of State Aid' in Harden, I. (ed.), State Aid: Community Law and Policy (Cologne: Bundesanzeiger Verlagsgesellschaft, 1993) 52.

Reich, N., 'The 'November Revolution' of the European Court of Justice: Keck, Meng and Audi Revisited' (1994) *Common Market Law Review*, 31(3):459.

Rodríguez Curiel, J.W., 'Giro jurisprudencial restrictivo del concepto de ayuda de Estado (sentencia del Tribunal de Justicia de las CC.EE. de 17-3-93)' (1993) *Gaceta Jurídica de la C.E. y de la Competencia*, 83:5.

Roeller, L.H., and Stehmann, O., 'The Year 2005 at DG Competition: The Trend towards a more Effects-Based Approach' (2006) *Review of Industrial Organization*, 29:281.

Rosas, A., and Armati, L., *EU Constitutional Law: An Introduction* (Oxford: Hart, 2012).

Ross, M., 'A Healthy Approach to Services of General Economic Interest? The BUPA Judgment of the Court of First Instance' (2009) *European Law Review*, 34:127.

Ross, M., 'Decentralization, Effectiveness, and Modernization: Contradiction in Terms?' (2004) in Biondi, A., Eeckhout, P., and Flynn, J. (eds), *The Law of State Aid in the European Union* (Oxford: Oxford University Press, 2004) 85.

Ross, M,. 'State Aids and National Courts: Definitions and Other Problems—a Case of Premature Emancipation?' (2000) *Common Market Law Review*, 37(2):401.

Ross, M., 'State Aids: Maturing into a Constitutional Problem' (1995) *Yearbook of European Law*, 15:79.

Ross, M., 'A Review of Developments in State Aids 1987–88' (1989) *Common Market Law Review*, 26(2):167.

Rossi-Maccanico, P., 'State Aid Review of Business Tax Measures Proposals for State Aid Control of Direct Business Tax Measures' (2007) *European State Aid Law Quarterly*, 2:215.

Rubini, L., 'The Elusive Frontier: Regulation under State Aid Rules' (2009) *European State Aid Law Quarterly*, 3:277.

Rubini, L., *The Definition of Subsidy and State Aid: WTO and EC Law in Comparative Perspective* (Oxford: Oxford University Press, 2009).

Rueff, J, 'La Cour et l'economie politique', in *Dix ans de jurisprudence de la Cour de justice des Commaunautes europeennes, Europäische Arbeitstagung* (Cologne: Heymanns, 1965) 13.

Runciman, W.L., 'The World Economic Conference at Geneva' (1927) *Economic Journal*, 37:465.

Rydelski, M.S. (ed.), *The EC State Aid Regime: Distortive Effects of State Aid on Competition and Trade* (London: Cameron May, 2006).

Ryziger, P-F. *Discriminations et subventions, first co-report, in Dix ans de jurisprudence de la Cour de justice des Communautés européennes, Europäische Arbeitstagung* (Cologne: Heymanns, 1965),

Salter, A., 'The League's Contribution' in Salter, A., Boyden, W., *The Economic Consequences of the League: The World Economic Conference* (London, 1927) 8.

Santamato, S., 'Advantage in the Context of Services of General Economic Interest under Altmark' in Mederer, W., Pesaresi, N., and Van Hoof, M. (eds), *EU Competition Law*, Volume IV, State Aid, Book One (Leuven: Claeys & Casteels, 2008) 369.

Saydé, A., *Abuse of Union Law and Regulation of the Internal Market*, Doctoral thesis defended at the European University Institute in 2012.

Scheuing, D.H., *Les aides financiers publiques aux enterprises en droit francaise et europeen AEE* (Paris: Editons Berger-Levrault, 1974).

Schina, D., *State Aids under the EEC Treaty, Articles 92 to 94* (Oxford: ESC, Oxford, 1987).

Schön, W., 'Taxation and State Aid Law in the European Union' (1999) *Common Market Law Review*, 36(5):910.

Schrans, G., 'National and Regional Aid to Industry under the EEC Treaty' (1973) *Common Market Law Review*, 12(2):174.

Sinnaeve, A., 'State Aid Procedures: Development since the Entry into Force of the Procedural Regulation' (2007), *Common Market Law Review*, 44(4):965.

Slot, P.J., 'NOx Emission Trading Rights: A Government Gift or Value Created by Undertakings?' (2013) *European State Aid Law Quarterly*, 12.

Slot, P.J., 'A View from the Mountain: 40 Years of Developments in EC competition law' (2004) *Common Market Law Review*, 41(2):443.

Slot, P.J., 'Joined Cases C-72/91 and C-73/91, Sloman Neptun Schiffahrts A.G. v. Seebetriebsrat Bodo Ziesemer der Sloman Neptun Schiffahrts A.G., Judgment of 17 March 1993' (1994) *Common Market Law Review*, 31(1):137.

Slot, P.J., 'Procedural and Substantive Compliance Required' (1991) *European Law Review*, 16:38.

Slot, P.J., 'Procedural Aspects of State Aids: The Guardian of Competition versus the Subsidy Villains?' (1990) *Common Market Law Review* 741.

Slotboom, M., 'State Aid in Community Law: A Broad or Narrow Definition?' (1995) *European Law Review*, 20:289.

Smith, A., *An Inquiry into the Nature and Causes of the Wealth of Nations* (Oxford: Clarendon Press, 1976, originally published 1776).

Smith, M.P., 'How Adaptable is the European Commission? The Case of State Aid Regulation' (2001) *Journal of Public Policy*, 21(3):219.

Smith, M.P., 'Autonomy by the Rules: The European Commission and the Development of State Aid Policy' (1998) *Journal of Common Market* Studies, 36:55.

Smith, M.P., 'Integration in Small Steps: The European Commission and Member-State Aid to Industry' (1996) *West European Politics*, 19(3):563.

Smits, C., 'La notion d'avantage et le critère de "l'opérateur en économie en marché"', in Dony, M., and Smits, C. (eds), *Aides d'État* (Brussels: Editions de l'Université de Bruxelles, 2005) 53.

Steenbergen, J., 'Trade Regulation since the Tokyo Round'. In Volker, E.L.M. (ed.), *Protectionism and the European Community* (Dewenter: Kluwer, 1987).

Stein, E., 'Lawyer, Judges and the Making of a Transnational Constitution' (1981) *American Journal of International Law*, 75(1):1.

Stein, E. (ed.), *The Art of Governance: Festschrift in Honor of Eric Stein* (Baden-Baden: Nomos Verlagsgesellschaft, 1987).

Steuart, J., *An Inquiry into the Principles of Political Economy* (Dublin: James Williams and Richard Moncrieffe, 1767).

Spierenburg, D., and Poidevin, R., *Histoire de la Haute Autorité de la Communauté du Charbon et de l'Acier: Un expérience supranationale* (Brussels: Bruylant, 1993).

Stuart, M., Lord, *The European Community and the Rule of Law* (London: Stevens & Sons, 1977).

Stuyck, J., Abraham, F., and Goemans, Ch. (eds), *Subsidies and Competition in the European Union: Generale Bank Lectures 1994–1995* (Leuven: Leuven University Press, 1996).

Sussman, M.J., 'Countervailing Duties and the Specificity Test: An Alternative Approach to the Definition of "Bounty or Grant"' (1986) *Law and Policy in International Business*, 18:475.

Sutton, A., Lannoo, K., and Napoli, C., 'Bank State Aid in the Financial Crisis Fragmentation or Level Playing field? A CEPS Task Force Report' (Brussels: CEPS, 2010).

Sykes, A.O., 'The Economics of WTO Rules on Subsidies and Countervailing Measures', Chicago John M Olin Law and Economics Working Paper No. 186 (2nd Series) May 2003.

Szyszczak, E. (ed.), *Research Handbook on State Aid* (Cheltenham: Edward Elgar, 2011).

Szyszczak, E., 'Financing Services of General Economic Interest' (2004) *Modern Law Review*, 67(6):982.

Taylor, B., 'The Brussels Sugar Convention', *North American Review* (1909) 347.

Temple Lang, J., 'The Development by the Court of Justice of the Duties of Cooperation of National Authorities and Community Institutions under Article 10 EC'(2007–2008) *Fordham International Law Journal*, 31(5):1483.

Thatcher, M., 'The Commission and National Governments as Partners: EC Regulatory Expansion in Telecommunications 1979–2000' (2001) *Journal of European Public Policy*, 8(4):558.

Tosato, G.L., 'L'evoluzione della disciplina sugli aiuti di Stato', in Schepisi, C. (ed.), *La modernizzazione della disciplina sugli aiuti di Stato: il nuovo approccio della Commissione europea e i recenti sviluppi in materia di public e private enforcement* (Turin: G. Giappichelli, 2011) 3.

Triantafyllou, D., 'Les règles de la concurrence et l'activité étatique y compris les marchés publics' (1996) *RTDE*, 32:57.

Tucker, J., *Instructions for Travellers* (London: 1757).

Van de Casteele, K., and Hocine, M., 'Favouring Certain Undertakings or the Production of Certain Goods': Selectivity' in Mederer, W., Pesaresi, N., and Van Hoof, M. (eds), *EU Competition Law*, Volume IV, State Aid, Book One (Leuven: Claeys & Casteels, 2008) 247.

Van Gerven, W. 'Twelve Years of EEC Competition Law (1962–73) Revisited' (1974) *Common Market Law Review*, 11(1):38.

Van Miert, K., 'Reflections on Seven Years as Commissioner Responsible for State Aid', in Ehlermann, C.D., and Everson, M. (eds), *European Competition Law Annual 1999: Selected Issues in the Field of State Aids* (Oxford: Hart Publishing, 2001) 3.

Verstrynge, J.F., 'Current Antitrust Policy Issues in the EEC: Some Reflections on the Second Generation of Competition Policy' (1984) in Hawk, B., *Annual Proceedings of the Fordham Corporate Law Institute 1985, Antitrust and Trade Policies in International Trade* (New York, NY: Matthew Bender, 1986), 673.

Vesterndorf, B., 'A Further Comment on the New State Aid Concept as this Concept Continues to be Reshaped—Pearle—A Further Piece of the State Aid Puzzle?' (2005) *European State Aid Law Quarterly*, 3:393.

Vicens Vives, J., *Manual de historia económica de España* (Barcelona: Editorial Vicens Vives, 1985).

Viner, J, *Studies in the Theory of International Trade* (Clifton, NJ: A. M. Kelley, 1975).

Viner, J., *Dumping: A problem in International Trade* (New York, NY: Kelley, 1966).

Vogelaar, F.O.W., 'The Impact of the Economic Recession on EEC Competition Policy, Part One: State Aids' (1985) *Swiss Review of International Competition Law*, 23:31.

von Danwitz, T., 'The Concept of State Aid in Liberalized Sectors', in Cremona, M. (ed.), *Market Integration and Public Services in the European Union* (Oxford: Oxford University Press, 2011) 103.

von Danwitz, A., 'The Concept of State Aid in Liberalised Sectors' (2008) EUI Working Paper 28, Fiesole: European University Institute, 2008.

Von der Groeben, H., *The European Community—The Formative Years: The Struggle to Establish the Common Market and the Political Union (1958–66)* (Luxembourg: Office for Official Publications of the European Communities, 1987).

Von der Groeben, H. *Competition in the Common Market*. Speech at the European Parliament. Strasbourg, 19 October 1961, European Commission.

Waelbroeck, M., 'Competition, Integration and Economic Efficiency in the EEC from the Point of View of the Private Firm', in *The Art of Governance: Festschrift in Honor of Eric Stein* (Baden-Baden: Nomos Verlagsgesellschaft, 1987), 1439.

Walsh, A.E., and Paxton, J., *Competition Policy: European and International Trends and Practices* (London: Macmillan, 1975).

Wathelet, M., and Partsch, P.E., 'Delimitation des contours de la notion d'aide d'état en Droit Communautaire' in *Les aides d'état en droit communautaire et en droit national* (Brussels: Bruylant, 1999) 1.

Weiler, J.H.H., *The Constitution of Europe* (Cambridge: Cambridge University Press, 1999).

Weiler, J.H.H., 'The Transformation of Europe' (1990–91) *Yale Law Journal*, 100(8):2403.

Weiler, J.H.H., and Wind, M., *European Constitutionalism beyond the State* (Cambridge: Cambridge University Press, 2003).

Wesseling, R., *The Modernisation of EC Antitrust Law* (Oxford: Hart, 2000).

Winter, J.A., 'Supervision of State Aid: Article 93 in the Court Of Justice' (1993) *Common Market Law Review*, 30(2):311.

Whish, R., and Sufrin, B., 'Article 85 and the Rule of Reason' (1987) *Yearbook of European Law*, 7(1):12.

Wyatt, D., 'National Price Fixing Rules and Article 30 EEC' (1978) *European Law Review*, 3:308.

Wulff, O., 'National Economic Policy: An Obstacle to the European Community?' In J. Schwarze, ed., *Discretionary Powers of the Member States in the Field of Economic Policies and Their Limits under the EEC Treaty* (Baden-Baden: Nomos Verlagsgesellschatft, 1988) 9.

Index

The manufacturer's authorised representative in the EU for product safety is Oxford University Press España S.A. of el Parque Empresarial San Fernando de Henares, Avenida de Castilla, 2 – 28830 Madrid (www.oup.es/en or product.safety@oup.com). OUP España S.A. also acts as importer into Spain of products made by the manufacturer.

www.ingramcontent.com/pod-product-compliance
Lightning Source LLC
LaVergne TN
LVHW011915200926
848484LV00002B/628

* 9 7 8 0 1 9 8 7 4 8 6 9 4 *